T0202788

Communications
in Computer and Information Science 1529

More information about this series at https://link.springer.com/bookseries/7899

Andrei V. Chugunov · Marijn Janssen ·
Igor Khodachek · Yuri Misnikov ·
Dmitrii Trutnev (Eds.)

Electronic Governance and Open Society: Challenges in Eurasia

8th International Conference, EGOSE 2021
Saint Petersburg, Russia, November 24–25, 2021
Proceedings

 Springer

Editors
Andrei V. Chugunov 🆔
eGovernance Center of ITMO University
St. Petersburg, Russia

Marijn Janssen 🆔
Delft University of Technology
Delft, The Netherlands

Igor Khodachek 🆔
North-West Institute of Management
St. Petersburg, Russia

Yuri Misnikov 🆔
eGovernance Center of ITMO University
St. Petersburg, Russia

Dmitrii Trutnev 🆔
eGovernance Center of ITMO University
St. Petersburg, Russia

ISSN 1865-0929   ISSN 1865-0937 (electronic)
Communications in Computer and Information Science
ISBN 978-3-031-04237-9   ISBN 978-3-031-04238-6 (eBook)
https://doi.org/10.1007/978-3-031-04238-6

This Springer imprint is published by the registered company Springer Nature Switzerland AG
The registered company address is: Gewerbestrasse 11, 6330 Cham, Switzerland

Preface

The 8th edition of the International Conference on Electronic Governance and Open Society: Challenges in Eurasia (EGOSE 2021) was held in an online format due to the COVID-19 pandemic constraints. It took place during 24–25 November, 2021. As previously, it was organized in St. Petersburg (Russia) by ITMO University's Centre for e-Government Technologies jointly with the North-West Institute of Management of the Russian Academy of National Economy and Public Administration (NWIM RANEPA). In addition to the traditional EGOSE conference topics, a specific feature of the 2021 event was the inclusion of the participatory budgeting theme, as an invitation to share experiences of the EU project "Empowering Participatory Budgeting in the Baltic Sea Region" (EmPaci). Overall, the conference agenda covered the same diverse list of topics that make EGOSE unique in the wider Eurasian region:

- Participatory Governance and Participatory Budgeting
- Social Media: Tools for Analysis, Participation, and Impact
- eGovernance and Policy Modeling
- Big Data, Computer Analytics, and Governance
- Cases and Perspectives of Government Transformations
- eGovernance and Eurasian Integration
- Open Government Prospects
- Information Society and eGovernance
- Citizen Centered E-Government
- Smart City and Quality of Life

In total, 69 papers from authors in 12 countries were submitted for review by the Program Committee, whose members selected 22 research papers for publication in this volume. Marijn Janssen representing the Delft University of Technology (The Netherlands) delivered the keynote plenary speech, "Adaptive Governance for a Resilient Digital Society", which was followed by three paper presentation sessions. Six papers were presented and discussed at the first session dedicated to digital technology and design in government services, policies, laws, and practices. The second session addressed the problematics of the digital society viewed from the perspective of openness, participation, trust and competences, as discussed in twelve papers. Another four papers presented at the third session reported research results in the field of digital government and Economy. Each session was concluded by discussion.

The trend of the rising prominence of research in the area of machine learning and computational linguistics that emerged a few years back was maintained at this conference as well. The area of digital government and society has revealed possible new emerging topics of research enquiry into surveillance and the silver economy, in addition to such traditional topics as digital services, policies, and comparative studies.

November 2021

Andrei Chugunov
Marijn Janssen
Igor Khodachek
Yuri Misnikov
Dmitrii Trutnev

Organization

Steering Committee

Andrei Chugunov	ITMO University, Russia
Marijn Janssen	Delft University of Technology, The Netherlands
Igor Khodachek	North-West Institute of Management, Russian Academy of National Economy and Public Administration, Russia
Yuri Misnikov	ITMO University, Russia
Dmitrii Trutnev	ITMO University, Russia

Program Committee

Olusegun Agbabiaka	Softrust Technologies Limited, Nigeria
Luis Amaral	University of Minho, Portugal
Dennis Anderson	St. Francis College, USA
Francisco Andrade	University of Minho, Portugal
Mohammed Awad	American University of Ras Al Khaimah, UAE
Maxim Bakaev	Novosibirsk State Technical University, Russia
Luis Barbosa	University of Minho, Portugal
Svetlana Bodrunova	St. Petersburg State University, Russia
Radomir Bolgov	St. Petersburg State University, Russia
Francesco Buccafurri	Mediterranea University of Reggio Calabria, Italy
Vytautas Čyras	Vilnius University, Lithuania
Luis M. Camarinha-Matos	NOVA University of Lisbon, Portugal
Sunil Choenni	Research and Documentation Centre (WODC), Ministry of Justice, The Netherlands
Andrei Chugunov	ITMO University, Russia
Cesar A. Collazos	Universidad del Cauca, Colombia
Shefali S. Dash	National Informatics Centre, India
Subrata Kumar Dey	Independent University, Bangladesh
Dirk Draheim	Tallinn University of Technology, Estonia
Olga Filatova	St. Petersburg State University, Russia
Enrico Francesconi	Institute of Legal Information Theory and Techniques (ITTIG-CNR), Italy
Fernando Galindo	University of Zaragoza, Spain
J. Paul Gibson	Institut Mines-Telecom, France
Dimitris Gouscos	University of Athens, Greece

Tongyi Huang	National Chengchi University, Taiwan
Diana Ishmatova	Waseda University, Japan
Marijn Janssen	Delft University of Technology, The Netherlands
Christos Kalloniatis	University of the Aegean, Greece
George Kampis	Eotvos University, Hungary
Vitalina Karachay	ITMO University, Russia
Sanjeev Katara	National Informatics Centre, India
Igor Khodachek	North-West Institute of Management, Russian Academy of National Economy and Public Administration, Russia
Bozidar Klicek	University of Zagreb, Croatia
Andreas Koch	University of Salzburg, Austria
Evgeny Kotelnikov	Vyatka State University, Russia
Christine Leitner	Centre for Economics and Public Administration, UK
Sandro Leuchter	Hochschule Mannheim - University of Applied Sciences, Germany
Olga Lyashevskaya	National Research University Higher School of Economics, Russia
José Machado	University of Minho, Portugal
Aleksei Martynov	Lobachevsky State University of Nizhny Novgorod, Russia
Ricardo Matheus	Delft University of Technology, The Netherlands
Mikhail Bundin	Lobachevsky State University of Nizhni Novgorod, Russia
Yuri Misnikov	ITMO University, Russia
Harekrishna Misra	Institute of Rural Management Anand, India
Kawa Nazemi	Darmstadt University of Applied Sciences, Germany
João Luís Oliveira Martins	United Nations University, Portugal
Prabir Panda	Independent Researcher, India
Manas Ranjan Patra	Berhampur University, India
Rui Quaresma	Universidade de Évora, Portugal
Alexander Raikov	Institute of Control Sciences, RAS, Russia
Aleksandr Riabushko	Office of the Affairs of the Ulyanovsk Region, Russia
Gustavo Rossi	La Plata National University, Argentina
Demetrios Sampson	Curtin University, Australia
Olga Scrivner	Indiana University Bloomington, USA
Shafay Shamail	Lahore University of Management Sciences, Pakistan
Irina Shmeleva	ITMO University, Russia

Evgeny Styrin	National Research University Higher School of Economics, Russia
Alexander Sungurov	National Research University Higher School of Economics, Russia
Neelam Tikkha	Rashtrasant Tukadoji Maharaj Nagpur University, India
Dmitrii Trutnev	ITMO University, Russia
Hsien-Lee Tseng	Taiwan E-Governance Research Center, Taiwan
Mario Vacca	Italian Ministry of Education, Italy
Costas Vassilakis	University of the Peloponnese, Greece
Lyudmila Vidiasova	ITMO University, Russia
Vasiliki Vrana	Technological Education Institute of Central Macedonia, Greece
Nikolina Zajdela Hrustek	University of Zagreb, Croatia
Sherali Zeadally	University of Kentucky, USA
Hans-Dieter Zimmermann	FHS St. Gallen University of Applied Sciences, Switzerland

Contents

Digital Government and Economy

Keynote

Adaptive Governance for a Resilient Digital Society

Marijn Janssen$^{(\boxtimes)}$![ORCID]

Faculty of Technology, Policy and Management, Delft University of Technology, Jaffalaan 5, Delft, The Netherlands
`m.f.w.h.a.janssen@tudelft.nl`

Abstract. Governments are confronted with all kinds of changes in their digital environment, such as pandemics, fake news, and security breaches. These changes come with many uncertainties and are hard to predict, whereas decisions need to be made quickly to avoid a negative impact. Adaptive governance embraces uncertainty and complexity by enabling continuous learning, involving a wide range of diverse actors, and being able to react within a short time frame. Adaptive governance can be viewed as a governance philosophy based on a range of instruments to create adaptability. The conflicting values of stability and adaptability can be balanced in different ways by governments. The variety in the environment and the variety of instrument to adapt to the environment needs to be in concert. Adaptive governance instruments can be combined to increase their effectiveness and to create a resilient society. Further research in governance instruments, their usage, and their effectiveness is needed.

Keywords: Adaptive governance · Adaptability · Agility · Information society · Cybersecurity · Law of requisite variety

1 The Need for Adaptive Governance

Governments are struggling to respond effectively to events that are hard to control. For example, the pandemic has had a large impact on our society and has resulted in the need to adapt continuously. The pandemic has shown various ways of responding to the crises by adopting all kinds of technology [1]. Another need to adapt comes from fake news. Policymakers are taking action to protect their citizens and institutional system from online misinformation [2]. Also, innovating and dealing with new technology developments like artificial intelligence (AI) and Internet of Things (IoT) results in the need to adapt by governments [3]. Governance is necessary to respond to these developments and the making of the necessary decisions. Yet the government is not always equipped to deal with this. Traditional governance is based on rules and regulation, a well-defined hierarchy of control, specialization and impersonality, clear accountability and authority, which is developed to ensure predictability, efficiency and stability [4]. This results in a discrepancy between the environment and the organization of the government. Regulations and policies for dealing with these challenges do not yet exist, and strict control

© Springer Nature Switzerland AG 2022
A. V. Chugunov et al. (Eds.): EGOSE 2021, CCIS 1529, pp. 3–7, 2022.
https://doi.org/10.1007/978-3-031-04238-6_1

is often not possible in these kinds of situations, whereas there is an urgent need for governments to adapt to the changing circumstances. To deal with with these kinds of uncertainties has resulted in the concept of 'adaptive governance'.

Adaptive governance refers to the ability of government to deal with complex societal issues having high levels of uncertainties and in which stakeholders having different and diverse interests are involved [5]. Uncertainty, complexity and many divergent stakeholders are the starting points for adaptive governance. Adaptive governance attempts to address *uncertainty* in a wicked situation through continuous learning, involvement of multiple actors in decision-making processes and self-organisation of the governance system [6]. Adaptive governance originates from dealing with natural disasters, extreme weather events, economic crises, and so on [7, 8] and has been introduced in digital government and information society by Janssen and Van der Voort [4]. This has been followed by other scholars [7, 8] using sometimes different names like agile governance, although they refer to different concepts. Whereas agility originates from software engineering and relates mainly to the speed of sensing and response within given structures, adaptivity is founded in evolution theory based on the core elements fitting and learning. Evolution implies system-level changes throughout government [6].

In this contribution, the concept of adaptive governance is investigated from multiple views. Adaptive governance can be viewed as a philosophical approach, but also from an instrumental perspective. Adaptive governance requires that predictability and stability on the one side, and adaptability and flexibility on the other hand, can be achieved. For this they need to be balancd. We argue that these can be combined by utilizing a combination of instruments. For this, we investigate Asby's law of requisite variety to investigate te diversity of instruments needed to deal with the various uncertainties in the environment.

2   Is Adaptive Governance an Oxymoron?

'Adaptive' and 'governance' might look contracting at first glance. Governance is about control, authorities and accountabilities, whereas adaptability is about informality, chaos, and change. From this perspective, these words can be viewed as an oxymoron. An oxymoron is a figure of speech in which apparently contradictory terms appear in conjunction.

The governance model of public administrations is often based on the ideas of Max Weber model of bureaucracy. Whereas traditional governance refers to aspects like control, monitoring, stability, accountability and institutional arrangements, this is not per se the way governance needs to be arranged. For example, in a complex adaptive system (CAS) independent entities can be guided by simple rules [9] which is based on a complete different type of governance. These simple rules can enable entities to form a cohesive and dynamic whole like a flock of birds. Furthermore also, in network governance strict control is not possible as there are various autonomous organizations involved. Network governance relies on a governance model based on bilateral communication and agreements instead of on formal hierarchies. Although adaptive conveys the idea of decentral, informality, simplicity, experimentation and might almost look like an anarchy, governance is possible, but it is arranged differently. Similar to network governance and the governance of CAS being different from Weber's model of governance, also adaptive governance is different from this model. Adaptive and governance are not contradictory and they can even strengthen each other. Adaptive governance is a governments' capacity to deal with change while protecting society from instability [4]. Adaptive governance can enhance traditional governance by providing a range of additional governance instruments.

3   Combining Values

In the previous section we argued that adaptive governance is not an oxymoron. This raises the question of how adaptive values on one side and stability on the other can be combined. Adaptive governance should enhance the capacity of an organization to deal with and adapt to changes while protecting the same organization from becoming unstable [4]. Adaptability might become chaos, whereas stability might result in bureaucracy and red tape. Both extremes are not desirable. As such, adaptability and stability are both needed at different times but need to be balanced, as shown in the figure below (Fig. 1).

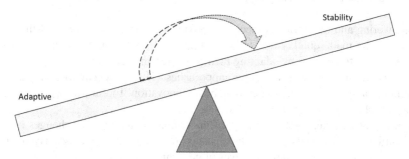

Fig. 1. Balancing and shifting between adaptability and stability

Essential for adaptive governance is the ability to balance the stability and adaptability values. Stability and adaptation alternate, and both are needed. This can be accomplished in various ways. For example, one strategy could be to change some part of the system, whereas to let some parts of the complete system to remain stable. This can be followed by changing other parts. Another approach is to adapt the whole system and to move to a new stable situation. Such a radical approach might be riskier in comparison to an incremental approach. Furthermore, changes can be incremental by bottom-up implementation via continuous improvement-oriented activities or by achieving radical organizational change by completely rethinking and adapting a new vision. In summary, different strategies can be employed to balance adaptability and stability in a way that they can be achieved simultaneously. For the governance, this implies that we do not have to get rid of the stable governance structures but that adaptive governance can enhance and enrich the range of governance instruments that can be used.

4 Creating Adaptive Governance

Ashby's law of Requisite Variety states that for a system to be stable, the number of states that its control mechanism is capable of attaining (its variety) must be greater than or equal to the number of states in the system being controlled [10]. Ashby's law should not be viewed as a kind of universal law but rather as an organizational principle. The interpretation of Ashby's law suggests that if governments want to deal with the uncertainties coming from the environments, then the governments need to have a repertoire of responses. Hence, the government systems should be able to handle the variability of its environment. In contrast, traditionally the strategy was to reduce the variability by standardizing responses [11]. For example, by creating standards form for applying for a permit or to standardize complain procedures. Such an strategy is feasible for situations within the own jurdisdiction, as the environment has to deal with the government by complying with regulations and policies. However, the type of uncertaincies mentioned at the start of this paper cannot be standardised as they are out of the control range. Variety reduction strategies are not feasible and other strategies need to be employed. Janssen and Van der Voort [4] provide a range of strategies. Below we summarize the main characteristics of these strategies.

- Empowering and decentralized decision-making and efforts. This ensures that decisions can be made quickly and close to where the uncertainties occur. Teams can quickly react to changes by adapting their priorities and capacity.
- Combine bottom-up and top-down approaches. Hierarchy can become a rigid command-and-control structure and can block innovation. Top-down approaches need to be enriched by bottom-up approaches.
- Detect early-warning signals. Signals of uncertainties and need for changes need to be heard at the early stages. Mechanisms and incentives for providing early-warning signals can enhance the adaptive power of governments.
- Wider participation. A variety of stakeholders are involved and by representing their voices, their ideas and thoughts can be heard. This can result in better interventions and also to the acceptance of these interventions.
- Focus on governance processes. Focus on procedures and governance processes instead of on rules and regulations. Ensure procedurally orientation instead of technically rational orientation to deal with more variety.
- Enhance local knowledge by supplementing them with scientific inquiry. Involve a diversity of researchers to gain and accumulate the knowledge needed.
- Diversity of skills, expertise and knowledge. People should be trained with new types of knowledge. Education and training will enhance the adaptive capacity. Furthermore, their ability to learn should be enhanced to seek for new ways of working and solutions to deal with the uncertainties.
- Experimentation. The measures and their consequences are often not known. Therefore learning by doing and experimenting in practice within a restricted environment can provide insight into what works and what does not work. Dealing with uncertainty by continuous adjustment.

In Asby's law the variety of the government must be at least as great as the variety of environment [11]. As the variety of the environment is unpredictable, this is hard to meet this requirement, nor is it necessary. Governance instruments and uncertainties do not have to be symmetric. Most important is to have a sufficient variety of adaptive governance instruments to deal with the variety of uncertainties. Furthermore, instruments can be combined, and it is likely that only a combination of instruments can be effective.

5   Conclusions

Although governance might be associated with hierarchy and control, a broader and richer view should be taken to associate governance also with adaptability. Adaptive governance is not an oxymoron and should be treated as something that is desirable at the same time. Adaptive governance accepts uncertainty by being prepared for change and surprise. An essential requirement for adaptive governance is the need to balance stability and adaptability. They can exist at the same time, or they can alternate. More research in strategies for combining stability and adaptability is needed.

Adaptive governance requires the embracing of a diversity of governance instruments. There should be a sufficient variety of governance instruments to deal with the variety of uncertainties. The variety of instruments and the environment can be asymmetric, as governance instruments are likely being able to deal with a range of uncertainties. Furthermore, instruments can be combined, and it is likely that only a combination of governance instruments will be effective.

References

1. Kummitha, R.K.R.: Smart technologies for fighting pandemics: the techno-and human-driven approaches in controlling the virus transmission. Gov. Inf. Q. 37(3), 101481 (2020)
2. Gaozhao, D.: Flagging fake news on social media: an experimental study of media consumers' identification of fake news. Gov. Inf. Q. 38, 101591 (2021)
3. Kankanhalli, A., Charalabidis, Y., Mellouli, S.: IoT and AI for smart government: a research agenda. Gov. Inf. Q. 36(2), 304–309 (2019)
4. Janssen, M., van der Voort, H.: Adaptive governance: towards a stable, accountable and responsive government. Gov. Inf. Q. 33(1), 1–5 (2016)
5. Bronen, R., Chapin, F.S.: Adaptive governance and institutional strategies for climate-induced community relocations in Alaska. Proc. Natl. Acad. Sci. U.S.A. 110(23), 9320–9325 (2013)
6. Janssen, M., Van Der Voort, H.: Agile and adaptive governance in crisis response: lessons from the COVID-19 pandemic. Int. J. Inf. Manag. 55, 102180 (2020)
7. Wang, C., Medaglia, R., Zheng, L.: Towards a typology of adaptive governance in the digital government context: the role of decision-making and accountability. Gov. Inf. Q. 35(2), 306–322 (2018)
8. Mergel, I., Gong, Y., Bertot, J.: Agile government: systematic literature review and future research. Elsevier (2018)
9. Lewin, R., Regine, B.: The Soul At Work: Unleashing the Power of Complexity Science for Business Success. Simon & Schuster, New York (1999)
10. Ashby, W.R.: An Introduction to Cybernetics. Chapman & Hall Ltd., London (1961)
11. Ashby, W.R.: Requisite variety and its implications for the control of complex systems. In: Klir, G.J. (ed.) Facets of Systems Science, pp. 405–417. Springer, Boston (1991). https://doi.org/10.1007/978-1-4899-0718-9_28

Digital Technology and Design

The Role of Service Design in Increasing Regional Innovation in the Silver Economy

Regina Erlenheim$^{(\boxtimes)}$ and Ingrid Pappel

Tallinn University of Technology, Tallinn, Estonia
{regina.erlenheim,ingrid.pappel}@taltech.ee

Abstract. Silver Economy in the world context is the third biggest economy, which generates the biggest opportunities in the public and consumer markets. The challenges that occur, and that are being investigated in the current short research paper, are the role and appropriation of service design in the silver economy. Furthermore, there are weak linkages of multiple and diverse stakeholders along with the lack of integrated innovation frameworks, which, in turn, creates challenges for the ageing society. Demographic change towards silver economy is a phenomenon that has a major impact and needs increased attention together with relevant practices of service design. The goal of the paper is to accentuate the changing role of service design in Silver Economy together with identifying the needs and requirements of the service ecosystem of seniors. This experience research paper draws initial conclusions from the experiences and the activities conducted throughout the entire Baltic Sea Region through a larger set of research activities of the OSIRIS project led by Tallinn University of Technology in Estonia and suggests further research for including more diverse stakeholder groups in the Silver Economy.

Keywords: Silver Economy · Public sector innovation · Service design · Digitalisation · e-governance

1 Introduction

Silver Economy (can also be addressed as the economy of the ageing population) is considered as a part of the general economy with the focus on the population of older adults of over 50 [1]. The members of the silver economy, e.g. people in the aging population have particular needs and demands, which will continue to evolve with the current rapid rate of technological, social, and demographic change. The baseline value of various services and goods in Europe's Silver Economy has been estimated of €3.7 trillion in 2015 and it is expected to potentially expand over the years across the EU to €5.7 trillion [2]. There is a tremendous range of interest areas that are related to challenges and opportunities, which are brought about by the growing aging population both in Europe and worldwide [1]. Together with the before mentioned changes, a call for more comprehensive way for addressing the Silver Economy is needed.

The more specific challenges in the Silver Economy are dominated by a disproportionate need for health services, which totals approximately up to €303 billion by people

© Springer Nature Switzerland AG 2022
A. V. Chugunov et al. (Eds.): EGOSE 2021, CCIS 1529, pp. 11–20, 2022.
https://doi.org/10.1007/978-3-031-04238-6_2

who are aged over 50 and totals 2/3 of all the health spending and 1/10 of all the public spending in 2015 [1]. In comparison, the Silver Economy spends on education only 0.2% of the education spending, which is only 0.03% of all government spending [1]. While the second most significant part of the public spending is going towards social protection (but varies depending on the specific country), then additional economic activities in a wide range of industries such as retail, restaurants, real estate, hotels, leisure services [1] together with education, culture, information and communication technologies and media, service robotics, mobility, insurances, and financial services among others [3] are all increasingly more significant for the members of the Silver Economy.

As shown above, there is an ever-growing need to address the shifting demands of the aging population. As mentioned above, the expected growth of Silver Economy (from €3.7 trillion in 2015 to €5.7 trillion in 2025) ensures that more attention on the wants, requirements, and demands of the aging population has to be put. Nowadays, one of the often spoken about approaches to understanding and meeting the needs of people in various stakeholder groups is service design, which in essence is a process during which sustainable solutions for both service users and service providers are generated in a human-centred approach [4]. While service design (SD) as a thinking tool and approach has been widely implemented in most sectors alike, it is argued here that it has not been utilised in its full potential when examining the Silver Economy. Authors (see [5–7]) have discussed the benefits of service design (for instance co-creation, co-design, visualisation, stakeholder involvement, and most definitely user-centred) in various contexts of service innovation amongst the seniors. To add upon that, the current experience research article sees the role of SD to increase in the coming years and benefit the Silver Economy sector tremendously. While focusing on Silver Economy, no specific distinction between public and private services is made in the context of this experience article. As mentioned above, Silver Economy is comprised of different significant members (from public, private and non-profit sectors) with the goal of meeting the ever-growing demands and needs of the aging population.

The current research centres around the changing role of service design that would support the process of digitalization of government as well private service ecosystems and draws from the experiences and activities of a research project (focus groups, interviews, hackathons, expert brainstorming sessions) conducted on Silver Economy in the Baltic Sea Region with increased attention on Estonia. The research paper relies on mixed research methods. The analysis has been combined based on workshops, interviews, surveys, and market research and provides an initial overview of the central emerging discussions on the role and function of service design within the larger phenomenon of Silver Economy. The current research is divided into three further sections. Firstly, it focuses on Estonia and its experience through a public sector lens and describes existing digital environment as a prerequisite for potential Silver Economy developments. The second section focuses on service design and its application in Silver Economy. Lastly, the third section focuses on the discussion of the previous two sections and showcases the roadmap for future research.

2 Estonian Background

Estonia has been working on ICT infrastructure to boost digital transformation since the beginning of 1990s. Many successful e-governance systems have been developed to provide digital service provision between government, entrepreneurs, and citizens. Moreover, it formed the country to be one of the more advanced countries in proving public services online [8]. However, while building e-governance related solutions, the complexity of how governments can satisfy the needs of their citizens in challenging times needs to be addressed. Thus, digital government ecosystems and investigating potential technologies have been focused on in Estonia, i.e. technologies that support digital transformation. Here the comprehension of architectural needs and requirements while developing e-Governance eco-system architecture to be homogeneous and interoperable need specific focus and inclusion [9]. Based on the experience gathered over the last decades one of the most critical components of Estonian e-governance development has been digital data exchange [9] together with digital signing as few of the most critical steps to move towards paperless government. Because of a well-developed e-governance ecosystem and publicly provided services, which keep developing further, administrative activities become increasingly more paperless. Furthermore, the local level, as the main public service provider to citizens, has applied digital means increasingly [10]. Moreover, paperless management enables the development and building of e-services that allow more often a fully digitalised interaction between citizens and local governments while adhering to both GDPR and eIDAS regulations.

That means, the digitalisation has involved additionally to the state level e-governance developments along with local governments where many developments have been built upon document management systems [11]. Estonian experience has shown that paperless management and digital records keeping has been essential foundation for service transformation and digitalisation [12]. In addition, seamless online services are possible because Estonia applied the use of a digital identity as one of the first priorities [13].

Thus, information management and smart (and repetitive) use of data allow enhanced monitoring of the procedural steps of the local authorities and that, in turn, allows effective as well as transparent service provision to the citizens. Although interdisciplinarity is one of the main considerations nowadays, technological solutions are still increasingly some of the dominating factors in the move towards e-governance realizations. Estonian practice has showed good evidence in that regard [14, 15].

As said above, The goal for the government is address and supply comfortability citizens' everyday life and making sure that all citizens know how, when, where and which services they need to use [16]. That involves also going more deeply into a service with the intention to make services efficiently accessible in most convenient way and Estonian experience is based on e-service transformation including making many services as proactive as possible. That approach should provide immediate access to other services, which require additional applications.

In case of a digital and proactive service, the government knows when somebody is entitled to a service, collects bits of necessary data from different registries, carries out necessary procedure and notifies the person about the proceeding process and results [17]. The goal is to bother the citizen as little as possible and only when inevitable. Although in some cases the government does not have data that is inevitable for completing the proceeding then it is justified approach citizen as many times as needed.

Raising the service accessibility is not the only way to serve citizens' needs. Moreover, instead of creating constantly new e-services within various channels for public services and waiting for the citizen to contact the local government, the focus should be on reaching out the citizen and proactively initiating service processes [18]. That also brings possibility to involve AI into service life cycle and automate the decision-making processes. However, the citizens' needs, especially the seniors' ones must be considered while developing and digitalising public services, which shows the necessity for service design to be involved.

Citizens needs and expectations towards public services are subject to change during their lifetime. Such changes could be mapped out as a life cycle of a person [19]. Services based on life events are becoming increasingly relevant [37]. This can also be witnessed by the focus of the European Commission to promote life and business events (LBEs) (and LBE based services) across Europe (See [20]). In Estonia, the Ministry of Economics and Communications has been focusing lately on the describing and harmonising 15 most used and central life and business events (these including but not limited to being born, going to school, getting married/divorced, applying for a disability, starting a business, and becoming a retired person) [21]. By implementing a life-event based logic to public services, governments, both central and local municipalities will be able to both anticipate the needs of people in the relevant service-user/stakeholder group and anticipate the resources that is needed to provide user-centred and relevant public services. It could be argued here, that by incorporating the insights from life-event based services together with tools and techniques of service design, the benefit for Silver Economy could be tremendous.

3   Service Design

The term "service design" was formulated by Lynn Shostack in 1982 [4]. Shostack [22] argued that SD should be the concern of the management and the marketing departments. Furthermore, she also claimed that a "service blueprint" needs to be introduced, which in turn would give an overview of how service systems as processes interact with other processes in a company, resources, and workflows. Now, almost forty years later, the use of service design has become frequent, popular, and widely accepted in many fields of life [23].

The objective of SD is to improve the quality of services, communication, and interaction between service providers and their customers, and users' experiences [23]. Service design in essence is set of tools, techniques, and thinking [18] a human-centred approach to service innovation [24]. The last years (even couple of decades) have shown that the attention has been growing on the needs of the users and growing interest in user-centric services. At the same time, little attention has paid to understanding users' preferences [25–27]. Firstly, one of the core components of service design is that it is deemed user-centric as it sets the user of the service at the centre of the design process and expects relevant and real understanding of the customer instead of just describing the statistically and analysing empirically their needs. Secondly, service design can be seen co-creative in nature because it looks into how to integrate service stakeholders into the process of designing it. Reflecting on the Silver Economy and what service design could offer in this context, the co-creativeness of service design will prove to be an invaluable asset to the stakeholders. Service design expects designers to consciously build an environment that facilitates the production and assessment of ideas within diverse set of stakeholders. Third, the sequencing (as suggested by Stickdorn and Schneider) tackles the steps of getting in touch with a service during its provision, and during the following post-service period. Service should hold customer's interest with a good narrative and keep the expectations without assuming too much of the customer. Fourthly, service design includes "evidencing". Physical artefacts continue to improve customers' observations and understanding of the service they have received. And finally, it is "holistic" - the big picture is prioritised [28]. Stickdorn and Schneider developed their work around service design further from thinking to doing ("This is Service Design Doing") [29] and suggested an updated approach to service design. Firstly, it should be human-centred and take into consideration all people who are affected by the service and all of their experiences, Secondly, instead of just being co-creative, service design should be collaborative and stakeholders from different backgrounds and functions should be actively involved in the service innovation process. Thirdly, service design should be iterative as the entire process is exploratory, adaptive, and experimental while maintaining its iterative characteristics. Fourthly, service design should be sequential and should be visualised and orchestrated as a sequence of interconnected activities. This is also supported by the notion of life and business events discussed briefly in the end of the previous section. Fifthly, the activities done during service innovation should be research and prototyped by reflecting on the perceived digital or physical reality. And lastly, service design needs to remain holistic and sustainably address the real needs of all stakeholders [29].

While we know increasingly more about the best practices and recommended routes to reach different stakeholders, the design of customer- (or user-) centred electronic public services will continue to be a complicated task in the light of changing demands and needs of citizens [25]. Service design could be explained as a sequence of activities such as planning and organising different resources (such as people, infrastructure, materials, communications) related to a service. Constant stress on public spending sets demands to keep finding ways to grow efficiency and addressing the needs of the citizens at the same time [30].

Through the recent years different service design methodologies have been developed for understanding what people need and want. While there are plenty of methodologies available, what is common among many of them is the understanding of the underlying problem with service provision. The Table 1 Below addresses three of methodologies briefly.

Double diamond as proposed by the UK Design Council in 2007 divides the design process into four distinguishable phases. This methodology is one of the more widely used approaches to service design currently [32]. Design Sprint that was developed by Google Ventures in 2010 proposes a five-day sequence of activities to solve, prototype, and test a solution during a five-stage/five-day process [33]. Iterative design process proposes a four-stage approach to service design [28].

Table 1. Service design methodologies

Methodology	Double diamond [31]	Google Sprint [33]	Iterative design process [28]
Stage 1	Discovery – understanding insights	Mapping and targeting	Exploration – clear understanding from different perspectives
Stage 2	Defining – making sense of possibilities	Sketching competing solutions	Creation – of many options and mistakes
Stage 3	Developing – creating, prototyping, testing, iterating	Deciding on the best solution	Reflection – prototyping in situation close to reality, role-playing
Stage 4	Delivering – finalising, producing, launching the project	Prototyping	Implementation – formulation and testing of a consistent concept
Stage 5	–	Testing	–

What is common is the previous three approaches is the central focus on understanding the problem with the current service process. There is a clear need to first understand the problems a service user or a service provider is dealing with. For that it is argued here in the current experience research paper that service providers who are operating both in and outside the Silver Economy and both in the public and private sector spheres need to include the aging populations more in their co-creative activities and allow wider participation during the consultation, preparation, delivery, and implementation stages of service innovation.

In order to provide value to different stakeholders of Silver Economy, i.e. public, private and non-profit sectors, academia, and the end-users, an integrated response from all of them is imperative [34]. Co-creation as a concept in essence, as mentioned above, suggests that all stakeholders work together to create products and services that the end-users would value. The experience of creating such a platform of collaboration would ensure that there would be a forum for mutual engagement and bridge the gap amongst different users of a service. This, in turn, would lead to building an environment where senior citizens and other stakeholders would be able to engage and innovate [34].

4 Discussion, Conclusions and Future Work

Effective SD needs cautious focus on different (often functional) issues such as costs, service levels, efficiency, sales, profits [35], and human aspects, such as emotions, preferences, needs, and wants (see [36, 37]. Burrows and others argue further in [37] that emotion-led goal modelling is often overlooked during the service development process, as technology developers often focus on the functional goals (i.e. what the solution does) as opposed to the quality and emotional functionality (i.e. the feel and pleasurability of the technological solution). They continue that emotional aspects are not thoroughly understood, and the stakeholders are blamed for the lack of engagement instead. This raises an interesting challenge for dealing with service design in the aging population. How to engage the seniors in the service design processes in order to provide emotionally appropriate and technologically adequate services both in the public and private sectors within the larger Silver Economy. It is argued here that service design can lends its techniques and tools for service innovation in these exact settings.

Estonia is working together with other countries' administrations and people, promoting its e-governance solutions and extending the knowledge about governmental digital transformation. That also means bringing in new innovative and sustainable services to the market. This, in turn, would allow contributing to Silver Economy by providing solutions to the problems of the ageing population to live more independently via ICT tools and have a healthy and comfortable life. This could be done by involving various stakeholders (as also suggested by Stickdorn and Schneider in [29]) to boost the economy with the services which are efficiently accessible within the digital environment while considering the technological acceptance and emotional aspects of innovative solutions. Even more so, barriers and limitations of what hinder public and private sector from developing and sharing services for seniors might be quite contradictory. While keeping up with the technological solutions of the rapidly changing world, seniors people may still experience distrust towards using digital technologies. Co-creation and co-design of public services is needed to assess the availability and access to services. Moreover, the lack of knowledge (and limited digital skills) is not only the limitation of the seniors but also a possible restriction for service providers and other crucial stakeholders.

As a conclusion as a result, we achieved an initial set of requirements to build an international collaborative platform that concentrates services and service providers together with the end users. SilverHub platform connects Baltic Sea Region countries through knowledge sharing in six regional Smart Silver Labs (ecosystems). In addition to the ecosystem the SilverHub is planned as a one-stop-shop for innovative supporting tools and financing instruments of each region. Based on the results achieved so far during the project (such as creating a common ground for the design of a collaborative platform) it will be able to give direction for further requirements' building for future collaborative activities within the Silver Economy such as a more extensive system design and system architecture.

We believe that as a future step including service design thinking together with co-creation and co-design principles will be used to guarantee that the needs of the seniors will be taken into account. The goal for the future will be to design an environment for publishing and directing (public) services and communication in the Silver Economy domain by the means of the digital technologies. The main concept will be a collaborative platform, which helps to develop innovative solutions to the problems faced by the aging population to help them live a more independent, healthy, and comfortable life and to be integrated into digital society. Private and public sector institutions, senior citizens, and other members in the Silver Economy should have the opportunity to collaborate and co-create innovative solutions. Furthermore, there are benefits associated with connecting financing stakeholders into the network to enable different actors of innovation monitor and accelerate the uptake of services while enabling seniors to continue aging gracefully. We see the platform tackling the challenges of meeting the needs of aging populations that the governments are currently facing.

Acknowledgments. The paper and this research could not have been done without the work and support of the OSIRIS project "Supporting Smart Specialization Approach in Silver Economy for Increasing Regional Innovation Capacity and Sustainable Growth (21.09.2018−30.09.2021)", in Tallinn University of Technology, School of Information Technologies, Department of Software Science and which is financed by the European Commission and the project team at Tallinn University of Technology.

References

1. Technopolis. The Silver Economy. Final report (2018). https://op.europa.eu/en/publication-detail/-/publication/a9efa929-3ec7-11e8-b5fe-01aa75ed71a1
2. European Commission. Silver Economy Study: How to stimulate the economy by hundreds of millions of Euros per year (2018). https://digital-strategy.ec.europa.eu/en/library/silver-economy-study-how-stimulate-economy-hundreds-millions-euros-year
3. Klimczuk, A.: Comparative analysis of national and regional models of the silver economy in the European Union. Int. J. Ageing Later Life (2016). https://journal.ep.liu.se/IJAL/article/view/1309
4. Interaction Design. Service Design (2021). https://www.interaction-design.org/literature/topics/service-design
5. Chen, S.-H.: Determining the service demands of an aging population by integrating QFD and FMEA method. Qual. Quant. Int. J. Methodol. **50**, 283–298 (2016). https://link.springer.com/content/pdf/10.1007/s11135-014-0148-y.pdf
6. DAA. Final report: Making ageing better. Design led innovations for active ageing. European Regional Development Fund Project (2014). https://idz.de/dokumente/DAA_FINAL_BOOK.pdf
7. Caic, M., Odekerken-Schroder, G., Mahr, D.: Service robots: value co-creation and co-destruction in elderly care networks. J. Serv. Manag. **29**(2), 178–205 (2018). https://www.emerald.com/insight/content/doi/10.1108/JOSM-07-2017-0179/full/html
8. UNDESA. United Nations E-Government Survey (2020). https://www.un.org/development/desa/publications/publication/2020-united-nations-e-government-survey
9. Saputro, R., Pappel, I., Vainsalu, H., Lips, S., Draheim, D.: Prerequisite for the adoption of the X-Road interoperability and data exchange framework: a comparative study. In: Proceedings of the Seventh International Conference on eDemocracy and eGovernment (ICEDEG). IEEE, Buenos Aires, Argentina (2020). https://ieeexplore.ieee.org/document/9096704
10. Pappel, I., Pappel, I., Tepandi, J., Draheim, D.: Systematic digital signing in Estonian e-government processes. In: Hameurlain, A., Küng, J., Wagner, R., Dang, T.K., Thoai, N. (eds.) Transactions on Large-Scale Data- and Knowledge-Centered Systems XXXVI. LNCS, vol. 10720, pp. 31–51. Springer, Heidelberg (2017). https://doi.org/10.1007/978-3-662-56266-6_2
11. Pappel, I., Tsap, V., Pappel, I., Draheim, D.: Exploring e-services development in local government authorities by means of electronic document management systems. In: Chugunov, A., Misnikov, Y., Roshchin, E., Trutnev, D. (eds.) EGOSE 2018. CCIS, vol. 947, pp. 223–234. Springer, Cham (2019). https://doi.org/10.1007/978-3-030-13283-5_17
12. Pappel, I., Tsap, V., Draheim, D.: The e-LocGov model for introducing e-Governance into local governments: an Estonian case study. IEEE Trans. Emerg. Top. Comput. **9**, 597–611 (2019). https://ieeexplore.ieee.org/document/8685129
13. Lips, S., Pappel, I., Tsap, V., Draheim, D.: Key factors in coping with large-scale security vulnerabilities in the eID field. In: Kő, A., Francesconi, E. (eds.) EGOVIS 2018. LNCS, vol. 11032, pp. 60–70. Springer, Cham (2018). https://doi.org/10.1007/978-3-319-98349-3_5

14. Gunaratne, H., Pappel, I.: Enhancement of the e-invoicing systems by increasing the efficiency of workflows via disruptive technologies. In: Chugunov, A., Khodachek, I., Misnikov, Y., Trutnev, D. (eds.) EGOSE 2020. CCIS, vol. 1349, pp. 60–74. Springer, Cham (2020). https://doi.org/10.1007/978-3-030-67238-6_5

15. Pappel, I., Pappel, I., Tampere, T., Draheim, D.: Implementation of e-invoicing principles in Estonian local governments. In: Borges, A., João, V., Rouco, J.C.D. (eds.) Proceedings of the 17th European Conference on Digital Government (ECDG): Military Academy, Lisbon, Portugal, 12–13 June 2017, pp. 127−136. Academic Conferences and Publishing International Limited (2017)

16. Sirendi, R., Mendoza, A., Barrier, M., Taveter, K., Sterling, L.: A conceptual framework for effective appropriation of proactive public e-services. In: Proceedings of 18th European Conference on Digital Government, ECDG 2018, Santiago de Compostela, Spain, pp. 213–221 (2018)

17. Kõrge, H., Erlenheim, R., Draheim, D.: Designing Proactive Business Event Services: A case study of the Estonian Company Registration portal. In Proceedings of the International Conference on Electronic Participation ePart 2019: Electronic Participation, pp. 73–84. San Benedetto del Tronto, Italy (2019)

18. Erlenheim, R.. Designing proactive public services. Ph.D. Dissertation. Tallinn University of Technology, Swinburne University of Technology (2019)

19. Kõrge, H.: Designing proactive business event services: a case study of the Estonian company registration. M.Sc. Dissertation. Tallinn University of Technology (2019)

20. European Commission. Core Public Service Vocabulary Application Profile 2.2.1, European Union (2021). https://joinup.ec.europa.eu/collection/semantic-interoperability-community-semic/solution/core-public-service-vocabulary-application-profile/release/221

21. Ministry of Economics and Communications (MEAC). In Estonina: Sündmusteenused viivad digiriigi järgmisele tasemele. Translation: Life and business events take the digital state to the next level (2020). https://www.mkm.ee/et/uudised/sundmusteenused-viivad-digiriigi-jargmisele-tasemele

22. Shostack, L.: How to design a service. Eur. J. Mark. 16(1), 49–63 (1982)

23. Steen, M., Manchot, M., de Koning, N.: Benefits of co-design in service design projects. J. Des. 5(2), 53–60 (2011). https://isfcolombia.uniandes.edu.co/images/2020-intersemestral/18_de_junio/Benefits-of-Co-design-in-Service-Design-Projects.pdf

24. Yu, E., Sangiorgi, D.: Service design as an approach to implement the value cocreation perspective in new service development. J. Serv. Res. (2017). https://journals.sagepub.com/doi/abs/10.1177/1094670517709356

25. Venkatesh, V., Chan, F.K.Y., Thong, J.Y.L.: Designing e-government services: key service attributes and citizens preference structures. J. Oper. Manag. 30, 116–133 (2012)

26. Jansen, A., Olnes, S.: The nature of public e-services and their quality dimensions. Gov. Inf. Q. 33(4), 647–657 (2016)

27. European Commission. eGovernment Benchmark 2017: Taking stock of user- centric design and deliver of digital public services in Europe. European Union (2017). https://op.europa.eu/en/publication-detail/-/publication/7f1b4ecb-f9a7-11e7-b8f5-01aa75ed71a1/language-en

28. Stickdorn, M., Schneider, J.: This Is Service Design Thinking: Basics, Tools, Cases. BIS Publishers, Amsterdam (2010)

29. Stickdorn, M., Schneider, J.: This is Service Design Doing (2017)

30. Karwan, K.R., Markland, R.E.: Integrating service design principles and information technology to improve delivery and productivity in public sector operations: the case of the South Caroline DMV. J. Oper. Manag. 24, 347–362 (2006)

31. Design Council. The Design Process: What is the Double Diamond? (2021). https://www.designcouncil.org.uk/news-opinion/design-process-what-double-diamond

32. Yu, E., Sangiorgi, D.: Service Design as an approach to New Service Development: reflections and future studies (2014). https://www.researchgate.net/publication/263088902_Service_D esign_as_an_approach_to_New_Service_Development_reflections_and_future_studies
33. The Sprint Book. The Design Sprint (2021). https://www.thesprintbook.com/the-design-sprint
34. Butt, S., Rava, K., Kangilaski, T., Pappel, I., Draheim, D.: Designing a digital collaborative platform for silver economy: inception and conceptualization. In: The Proceedings of Eight International Conference on eDemocracy and eGovernment (ICEDEG) (2021)
35. Narasimhan, R., Talluri, S., Sarkis, J., Ross, A.: Efficient service location design in government services: a decision support system framework. J. Oper. Manag. **23**, 163–178 (2005)
36. Miller, T., Pedell, S., Lopez-Lorca, A.A., Mendoza, A., Sterling, L., Keirnan, A.: Emotion-led modelling for people oriented requirements engineering: the case study of emergency systems. J. Syst. Softw. **105**, 54–71 (2015)
37. Burrows, R., Pedell, S., Sterling, L., Miller, T., Mendoza, A.: Motivational goals for using electronic health record applications. In: Proceedings of European Network of Living Labs, OLLD 2018 (2018). https://www.researchgate.net/publication/327891156_Motivatio nal_Goals_for_using_Electronic_Health_Record_Applications/download
38. Erlenheim, R., Draheim, D., Taveter, K.: Identifying design principles for proactive services through systematically understanding the reactivity-proactivity spectrum. In: Proceedings of ICEGOV2020: Proceedings of the 13th International Conference on Theory and Practice of Electronic Governance (2020). https://dl.acm.org/doi/10.1145/3428502.3428572

Unraveling the Social-Technical Complexity of Dashboards for Transformation

Florian Lemke[1]([⊠]), Marijn Janssen[2], and Dirk Draheim[3]

[1] Capgemini, Business and Technology Solutions – Public Sector, Berlin, Germany
florian.lemke@capgemini.com
[2] Technology, Policy and Management Faculty, Delft University of Technology, Delft,
The Netherlands
M.F.W.H.A.Janssen@tudelft.nl
[3] Information Systems Group, Tallinn University of Technology, Tallinn, Estonia
dirk.draheim@taltech.ee

Abstract. The need for standardized and visualized performance monitoring on a wide range of topics has become apparent in recent years. In the public sector, there has been an increase in the number of dashboards to create transparency into the progress. Yet, the design of dashboards encounters many challenges ranging from technical to social. The goal of this research is to unravel the social-technical complexity of dashboards and outline their basic requirements and a process for creating dashboards. In addition to explicit project milestones, these also visualize digital implementation programs at the policy level.

Keywords: Dashboard · Performance Monitoring · Stakeholder · e-Government (eGov) · Digital Government · Complexity · Design Dimensions

1 Introduction

A crucial success factor in any digital transformation is a deep understanding of adequate key performance indicators and their systematic utilization. Measurements and performance indicators and the usage of data as a basis for private and public decision-making have become more important to provide insight into the progress of digital government initiatives. Public sector CIOs and ministers are requesting key performance indicators (KPI) from different public organizations to build up dashboards that can present and quickly offer information about their transformation projects for internal use or to the public [1–3].

The transformation is often guided by the development of metrics presented on dashboards [4]. A dashboard is a graphical user interface which provides at-a-glance views as well as data and information on a particular topic. The underlying data and information can often be understood as key performance indicators that are relevant to a particular objective of a process. Dashboards are used more and more as an alternative to the annual "progress report". Whereas reports are provided in discrete points in time, dashboards can always give the actual situation. A dashboard provides a means to track

© Springer Nature Switzerland AG 2022
A. V. Chugunov et al. (Eds.): EGOSE 2021, CCIS 1529, pp. 21–34, 2022.
https://doi.org/10.1007/978-3-031-04238-6_3

progress, however, its indicators might also easily give wrong impressions. Data might not be correct, might give a wrong picture or can be interpreted in the wrong way as they are from social-technical nature [5]. Also, people might fill in data politically [6, 7]. As such, managing digital transformation using measures such as KPIs and dashboards is challenging.

While dashboards are by no means a new phenomenon, we can nowadays observe a wide-spread and increasing proliferation and utilization of such tools throughout the public sector. For example, they are used to display use of financial resources, reform progress, health data, and geospatial and environmental data. Currently, managing government officials request measures and dashboards to make their initiated changes (such as digital strategies and programs) and their daily work more visible and transparent to the citizen. A good example is the visualization of vaccination progress in various countries in the context of the global COVID-19 pandemic [8]. Hence, consultancies are engaged and consult the relevant public institutions and set up measures that outline current situations and trail measures that mostly show obvious and biased outcomes. However, those situations will not bring digital transformation to a further stage and will not contribute significantly to the transparency requested by the citizen as they do not provide the information that is required, or only provide it in part in order to withhold information. This approach does not create change in terms of building trust and openness with governments [9].

In order to better understand these social-technical challenges and to provide dashboard creators with a targeted approach to their creation, this paper will unravel the social-technical complexity of dashboards and outline basic requirements for dashboards to understand the complexity and counteract existing challenges to make them successful.

In Sect. 2, we provide the conceptualization of the development of a dashboard from its data generation to implementation based on five expert interviews to put the information provided in the interviews into an overall structure. In Sect. 3, at first, we will have a look at two different cases and outline the results of the five expert interviews regarding the outlined challenges for the development of a dashboard by introducing and presenting an overview of generic challenges. We finish the paper with a conclusion in Sect. 4.

Our suggested generic overview of challenges in the development of current dashboards is based on evidence from a short literature review, an analysis of two presented cases (Sect. 3) and, furthermore, evidence from five anonymous personal open expert interviews – each one hour – that we have conducted in Germany and the People's Republic of China (PRC). The interviewees are senior practitioners in the development and implementation of dashboards and specialists in the R&D sector on a national and European level.

The five experts were identified according to their experience in the national and international context as well as their involvement in the process of creating a dashboard. The respondents included people involved in the conceptual design of dashboards, experts involved in the technical implementation and creation of the data engine, and experts focused on the creation of the interfaces.

In the area of dashboard conceptualization, the experts were two German senior business analysts who are involved in the creation of public dashboards (1) and the creation of public and private dashboards (2). For the analysis of technical questions, a Chinese data scientist from a public research institute in Guangzhou was interviewed (3), who deals with the provision of utility data. Furthermore, a German data engineer was interviewed who deals with the development of system architectures of the data engine based on the data of the dashboards to be used (4). Finally, a German frontend designer of a private research institute was interviewed, who deals with the creation of interfaces (5).

2 Conceptualizing Dashboards: From Data Generation to Implementation

In order to obtain a clear and unambiguous definition of a development process of a dashboard and corresponding terms (e.g., the types of dashboards identified), the information provided is conceptualized based on literature, interviews and the authors' own knowledge.

To meet the main goal of a dashboard, the automated and visualized provision of reports should be based on available resources (and thus enable a significant reduction of effort for the creation of those reports). A generic process should also be created which represents the development of a dashboard. Based on the authors' personal experience, interviewees were asked to comment on and expand a given high-level process in a joint conversation with the authors. During the interviews, clear process steps for the overall development of a dashboard emerged.

Based on the conducted expert interviews, a generic process for the development of dashboards was derived. In the process, two different approaches for the public sector were identified that make necessary a distinction necessary in the development of a dashboard, i.e., open-oriented dashboards and goal-oriented dashboards:

- *Open-oriented dashboards* are the visualization of data that show a development without a previously defined goal. Good examples are the presentation of infection figures and the vaccination rate during the COVID-19 pandemic. Likewise, dashboards that show the distribution of age cohorts and population development can be classified as open-oriented.

- *Goal-oriented dashboards* are visualizations of data that work towards an explicit goal. For example, policy efforts can be visualized and the extent to which policy goals have been achieved can be recognized. These dashboards usually show the development of thematic projects such as digital transformation or the fight against poverty among the elderly. However, this requires a clear definition of the measurability of these goals.

Both identified types of dashboards differ in the framework of information provision and the extent to which transparency is created, as goal-oriented dashboards are located within predefined frameworks. Depending on the user orientation, the data provided can be used to visualize information on the fulfillment of goals. However, the user should be responsible for evaluating the visualized data of the dashboard. In the case of open-oriented dashboards, the creation of transparency is purely dependent on the information provided and is not influenced by a defined target direction.

It is not necessary to define the user groups for one of the identified types of dashboards. Depending on their content, both types of dashboards can address the same or different user groups at the very same time.

In the case of open-oriented dashboards, the first step is to define the correct measures after the major question and objective has been posed. It may be that already existing data sets and indicators must be visualized, or that new data sets and logics have to be developed, which enable a visualization of the major question and objective with the help of data.

In the case of goal-oriented dashboards, a translation from policy goals, characteristics or milestones that should be achieved must take place at the beginning to enable data-driven measurability to subsequently merge these two types of dashboards and facilitate a clear definition of the targeted audience.

The following step focuses on the involvement of different stakeholders. Some of the relevant stakeholders can be found in Fig. 1.

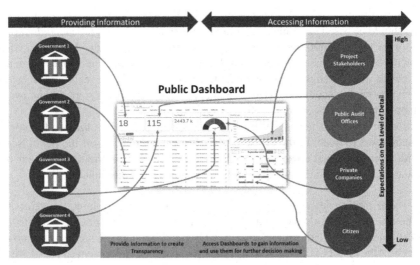

Fig. 1. Example of a dashboard: the provision of dashboards and the different expectations at the level of information provided for different user groups.

Here, it is important to involve not only the participating institutions but also future users and audience. In the conducted interviews, clear comments were made in this regard, which referred to the fact that the involvement of stakeholders was primarily concerned with setting goals and user centeredness. The focus in this step is not yet on the provision of data and the close involvement of data suppliers, so as not to jeopardize or restrict the creative and iterative process for answering the major question and objective.

After completion of this process step, various activities are carried out in parallel. The definition of the individual steps is usually carried out in interactive workshops with all stakeholders and various methods such as design thinking [10] and co-creation [11, 12]. In addition to the definition of the user journey, the determination of relevant data and the form of visualization of corresponding data, multivariate tests are carried out in this step in order to achieve a satisfactory result for the user. After completion of this phase, the result may differ significantly from the objectives that were defined at the beginning of the process.

In the following step, the necessary data quality is defined together with corresponding data providers and appropriate data sources are identified to ensure the development of the key elements of a dashboard, i.e., the data engine. From the developer's point of view, the preparation and participation of the data suppliers are fundamental, since they have an overall view of the data available to them and at the same time also have the knowledge regarding the data quality, according to the statement of one interviewee (4).

The development of the data engine is described by the interviewees (3–5) as the key element of the process. The development of the data engine includes the definition of the system architecture, whose structure is dependent on the data provided. System architectures that exclusively process static data differ from those that also process dynamic data. At the same time, the data engine also serves as a data storage to enable the manual provision and storage of non-dynamic data from corresponding data-registers. A data-register is a data storage or set of data that can be assigned to a variety of functions by a data engineer. To merge these data-registers in a meaningful and value-creating way, a corresponding data-register linking takes place within the data engine. To check the plausibility and quality of the data provided, the data engine also includes a data plausibility logic and a data linking logic. A data linking logic only becomes significant if different raw data sets are merged to obtain new insights and create new indicators for statements. This is especially necessary when goals have to be made measurable within goal-oriented dashboards. The same procedure can be seen when developing complex indexes. Some of the data that is made available and processed within the data engine may not be public. For security reasons, appropriate data security measures must therefore be considered as early as in the stage of creating the data engine to guarantee the security of the data. According to the interviewees (4–5), this process step poses challenges, since access to the final interface for visualization is usually protected, however the security of the data engine has not been sufficiently considered.

After the basic development of the data engine, the implementation of previous results and decisions on the strategic orientation, the results of the user tests as well as the definition and creation of relevant data together with their quality take place in a major visualization interface designed for this purpose. Many different visualization tools are available for this purpose. Besides commercial providers, there are also open-source libraries with ready-made visualization options and interfaces. The selection of the appropriate visualization tool depends on the requirements of the interface. The use of open-source interfaces makes it possible to improve the visual design, the standardization and professionalism of the representations and to enable a better user experience.

After the first visualization of data, an important milestone within the project implementation can be achieved with the go-live of the visualization interface as a minimal viable product (MVP).

With the help of user feedback and further usability workshops, further requirements and design elements can be implemented in the interface following an iterative process to increase its quality. With this step, the basic process for the development of a dashboard is completed.

During the interviews, an expert (2) offered the thought of a "next generation" development of dashboards. With this statement, she underlined the further development and decoupling of interfaces with further reference to the already existing major data engine. This spin-off serves the possible representation of regional specifics and is to be fundamentally dependent on the main dashboard. One interviewee (2) emphasizes that in the private sector, spin-off dashboards could be the upgrading of a supply chain process, which could be enriched with internal company data and thus offer new possibilities for presentation and, in addition to a better basis for management decisions, could also enable a competitive advantage.

The interviewee (2) affirms the provision of different spin-off minor visualization interfaces with the statement that the necessary data and representations must be brought to the place where they are needed. One interviewee (1) supported this with the statement: *"The data has to follow the citizens and not the citizen its data."*

For the public sector, this development of a "next generation" dashboard could be a trustworthy, comprehensible, region-specific visualization of information for citizens, especially in the context of responsibility and provision of valid data and information. An example of this could be the creation of a major dashboard, which would visualize general information about the infection rates and general regulations in the context of the COVID-19 pandemic at the national level. Possible spin-off dashboards would be specific dashboards at the regional and municipal level, showing targeted information and regulations in the regions and thus improving the comprehensibility for users and ensuring that the data are up-to-date.

Public institutions are enabled to provide up-to-date information at low cost and thus create added public value due to open-data. At the same time, this also means a reduction in the complexity of corresponding interfaces since those spin-offs are tailored to the requirements of the users.

Figure 2 shows the open- and goal-oriented approaches from their beginning, which results in two different steps for the further creation of a dashboard. The process visualization was designed using the Business Process Model and Notation (BPMN 2.0), which is a graphical specification language in business informatics and process management [13].

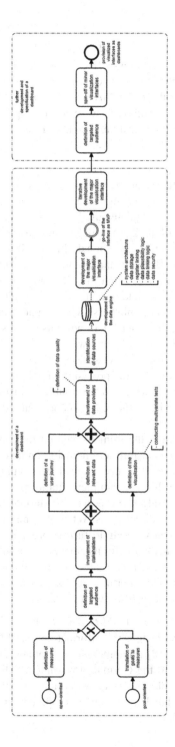

Fig. 2. The development process of a dashboard.

3 Challenges

For the analysis of challenges in the creation of dashboards, the authors conducted interviews as well as an examination of two cases. Here, the purpose and the framework conditions were elaborated and special aspects during the development were analyzed. The analyses were carried out on the *OZG Dashboard Germany* and the *Dashboard "Digital Made in Germany"*. These dashboards were chosen explicitly because the corresponding background information was available and because they were open-oriented and goal-oriented dashboards.

OZG Dashboard Germany (Open-Oriented) [14]
The dashboard on the implementation of the Online Access Act in Germany (OZG) presents the development of administrative digitization based on a uniform federal law. The law, which was passed in 2017, regulates the legally binding provision of digital administrative services by the end of 2022 [15, 16]. The initially very slow implementation of the law is also reflected in the provision of a dashboard. It was not until 2020 that the Federal Ministry of the Interior, Building and Community began providing an initial version of a dashboard. This dashboard, which initially had a strong goal-orientation, was heavily criticized by experts in the field of administrative digitization and misinterpreted by third parties (e.g., newspaper publishers). The misunderstanding was based on the visualization of data regarding the provision of administrative services in Germany. At the beginning of the implementation of the law, 575 OZG-services were set. The visualization showed that the provision of OZG-services was progressing rapidly. However, a closer look at the data showed that the provision of a digital service was already considered complete as soon as the service was available in just one municipality in Germany. This is highly controversial in the federal context and distorts the provision of the actual information.

Based on the criticism expressed, the ministry started to relaunch the dashboard at the beginning of 2021, taking a clear turn and focusing on an open-oriented format of the dashboard provision. This has the advantage that changing goals based on a possible deprioritization of services during the implementation process and the dedicated presentation of regional aspects of the Länder (term of the German federal states) can be better presented without focusing on direct goals. While the analysis for this paper was still underway, the ministry has been working to further provide information within a new dashboard on the OZG-implementation for its citizens. This will focus primarily on the general provision of OZG-services in the Länder, listing the provision of technical services and basic functionalities of the portal network, and at the same time clearly showing the corresponding go-live dates of individual OZG-services on a timeline.

Dashboard "Digital Made in Germany" (Goal-Oriented) [17]
The "Digital Made in Germany" website is the information portal for the German government's "Shaping Digitization" [18] implementation strategy. The website provides interactive and data-based access to the German government's digital policy priority projects and to the federal policy players in digital policy. The core of the site is the Digital Policy Dashboard, which has been under development since March 2019 and was published in September 2020.

With the help of a process similar to that described above for the creation of a goal-oriented dashboard, 140 central digital policy projects in five fields of action were brought together and made measurable on the basis of the "Shaping digitization" implementation strategy. For the first time, an interactive dashboard on the German government's digital policy was developed for the website. The dashboard is a visual progress indicator for the implementation of digital policy projects in the implementation strategy. It supplements the strategy and underpins the projects with current data where quantitative visualization and measurement is suitable. It is intended to improve the visualization of progress in individual projects and make it more comprehensible. Further indicators on the topics of digital policy in the implementation strategy have been added. Hence, the dashboard is the entry point to the measurability of the federal government's digital policy.

Right at the beginning of the creation of the dashboard, a particular challenge arose in the supply of measurable data relating to the individual initiatives in the various federal ministries that were involved. It became apparent that the number of data suppliers posed a particular challenge in order to obtain an overall view of the implementation of the strategy and the individual initiatives. Over time, it also became apparent that less and less data was available from the relevant ministries or that there were no longer any updates to the information. In the run-up to the September 2021 federal elections in Germany, a decrease in information within the dashboard became clear. Thus, the information provided was reduced and it was not visible whether corresponding initiatives were ended earlier or were completed. This may be an example of a recurring challenge that arises from the provision of dashboards [6]. Institutions are now subject to direct external monitoring, as information is proactively provided that can lead to poor results in the context of a review of past years (e.g., before the end of a legislative period) and put political parties and ministers under pressure.

During the development of the generic process for creating a dashboard as described in Sect. 3 and visualized in Fig. 2, various challenges and requirements emerged during the expert interviews and were subsequently clustered by the authors. Based on the analyses of existing dashboards and the interviews conducted in Germany and the PRC, various design dimensions have been identified.

The design dimensions have been consolidated and defined in Table 1. Six dimensions emerged that the interviews identified as particularly important. These are (1) the *strategic* orientation of dashboards, (2) the holistic consideration of *stakeholders*, (3) the targeted *use of data*, (4) the form of *visualization*, (5) the provision of a *feedback* component, and finally also (6) the *technical* requirements for the subsequent visualization of data.

In addition to the consolidation of challenges into corresponding design dimensions, a prioritization could be carried out. This means that, depending on the urgency or weighting in the overall process of creating a dashboard, a particular dimension is assigned a special priority. The analysis showed that the complexity of implementing dashboards results from the evaluation of the design dimensions, which can vary greatly in some areas. The main factors here are the type of a dashboard, its strategic alignment, the user group it will refer to, and the technical requirements for the data engine.

During the analysis following the interviews, it was found that interviewees (1–2) who had an overall view of the process of creating a dashboard were the most likely to indicate that the defined design dimensions are mutually interconnected and that there are

Table 1. Design dimensions for the development of dashboards.

Priority	Design dimensions
1	Strategic
	How will the dashboard support or challenge the current strategic alignment of the institution? What type of information will be provided? Will the information provide insights? What is the intention of the information provided? Is the information relevant and does it integrate into the political sphere? What will be the cost for collecting the data, the development of a data engine and the interface?
2	Stakeholder
	Are future users, data suppliers and data owners involved? Will the dashboard have an internal or external benefit for the stakeholders? What are the internal and external requirements for the dashboard from the perspective of the individual stakeholders? What should the dashboard be used for by each stakeholder? Who is the addressee of the dashboard from the perspective of each stakeholder? How can the different requirements of the stakeholders be consolidated and aligned in a user-centric way?
3	Use of Data
	Is the data publicly available? Do data sets need to be merged? What is the quality of the data? Who collected the data? How was the data collected? In what format is the data provided and how often is it updated? How valuable is the data? Is a description and source of data sets available? Who is the owner of the data?
4	Visualization
	Is the purpose of the visualization more informative or interpreted as a control element? Which data must be visualized in which form and is it relevant to visualize all available data? Does the visualization create transparency? Is the visualization an exclusive pre-selection or should users have the possibility to choose the visualization themselves? Should there be the possibility to visually display comparisons, and can data sets be merged by the user for this purpose?

(continued)

Table 1. (*continued*)

Priority	Design dimensions
5	Feedback for Continuous Improvement
	Is the possibility of user feedback desired? In which format should the user have the possibility to give feedback? (open questions, questionnaire, scale) Should there be barriers to giving irrelevant feedback? Is there a special focus for the corresponding feedback? (feedback on selection of data, visualization, handling of the interface)
6	Technical
	Is the data provided in a machine-readable and standardized form? What are the requirements for the system architecture based on the data sets used? What are the technical requirements for the data engine in terms of data-register linking, data plausibility logic, data linking logic, and data backup? What measures are taken to increase IT-security and privacy? Is a ready-made tool used to create the interface or is it a proprietary development? Are interfaces required that enable third-party access to a data engine?

various dependencies. At the same time, this also means that there is a certain potential for conflict among the existing design dimensions, which also has an influence on the complexity of developing a dashboard. This is already evident in the strategic orientation of some dashboards, as a clear decision is made in favor of exclusive visualization, the possibility of compiling one's own data sets and the associated juxtaposition of data for a self-directed conclusion of new insights, or even the possibility of proactively requesting feedback to improve data and user quality.

It has been shown that the challenge to requirements engineering also becomes a challenge in the context of deciding on a clear standardization (compare with Sect. 2). This limits the individuality and specific characteristics of representations and the provision of data. Therefore, it is important to opt for an iterative process of defining measures and corresponding data based on user requirements. Two interviewees (2, 5) clearly summarizes this in a statement saying that standardization limits innovation and individuality and thus couples the overall process to narrow framework conditions.

To counteract this, it is more important to actively involve users in the process of developing the dashboard and to focus on a further step on the development of "next generation" dashboards as proposed by an interviewee (2). In this way, the complexity of the functionalities for spin-off dashboards can be adapted according to the user groups. This means that, in addition to simplifying functionalities, citizens for example, who are solely interested in viewing the information on the dashboard, can be provided an increase in functionality in order to meet the requirements of specialists and scientists who want to merge or compare a wide variety of data sets in order to arrive at new insights [19].

Against this background, it is therefore important that the afore mentioned design dimensions are relevant, during and after the creation of dashboards. According to the interviewees (1–3), fundamental strategic decisions play a special role here, because a decision in favor of predefined measures severely limits the possibilities for gaining knowledge. Of course, other considerations must also be made that deal with the complexity and simplicity of use. However, this is entirely up to the prior analysis of the audience and subsequent user groups. In conclusion, the analysis of the requirements shows that an imbalance can build up between the design dimensions, thus complicating the development and the not bringing the desired success when used later. One example is the recurring challenge of the misalignment of the used data and the actual data to be used to answer the previously defined questions and requirements from the users' perspective.

The overview given in this paper cannot be considered exhaustive, as the requirements for a dashboard differ greatly depending on the dashboard and the particular use case. However, the expert interviews and our own analyses during the creation of various government dashboards have shown these areas of complexity.

4 Conclusion

The creation of dashboards goes through a recurring process that has explicit characteristics and requirements depending on its particular environment and demands. The complexity of the creation process depends on various framework conditions and requirements from a social-technical point of view. The interviews have shown that in addition to the current process models, there are also future approaches for the development of dashboards. In this context, the major role of data engines will be elevated to a new level, and dashboards will become corresponding media output for the data lakes that are being created within the framework of open-data [20]. Data lakes are the future for the provision and processing of mass data. In contrast to data portals, they allow data to be made available in a timely and flexible manner [21].

We found two types of dashboards, i.e., open- and goal-oriented dashboards. The process of creating dashboards somewhat differs based on the type of dashboard, and the special requirements for user-friendliness that are neglected to cope with the mass of data. However, the advantages are the highly added value of the data used for visualization since the actuality of the data reflects the requirements of today. To address the related challenges of user-friendliness, this paper proposes the development of a "next generation" dashboard that focuses on regional characteristics and specific requirements of an audience.

These requirements are reflected in the six design dimensions and show how interconnected the various questions and requirements of the design dimensions are and how strongly they depend on each other. At the same time, it also shows how high the potential for conflict is between the individual design dimensions. These design dimensions are (1) the *strategic* orientation of dashboards, (2) the holistic consideration of *stakeholders*, (3) the targeted *use of data*, (4) the form of *visualization*, (5) the provision of a *feedback* component, and finally (6) the *technical* requirements for the subsequent visualization of data.

Based on the requirements for the creation of dashboards resulting from the process analysis, which were clustered and prioritized within the design dimensions, extensive questions about their interaction, interdependence, and potential for conflict emerged. For this purpose, it will be necessary to continue addressing these issues in further scientific research.

References

1. Lewis, J.M., Triantafillou, P.: From performance measurement to learning: a new source of government overload? Int. Rev. Adm. Sci. **78**(4), 597–614 (2012). https://doi.org/10.1177/0020852312455993
2. Janssen, D., Rotthier, S., Snijkers, K.: If you measure it they will score: an assessment of international eGovernment benchmarking. Inf. Polity **9**(3, 4), 121–130 (2005). https://doi.org/10.3233/ip-2004-0051
3. Sarikaya, A., Correll, M., Bartram, L., Tory, M., Fisher, D.: What do we talk about when we talk about dashboards? IEEE Trans. Vis. Comput. Graph. **25**(1), 682–692 (2019). https://doi.org/10.1109/tvcg.2018.2864903
4. Matheus, R., Janssen, M., Maheshwari, D.: Data science empowering the public: data-driven dashboards for transparent and accountable decision-making in smart cities. Gov. Inf. Q. **37**(3), 101284 (2020). https://doi.org/10.1016/j.giq.2018.01.006
5. Maheshwari, D., Janssen, M.: Measurement and benchmarking foundations: providing support to organizations in their development and growth using dashboards. Gov. Inf. Q. **30**, S83–S93 (2013). https://doi.org/10.1016/j.giq.2012.11.002
6. de Bruijn, H.: Performance measurement in the public sector: strategies to cope with the risks of performance measurement. Int. J. Public Sect. Manag. **15**(7), 578–594 (2002). https://doi.org/10.1108/09513550210448607
7. Bourne, M., Neely, A., Platts, K., Mills, J.: The success and failure of performance measurement initiatives. Int. J. Oper. Prod. Manag. **22**(11), 1288–1310 (2002). https://doi.org/10.1108/01443570210450329
8. German Federal Ministry of Health. The official dashboard for the vaccination campaign of the Federal Republic of Germany. Current Vaccination Status, 20 August 2021 (2021). https://impfdashboard.de/en/
9. Lemke, F., Taveter, K., Erlenheim, R., Pappel, I., Draheim, D., Janssen, M.: Stage models for moving from e-Government to smart government. In: Chugunov, A., Khodachek, I., Misnikov, Y., Trutnev, D. (eds.) EGOSE 2019. CCIS, vol. 1135, pp. 152–164. Springer, Cham (2020). https://doi.org/10.1007/978-3-030-39296-3_12
10. Object Management Group. Business Process Model and Notation (BPMN), version 2.0, OMG Document Number formal/2011-01-03. OMG (2011)
11. Lewis, J.M., McGann, M., Blomkamp, E.: When design meets power: design thinking, public sector innovation and the politics of policymaking. Policy Polit. **48**(1), 111–130 (2020). https://doi.org/10.1332/030557319x15579230420081
12. Edelmann, N., Mergel, I.: Co-production of digital public services in Austrian public administrations. Adm. Sci. **11**(1), 22 (2021). https://doi.org/10.3390/admsci11010022
13. Lember, V., Brandsen, T., Tõnurist, P.: The potential impacts of digital technologies on co-production and co-creation. Public Manag. Rev. **21**(11), 1665–1686 (2019). https://doi.org/10.1080/14719037.2019.1619807
14. Federal Ministry of the Interior, Building and Community. OZG-Dashboard, April 2021 (2021). https://www.onlinezugangsgesetz.de/Webs/OZG/DE/umsetzung/ozg-dashboard/ozg-dashboard-node.html
15. Proll, E.-C.: Die umsetzung des OZGs in Deutschland. In: Stember, J., Eixelsberger, W., Spichiger, A., Neuroni, A., Habbel, F.-R., Wundara, M. (eds.) Aktuelle Entwicklungen zum E-Government: Neue Impulse und Orientierungen in der digitalen Transformation der öffentlichen Verwaltung, pp. 29–52. Springer, Wiesbaden (2021). https://doi.org/10.1007/978-3-658-33586-1_2
16. Lemke, F., Ehrhardt, K., Popelyshyn, O.: Support and resistance of public officials towards current eGovernment initiatives – a case study on Ukraine and Germany. dms – der moderne staat **14**(1), 61–80 (2021). https://doi.org/10.3224/dms.v14i1.08

17. Federal Chancellery of Germany. Dashboard Digitalpolitik, September 2020 (2020). https://www.digital-made-in.de/dmide
18. Federal Chancellery of Germany. Digitalisierung gestalten - Umsetzungsstrategie der Bundesregierung (6th Version), June 2021 (2021). https://www.digital-made-in.de/resource/blob/1793046/1794318/339a38c264fd50ff9efca6ad8da64bae/2021-digitalisierung-gestalten-aktualisierung-juni-2021-pdf-data.pdf?download=1
19. Yigitbasioglu, O.M., Velcu, O.: A review of dashboards in performance management: Implications for design and research. Int. J. Acc. Inf. Syst. 13(1), 41–59 (2012). https://doi.org/10.1016/j.accinf.2011.08.002
20. Janssen, M., Charalabidis, Y., Zuiderwijk, A.: Benefits, adoption barriers and myths of open data and open government. Inf. Syst. Manag. 29(4), 258–268 (2012). https://doi.org/10.1080/10580530.2012.716740
21. Ravat, F., Zhao, Y.: Data lakes: trends and perspectives. In: Hartmann, S., Küng, J., Chakravarthy, S., Anderst-Kotsis, G., Tjoa, A.M., Khalil, I. (eds.) DEXA 2019. LNCS, vol. 11706, pp. 304–313. Springer, Cham (2019). https://doi.org/10.1007/978-3-030-27615-7_23

Segregation of Duties in Business Architecture Models

Małgorzata Pańkowska[(⊠)] [iD]

University of Economics in Katowice, Katowice, Poland
pank@ue.katowice.pl

Abstract. Business institutions manage their employees and particularly monitor if they responsibly realize their tasks. Business process modelling supports the responsibility management, as well as controls realization of business tasks assigned to particular employees. For security reasons as well as for business effectiveness and efficiency, the segregation of duties (SoD) is implemented in business units. This paper covers literature review on the segregation of duties in business organizations. Next, this paper includes an original business model for SoD management support. This model is complement with business process and business architecture models. The proposed model comprises duties' controlling, task execution, registration, and verification. This model is applied for SoD analysis in a law firm. Findings concern the applicability of SoD model for small enterprises and justification of multi-method modelling.

Keywords: Segregation of duties · Business architecture · ArchiMate · Business process modelling · BPMN · Assurance map

1 Introduction

Enterprise architecture (EA) concept is defined as the business organization's scheme for aligning its vision and goals, business processes and information communication technology (ICT). The issue of modelling a business architecture that can support the adoption of EA's capabilities, as well as vision of EA in a complex development project with the ICT, applications, and data components is the key question in this study.

Enterprise architecture is perceived as an integrated complex of principles, methods, languages, notations, and models that are used in the modeling and realization of the enterprise's organizational structure, business processes, data, software, and hardware. In principle, EA is an integrated procedure of aligning business strategies with ICT architecture. Modeled organization covers standardized business operations and incorporates systems in different, but integrated layers, i.e., business architecture, data, information, applications and computer infrastructure layers. EA is a certain framework that helps to design, implement, and manage a business plan and to incorporate it with the ICT domain efficiently and effectively. EA is developed for many reasons, e.g., digital transformation, creating organizational benefits, for business model implementation, information safety and security assurance, or for business value generation. In

A. V. Chugunov et al. (Eds.): EGOSE 2021, CCIS 1529, pp. 35–49, 2022.
https://doi.org/10.1007/978-3-031-04238-6_4

practice, EA is a collection of artefacts presenting various aspects of an organization from an ICT perspective. The development of enterprise architecture in business organizations implies using these artefacts to facilitate business information systems' design. Among the EA visualization notations, just ArchiMate, UML, and SysML (System Modelling Language) belong to basic architecture-based modelling notations. Beyond that, the Business Motivation Model (BMM) and Case Management Model and Notation (CMMN), or goal-based modelling notation are rarely applied, but Business Process Model and Notation (BPMN) is a very popular. ArchiMate language provides the visual icons for business stakeholders, actors, problems, principles, requirements, products, information assets, business processes, as well as for interrelationships among these items. The Unified Modelling Language (UML) covers visual icons for business actors, triggers, flows, assets, information, and processes. Although UML does not provide means for representing the concern, goal, value chain, problem, risk, product, nor cost structure, it is applied for EA modelling. It should be noticed that none of these modelling techniques are oriented towards business actor's duties, responsibilities, nor conflicts of interests. Within EA domain, business architecture is a process of transforming a business strategy and business requirements into information systems for data processing and decision making support. In this paper, ArchiMate 4.9 as the Open Group modelling language is applied to represent the business architecture. This modelling is supplement by business process presented in BPMN. However, the research question is how to model information access privileges and employees' duties in an organizational structure. Therefore, this paper shows that CERI (Controlling, Execution, Registration, and Investigation) model supports business architecture modelling through emphasizing the features like conflict avoiding, task controlling, task assignment, traceability of activities, and multi-dimensional view capability.

The paper includes four sections. The second section covers literature review on segregation of duties (SoD) as a concept important in business organization design. Next, the CERI model is presented and confronted with other similar business models, i.e., RACI (Responsible, Accountable, Consulted, and Informed) and RASCI (Responsible, Accountable, Supportive, Consulted, and Informed). In the fourth part, business architecture for a law firm acting on small and medium enterprises' market is presented and discussed. Finally, conclusions and future work proposals are included.

2   Segregation of Duties in Literature Review

According to Repa and Svatos [1] digital business architecture is a composition of the business processes and structures. Their specifications are included in business plans, strategy, and vision. Hence, these documents include the premises of business architecture motivations, presentation and discussions. Business goals are fundamental determinants of activities, which constitute processes. Business processes, after confrontation with procedures and politics, can be modelled in ArchiMate and BPMN notations. Once the tasks are specified, one has to identify their performers and so, the organization structure should be modelled. BPMN business processes include actors' specification. Actors are assigned to tasks and assets. They are responsible for task execution and appropriate resource usage.

Actors are mutually dependent and having impact on one another. They have competencies, privileges, and duties. In ArchiMate, each business actor has their own profile. General characteristics of this profile are modelled in Fig. 1.

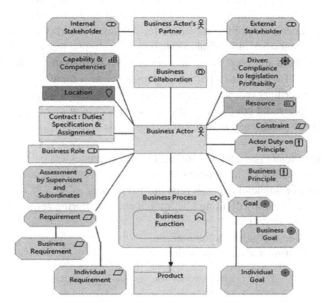

Fig. 1. Business actor profile.

Modelling the business organization stakeholders and particularly actors in business architecture requires considering their segregation of duties. In Merriam-Webster Thesaurus (www.merriam-webster.com) duty is identified with moral or legal obligation. It is the force of moral obligation. Duties should be segregated, because they are related to assets. According to Ferroni [2] the segregation of duties is to provide compliance with laws and regulations. Management of duties covers granting the proposer rights to the chosen people, controlling and reporting exceptions to the processes. Business actors are specified to perform compatible duties. Governance of duties includes evaluating and directing them as well as monitoring the SoD rules and procedures in accordance with business governance. Segregation of duties is necessary to avoid conflicts in accessing and usage of resources. Segregation of duties results from the typology of goals and may concern:

- Individuals: different actors performing separated duties.
- Functions or business units: different functions requiring separated duties.
- Companies: business organization operations performed by different legal entities.

Duties assigned to a particular business actor constitute their profile, which also defines sets of permissions granted. A role is described as a collection of actor profiles. In business organizations, actors' roles are to be controlled, and needless and redundant roles should be detected, and eliminated or modified.

Roles represent certain expectations connected with social positions, responsibilities, and duties [3]. Understanding the relationships among roles and the role structures allows people to acquire an understanding of social duties in the business processes. Particularly, monitoring and updating practice is to ensure duties segregation and analyzing. The practice of business task complementarity and substitution means that individuals, i.e., organization members, are able to substitute for one another in task execution. That is particularly important when individuals rotate between different teams and business units or when some of them are temporarily unavailable. SoD allows to assign responsibility for different parts of a process to particular people. Hence, there is no one employee able to control the critical functions or resources. No single individual should have the authority to execute some conflicting transactions nor critical tasks with the potential impact on financial statements. Benefits of SoD include [4]:

- Effective and efficient realization of critical business processes.
- Appropriate protection of information assets.
- Minimized risk of financial loss and reputational damage.
- Reduced business risk, by dividing operational and monitoring responsibilities.
- Balancing critical activities.
- Preventing confidential information leaks.
- Savings in consulting and auditing hours.

Table 1. Findings in publications on SoD.

No	Author	Findings	Nc[1]
1	[6]	Author identifies a scheme for classifying duty combinations and measures of their effectiveness	6
2	[7]	Authors present a formal modeling framework and they verify business processes in aspect of their compliance to SoD and privacy protection policies	31
3	[8]	Author discusses the organizational requirements for implementation of a control system through a segregation of duties. Author argues that failures, which arrived in process of control, compromise compliance	5
4	[5]	The paper describes model for SoD. The synthesized model includes segregation of six sets of duties among a minimum of five employees. The analyzed duties were for manual as well as for computer-supported processes	5
5	[9]	Author proposes principle of a segregation of duties on non-executive boards in banking sector. Beyond that, author provides an outline of relevant legislative requirements	2
6	[10]	Authors explain why corporate strategy changes negatively influences design and effective operation of ICT controls	2

[1]Nc - number of citations in Scopus

Unfortunately, there are also some risks connected with inappropriate segregation of duties, e.g., misappropriation of assets, inaccurate financial documentation, inappropriate processes, or reputational damage. Although the SoD seems to be important, this issue is not sufficiently well emphasized in management science literature. In this study, the literature review research question (RQ1) is presented as follows: How is SoD modelled for business architecture development?

The rudimentary reviews have been done using the following repositories: Association for Information Systems Electronic Library (AIS eLib), IEEE Xplore Digital Library (IEEE Xplore), SAGE Journals, Science Direct and Scopus. In these databases, the phrase "segregation of duties SoD" was searched. However, the number of received results was not very high. Just 92 publications, for years 2010–2021, were found. Also Kobelsky [5] has noticed a limited number of research papers describing the cognitive fundamentals for identification, determining and assignment of duties in organizations. The word "segregation" and the second word "duties" have different interpretations, applications, and connotations. Next, after removal of inappropriate papers, only 6 cited papers were selected as representative and valuable examples of discussions on the segregation of duties (Table 1).

3 Combining Business Architecture Modelling Methods

Although authors of the reviewed papers and auditing organizations, e.g., COSO, emphasize the value of SoD, there is a need to reduce the gap concerning the SoD model in business architecture. This model has been developed in a study, where group of user representatives and professionals collaborate to achieve particular business goals. In publications, business architecture modelling is not based on a single method approach. The mixed methods approach is popular and provides additional value and a synergy effect. Fetters and Molina-Azorin [11] have considered methods' integration in different ways. Hence, integration through comparing is developed to examine a specific phenomenon by collecting both qualitative and quantitative data. In principle, it is a process similar to triangulation of methods. The triangulation of methods concerns various aspects of research and implies the combination of different insights in an investigation [12]. Beyond that, there are integration different domain concepts and constructs, integration through data expanding [13] and integration through construction of a case. Mixed methods are applied in case study as it is presented in this paper, and as it was emphasized by Yin [14]. In general, different configurations of integrated methods allow to receive a holistic view of the business organization, but also reveal models' complementarity, their weaknesses and gaps in modelling. The discussion on business architecture models and methods integration should be supported by literature review. Hence, the second research question (RQ2) was formulated as follows: How does complementarity of methods support business architecture modelling? In this review, the searching phrase included "method complementarity" AND "business architecture". In repositories, i.e., Scopus, Sage Journals, Science Direct, IEEE Xplore, and AIS eLibrary, in years 2010–2021, 5410 publications were stored. However, this huge number of publications have not precisely answered that question.

The most suitable and highly cited publications are included in Table 2. That table covers important findings and original approach revealed in each publication.

Table 2. Findings in publications on method complementarity.

No	Author	Findings	Nc[1]
1	[15]	Authors explore social, financial, and environmental sustainability as the fundamentals of a holistic approach to value creation	23
2	[16]	Authors present a methodological guideline for developing design principles that address the particular class of heterogeneity problems in enterprise architecture (EA) management	8
3	[12]	Authors perceive that mixed-method, multi-method, and triangulation are used interchangeably	7
4	[17]	Authors argue that multi-methodologies facilitate problem structuring, alternative process design, and solution implementation. They apply an action research process in their research	17
5	[18]	Authors describe multilevel modelling and mixed methods' application for support of theoretical advancements. They focus on micro foundation strategy development. The mixed methods are from the field outside the strategy management (e.g., psychology, education, health science)	28
6	[19]	Authors discuss applicability of mixing methods. Such approach permits capture new observations and communicate experiences that are difficult to verbalize	12

[1]Nc - number of citations in Scopus

Beyond that, many other researchers discuss multi-methodology applicability and its internal complementarity. For example, Pashkevich and Haftor [20] argue that the use of multiple and different research methods in a complementary manner allows to uncover new insights that cannot be derived from any single study. Schwarz et al. [21] have reviewed literature on multiple business models and they show that firms develop business models' composition as a result of challenges in contemporary ICT-driven environment. In their opinion, the coordination of multiple business models can complement very popular customer-centric perspective in business management. Belucio et al. [22] highlight that multi-methodological approach provides more extensive recommendations to designers, manufacturers and decision-makers. Lame et al. [23], as many other authors, propose multi-methodology for process redesign. Their approach includes process management and Soft Systems Methodology (SSM). San Cristobal et al. [24] argue that multi-methodology is perceived as a means to support research problem structuring as well as a suitable combination of methodologies to manage project successfully. Salahat and Wade [25] presented that combining Soft Systems Methodology (SSM), the Unified Modelling Language (UML), and the Naked Objects approach improves the business process modeling and implementation. Mingers [26] has strongly supported the idea of multi-methodology and has defined it in very general, but effective way, as "the whole area of utilizing a plurality of methodologies or techniques within the practice of taking actions in problematic situations" [26, p. 2]. Brocklesby expands this concept by pointing that methodologies and techniques can be developed within different paradigms [27]. Jochemsen et al. [28] suggest standardization approach application for better understanding and modelling the complex information systems and enterprise architecture at different levels.

However, in this paper, computer science system analysis methods, i.e., ArchiMate language-based analysis and BPMN process modelling are combined with SoD model derived from management science. In this study, RACI and RASCI models are a premise of SoD model, which follows the employee responsibility modelling. RACI matrices provide information on task details and owners. In this model, researchers focus on responsibility for the resources, task execution, and approval of what has been done. Caniballas et al. [29] have proposed to combine RASCI matrices and BPMN models. They argue that just BPMN notation is a commonly well-known standard for business process modelling. Therefore, they have focused on a particular type of RACI model named RASCI and they have introduced RASCI-aware business process models in BPMN notation. RACI models are used to associate activities with business organization resources. In these models, Responsible (R) is a person, who has to perform a work on the task. They are assigned to do the work. Accountable (A) is a person who has to approve the work performed by the person Responsible for an activity. So, the individual is accountable for the successful completion of the task and they have the authority to delegate the work to the Responsible person. Consulted (C) role includes all these people, whose opinion is needed while carrying out the work. They are experts who are asked to provide an opinion about the task. Finally, Informed (I) role is kept for the persons with whom there is only one-way communication. In RASCI model, the Supportive (S) people assist in completing any activities. However, in comparison with Consulted (C), they are only asked to provide necessary information to complete tasks. Unfortunately, the RACI nor RASCI models do not sufficiently well highlight the segregation of duties. Therefore, this paper proposes a CERI model, where:

- Controller (C) represent board, top management, authority or power to determine duties and regulations, which are included in each employee contract.
- Executor (E) is the performer, task owner, task custodian, employee, worker, having a particular task to carry out.
- Receptionist (R) is the front desk officer, clerk, office administration employee responsible for data registration, information processing, and internal communication.
- Investigator (I) represents verifying authority, who is responsible for the validation and verification of the accomplishment of duties.

In general, this study scheme is included in Fig. 2. This proposed multi-model (Fig. 2) is a description of business architecture. It identifies business goals and principles, functions, active elements (in ArchiMate language) (i.e., **A**), critical processes (BPMN processes) (i.e., **B**), contracts (i.e., **C**), SoD (i.e., **D**), and application of the SoD for information access rights distribution and assurance mapping (i.e., **E**). In principle, the business architecture is presented in ArchiMate language model. Contracts included in ArchiMate model are the base for CERI matrix specification, which further can be used for information access rights distribution in the business organization as well as for assurance mapping, which is an operational management method. Explanation of these symbols and small diagrams is included in the next section.

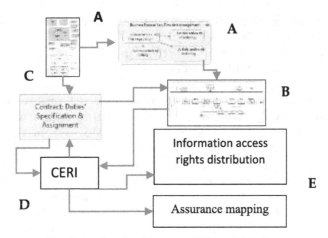

Fig. 2. Business architecture multi-model outline.

4 Law Firm Business Model – Illustrative Case Study

Zivkovic et al. [30] argue that conceptual modelling is a key discipline of business informatics. However, this conceptual modelling is also useful for organization design and business process reengineering. Business models facilitate communication between business organization designers and information systems' developers, or in general between stakeholders focused on the essentials of any problem under consideration, e.g., business organization audit, managerial decision making. The business architecture models, and following them – enterprise architecture models can be elaborated for huge companies, as well as for small and medium enterprises (SMEs). This case study concerns small Law Firm working on local market. Lawyers in this Law Firm utilize their litigation, administrative, and investigative competencies in providing high-quality legal services. This Law Firm is comprised of a Litigation Department and an Alternative Dispute Resolution Department. They handle commercial and civil prosecutions in local community. They represent interests of citizens, small and medium business units, and governmental institutions. They are oriented towards providing ethical and personalized representation to its clients. The goals of the Law Firm are argumentative advocacy, rational counselling, and ethical behavior. They work to provide honest and ethically justified solutions to their clients. They are interested in offering services that are understandable and provided on time to clients, but first currently managed and secured. Each legal case has its number, dossier set up date, its subject, type, legal status, description, paymaster, and executor. The legal acts have to be stored and protected in computerized systems. Publicly accessible schedule supports this Law Firm, judicial actions' management and introduction of new orders. The dossier management information system is to support the management of payments, which depend on type of case. Hence, taking into account the above presented description, the ArchiMate model has been elaborated and included in Fig. 3. The ArchiMate Motivation Layer and the ArchiMate Contracts are included in Fig. 2 as elements A and C, respectively.

This model (Fig. 3) includes only the elements of one layer of TOGAF enterprise architecture, i.e., Business Architecture layer. The Open Group Architecture Framework, TOGAF 9 (www.opengroup.org/togaf) standard, is a proven Enterprise Architecture methodology and framework. In TOGAF, there are four architecture domains that are commonly accepted as parts of the overall enterprise architecture:

- The Business Architecture defining the actors, contracts, roles, processes, and products (see Fig. 3).
- The Data Architecture describing the structure of logical and physical data assets and data management components in a business organization.
- The Application Architecture including business software systems, their integration and their relationships to the business processes of the organization.
- The Technology Architecture presenting the system software and hardware capabilities needed for data processing in this business organization.

The Data, Application, and Technology Architecture are important for EA modelling and information systems' implementation. However, in the studies on organization design the Business Architecture layer is sufficient, although it should be supplemented by the motivation analysis. In the ArchiMate language, the Motivation is expressed by considering stakeholders, goals, drivers, principles, and requirements (see Fig. 3).

The ArchiMate language business processes can be also presented in a more specific BPMN notation (see Fig. 4). In ArchiMate model (Fig. 3) there are 4 identified sub-processes, i.e., judicial action scheduling, judicial action files registration, judicial action archiving, and billing. The same sub-processes are included in the BPMN model (Fig. 4), which is marked as element B in Fig. 2. The analysis of contracts and business process, as well as mutual dependencies of business actors allow for the specification their duties and including them in the CERI matrix (see Table 3).

In the CERI matrix, each Receptionist (R) is obliged to data registration. They are not able to establish principles, rules, or duties for others. Only top management can create, select, make decisions and control the other employees. They provide orders to subordinates, represent the firm in the business environment, and establish the future business strategy. Hence, the legal firm president is the Controller (C). The directors of departments play a role of a mediator between top management and employees, i.e., lawyers and paralegals. They have tasks to execute as well as the ability to verify work of other employees. Therefore, department directors and lawyers are Executives (E).

Administrative staff is to assist in judicial actions' management, particularly in case scheduling, registration, and archiving. Paralegal is assistant supporting the firm clerks. Finally, only the department director and president can be defined as Investigators (I), as they are responsible for the compliance, quality of work and future development of that firm. So far, none of the available technique of conceptual modelling of an enterprise enables modelling of segregation of duties. That issue is important in particular for security and privacy protection system development.

Therefore, the proposed CERI matrix can be further used for the specification of computerized information system user profiles. Taking into account the necessity of confidential information security and personal data protection, the Law Firm should plan the accessibility to data and information. Therefore, access rights should be included in

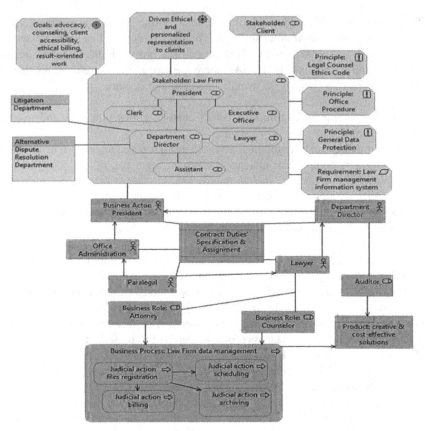

Fig. 3. Business Architecture layer (yellow) and Motivation layer in ArchiMate language. (ArchiMate 4.9 default colors)

employee contracts and specification of duties as well as in accessibility rights matrix (Table 4, where "x" means permission assigned to the actor).

The database management CRUDA model can be used for determining the access rights to the Law Firm. Therefore, in Table 4, the Law Firm top management is obliged to create (C), read (R), update (U), delete (D) or archive (A) information. So, in this model, archiving is left for other subordinates. The same privileges are specified for directors of department. Lawyer is assumed unauthorized to delete information, while administrative staff can create, read and archive information. Paralegal is assumed to support archiving. The segregation of duties cannot be neglected in the risk management practices as well as in controlling the business tasks. Therefore, the CERI matrix can be considered as a premise for an assurance map development. The assurance map is the objective examination technique applied in operational management to perform an independent assessment of business activities. Since the board is responsible for ensuring the internal control arrangements across the whole organization, assurance is a key compliance issues. An assurance map represents key activities over which assurance is required, four lines of defense, the gaps of no assurance providing, and

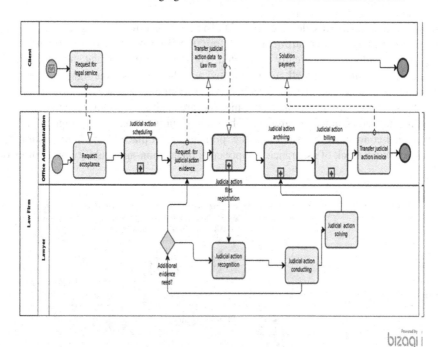

Fig. 4. The BPMN main business process for the Law Firm. (Bizagi Modeler default colors)

Table 3. The CERI matrix for the Law Firm.

Position	C	E	R	I
President	x	x		x
Department director		x		
Lawyer		x	x	
Paralegal			x	
Administrative staff		x	x[a]	

[a]x - means the roles and duties connected with this role.

Table 4. Permissions to process the confidential information in the Law Firm.

Position	Confidential information records access rights				
	C	R	U	D	A
President	x	x	x	x	
Department director	x	x	x	x	
Lawyer	x	x	x		
Paralegal					x
Administrative staff	x	x			x

the level of assurance provided (see Fig. 5). The assurance level rating represents the quality evidence by each department. Therefore, the High Assurance (i.e., H on green in Fig. 5) is detailed and cyclically conducted. The controls are in place and adequately mitigate risks. Policies are well communicated and the business intelligence tools are deployed to automatize controls and reports. The Medium Assurance (i.e., M on yellow in Fig. 5) is not regularly performed, so some risks are neglected, policies are not entirely communicated, and controls are manual. The Low Assurance (i.e., L on orange in Fig. 5) is occasional control. In this situation, few policies are in place. The None Assurance (N on Red) means lack of assurance. Empty cells means non-applicability of assurance in Fig. 5.

Assurance Activity	Risk evaluation	Management first line -Risk Owners		Functions second line - Oversight Assurance		Independent third line - Independent Assurance	External fourth line - External Assurance	
		Lawyer	Legal Firm Department Director	Risk Management	Legal Firm President Review	Internal Audit	External Audit	Other Third Party
Strategy, Vision & Mission	L	N	H	N	H	M	L	
Conduct, Culture, Behaviour, Ethics	L	L	M	M	M	H	N	M
Financial Reporting	H	H	H	M	M	H	H	
Financial Controls	H	H	H	M	M	H	H	
Business Legal Resilience	L	L	L	M	M	L	M	L
Information Communication Technology (ICT)	M	L	L	M	H	L	L	
Treasury	H	M	M	H	M	N	L	
Tax, Pensions & Insurance	L	M	M	L	L	N	L	
Human Resources	M	M	H	L	M	L		
Fraud	M	M	L	L	L	M	L	
Health, Privacy Protection & Safety	M	M	M	H	H	L		H
Quality Management	M	M	H	M	L	L		
Research & Development	M	L	M	H	M	L		
Social Responsibility, Corporate Image	L	N	L	L	H	M	N	

Fig. 5. Activities, risks, actors, and assurance level in assurance map. (ICAEW default colors) [31]

The assurance map permits for controlling the current activities and as such is a conceptual model of this firm. The business architecture modelling researchers do not reject the idea of model complementarity, therefore the ArchiMate and BPMN process models can be supplemented by other modelling considerations. For example, Ross et al. [32] have noticed relationships among enterprise architecture and management practices, i.e., Balanced Scorecard, Quality Management, Capability Maturity Model integration (CMMI).

5   Conclusions

In the EA development domain, methods and models are needed at the conceptualization stage for business organization design and its information systems' development. Method and model engineering covers procedures, languages, and tools to support the EA development. Thanks to Odell and other researchers involved by Brinkkemper, the method engineering is defined as a coordinated and systematic approach to establish work methods [33]. For models, the research process can be realized in a similar way.

Hence, that process covers the recognition and description of business environment, review of model base repositories, identification of gaps in business domain modelling, recognition of the circumstances of this new identified dimension modelling, specification of the model components and their inter-relationships, visualization of the model, and verification of the proposed model in practice. Studying the business organization activities allowed to emphasize the gap concerning just the segregation of duties. The issue is important in the aspect of organization governance and business value creation. In project-oriented organizations, the SoD determines the quality of consortium and – subsequently the whole project's success. Therefore, in this domain the future research should be carried out.

References

1. Repa, V., Svatos, O.: Model consistency as a tool for digital business architecture verification. Proc. Comput. Sci. **159**, 2144–2153 (2019). https://doi.org/10.1016/j.procs.2019.09.388
2. Ferroni, S.: Implementing segregation of duties: a practical experience based on best practices. ISACA J. **3**, 1–9 (2016). https://www.isaca.org/resources/isaca-journal/issues/2016/volume-3/implementing-segregation-of-duties-a-practical-experience-based-on-best-practices. Accessed 21 May 2021
3. Gustavsson, T.: Practices for vertical and horizontal coordination in the Scaled Agile Framework. In: ISD 2018 Proceedings, pp. 501–522. Lund University, Lund (2018). http://kau.diva-portal.org/smash/record.jsf?pid=diva2%3A1266106&dswid=-835. Accessed 15 May 2021
4. Guide to Internal Control over Financial Reporting. Center for Audit Quality (2019). https://www.thecaq.org/wp-content/uploads/2019/05/caq_guide_internal_control_over_financial_reporting_2019-05.pdf. Accessed 15 May 2021
5. Kobelsky, K.W.: A conceptual model for segregation of duties: integrating theory and practice for manual and IT-supported processes. Int. J. Acc. Inf. Syst. **15**(4), 304–322 (2014). https://doi.org/10.1016/j.accinf.2014.05.003
6. Srinidhi, B.: The influence of segregation of duties on internal control judgments. J. Acc. Audit. Finan. **9**(3), 423–444 (1994). https://doi.org/10.1177/0148558X9400900303
7. Kokash, N., Arbab, F.: Formal behavioral modeling and compliance analysis for service-oriented systems. In: de Boer, F.S., Bonsangue, M.M., Madelaine, E. (eds.) FMCO 2008. LNCS, vol. 5751, pp. 21–41. Springer, Heidelberg (2009). https://doi.org/10.1007/978-3-642-04167-9_2
8. Engdahl, O.: Ensuring regulatory compliance in banking and finance through effective controls: the principle of duality in the segregation of duties. Regul. Gov. **8**(3), 332–349 (2014). https://doi.org/10.1111/rego.12027
9. Georg, L.: Information security governance: pending legal responsibilities of non-executive boards. J. Manag. Governance **21**(4), 793–814 (2016). https://doi.org/10.1007/s10997-016-9358-0
10. Tanriverdi, H., Du, K.: Corporate strategy changes and information technology control effectiveness in multibusiness firm. MIS Q. **44**, 1573–1617 (2020)
11. Fetters, M.D., Molina-Azorin, J.F.: The mixed methods research integration trilogy and its dimensions. J. Mixed Methods Res. **11**(3), 291–307 (2017). https://doi.org/10.1177/1558689817714066
12. Zachariadis, M., Scott, S., Barrett, M.: Methodological implications of critical realism for mixed-methods research. MIS Q. **37**(3), 855–879 (2013). https://doi.org/10.25300/MISQ/2013/37.3.09

13. Uprichard, E., Dawney, L.: Data diffraction: challenging data integration in mixed methods research. J. Mixed Methods Res. **13**(1), 19–32 (2016). https://doi.org/10.1177/155868981667 4650
14. Yin. R.K.: Case Study Research: Design and Methods, 5th edn. Sage, Thousand Oaks (2014)
15. Laszlo, A., Castro Laszlo, K., Dunsky, H.: Redefining success: designing systemic sustainable strategies. Syst. Res. Behav. Sci. **27**(1), 3–21 (2009). https://doi.org/10.1002/sres.982
16. Widjaja, T., Wayne Gregory, R.: Design principles for heterogeneity decisions in enterprise architecture management. In: ICIS 2012 Proceedings, Thirty Third International Conference on Information Systems, Orlando, pp. 1–11 (2012). https://citeseerx.ist.psu.edu/viewdoc/dow nload?doi=10.1.1.665.4259&rep=rep1&type=pdf. Accessed 15 May 2021
17. Small, A., Wainwright, D.: SSM and technology management: development multimethodology through practice. Eur. J. Oper. Res. **233**(3), 660–673 (2014). https://doi.org/10.1016/j. ejor.2013.08.049
18. Aguinis, H., Molina-Azorin, J.F.: Using multilevel modeling and mixed methods to make theoretical progress in microfoundations for strategy research. Strateg. Org. **13**(4), 353–364 (2015). https://doi.org/10.1177/1476127015594622
19. Shannon-Baker, P., Edwards, C.: The affordances and challenges to incorporating visual methods in mixed methods research. Am. Behav. Sci. **62**(7), 935–955 (2018). https://doi.org/ 10.1177/0002764218772671
20. Pashkevich, N., Haftor, D.: Exploring complementarities of productive IT use through methodological complementarism. Electron. J. Bus. Res. Methods **16**(3), 128– 138 (2018). https://issuu.com/academic-conferences.org/docs/ejbrm-volume16-issue3-articl e496. Accessed 21 May 2020
21. Schwarz, J., Terrenghi, N., Legner, Ch.: From one to many business models: uncovering characteristics of business model portfolios. In: Proceedings of the 25th European Conference on Information Systems (ECIS), Guimaraes, Portugal, pp. 2285–2300 (2017). https://serval. unil.ch/resource/serval:BIB_F22A0A91EDA7.P001/REF.pdf. Accessed 17 May 2021
22. Belucio, M., Ridrigues, C., Henggeler, A.C., Freire, F., Dias, L.C.: Eco-efficiency in early design decisions: a multimethodology approach. J. Clean. Prod. **283**, 124630 (2021). https:// doi.org/10.1016/j.jclepro.2020.124630
23. Lame, G., Stal-Le Cardinal, J., Jouini, O., Carvalho, M., Christophe Tournigand, Ch., Wolken-stein, P.: A multimethodology for hospital process redesign. In: Proceedings of the International Conference on Engineering Design, ICED, vol. 3, no. DS87-3, pp. 41–50. University of British Columbia, Vancouver (2017)
24. San Cristobal, J.R., Diaz, E., Gonzalez, M.A., Madariaga, E., Lopez, S., Trueba, M.: From the hard paradigms towards multimethodology in project management. Proc. Comput. Sci. **100**, 1228–1234 (2016). https://doi.org/10.1016/j.procs.2016.09.152
25. Salahat, M., Steve Wade, S., Lu, J.: A systemic framework for business process modelling and implementation. In: International Conference on Innovations in Information Technology, IIT 2008, vol. 4781657, pp. 247–251 (2008). https://doi.org/10.1109/INNOVATIONS.2008. 4781657
26. Mingers, J.: Multi-paradigm multimethodology. In: Mingers, J., Gill, A. (eds.) Multimethodology, the Theory and Practice of Combining Management Science Methodologies, pp. 1–22. Wiley, Chichester (1997)
27. Brocklesby, J.: Becoming multimethodology literate: an assessment of the cognitive difficulties of working across paradigms. In: Mingers, J., Gill, A. (eds.) Multimethodology, the Theory and Practice of Combining Management Science Methodologies, pp. 189–216. Wiley, Chichester (1997)
28. Jochemsen, E., van den Hooff, B., Plomp, M., Rezazade Mehrizi, M., Derks, L.: The effects of standardization on architecture complexity. In: ECIS 2021 Conference Proceedings, Research Papers, p. 102 (2021). https://aisel.aisnet.org/ecis2021_rp/102. Accessed 21 May 2021

29. Cabanillas, C., Resinas, M., Ruiz-Cortes, A.: Mixing RASCI matrices and BPMN together for responsibility management. In: VII Jornadas en Ciencia e Ingenieria de Servicios, JCIS 2011 (2011). https://doi.org/10.13140/2.1.4769.6960
30. Zivkovic, S., Kuhn, H., Karagiannis, D.: Facilitate modelling using method integration: an approach using mappings and integration rule. In: ECIS 2007 Conference Proceedings, p. 122 (2007). http://aisel.aisnet.org/ecis2007/122. Accessed 20 May 2021
31. 10 steps to create an assurance map. https://www.icaew.com/technical/audit-and-assurance/assurance/assurance-mapping/10-steps-to-prepare-your-assurance-map. Accessed 20 May 2020
32. Ross, J.W., Weill, P., Robertson, D.C.: Enterprise Architecture as Strategy, Creating a Foundation for Business Execution. Harvard Business School Press, Boston (2006)
33. Odell, J.J.: A primer to method engineering. In: Brinkkemper, S., Lyytinen, K., Welke, R.J. (eds.) Method Engineering, Principles of Method Construction and Tool Support, pp. 1–8. Chapman & Hall, London (1996)

Standard Cloud Solution for Control and Supervision in Russia

Mikhail Bundin$^{(\boxtimes)}$ ⓘ and Aleksei Martynov ⓘ

Lobachevsky State University of Nizhny Novgorod (UNN), Nizhny Novgorod 603022, Russia
mbundin@mail.ru

Abstract. The introduction of cloud computing technologies in the field of public administration has become a global trend. In Russia the prospects of using various solutions and services to optimize the activities of control and supervision bodies are actively being considered. Since 2017, as part of the Administrative Reform, the issue of using unified cloud services for control and supervision bodies has been continuously discussed. Since 2018, within the framework of this initiative, a unified information system is being implemented – a Standard Cloud Solution for control and supervisory activities. The article discusses the content of program and legal documents regulating the implementation of this Standard Cloud Solution, as well as the current practice of its implementation from the point of view of existing trends in the use of cloud computing technologies for the needs of public administration in the world. In conclusion, it is stated that it is still impossible to unambiguously assess the effectiveness of these digital solutions. At the same time, it could be admitted that the necessary legal framework for their application is appeared and it is high time to consider more attentively issues on security and openness of such information systems.

Keywords: Public administration · e-government · Digital public administration · State control and supervision · Cloud technologies · Standard cloud solution

1 Introduction

Building digital society and digital economy, which is now spoken of almost everywhere, is unthinkable without an effective system of public administration, which must also meet the current social transformations and use actively the top-level information technologies.

This is what logically explains the emergence in Russia of the sub-program "Information State" of the State National Program "Information Society 2011–2020" [35] and what is more relevant now is the National Project "Digital Economy" which includes the federal project "Digital Public Administration" [31].

An important point for the digital economy's development is the reduction of administrative barriers, which is directly related to the further reform of state control and supervision by improving its outfit through new information technologies.

© Springer Nature Switzerland AG 2022
A. V. Chugunov et al. (Eds.): EGOSE 2021, CCIS 1529, pp. 50–61, 2022.
https://doi.org/10.1007/978-3-031-04238-6_5

Developed in 2016, the Passport of the Priority Program "Reform of Control and Supervisory Activities" (hereinafter referred to as the Passport of the CSA Reform) [32] contains several quite important measures to improve the "outfit" of control and supervisory activities with new information technologies. In fact, this gave a start to a comprehensive, consistent and qualitatively new stage of the introduction of digital technologies into the control and supervisory system in Russia. According to the above-mentioned Passport of the CSA reform, in 2018, it was planned to introduce a standard cloud solution for control and supervisory activities (SCS CSA), which was implemented based on the Regulation on the state information system "Standard Cloud Solution for Automation of Control (Supervisory) Activities" (Hereinafter - SIS SCS CSA). Since 2020, a new version (version 2.0) of SIS SCS CSA has been introduced in a demo version on the Portal of Control and Supervisory Activities of Russia [33].

Such significant changes quite reasonably raise many questions about the formation of an appropriate legal environment for further introduction of cloud services for control and supervision, as well as about the effectiveness of such solutions and their safety both for the control and supervisory bodies and their functioning, and for the objects of control/inspections and related controlled persons.

2 Literature Review

In particular, the advantages and disadvantages of cloud computing for economics and business have been studied in sufficient detail [46]. Many studies note the significant advantages that cloud solutions can provide for businesses, especially for small and medium-sized, by increasing efficiency and reducing the overall cost of maintaining IT infrastructure [28].

The legal aspects of the cloud solutions' use are also quite well developed [36], especially in terms of protecting the rights of the individual, personal data [10, 25, 40, 41], ensuring information security and confidentiality of information [38]. Also, a considerable attention is paid to the problems of private law regulation of the provision of services based on cloud solutions and conclusions are drawn regarding the possible legal nature of such agreements between the provider and the user, which may have different characteristics depending on the model of cloud services: a lease (infrastructure lease) agreement, a license agreement, a contract on the paid services' provision, a mixed agreement and an unnamed agreement [37].

The use of cloud computing technologies for public administration purpose is still relatively poorly understood. A large part of existing studies explores the problems of ensuring information security [12, 20] and data confidentiality, personal data protection, information openness, as well as the advantages of cloud solutions and the prospects for improving the efficiency of public administration with their help [3, 4, 16, 27, 46]. At the same time, the issue of the targeted application of cloud solutions in relation to control and supervision remains unexplored, which explains the relevance of the topic.

3 Current Cloud Computing Models

Current studies rightly note the lack of clear terminology in the description of cloud computing/solutions [37], including in the context of the variety of their implications and forms. In fact, the term "cloud service (cloud solution)" is used to refer to digital services based on the "cloud computing" technology – cloud services [37].

Quite often, to describe these phenomena, the terminology of ISO/IEC 17788/2014 is used. According to this international standard document, cloud computing is a "paradigm for enabling network access to a scalable and elastic pool of shareable physical or virtual resources with self-service provisioning and administration on-demand" [21].

It is customary now to distinguish three main models of cloud services:

1. "Software as a service" (SaaS). The consumer receives software tools—the provider's applications that operate on the cloud infrastructure.
2. "Platform as a service" (PaaS). The consumer receives funds on the cloud infrastructure to deploy their own or purchased applications developed by program solutions and tools supported by the provider.
3. "Infrastructure as a service" (IaaS). The consumer receives data processing, storage, networking, and other basic computing resources and can deploy and execute arbitrary software, including operating systems and applications, on them [17].
4. Recently, it becomes common to mention two more models for providing cloud solutions, which in many ways are superstructures to the three main ones:
5. "Data Storage as a Service" (DSaaS). The consumer gets the data storage capabilities and the associated capabilities.
6. "Network as a Service" (NaaS). The consumer has the possibility of transport connectivity and associated network capabilities.

The creation and use of cloud solutions is a global trend and provides many advantages. The cloud solution minimizes or completely diminish IT costs for server administration, storage organization, troubleshooting, etc.

On the eve of the World Mobile Congress 2017 in Shanghai, two well-known companies Huawei and IDC prepared a report, which emphasized that the basis of corporate communications in the nearest future will be cloud computing technologies, which will help to increase significantly their market share [22].

In Russia, the "Digital Public Administration" project envisages the use of cloud computing by executive authorities. It is intended to create, develop and operate a software solution (a platform) for the performance of state functions, including the creation and operation of a single register of mandatory requirements of a standard cloud solution for the automation of control and supervisory activities, to guarantee the management of the activities of employees of state bodies.

4   Current International Practice of the Use of Cloud Computing for Public Administration

4.1   USA

The United States can be considered one of the few countries that have been actively promoting the use of cloud solutions for a long time, including for the needs of public administration.

One of the first steps in defining a nationwide strategy for widespread adoption of cloud solutions was the development in September 2011 by the National Institute of Standards and Technology (NIST) of the conceptual apparatus – the definition of cloud computing. It was this document that proposed three main models of cloud solutions and classified cloud services into public, private, public and mixed (hybrid) "clouds" [45].

In February 2011, the U.S. government adopted the Federal Cloud Computing Strategy, now sometimes referred to as "Cloud First" [13]. This document provides in sufficient detail not only an analysis of the then cloud solutions market, but also actively suggests implementing cloud solutions in the field of public administration. The strategy assumed a reduction in government spending on IT infrastructure by 4 times in the case of its transfer to the "cloud".

In 2017, the Administration of the US President prepared a Report to the President on Federal IT Modernization, which gave impetus to a significant update of the Federal Cloud Computing Strategy [34]. In 2019, a new version was approved, called "Smart Cloud" [42]. The strategy envisions a long-term model for the safe transition of federal agencies to the use of cloud technologies in order to further reduce costs, improve security and speed of service delivery.

An important role in introducing technological innovations in the public administration system at the federal level is played by the Federal Risk and Authorization Management Program (FedRAMP) [43], the essence of which is expert risk assessment and standardization in the implementation of cloud services by federal agencies. In fact, any decision to use cloud solutions that involves the use of federal data must be verified under a special program procedure. Currently, the program involves more than 220 cloud solution providers and 150 federal agencies, and 35 experts, as well as independent auditors, who can also be engaged for initial and periodic checks of compliance of cloud solutions with FedRAMP standards.

4.2 European Union

The European Union in 2012 developed the European Cloud Strategy, which became the first pan-European document defining the development directions of the European IT market for cloud solutions. The strategy itself involved the implementation of three key steps towards overcoming possible regulatory and administrative barriers to the introduction of cloud technologies:

1. "breakthrough the jungle of standards" – harmonization and development of a unified system of standardization and certification of cloud services;
2. "secure and fair contract terms" – development of the necessary legal framework at the pan-European level for the conclusion of cloud service agreements, including model and model agreements, including provisions on the protection of personal data;
3. "building a European Cloud Partnership to drive innovation and growth in the public sector" – ensure that Member States, public sector suppliers and users work together to develop common, open and transparent public procurement requirements for cloud solutions [6].

In 2014, the governing body of the European Cloud Partnership developed recommendations for defining the EU's cloud computing policy [11], which were considered in the development of the Digital Single Market Strategy [7]. In 2020, as a continuation of the work already started in the EU, the European Data Strategy was adopted, which contained significant provisions concerning the further implementation of cloud computing technologies in the public sector [8]. In the document a still low level of "use" of cloud solutions in the public sector is admitted, which could potentially provoke a decrease in the efficiency of public services providing. As a solution, the Strategy involves several steps aimed at developing an appropriate legal framework for the creation of pan-European data pools, further steps to develop partnerships between the public sector and providers of digital services. A special role in the document was assigned to the elaboration of a legal framework for data clouds and cloud services for the system of public procurement and law enforcement.

Some European countries have adopted their policy and strategic documents on the implementation in the public sector of cloud computing technologies. In particular, the UK adopted a Strategy in the field of cloud computing in 2011 (English Government Cloud Strategy) [18], and developed recommendations for the use of cloud computing services for public administration needs in 2020 (English Cloud guide for the public sector) [5]. The implementation of these strategic documents is directly related to the G-Cloud project, which is a system of voluntary certification of cloud services by their suppliers if they plan to offer their services and products to government services. France also adopted its public sector cloud solutions strategy in 2018, focusing on creating a single hybrid cloud service for the public sector. In Germany, there is a somewhat similar Trusted Cloud service provided by the German Ministry of Economy and Energy [2].

4.3   Asia and Pacific

China has long been relatively closed to foreign IT companies, including in the provision of cloud services. Certain changes occurred in 2015, when foreign companies were allowed to offer their cloud solutions in China through the opening of joint ventures with national partners (no more than 50%). In 2011, the Twelfth Five-Year Plan provided guidelines for almost all aspects of China's economic, political, and social systems nationwide for the five-year period 2011–2015. The Chinese government paid great attention to education, economic transformation, industrial modernization, and environmental protection. It considered information technologies and cloud computing as key elements of its implementation [9, 15]. Since 2015, China has developed several strategic and policy documents concerning the use of cloud solutions for public administration needs. These documents stipulate that cloud computing platforms and data processing centers providing services to the party and the government are located exclusively in China, while all confidential information cannot be transmitted, processed or stored outside the state. Government services and departments have the right to enter into security or confidentiality agreements with service providers. At the same time, there is a ban on the use of cloud services by enterprises and institutions related to state or official secrets [29].

One of the market leaders in cloud solutions for the Chinese government is Huawei, which has implemented more than 350 governmental cloud projects in China, including

22 national, 18 provincial, and 310 local clouds. In 2017 Huawei ranked first in both the e-government cloud technology market and China's Big Data market [26]. Huawei is now actively promoting the "one cloud + one lake + one platform" strategy. The latter helps speed up data integration and exchange between different government information systems [47].

Among Asian countries, *South Korea* is still one of the world top leaders in the information technologies' implementation in the public sector, which fully applies to the leadership in the development of cloud computing technologies, which have long been used with great success to provide public services.

This largely explains a certain leadership of the Republic of Korea in the development and adoption of appropriate regulatory frameworks for the use of cloud services, and at the level of legislation. In 2015, the country adopted one of the first in the world [23] the Law on Cloud Computing, which sets out in art. 20 the responsibility of authorities and government agencies to make efforts to implement cloud computing and recommends using cloud information systems developed by private campaigns, rather than developing their own cloud solution [48].

Another country that began to actively adapt cloud computing technologies to the field of public administration at an early stage was the *Philippines*. The current IaaS cloud infrastructure was launched in 2013 as part of the Integrated Government Program of the Philippines (iGovPhil) [44], jointly implemented by the Department of Science and Technology – Advanced Science and Technology Institute (DOST-ASTI) and the Department of Information and Communication Technology (DICT). Due to the placement of software solutions, servers, data storages in the cloud, it becomes possible to improve the quality of services provided to the public and business. Currently, GovCloud offers such services as GovMail (an email system), PhPay (a universal payment service for paying for government services), ARMIS (a cloud storage system for documents and archives), PMGov (an infrastructure project management system), a registry of agency services, and web hosting for government agencies. Soon, the cloud is also planned to host a common service Forms Builder (a designer of documents and electronic forms) and Single Sigh On (a single system for identifying and accessing cloud services).

Other countries in the region are also actively developing relevant policy and strategic documents that define various dimensions of the implementation of cloud solutions in the public sector. Among the leaders of this direction, we can note *Australia* [39], *Singapore* [49], and *Malaysia* [1].

5 Forming Legal Framework for Cloud Computing Solutions for Control and Supervision in Russia

The key document that launched the next stage for control and supervisory activities' reform is the Passport of the priority program Reform of control and supervisory activities adopted in December 2016 [32].

One of the areas of reform related to the automation of control and supervisory activities (hereinafter – CSA) is the introduction of a new digital technology solution – a standard cloud solution for control and supervisory activities (SCS CSA) with the main tasks:

- completeness, reliability and timeliness of providing information (data) on CSA;
- digitalization of administrative procedures of CSA;
- ensuring interdepartmental electronic interaction between control and supervisory bodies (hereinafter referred to as CSB);
- development of electronic interaction between officials of control and supervisory bodies and audited individuals and legal entities;
- improving the quality of state and municipal control and supervision by optimizing the work of state control bodies, increasing the openness of their work and reducing the financial costs of their activities;
- prevention of corruption;
- the possibility of appealing the results of control and supervisory activities in electronic form.

It is assumed that this "standard solution" will be an automated solution that helps to support the activities of the inspection staff of control and supervisory bodies, containing a complete and up-to-date description of administrative procedures, templates and forms of documents, decision-making models, which will eliminate an excessive degree of discretion and directly affect the quality index growth of administration of control and supervisory functions.

The use of SCS CSA by the regional bodies is possible at their choice, which can potentially ensure effective implementation of legislative requirements. If regional authorities use their own information systems for the CSA, their integration (compatibility) with federal information resources should be ensured.

In 2017, the Russian Government approved the action plan (Roadmap) on the creation, development and commissioning of the information system "Standard cloud solution for automation of control (supervisory) activities" for 2017–2019 [30].

The main goal of the "road map" is to optimize the labor, financial and material resources used in the realization of public (state and municipal) control and supervision, including reducing on spot visits by inspectors of control (supervisory) bodies of audited organizations, transferring document flow from paper to electronic form, reducing the number of conflict situations using the federal information system for pre-trial (out-of-court) appeals.

The main results of its implementation should be:

- creation, development and commissioning of SIS SCS CSA;
- development and adoption of a regulatory framework for establishing the requirements for the informatization of CSA.

An important stage in the formation of the appropriate regulatory framework for the functioning of the SCS CSA was a special Decree of the Government "On the state information system "Standard Cloud Solution for the Automation of Control (Supervisory) Activities" introducing the Regulation on the state information system "Standard Cloud Solution for the automation of Control (supervisory) Activities" (SIS SCS CSA).

The latter is designed to automate processes:

- the implementation of a risk-based approach in the realization of state control (supervision);
- assessment of the effectiveness and efficiency of public control (supervision) and municipal control;
- systematization and accounting of mandatory requirements;
- information interaction between public (state and municipal) control (supervision) bodies, prosecutor's offices, other state bodies, as well as organizations during the CSA by giving access to data on the activities of the inspected persons and about the production facilities used by them and information obtained using special technical means;
- carrying out measures for the implementation of state and municipal control.

6 Current Practice of Introducing SIS SCS CSA

On May 8, 2019, the SIS SCS CSA was put into operation. It is a digital platform that has the name "PortalKND" and official web address: https://knd.gov.ru.

In 2019 the Russian Ministry of Digital Development ("Mintsifry Rossii") approved the common functional and technical requirements for automation of priority regional state control (supervision) in order to implement a risk-based approach.

Functionally, the KND Portal consists of the following sections: 1) News; 2) Documents; 3) Instructions; 4) Organizations of the CSA; 5) Questions and Answers.

The main page of the portal lists the priority types of regional state control and supervision activities.

Working with the portal is possible after passing authorization using the unified identification and authentication system (UIAS) of the portal "Gosuslugi" (General Russian e-Government services portal), as well as providing the necessary permissions to use the user's personal data contained in the portal's personal account.

In fact, the use of the portal is possible only with the appropriate permission of the administration/operator, provided by employees of the relevant control and supervisory authorities.

Since the beginning of 2020, work has begun on updating the KND Portal [24] and the launch of trial operation of its modified version 2.0 [19]. It is planned to significantly update the design of user interfaces and their functionality according to Gosweb 2.0 (National Russian e-Government brandbook). The updated portal will have tools for information interaction of CSB with citizens and organizations, and will also have the necessary functionality for posting publicly available information and open data. Thus, the portal will be functionally divided into two parts: open and restricted assess.

The open part should be accessible to all users of the portal and have a navigation mechanism. In the main, the open part is planned to post up-to-date methodological and legal-reference documents that define the relationship between the audited persons and the CSB, in particular: lists of CSB, preventive and training materials, instructions, video tutorials on working with SIS SCS CSA, lists of mandatory requirements, scenarios for inspections, etc.

Unfortunately, considering the relatively short time that has passed since the beginning of the operation of the SIS SCS CSA, there is no analytical data on its use by CSB it at the moment, although such functionality is provided and laid down in the open part of the Portal in the future.

7 Conclusion and Results

Considering the inability now to conduct a detailed assessment of the effectiveness of the implementation of the SIS SCS CSA as the transition process will take some time, it is already possible to envisaged its development.

In general, as the analysis of the existing regulatory environment shows the legal basis for the use of cloud computing technology in control and supervisory activities has been formed, including the new federal law that will come into force soon in 2021 [14].

Based on current foreign practices' analysis it is possible to highlight some suggestions for improving the legal framework for the implementing of cloud solutions in control and supervisory activities in Russia:

1. The current documents describe relatively poorly the problems of creating a competitive environment for cloud solution providers, including import substitution, priority for Russian developers, and the admission of foreign suppliers;
2. In fact, the general requirements for cloud solutions and their admission to use in the public sector, including through the public procurement system, are very vaguely formulated;
3. The implementation of SIS SCS CSA clearly touches upon the use of IoT technologies, but these issues remain practically untouched and clearly require further work on them, especially from the point of information security;
4. Current program documents do not treat sufficiently the issues of training staff and personnel to work with cloud solutions. Despite the abundance of instructions, it is not entirely clear how the system of professional training will be built and whether this will be a condition for access to the system.

Funding.   The reported study was funded by RFBR, project number 20-011-00584.

References

1. 1GovCloud, My Government (the Government of Malaysia's Official Gateway). https://www.malaysia.gov.my/portal/content/30097. Accessed 21 Oct 2021
2. About Trusted Cloud, Trusted Cloud. https://www.trusted-cloud.de/en/about-trusted-cloud
3. Aubakirov, M.Z., Nikulchev, E.V.: Tasks of developing cloud platforms for ensuring information needs of the public sector. Electron. J. Cloud Sci. 2(2) (2015)
4. Chemerkin, Y.: Cloud computing as a tool for processing confidential information. Hist. Arch. 14(94), 53–65 (2012)
5. Cloud guide for the public sector, UK Government. https://www.gov.uk/government/publications/cloud-guide-for-the-public-sector/cloud-guide-for-the-public-sector. Accessed 21 Oct 2021

6. Communication from the Commission to the European Parliament, the Council, the European Economic and Social Committee and the Committee of the Regions COM (2012) 529 final (Brussel, 27.09.2012) "Unleashing the Potential of Cloud Computing in Europe", EUR-Lex.europa.eu. https://eur-lex.europa.eu/LexUriServ/LexUriServ.do?uri=COM:2012:0529:FIN:EN:PDF. Accessed 21 Oct 2021

7. Communication from the Commission to the European Parliament, the Council, the European Economic and Social Committee and the Committee of the Regions "A Digital Single Market Strategy for Europe" COM(2015) 192 final, EUR-Lex.europa.eu. https://eur-lex.europa.eu/legal-content/EN/TXT/?uri=COM%3A2015%3A192%3AFIN. Accessed 21 Oct 2021

8. Communication from the Commission to the European Parliament, the Council, the European Economic and Social Committee and the Committee of the Regions A European strategy for data COM/2020/66 final, EUR-Lex.europa.eu. https://eur-lex.europa.eu/legal-content/EN/TXT/?qid=1593073685620&uri=CELEX%3A52020DC0066. Accessed 21 Oct 2021

9. Craig, J.: Cloud computing in China. Daxue Consulting, 21 May 2020. https://daxueconsulting.com/cloud-computing-china/. Accessed 21 Oct 2021

10. Elin, V.M.: Cloud services and features of their legal regulation in the Russian Federation. Inf. Law **4**, 28–33 (2017)

11. Establishing a trusted cloud Europe, Publication Office of the European Union. https://op.europa.eu/en/publication-detail/-/publication/b5c80ddb-fa1a-465b-a8f3-3e6c90af4a3b. Accessed 21 Oct 2021

12. Fabrichnov, A.G.: Legal bases of application of "cloud technologies" as an innovative form of providing public services. Innov. Invest. **7**, 134–136 (2014)

13. Federal Cloud Computing Strategy. https://obamawhitehouse.archives.gov/sites/default/files/omb/assets/egov_docs/federal-cloud-computing-strategy.pdf. Accessed 21 Oct 2021

14. Federal Law No. 248-FZ of 31.07.2020 "On State Control (Supervision) and Municipal Control in the Russian Federation". http://publication.pravo.gov.ru/Document/View/0001202007310018. Accessed 21 Oct 2021

15. Feng, F.: China's Plan: What does it mean to cloud computing? IBM, 03 Apr 2012. https://www.ibm.com/blogs/cloud-computing/2012/04/03/chinas-plan-what-does-it-mean-to-cloud-computing/. Accessed 21 Oct 2021

16. Gasser, U., O'Brien, D.: Governments and Cloud Computing: Roles, Approaches, and Policy Considerations, Berkman Center Research Publication, 2014-6 (2014). https://doi.org/10.2139/ssrn.2410270

17. Glazunov, S., Biznes v oblakah: What are the benefits of cloud technologies for an entrpreneur? J. "Countur", 22 February 2013. https://kontur.ru/articles/225. Accessed 21 Oct 2021

18. Government Cloud Strategy, UK Government. https://www.gov.uk/government/publications/government-cloud-strategy. Accessed 21 Oct 2021

19. Gryzunova, A.: IT company will create a cloud for "Electronic government". Rossiyskaya Gazeta, 11 September 2020. https://rg.ru/2020/09/11/reg-pfo/saranskaia-it-kompaniia-sozdast-oblako-dlia-elektronnogo-pravitelstva.html. Accessed 21 Oct 2021

20. Irion, K.: Government cloud computing and national data sovereignty. Policy Internet **4**(3–4), 40–71 (2012). https://doi.org/10.2139/ssrn.1935859

21. ISO/IEC 17788/2014: Information technology—Cloud computing—Overview and vocabulary. https://www.iso.org/standard/60544.html. Accessed 21 Oct 2021

22. Kaadze, A.G.: Sky-high prospects of cloud technologies. 8 trend solutions for business. Arguments and Facts. https://aif.ru/boostbook/oblachnye-tekhnologii-i-reshenija.html. Accessed 21 Oct 2021

23. Kelleher, J.: How world's first cloud-specific law will impact South Korea's Public Sector. OpenGov, 26 October 2018. https://opengovasia.com/how-worlds-first-cloud-specific-law-will-impact-south-koreas-public-sector/. Accessed 21 Oct 2021

24. Korolev, I.: The cloud for supervisor officials will cost 1.3 billion. Cnews, 04 February 2020. https://www.cnews.ru/news/top/2020-02-04_oblako_dlya_proveryayushchih_chi novnikov. Accessed 21 Oct 2021
25. Kuan, H.W., Millard, C., Walden, I.: The problem of personal data in cloud computing - what information is regulated? The cloud of unknowing. Int. Data Priv. Law 1(4), 211–214 (2011)
26. Liddle, J., Chipman Koty, A.: Weathering China's Cloud Computing Regulations. China Briefing, 12 July 2016. https://www.china-briefing.com/news/weathering-chinas-cloud-com puting-regulations/. Accessed 21 Oct 2021
27. Mackay, M., Baker, T., Al-Yasiri, A.: Security-oriented cloud computing platform for critical infrastructures. Comput. Law Secur. Rev. 28(6), 679–686 (2012). https://doi.org/10.1016/j. clsr.2012.07.007
28. Mell, P., Grance, T.: The NIST Definition of Cloud Computing: Recommendations of the National Institute of Standards and Technology (Special Publication 800-145), September 2011. NIST. http://csrc.nist.gov/publications/nistpubs/800-145/SP800-145.pdf. Accessed 21 Oct 2021
29. Murphy, M., Dang, F.: Cloud computing in China, Lexology, 21 March 2019. https://www. lexology.com/library/detail.aspx?g=998fe1a0-6634-41e7-a670-19ca406709e5. Accessed 21 Oct 2021
30. Order of the Government of the Russian Federation No. 2049-r of 26.09.2017, Official Internet portal of legal information. http://publication.pravo.gov.ru/Document/View/000120170929 0019. Accessed 21 Oct 2021
31. Passport of the national project National program "Digital Economy of the Russian Federation" (approved by the minutes of the meeting of the Presidium of the Council under the President of the Russian Federation for Strategic Development and National Projects dated June 4, 2019 No. 7), Ministry of Digital Development, Communications and Mass Communications of the Russian Federation. https://digital.gov.ru/uploaded/files/natsionalnaya-progra mma-tsifrovaya-ekonomika-rossijskoj-federatsii_NcN2nOO.pdf. Accessed 21 Oct 2021
32. Passport of the priority program "Reform of control and supervisory activities". Government of Russian Federation. http://static.government.ru/media/files/vu4xfkO2AdpTk1NaJN 9gjDNtc69wa5fq.pdf. Accessed 21 Oct 2021
33. Portal of control and supervisory activities. https://demo.knd.gov.ru/. Accessed 21 Oct 2021
34. Report to the President on Federal IT Modernization, Chief Information Officer. https://www. cio.gov/assets/resources/Report-to-the-President-on-IT-Modernization-Final.pdf. Accessed 21 Oct 2021
35. Resolution of the Government of the Russian Federation of April 15, 2014 No. 313 " On Approval of the State Program of the Russian Federation "Information Society (2011–2020)". Ministry of Digital Development, Communications and Mass Communications of the Russian Federation. https://digital.gov.ru/ru/documents/4137/. Accessed 21 Oct 2021
36. Romashkina, P.P.: The use of the term cloud technologies in the legal field. E-Scio 3(42) (2020). https://cyberleninka.ru/article/n/ispolzovanie-termina-oblachnye-tehnologii-v-pravovom-pole. Accessed 21 Oct 2021
37. Savelyev, A.I.: The Legal nature of the "cloud" services: freedom of contract, copyright, and high technology. J. Civil Rights 5, 62–99 (2015)
38. Savelyev, A.: Software-as-a-service - legal nature: shifting the existing paradigm of copyright law. Comput. Law Secur. Rev. 30(5), 560–568 (2014). https://doi.org/10.1016/j.clsr.2014. 05.011
39. Secure Cloud Strategy (Version: 1704). https://dta-www-drupal-20180130215411534000 00001.s3.ap-southeast-2.amazonaws.com/s3fs-public/files/cloud/secure-cloud-strategy.pdf. Accessed 21 Oct 2021
40. Sun, P.J.: Security and privacy protection in cloud computing: discussions and challenges. J. Netw. Comput. Appl. 160, 102642 (2020). https://doi.org/10.1016/j.jnca.2020.102642

41. Svantesson, D., Clarke, R.: Privacy and consumer risks in cloud computing. Comput. Law Secur. Rev. **26**(4), 391–397 (2010). https://doi.org/10.1016/j.clsr.2010.05.005
42. The 2019 Federal Cloud Computing Strategy, Cloud Smart, the Whitehouse. https://www.whitehouse.gov/wp-content/uploads/2019/06/Cloud-Strategy.pdf. Accessed 21 Oct 2021
43. The Federal Risk and Authorization Management Program (FedRAMP), FedRAMP. https://www.fedramp.gov/. Accessed 21 Oct 2021
44. The Integrated Government Philippines (iGovPhil) Program, iGov Philippines. https://i.gov.ph/about-us/. Accessed 21 Oct 2021
45. The NIST definition of cloud computing. https://nvlpubs.nist.gov/nistpubs/Legacy/SP/nistspecialpublication800-145.pdf. Accessed 21 Oct 2021
46. Viktorova, N.G., Shukhov, F.G.: Digital economy: the development of cloud technologies in Russia and abroad. Age Qual. **2**, 80–89 (2019). https://cyberleninka.ru/article/n/tsifrovaya-ekonomika-razvitie-oblachnyh-tehnologiy-v-rossii-i-za-rubezhom. Accessed 21 Oct 2021
47. Xin, W.: e-Government: Contributing to a Digital China. Huawei (2020). https://e.huawei.com/ru/publications/global/ict_insights/201902271023/Cooperation-Focus/201904151626?utm_medium=affiliate&utm_source=Adcell&utm_campaign=deeplink&utm_content=15554&bid=211178-26134-at107565_a186044_m4_p104552_t3_cRU_sf6a65c63-2cca-43f1-869f-6055ae6c968a&adcref=. Accessed 21 Oct 2021
48. Young-Hee, J.: Snapshot: cloud computing regulation in South Korea. Lexology, 18 November 2019. https://www.lexology.com/library/detail.aspx?g=06739e34-8d0e-4c33-8f0e-b4f3c0e970d5. Accessed 21 Oct 2021
49. Yu, E.: Singapore government pushes on with cloud migration. ZdNet, 21 July 2020. https://www.zdnet.com/article/singapore-government-pushes-on-with-cloud-migration/. Accessed 21 Oct 2021

The Concept and the Roadmap to Linked Open Statistical Data in the Russian Federation

Yury Akatkin[1] (ID), Konstantin Laikam[2] (ID), and Elena Yasinovskaya[1(✉)] (ID)

[1] Plekhanov Russian University of Economics, Moscow, Russia
{u.akatkin,elena}@semanticpro.org
[2] Russian Federal State Statistics Service, Moscow, Russia
laikam@gks.ru

Abstract. Statistics is the main domain of government data. It represents the important information and should meet customer requirements, including simple navigation and search, enriched visualization, and deep analysis. Linking helps improve the quality and accessibility of statistical data, ensuring its unambiguous interpretation due to the implementation of semantic methods. Russian Federal Statistics Service targets to provide data as LOSD. The Concept and the Roadmap for Development and Dissemination of Linked Open Statistics in Rosstat, presented in this paper, is the first step to achieve the assigned task.

Keywords: Data centricity · Data-driven government · Semantic interoperability · Linked open data · Open Government Data · Linked open statistical data · LOSD · Semantic assets

1 Introduction

International, public, and private organizations increasingly open their data for further reuse. Most of the Open Government Data (OGD) belongs to statistics: demographic (e.g., census data [1]), economic and social indicators (for example, the number of new enterprises, unemployment rate). Multidimensional statistical OGD today constitute an important ground for accelerating socio-economic development by creating new significant public, municipal, non-profit, commercial services, or products [2–4].

Assessing the current state of OGD publishing, the experts [3, 5, 6] identify the following barriers, constraining the formation of a complex data landscape:

- low consumer awareness of data available in general (lack of a starting point providing systematic information about the composition and content of data necessary for research and analysis);
- insufficient functionality of search mechanisms and access organization (lack of services providing a single access point to OGD for external information systems);
- limited ability to OGD interpretation considering semantic meaning (low quality of metadata, lack of metadata in machine-readable formats).

A. V. Chugunov et al. (Eds.): EGOSE 2021, CCIS 1529, pp. 62–76, 2022.
https://doi.org/10.1007/978-3-031-04238-6_6

The efforts to achieve the openness and transparency of OGD (highlighting statistics as its key domain[1]) are aimed to ensure easy access, research, and (re) use of data for public administrations, citizens and businesses, non-profit organizations, as well as scientific communities or media. These consumers have already formed a certain demand for more efficient ways to search, integrate and process statistical data.

Modern research and practice of such international organizations as the UNECE[2], the Eurostat[3], the World Bank[4], as well as the experience of some national statistical institutes [1, 7] prove it is Linked Open Statistical Data (LOSD) that provides an effective way to overcome the above barriers and to meet customer requirements.

However, despite a noticeable set of conceptual documents and rather thorough research, the practice of LOSD publication is still fragmentary. Unfortunately, the datasets (e.g., published by Eurostat) declared as LOSD are often unavailable or impossible to discover, and the observable academic projects have not led to significant practical results or haven not presented them yet. Development and dissemination of linked data is a complex, time-consuming, and multidimensional task, requiring efforts both in creation and (re) use of semantic assets[5] (SA) and in visualization of datasets represented as LOSD. There is the need for integrated approach, combining the application of semantic methods supported by appropriate tools (platforms) connected with the existing infrastructure of statistical institutions. It is important to organize the collaboration of expert community based on the use of semantic platforms, as well as to improve legal regulation and to support knowledge building. Only such strategy could lead statistics providers to a "transparent" way of presenting data, supporting its multiple reuse, unambiguous interpretation, and ensuring high quality. This, in its turn, will give to analysts and researchers the opportunity of expending the range of academic and applied problems to be solved by using extended associations of data obtained from heterogeneous sources.

In 2020, Russian Federal State Statistics Service (Rosstat) initiated the research with the aim to develop the Concept and the Roadmap for LOSD development and dissemination based on the study of international experience in terms of the applied regulatory, scientific, methodological, and technical approaches with the implementation of semantic methods. The results of this work, carried out by the Plekhanov University of Economics, the authors present in this paper.

---

[1] Open Data Maturity in Europe, 2016, https://data.gov.ru/sites/default/files/documents/edp_lan dscaping_insight_report_n2_2016.pdf.

[2] High-Level Group for the Modernisation of Official Statistics, UNECE Statswiki, https://sta tswiki.unece.org/pages/viewpage.action?pageId=187891840.

[3] ESSnet Linked Open Statistics. CROS, https://ec.europa.eu/eurostat/cros/content/essnet-lin ked-open-statistics_en.

[4] IEG. Data for Development: An Evaluation of World Bank Support for Data and Statistical Capacity, https://ieg.worldbankgroup.org/evaluations/data-for-development.

[5] *The authors determine semantic assets as data descriptions prepared for multiple reuse: (1) metadata such as XML and RDF schemas; (2) common data models, (3) ontologies, (4) thesauri, (5) reference data such as code lists, taxonomies, vocabularies, glossaries. SA should be published as data standards.*

2   Methods

The authors conducted this research following the methods of internationally used Design Science Research Methodology for Information Systems Research (DSRM).

At the *problem identification stage*, the first part of the research covered the following areas: (1) the study of international experience in the production, storage, and dissemination of LOSD and the application of semantic methods for these tasks; (2) the study of international and domestic technologies, approaches, and solutions for LOSD development using semantic assets. The results of this stage the authors represented earlier in some papers and EGOSE Conference reports [2, 8], characterizing the current state of OGD in Russia together with the analysis of possible ways of LOSD implementation in Russian statistics. The authors shortly summarize them in Sect. 3. In review the authors describe the actual strategic documents, regulating government data management, publishing and representing statistical data in Russia, as well as existing approaches to the improvement of data quality and LOSD development, setting the ground for initial proposals of LOSD formation in Rosstat corresponding to established practice.

Due to obtained results and analysis the authors have identified the *main objectives* as the following: (1) to improve the quality of open statistical data, provided by Rosstat; (2) to ensure the possibility of Rosstat LOSD multiple reuse, especially in creating the third-party applications and services; (3) to provide an unambiguous interpretation of statistical data during its analysis, visualization and comparison through the use of semantic methods and Semantic Web rules [10], thus (4) to achieve semantic interoperability in cross agency and international interaction and (5) to increase the demand for Russian statistics.

At the design and development stage, the authors prepared the drafts of the Concept and the Roadmap for the development and dissemination of linked open statistical data in Rosstat, represented *for demonstration* at the meeting of the Scientific and Methodological Council of Rosstat in October 2020. As a result of *expert discussion and communication*, at the second part of the research the authors have made: (1) the proposal for legal and technical regulation; (2) the proposal for methods, based on semantic approach, and selected (3) technologies and tools suitable for LOSD formation in Rosstat using semantic assets.

Currently, the Concept and Roadmap Drafts are at the stage of approval and publication. This paper represents basic provisions of the Concept, including its goals and objectives (Sect. 4.1), principles for the creation and dissemination of LOSD (Sect. 4.2), as well as the Action Plan (Sect. 4.3), which formed the basis for a detailed Roadmap for the Concept implementation.

3   Review

The Action Plan "Open Data of the Russian Federation" [11] determines a strategic goal to increase the transparency and openness of public administration activity, as well as the raise the level of compliance with the criteria for cross-country comparisons.

To achieve the strategic goal, this Action Plan sets the focus to "fulfill the following sub-goals:

- to improve the quality of open data sets preparation and publication;
- to stimulate the growth of commercial companies and public organizations using information represented in the form of open data;
- to create the market for applications and services based on the information represented in the form of open data;
- to ensure the semantic interoperability of open data sets".

The main goal of the National System for Data Management (NSUD) [12] is to increase the efficiency of OGD creation, collection and use for (1) the provision of public and municipal services: (2) the implementation of public and municipal functions, (3) the provision of access to information in accordance with the demand of citizens, business, or public entities. "The achievement of the specified goal will be carried out through legal, methodological, information technology, organizational and personnel mechanisms by means of: (1) increasing the availability of government data; (2) ensuring the completeness, relevance, consistency and coherence of government data" [12].

At the same time the adoption of FAIR principles becomes an important task supporting the availability and reuse of OGD. These principles, primarily defined for eScience ecosystem, provide the guidelines to improve the Findability, Accessibility, Interoperability, and Reuse of digital assets [13]. The compliance with FAIR principles is one of the key OGD quality indicators, assessing the provision of rich and adequate metadata making OGD datasets fully traceable, accessible, interoperable, and reusable for both humans and machines [14].

The Concept of creating a Digital Analytical Platform for the provision of statistical data (as one of the main NSUD components) reviews current methods of collecting and processing statistical information in Russian and conveys that they have led to a situation "in which consumers are provided with aggregated statistical information … having low value for some stakeholders and not representing the possibility of flexible use for various purposes" [15]. At the same time, there is the lack of conditions releasing the potential for reuse of primary statistical data collected from respondents. In addition, the developers of this concept agree that at present the official statistical information is primarily focused on the demands of the government and the requests of federal public agencies. On the other hand, it is the society that feels the need for reliable, scientifically grounded, and timely provided official statistical information. These requirements are not fully satisfied, especially when they change rapidly due to velocity of digital era.

Rosstat cooperates and exchanges data with several types of data consumers, such as government, business, academia, media, non-profit and other organizations, including international statistical institutes. These consumers often combine statistics with other types of data, e.g., geospatial, to provide value-added services and mobile applications in accordance with internal or external demand [2].

The expansion of data sharing and integration is significantly limited by the incompatibility of interacting information systems at the semantic level, as well as the complexity of unambiguous data interpretation. To achieve semantic interoperability[6], to

---

[6] *The authors determine Semantic interoperability as the ability of interacting information systems to interpret the meaning of the information they exchange in the same way.*

enable the use and analysis of data from various internal or external sources, semantic assets, describing data, must be consistent with each other [8, 16].

It seems rather difficult to produce the statistics available for effective use on the web [4]. Responsible agencies determine the formats of published data, they use different structures, as well as irregular formatting and discording standards. There is a lack of documentation, describing published data, it is even not provided at all [8]. It is quite challenging for consumers (both people and machines) to understand and use statistics: it is not always clear what it means and whether it is possible to compare data obtained from different sources.

Nowadays, Rosstat uses SDMX[7] in the Unified Interdepartmental Information and Statistical System (EMISS)[8], and applies the DDI[9] standard when disseminating the results of various sample surveys of the population. The use of the object models on (the basis for SDMX and DDI) improves user understanding of data and increases interoperability of statistical information systems.

However, the use of the object approach does not allow to overcome the high fragmentation and heterogeneity of the information landscape. It is possible to provide linking and increase the connectivity of statistical data by using elements of the Semantic Web (SW) technological stack, such as RDF, OWL, SPARQL and others. SW presents data in linked format, i.e., considering the relations (associations) between entities, described in accordance with the SW rules [10]. Semantic annotation allows not only a person, but also a computer, adequately interpret the meaning of data using semantic assets, having no restrictions on complexity, coherence, or variability [17]. Publishing linked statistics simplifies the search and integration of data, and SW technologies provide the environment where applications can query and manipulate data, build interfaces, and infer knowledge with semantic attributes [4, 9].

Semantic assets describing data in the domain context set the basis for searching, collecting, complex analysis and visualization of LOSD, considering semantic properties. Moreover, it is the quality of such semantic assets that decisively affects the possibility of machine data interpretation [16]. To produce and spread LOSD, it is necessary to provide the development of interconnected semantic assets (e.g., ontologies [18, 19]) based on a unified methodology ensuring SA management throughout the life cycle, providing SA reuse, delivering them as services or architectural building blocks [20].

Despite the significant labor demanded for formalization of statistical knowledge, linked data, and the SA, used for its description, provide a better opportunity to interconnect heterogeneous data sets of official statistics (covering both data and metadata) located in different databases and warehouses, belonging to various providers.

The result of these efforts serves to create conditions for the joint processing of statistics with internal data and external, obtained from consumers. This approach provides the semantic interoperability of information systems, including their capability for cross-agency interaction.

---

[7] Statistical data and Metadata Exchange, https://sdmx.org/.

[8] Unified Interdepartmental Information and Statistical System (EMISS), https://www.fedstat.ru/.

[9] The Data Documentation Initiative (DDI): An Introduction for National Statistical Institutes//Open Data Foundation July 2011, http://odaf.org/papers/DDI_Intro_forNSIs.pdf.

International organizations, national statistical institutes and government agencies are linking data to publish statistics on the Internet. Using LOSD, statistical organizations strive to ensure:

- integrity and transparency: in addition to easy access and openness, linked data allows searching, cross-referencing and verification of data represented by public administrations;
- interoperability and unification of cross-agency interaction: LOSD provides tools for publishing data as RDF with consistent semantics, using SA developed within global and national initiatives, including international cooperation. This facilitates the identical interpretation of open data obtained from various information resources, since it provides the possibility to extend or enhance datasets by linking data and metadata, common to some departments;
- economic efficiency: LOSD reduces labor and time costs, provides effective management of information resources in the processing and production of OGD, due to its reuse. For example [21], there is no need to conduct annual statistical surveys collecting data about import-export transactions if customs service or another related agency has already collected and processed such data and made it available for sharing;
- added value in statistical data production, new ideas for government procedures due to cross-agency information sharing: combining data and correlation analysis for exploring data more deeply and answering more complex questions required by machine-processing and decision-making services;
- improved quality of statistical data: development and dissemination of LOSD helps to eliminate such problems as: (1) errors in the data presented in tabular form and the need to convert data into a standard format; (2) inconsistency of data; (3) heterogeneity of data sources; (4) incoherence in the terminology used to describe data [4, 21, 22].

To meet LOSD perspectives, some standard vocabularies have been already developed (such as the RDF Data Cube Vocabulary and XKOS [23]) and there is an ongoing process of necessary semantic assets creation (e.g., in the LOD2 project [18]). In addition, such important semantic models as ontologies take a great part in the initiatives devoted to LOSD [19].

The development of linked open data in statistics will facilitate wider implementation of linked open data in the public sector in general. This can help government officials and policymakers understand the opportunities and benefits of publishing data in linked open format [5]. Therefore, the proposed methods and solutions should not only reveal regulatory, methodological, and technological aspects, but also should boost the growth of information sharing culture, support (meta)data management and (re)use, improve competencies and technological skills, as well as to consolidate the efforts of the expert community and strengthening the interests of statistical data consumers.

4 Results and Discussion

4.1 Development and Dissemination of Linked Open Statistics in Rosstat. Aims and Objectives

In accordance with the current international experience and the prevailing trends in statistics, the goal of the Concept is set to increase the efficiency and expand the reuse of statistical data due to the possibility of its integration and joint processing, providing an unambiguous meaningful interpretation of data in digital services, applications, and other information systems. To achieve this goal, it is necessary to:

1. To raise the awareness of data providers and consumers, expanding their abilities to discover, search, navigate and compare statistics obtained from various sources.
2. To improve the organization, integration, and provision of data on the Internet by structuring the statistical data landscape using semantic methods.
3. To create basic semantic information resources, as well as to develop the methods and technologies focused on spreading the culture of using LOSD in all areas of public administration.
4. To standardize the interaction between public administrations or other public sector organizations, providing effective information sharing, increasing the level of semantic interoperability of government systems.
5. To introduce automation methods for getting data ready for processing and, as a result, to reduce labor contribution, time and cost of analyzing statistical data.

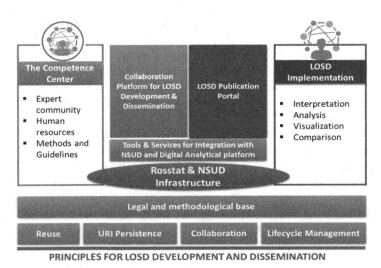

Fig. 1. The LOSD Concept of Rosstat. Overall approach.

The implementation of the Concept (see Fig. 1) follows the basic principles of LOSD development and dissemination, specified in the next section.

The Roadmap determines the sequence of actions to achieve the Concept goal, in accordance with the current level of OGD evolution in the Russian Federation [8].

For the successful realization of the Concept, it is important to revise the existing model of statistical data publishing, with the focus on simplifying the processes of information sharing and cross-agency data exchange, emphasizing the possibility of its reuse. It is necessary to formalize this new model of LOSD publication within the relevant legal and methodological documents, providing an upgraded set of regulations and guidance.

The key enabler of LOSD implementation in Rosstat is the formation of an expert community. The community should bring together the specialists in semantic integration and semantic analysis with domain experts in statistics and related areas. It is proposed to establish a Competence Center, responsible for collaboration, academic research, methodological support, testing or inventing methods and tools for SA creation, dissemination, and reuse, as well as the application of semantic assets for linking and processing statistical data. The other objective of the Competence Center is to research and develop the technologies for LOSD publication, visualization, and analysis, aimed at improving the possibility of data discovery, search, navigation, and comparison. This would simplify the understanding of data, provide its interpretation in the domain context, and eliminate fragmentation or heterogeneity of statistical data landscape. The modernization of statistical processes should consider the joint use of common data semantics.

To gain the interest of consumers and stimulate the ability to create their own applications and services, using LOSD, it is also necessary to provide end users with advanced functions for working with datasets published as LOSD, such as navigation queries, information search, data mapping.

Modern digital platforms should form the basis for the fulfillment of assigned tasks. We suggest building of Collaboration Platform for LOSD development and dissemination and LOSD Publication Portal, integrated into the existing Rosstat infrastructure and the National Data Management System (NSUD), including its Digital Analytical Platform, via special interaction services.

In addition, Rosstat, supported by the participation of expert community, should focus on the growth of human capabilities, educating, training, and improving the qualification of existing employees and future specialists through educational programs, training courses and academic disciplines.

Such integrated approach, presented in the Concept, along with the suggested system of actions (see Sect. 4.3), realized in the Roadmap, will enhance the culture of OGD management and use using the example statistics domain. It will promote open statistical data in Russia to a higher maturity level (in accordance with 5-star model: data is open, linked and published in a machine-readable format, providing the context[10]). The positive experience gained within the framework of the Concept implementation will display the successful application of semantic technologies in one of the most significant domains and will initiate its extension to other OGD domains.

---

[10] Berners-Lee T. 5-Star Open Data, http://5stardata.info/en/.

4.2 Principles for LOSD Development and Dissemination

Principle 1. Reuse

Official statistics has an extremely high potential for reuse, especially when combined with other data, for example, (1) in conjunction with data from other sources in the field of political and economic analysis, (2) in integration of statistical and geospatial data, supporting monitoring, planning, or emergency control, (3) in combination of official statistics with commercial markets data, facilitating business investment decisions[11].

Development, cataloging and dissemination methods should ensure reuse of linked open statistical data and semantic assets. LOSD and SA should be available at required time, with the necessary level of detail and in the correct distribution formats. It is important to provided them in compliance with clearly defined copyright licenses, providing sustainable access over a long period of time.

Principle 2: URIs Persistence

The persistence of URIs, i.e., the immutability and stability of links to resources, is necessary to ensure multiple (repeated) use of those resources that they identify. Using URIs, a user agent can request an identified resource and receive back a meaningful response. It is necessary to define the rules for using such technologies as HTTP to check the correct request's processing. If the user agent is a web browser, then a readable HTML document should be returned. If a resource is requested by an RDF client, then an RDF file must be returned with the URI of the requested resource. URIs belong to the technical architecture of the Internet. In this regard, technical features are important in the development of identifiers intended for further reuse by a wide range of consumers [24].

During the future research in formulating the guidelines and rules of persistence, it is necessary:

- to analyze the current practice of publishing URIs;
- to systematize best practices in the development and publication of persistent URIs;
- to highlight the stability problems arising in applying design rules and URIs management;
- to identify technical issues related to the design of persistent URIs;
- to consider the possibility of generating URIs in Russian.

Principle 3. Lifecycle Management

The management of LOSD and applied semantic assets demands the joint work and ownership, regulation of data and SA management processes, as well as the life cycle support (for example, during such processes as localization, archiving, coordination, updating, publication, and distribution of both LOSD and SAs).

General approaches and processes performing LOSD management should be built into the activity of existing or specially created structures of Rosstat. It is necessary to develop appropriate lifecycle management methods, reflecting all LOSD and SA business processes: from data collection, refining, modeling, identification and anonymization to harmonization, version control, dissemination, and archiving. This will have a

---

[11] https://5stardata.info/en/.

positive impact on the organization of LOSD production processes, together with clear division of roles and responsibilities. It will also influence the choice of technologies, the coordination of capacity building, community formation and the promotion of promising solutions.

It is necessary to conduct the next study of existing practices and methodologies, arranging the interaction and experience exchange with international organizations participating in LOSD projects and programs like ISA2[12], ESS and others[13], as well as with standardization organizations such as W3C[14], the Open Group[15] or The Open Geospatial Consortium[16].

Principle 4. Collaboration
To ensure the semantic interoperability of information systems, it is essential to combine the efforts of IT specialists (system engineers, specialists in modeling and design of information sharing, developers of integration and data exchange services) and domain experts (specialists responsible for formalizing industry domains, formation of knowledge bases, description of entities and relationships in the process of scientific activity). At the same time, during the collaboration, an interaction "gap" often appears. Associated with misunderstandings, it leads to multiple improvements and unsatisfactory results.

That is why there is the need to support the consolidation of expert community within the framework of collaboration platform for the development and dissemination of linked open statistics. This platform should also provide access to information resources, methodological materials and training courses, including various guidelines for processes, standards, and tools for LOSD. It should also open the channel for sharing experience, involvement of the scientific community and business partners (for example, R&D sector).

During the implementation of the Concept the authors consider the further development or extension these principles in compliance with FAIR approach and the experience of its adoption on OGD domain.

4.3 The System of Actions for the Implementation of the Concept

Following the study of methodological and technological approaches to linking of open statistical data using semantic methods, the authors have developed a system of actions for the implementation of the Concept (see Fig. 2).

Along with the framing of federal and institutional regulatory legal acts governing LOSD in Rosstat, organizational and methodical support demands focused attention. It includes building and implementation of LOSD architecture (we suggest using

---

[12] Interoperability solutions for public administrations, businesses and citizens, https://ec.europa.eu/isa2/home_en.

[13] For example, Connected Open Government Statistics, https://gss.civilservice.gov.uk/guidance/the-gss-data-project/.

[14] World Wide Web Consortium (W3C), https://www.w3.org/.

[15] The Open Group Website, https://www.opengroup.org/.

[16] OGC Standards and Resources | OGC, https://www.ogc.org/standards.

TOGAF[17] approach to fulfill this action), which represents a description of models, policies, rules, or standards at the conceptual level, as well as the production of various solutions and technologies in compliance with the basic principles represented in Sect. 4.2.

The development and cataloging of semantic assets required for linking statistical data should be based on the implementation and publication of open standards. To realize this, the authors suggest organizing the work of expert community, including international academic, institutional, and technical cooperation. The formation of LOSD Competence Center should support the collaboration of IT specialists and domain experts, working on SA modeling and LOSD development, publication, visualization, and analysis. The growth and expansion of expert community should boost the promotion of LOSD principles to other OGD domains, attract interested LOSD consumers and involve them into creation of new digital services based on linked open statistics.

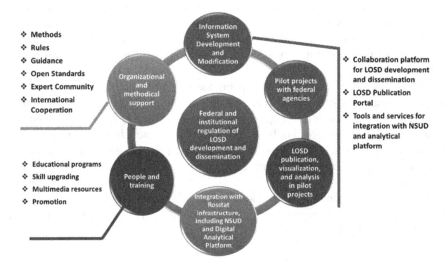

Fig. 2. The System of Actions for the implementation of the Concept.

To fulfill the tasks assigned by LOSD architecture, it is necessary to build IT infrastructure, including software platforms and services for integration with the existing platforms of Rosstat and NSUD.

The Collaboration Platform for LOSD development and dissemination should perform the following key functions:

– cataloging, management and reuse of semantic assets;
– building the information exchange models for LOSD development services, supporting the work of public agencies (external providers of data);
– linking statistical data using semantic assets for further comparison, analysis and visualization based on a set of tools and processes supporting LOSD development and dissemination;

---

[17] The Open Group, TOGAF Standard, https://www.opengroup.org/togaf.

- representing educational materials, courses, guidelines, providing basic functions of training platform, which in the future may become a separate component of infrastructure;
- providing information, methodological, organizational, and regulatory support of the LOSD expert community, promoting general approaches to semantic integration and semantic analysis.

It is planned to create a Portal for LOSD publication, representing the catalog of linked open statistical datasets and visualization tools suitable for various user categories. In addition, this portal should solve the problem of popularizing and promoting LOSD among the audience, representing LOSD benefits, demonstrating tools and services via the capabilities of existing projects and developed solutions, as well as attracting experts to collaboration, establishing the pool of interested LOSD consumers and providers.

Ongoing international LOSD projects (e.g., in ESS Net) pay particular attention to human resource skill improvement and education, Therefore, a significant part of the actions refers to the creation of guidelines and rules, expanded into advanced training courses and multimedia resources, special programs of higher education, forming the Rosstat personnel reserve and spreading the culture of information sharing.

The concept implementation period is set up to 2024 and includes four stages presented in Table 1.

Table 1. Stages of the Concept implementation

Stage	1	2	3	4
Year	2021	2022	2023	2024
Goal	Preparatory stage of the Concept implementation	Methods creation and tools testing for LOSD development and dissemination	Infrastructure for LOSD development and dissemination	Implementation and integration with NSUD & digital analytical platform
Main objectives	Regulations LOSD Architecture Cooperation	Experimental LOSD development Basic methods, tools and guidelines Expert groups working on SA sufficient for linking existing datasets	Concepts and Strategies Expert Community Primary training Pilot projects Infrastructure design Basic catalog of semantic assets	Collaboration platform LOSD publication portal Integration services SA Catalog Educational programs Skills training Pilot projects with federal agencies

The proposed System of Actions forms the basis for a detailed Roadmap, specifying the activities, deadlines, stakeholders, as well as documents and planned results in the following areas determined for each stage: (1) regulatory support; (2) organizational and methodological support; (3) human resources; (4) research competencies and technological groundwork; (5) IT infrastructure.

5 Conclusion

This paper presents the results of the study carried out by the Plekhanov University of Economics in the interests of the Federal State Statistics Service of the Russian Federation. The analysis of international experience, discovery, and systematization of existing approaches towards LOSD development, including semantic methods and tools used to improve the quality of statistical data, as well as its dissemination and reuse, comprises the backbone of the Concept and the Roadmap for linked open statistical data in Rosstat.

From the perspective of the obtained results, the authors outline the current state of the problem and reflect the main directions for LOSD development in Russia based on the formulated principles. The paper highlights basic provisions of the developed Concept, and presents the system of actions, necessary for its implementation, elaborated in the Roadmap steps and timeline.

As a result of concept implementation and roadmap realization it is planned to achieve the following target state:

1. *Normative level.* There are developed and adopted legal acts regulating the creation, dissemination, and application of LOSD in Rosstat.
2. *Organizational level.* In Rosstat there are structural units responsible for the development and publication of LOSD. The established Competence Center unites IT specialists and experts, gathered for collaboration, using the platforms for LOSD creation, publication, visualization, and analysis. It promotes LOSD principles for the audience, organizes expert community and attracts interested consumers. The expert collaboration follows the developed methodologies, best practices and solutions represented for reuse.
3. *Methodological level.* There is a set of developed or adopted methodological documents regulating LOSD in Rosstat. Students and graduates of specialized universities use training courses as a part of higher education programs or advanced training programs for specialists in statistics. Multimedia resources promote the advantages of LOSD, inform and educate users.
4. *Semantic level.* There is a constantly expanding catalog of localized and/or developed semantic assets, including international ones, used for the creation, dissemination, and publication of LOSD. The set of basic SA is developed by means of collaboration platform tools and services, implemented for the pilot LOSD projects.
5. *Technical level.* There is a set of developed or adapted embedded tools for LOSD, including the Collaboration Platform and LOSD Publication Portal, implemented together with necessary services. These platforms, mechanisms and tools are integrated into the existing Rosstat IT infrastructure.

References

1. Aracri, R.M., Radini, R., Scannapieco, M., Tosco, L.: Using ontologies for official statistics: the ISTAT experience. In: Garrigós, I., Wimmer, M. (eds.) Current Trends in Web Engineering, pp. 166–172. Springer, Cham (2018). https://doi.org/10.1007/978-3-319-74433-9_15 Accessed 12 Oct 2021

2. Akatkin, Y.M., Laykam, K.E., Yasinovskaya E.D.: Linked open statistical data: relevance and prospects. Voprosy statistiki **27**(2), 5–16 (2020). (in Russian). https://doi.org/10.34023/2313-6383-2020-27-2-5-16. Accessed 12 Oct 2021

3. Cyganiak, R., Hausenblas, M., McCuirc, E.: Official statistics and the practice of data fidelity. In: Wood, D. (ed.) Linking Government Data, pp. 135–151. Springer, New York (2011). https://doi.org/10.1007/978-1-4614-1767-5_7. Accessed 12 Oct 2021

4. Kalampokis, E., Zeginis, D., Tarabanis, K.: On modeling linked open statistical data. J. Web Semant. **55**, 56–68. (2019). https://www.sciencedirect.com/science/article/pii/S1570826818300544?via%3Dihub. Accessed 12 Oct 2021

5. Janssen, M., van den Hoven, J.: Big and open linked data in government: a challenge to transparency and privacy? Gov. Inf. Q. **32**(4), 363–368 (2015). http://www.sciencedirect.com/science/article/pii/S0740624X15001069. Accessed 12 Oct 2021

6. Toots, M., Mcbride, K., Kalvet, T., Krimmer, R.: Open data as enabler of public service co-creation: exploring the drivers and barriers. In: International Conference for E-Democracy and Open Government, pp. 102–112 (2017)

7. Chaniotaki, E., Kalampokis, E., Tambouris, E., Tarabanis, K., Stasis, A.: Exploiting linked statistical data in public administration: the case of the Greek ministry of administrative reconstruction. In: Emergent Research Forum (ERF) (2017). https://aisel.aisnet.org/cgi/viewcontent.cgi?article=1278&context=amcis2017. Accessed 12 Oct 2021

8. Akatkin, Y., Yasinovskaya, E.: Data-driven government in Russia: linked open data challenges, opportunities, solutions. In: Chugunov, A., Khodachek, I., Misnikov, Y., Trutnev, D. (eds.) EGOSE 2020. CCIS, vol. 1349, pp. 245–257. Springer, Cham (2020). https://doi.org/10.1007/978-3-030-67238-6_18, https://www.springerprofessional.de/en/data-driven-government-in-russia-linked-open-data-challenges-opp/18742244. Accessed 12 Oct 2021

9. Cognini, R., Falcioni, D., Maccari, M., Polzonetti, A., Re, B.: Scrivania: public services execution and semantic search. In: The 2014 International Conference on e-Learning, e-Business, Enterprise Information Systems, and e-Government (2014). http://worldcomp-proceedings.com/proc/p2014/EEE2928.pdf. Accessed 12 Oct 2021

10. Bizer, C., Heath, T., Berners-Lee, T.: Linked data: the story so far. In: Semantic Services, Interoperability and Web Applications: Emerging Concepts, pp. 205–227. IGI Global (2009). https://doi.org/10.4018/978-1-60960-593-3. Accessed 12 Oct 2021

11. The Government Commission for the Coordination of the Open Government Activities, Action Plan, Open Data in Russian Federation, Meeting protocol 25.12.2014 No 10 (2014). (in Russian). http://rulaws.ru/goverment/Plan-meropriyatiy-Otkrytye-dannye-Rossiyskoy-Federatsii/. Accessed 12 Oct 2021

12. Government of the Russian Federation Decree № 1189-r dated 03/06/2019. On approval of the Concept of Creating and functioning of the National Data Management System and the action plan ("Roadmap") on the creation of a national data management system for 2019–2021. (in Russian). http://static.government.ru/media/files/jYh27VIwiZs44qa0IXJlZCa3uu7qqLzl.pdf. Accessed 12 Oct 2021

13. Quarati, A.: Open government data: usage trends and metadata quality. J. Inf. Sci. 1–24 (2021). https://doi.org/10.1177/01655515211027775, https://www.researchgate.net/publication/355162638_Open_Government_Data_Usage_trends_and_metadata_quality. Accessed 12 Oct 2021

14. Wilkinson, M.D., Dumontier, M., Aalbersberg, I.J., et al.: The FAIR guiding principles for scientific data management and stewardship. Sci. Data 3, Article no. 160018 (2016). https://www.nature.com/articles/sdata201618. Accessed 12 Oct 2021

15. Government of the Russian Federation Decree № 956 dated 06/22/2021. On the State Information System "Digital analytical platform for providing statistical data". (in Russian). http://static.government.ru/media/files/FFzGVA88Y6O099MEBBu45eG3nOjnkRLA.pdf. Accessed 12 Oct 2021

16. Ryhänena, K., Päivärintab, T., Tyrväinenc, P.: Generic data models for Semantic eGovernment interoperability: literature review (2014). https://www.diva-portal.org/smash/get/diva2:993528/FULLTEXT01.pdf. Accessed 12 Oct 2021

17. Akatkin, Y., Yasinovskaya E.: Digital transformation of the government. Data centricity and Semantic Interoperability. In: LENAND, 724 c (2019). (in Russian). ISBN 978-5-9710-6185-4, https://urss.ru/images/add_ru/246958-1.pdf. Accessed 12 Oct 2021

18. Janev, V., et al.: Supporting the Linked Data publication process with the LOD2 Statistical Workbench, Semantic Web – Interoperability, Usability, Applicability (2013). http://www.semantic-web-journal.net/system/files/swj591.pdf. Accessed 12 Oct 2021

19. Cotton, F.: Core ontology for official statistics. In: Conference of European statisticians. Modern Stats World Workshop Geneva, Switzerland (2019). https://www.unece.org/fileadmin/DAM/stats/documents/ece/ces/ge.58/2019/mtg2/MWW2019_COOS_Cotton_Abstract.pdf. Accessed 12 Oct 2021

20. EUROSTAT LOSD Publication and Capacity Building: LOSD Publication Pipeline and Overall LOSD Service Architecture (2018). https://ec.europa.eu/eurostat/cros/system/files/d2.1_p_losd_publication_pipeline_and_overall_losd_service_architecture.pdf. Accessed 12 Oct 2021

21. Petrou, I., Meimaris, M., Papastefanatos, G.: Towards a methodology for publishing linked open statistical data. JeDEM – eJournal of eDemocracy Open Gov. 6(1), 97–105 (2014). https://doi.org/10.29379/jedem.v6i1.322. Accessed 12 Oct 2021

22. Feitosa, D., Dermeval, D., Ávila, T., Bittencourt, I.I., Lóscio, B.F. Isotani, S.: A systematic review on the use of best practices for publishing linked data. Online Inf. Rev. 19(1), 107–123 (2018). https://doi.org/10.1108/OIR-11-2016-0322, https://www.semanticscholar.org/paper/A-systematic-review-on-the-use-of-best-practices-Feitosa-Dermeval/47566cbf91846b06d1242c4411b579198c69d287. Accessed 12 Oct 2021

23. Cotton, F., Cyganiak, R., et al.: XKOS: an SKOS extension for statistical classifications. In: Conference: ISI 2014, 59 World Statistics Congress At: Hong Kong, China (2014). https://www.researchgate.net/publication/280740700_XKOS_An_SKOS_Extension_for_Statistical_Classifications/stats. Accessed 12 Oct 2021

24. Archer, Ph., Goedertier, S., Loutas, N.: Study on persistent URIs, with identification of best practices and recommendations on the topic for the MSs and the EC (2013). https://joinup.ec.europa.eu/sites/default/files/document/2013-02/D7.1.3%20-%20Study%20on%20persistent%20URIs.pdf. Accessed 12 Oct 2021

Legal Issues on the Use of "Digital Twin" Technologies for Smart Cities

Mikhail Bundin$^{(\boxtimes)}$ ⓘ, Aleksei Martynov ⓘ, and Ekaterina Shireeva ⓘ

Lobachevsky State University of Nizhny Novgorod (UNN), Nizhny Novgorod 603022, Russia
mbundin@mail.ru, avm@unn.ru

Abstract. The "digital twin" technology refers to advanced digital technologies that form the basis for the digital economy and digital transformation of central and local governments engaged in public administration. Among the many advanced technologies, "digital twin" technology is an integratory technology of almost all end-to-end digital technologies and sub-technologies and usually acts as a driver that provides technological breakthroughs and allows high-tech companies to move to a new level of technological and sustainable development. The increasing complexity of social and economic processes forces the state to look for effective tools for assessing possible risks in decision-making, especially in the management of complex systems, such as the urban economy of large cities, large industrial facilities, and critical infrastructure. The use of such solutions is already actively introduced or actively discussed by many countries, including Russia. Since 2019, a major project "Smart City" has been announced in Russia, within the framework of which it is planned to digitalize more than 200 large localities, using the "digital twin" technology as well. The article deals with the formation of legal regulation and the problems of using digital twin technologies for public administration. The most significant issues are considered to be information security, protection of personal data, ensuring individuals' rights and freedoms, and issues of liability-sharing.

Keywords: e-Government · Legal aspects · Digital twin · Public administration · Smart cities

1 Introduction

Modern public administration is increasingly focused on the use of the most advanced technological solutions. Moreover, with the increasing complexity of social and social processes, it is essential not to search for *ad hoc* tools and options, but to strive for systematic and comprehensive solutions that act "ahead of the curve", allowing you to model situations and anticipate their consequences and avoid serious damage.

In practice, in industry as well as in other economic domains, the construction of digital models of complex processes – "digital twins" - has long been considered as the most appropriate solution, which help to better understand and predict development and improve the efficiency of their management. Such technologies have become even more

© Springer Nature Switzerland AG 2022
A. V. Chugunov et al. (Eds.): EGOSE 2021, CCIS 1529, pp. 77–86, 2022.
https://doi.org/10.1007/978-3-031-04238-6_7

widely used for the management of large cities [29]. There could be mentioned dozens of successful projects with a high degree of detail of digital models of major cities: Singapore, Amaravati, Boston, Newcastle, Jaipur, Helsinki, Rotterdam, Stockholm, Rennes and Antwerp [21].

Starting in 2019, Russia is also developing solutions for the use of "digital twins" technology for managing large cities. Such cities as Moscow, St. Petersburg, Yekaterinburg, Vladivostok, etc. became pioneers. In 2020, Ministry of Construction and Housing and Communal Services (Minstroy) developed the Concept of digitalization of urban economy – "Smart City", which involves the creation of "digital twins" of cities [20]. As of 2020, more than 200 Russian cities have already joined the project.

Considering such rapid prospects, the authors suggest to consider the formation of an adequate legal environment for the implementation of those "digital twins" projects as well as to assess possible legal risks.

2 Methodology and Literature Review

The authors used methods of qualitative analysis of foreign and Russian studies, official and legal texts, policy documents in open sources, international science-citation databases and media sources: abstraction, synthesis, induction, deduction, dialectical, formal-logical, comparative-legal. Considering some practical implications authors also analyze existing practices of "smart cities" projects and existing statistical reports and figures from open sources, concerning the development of smart city projects.

Now, the most developed topics on the use of digital twin technologies are the general issues on the applicability of this technology in various spheres of economics [13, 14, 16, 23, 26]. The most promising areas in this regard are industry, critical infrastructure modeling [15, 29, 34], security management [5, 16, 32], transport [24], aircraft manufacturing [18, 30], and smart cities [4, 11, 16, 25, 32].

It should be noted that most of the studies are rather focused on the technical, technological, organizational and other aspects of the use of "digital twins" technologies. While the legal aspects are increasingly outside the scope of modern research [17, 30].

The most actively developing legal regulation of IOT [26] as one of the components of building a system of "smart cities", while in general, legal issues of "digital twins" in public administration are still poorly understood.

3 Foreign and International Experience

There is globally a very high interest of the industry in the technology of "digital twins". According to various estimates, the market for these technological solutions, according to some forecasts, can reach the level of $48.2 billion by 2026 [12]. General Electric has developed a digital dual platform-PREDIX, which can better understand and predict the efficiency of the production base. The special intelligent platform of the SIEMENS company helps to control practically all process of design, production and operation of production. ABB focuses on creating new opportunities for decision-making based on data obtained using similar technology. Microsoft has also expanded its digital twin product portfolio by offering a versatile platform based on the Internet of Things for modeling and analyzing interactions between people, spaces, and devices. The initiatives of these technology leaders have significantly pushed the boundaries of the use of "digital twin" technologies in the industry.

One of the first major and successful projects was the creation of the National Aeronautics and Space Administration (NASA) "digital model/twin" in the field of aircraft construction [18]. This system allows you to check the compatibility and reliability of components and assemblies used in the aviation industry, and simulate various options for their operation and/or operating conditions. It is the use of this digital model that helps to solve many issues related to the reliability and maintenance of aircraft components, aircraft and spacecraft, and to ensure aviation safety.

Another striking example is the creation of a "digital double/image" of an entire city – Singapore [17]. Large cities are usually characterized by dynamism, which complicates the management of urban infrastructure. One has only to think of the millions of people who live in large cities, or of the schools, offices, shops, hospitals, or transportation systems that require the constant attention of city authorities. "Virtual Singapore", created by the National Research Foundation (NRF), offers 3D semantic modeling of the urban environment, in which the meaning of the data can be directly related to the real world, displaying real places or characteristics of various modes of transport, or components of buildings and urban infrastructure. In addition to the typical map and ground data, the platform also includes a variety of dynamic real-time indicators, as well as information about demographics, climate or traffic, making it an extremely versatile tool with huge potential.

With this in mind, "Virtual Singapore" is also useful for simulating emergencies in stadiums or shopping malls and developing the most appropriate evacuation protocols. It can also be used to simulate the operation of transport and the movement of pedestrians to adapt them to real-world requirements. The platform also provides real-time environmental monitoring, using solar panels, LED lights, pneumatic waste transport systems, pedestrian traffic systems, and bicyclist movement.

"Virtual Singapore" in the future will allow the public and private sectors to use the platform together with researchers and civil society institutions to develop applications and test possible models of city development, which will serve to improve the quality of life and the urban environment.

In general, we can name dozens of modern cities that are actively implementing the technology of "digital doubles" for a variety of purposes: Amaravati, Boston, Newcastle, Jaipur, Helsinki, Rotterdam, Stockholm, Rennes and Antwerp [21].

4   Smart Cities with Digital Twins in Russia

Moscow is one of the most developed Russian cities in terms of infrastructure, which was one of the first to announce the "Smart City" direction as one of the key areas of urban planning and development. In 2017, the Moscow Government developed the Strategy "Moscow-Smart City 2030" [19], which also involves improving the urban management system. It is assumed that deep digitalization will take some time and in order to ensure a safe transition to them, they are supposed to be pre-tested with the help of a "digital twin" of the city. In particular, the first stage is planned to use BIM (Building Information

Modeling) technology [8], which allows you to build models of buildings and understand how they fit into the urban environment, which is especially important at the beginning of construction and urban planning. In the future, this will allow to gradually move from building to larger models of the districts and the city as a whole. The primary task is to improve the quality of the urban environment and significantly facilitate its planning and management, including the management of city communications, logistics, transport, etc. The Russian capital was awarded the International Society of City and Regional Planners (ISOCARP) award for outstanding achievements in 2020 [28].

St. Petersburg is the second city where the large-scale use of the "digital twin" technology is considered [33]. Now, the most significant achievement was the creation of the "Digital Kronstadt" (Kronstadt is a district of St. Petersburg, located on an island in the Gulf of Finland) [1]. The project was implemented jointly with Megafon, one of the IT-leaders and mobile operators in Russia. The creation of the Kronstadt's "digital twin" made it possible to analyze the state of the urban environment in more detail, as well as to think about its further development on the example of several most relevant areas: education, health, transport infrastructure, the state of housing and communal services, the number of communal apartments, the number of residents in houses requiring major repairs, etc. In the future, the project involves integration with other urban systems containing data on the urban environment, including surveillance cameras, as well as data from laser scanning of buildings and structures. The project can then cover the entire city and provide a comfortable and safe environment.

Other cities are also considering deep digitalization of urban governance, including the creation of digital twin cities. The federal project "smart city" has already been supported by 209 Russian cities [22]. At the same time, it is still extremely difficult to judge the status of the project, the first report on which is planned to be submitted by the end of 2021. The most successful projects among large cities are Yekaterinburg [27], where a digital model of the city's heat and power networks system and a digital model of one of the city's districts were created, and the city of Vladivostok, which together with MTS (another major Russian telecom service operator) implements a universal digital model of the city based on geodata, data from the telecom operator and government data, with extensive capabilities [2].

5   Legal Framework for Digital Twin Technologies in Russia

In the current legislation of the Russian Federation, there are various interpretations of the digital technology "digital twin". In accordance with the Order of the Federal State Statistics Service of July 30, 2020 No. 424, a digital double is proposed to mean a digital model of a product or process, which includes design requirements and technical models describing its geometry, materials, components, assembly and conduct; technical and operational data that is unique to each individual physical asset [21].

According to the Comprehensive Plan for the Modernization and Expansion of the Main Infrastructure for the period up to 2024 [10], it is proposed to understand "digital twin" as virtual images of vehicles and transport infrastructure objects, including for managing their life cycle.

As follows from the Concept of the urban digitalization project "Smart City" [22], "digital twin" is defined as a virtual prototype of a real urban object or process, the essence of which is continuous data collection, standardization of data and relationships of elements, their visualization and complex analysis.

It can be stated that currently there is no single understanding of the digital technology "digital twin" in the legislation of the Russian Federation. At the same time, it should be considered that the Decree of the Government of the Russian Federation of October 10, 2020 No. 1646 approved the Regulation on departmental digital transformation programs [9]. According to this document, "digital transformation" is understood as a set of actions carried out by a state body aimed at changing (transforming) public administration and the activities of a state body to provide them with public services and perform public functions through the use of data in electronic form and the introduction of information technologies in its activities in order to: (a) increasing citizens' satisfaction with public services, including digital ones, and reducing business costs when interacting with the state; (b) reducing the costs of public administration, economic sectors and the social sphere; (c) creating conditions for increasing revenue collection and reducing the shadow economy through digital transformation; (d) increasing the level of reliability and security of information systems, technological independence of information and technological infrastructure from equipment and software originating from foreign countries; (e) ensuring the level of reliability and security of information systems, information and telecommunications infrastructure; (f) elimination of excessive administrative burden on business entities within the framework of control and supervisory activities.

In 2019, a new article (Art. 57.5) was introduced in the Urban Planning Code of the Russian Federation [3], which provides from 2022 for the mandatory creation of BIM models of capital construction projects and submitting it among other documents in order to get a construction permit. The information put into the digital double should include a 3d model of the building, information about the geological and engineering expertise of the object, and other characteristics. In fact, we are talking about some small spatial element for the inclusion in other information systems of the "smart city", including its "digital twin".

In the end, it is worth considering these documents as the first steps towards building a legal framework for the use of a "digital twin" in the field of urban planning and urban management. At the same time, when further forming the legal framework, a number of significant legal risks should also be more carefully assessed.

6 Legal Issues for the Use of Digital Twin in Smart Cities

6.1 Personal Data Protection

A digital twin is sometimes a fairly detailed software-based copy that simulates a physical system or product, such as complex equipment, technological process, enterprise, vehicle, complex social and logistics infrastructure (airport, hospital), and today entire cities. An analysis of current, used solutions and services suggests that the digital twin will be integrated with IoT and BigData technologies [32]. The relevance and effectiveness of the digital model will depend on the quality and relevance of data obtained from urban infrastructure and many other sources, including urban cameras, metering devices, monitoring devices, etc. [24]. In fact, such a model can often be directly connected to the real world, and this can conceal a significant concern about collecting personal data about people's behavior, through numerous sensors and cameras. This will require the adoption of the necessary technical, organizational and legal measures to control access to those elements or data of the digital double that may contain personal data and other confidential information [31]. At a minimum, a "privacy by design" principle should be used when granting access to "real information" through a "digital twin" [6].

6.2 Cybersecurity

The relationship of a digital double with a real object can be used not only for good purposes, but potentially to damage the urban infrastructure, its normal functioning, and even lead to serious consequences and human losses. It will be easier for an attacker to understand how a particular infrastructure object is functioning and reproduce an unfavorable physical scenario in reality. This can be particularly dangerous for critical urban infrastructure: transport, energy, healthcare, communications, etc. [24]. This determines the need for careful regulation of the use of technological components of the "digital double", and the granting of rights to use them with caution. Moreover, it is necessary to anticipate and exclude the possibility of access through the "digital twin" to the real management systems of the urban infrastructure, which can be integrated or interconnected with it.

6.3 Intellectual Property and Trade Secret

Protection of intellectual property and trade secrets may arise on the technologies and solutions used in the digital twin. To a certain extent, it is worth talking about the rights to the final product and the solutions used in it, received, initial and intermediate data from developers, suppliers, main customer operators (municipal authorities, organizations managing urban infrastructure), users (legal entities and individuals), and third parties. In this case, decisions on the protection of trade secrets must be necessarily integrated into the "digital twin" model, as well as the relevant provisions of in the legislation should introduced [26].

6.4 Distribution of Liability

It is safe to assume that the final product of the "digital twin" of a city or possibly a larger object (a region or even in the future an entire country) [20] will also be a complex object. In this case, it is quite possible to assume a lot of disputes between customers, suppliers, operators and users of the final product. The development of standards in this area could be considered as a possible measure in the future [7]. However, this will generally require careful consideration of the terms of contracts, public procurement and user agreements, etc. documents.

6.5 Decision-Making

In addition, the use of a "digital double" for making certain urban management decisions by the relevant public authorities [25] will also require the creation of certain procedural assessment documents and criteria for evaluation of the information received from the "digital twin". In this case, it may be necessary to develop regulations for decision-making on urban management or infrastructure facilities and specify at least in which cases the use of a "digital twin" will be mandatory, recommended or optional, etc. There may also be an issue of assessing, reviewing, or rejecting the information obtained with the help of a "digital twin", perhaps using other technological solutions or a human being (expert). In this case, it will be extremely important to evaluate the actions of incorrect configuration and operation of the "digital double" or incorrect evaluation of the result obtained.

6.6 Impact Assessment

Closely related to the previous ones may be the question of using a "digital twin" to ensure the search for the perpetrators and ultimately as proof of their guilt in making managerial decisions. It is quite possible that the "digital twin" can be used to model and analyze the situation in detail, as well as to find the causes – the actions of subjects (public official, infrastructure operators) that led to certain consequences in real life. This may well be relevant for the analysis of logistics, management and other errors and the identification of the perpetrators.

6.7 Openness of Information

Considering that the main operator of the "smart city" should be a public authority (municipality), it will be quite obvious not only to address the issue of restricting access, but also the reverse issue of ensuring the openness of information obtained with the help of a "digital twin". The principle of open government will be equally applicable to digital models of cities. This will require, among other things, legal, organizational and technical solutions that would ensure the access of citizens and legal entities to the part of the system for which there are no confidentiality requirements.

7 Conclusion and Future Work

It seems logical that the formation of the necessary legal environment, as well as the overall assessment of the existing challenges and dangers that may arise in connection with the further mutual integration of the information systems of the smart city and its digital counterpart, is just beginning. Some of the issues concerned here may well be related to existing solutions and positions, such as the Internet of Things, data protection, the openness of information, etc.

However, given that the "digital twin" is an independent complex product/service, so to say, has its own specific properties and features, it is quite obvious that this will require further systematization of knowledge about the legal aspects and challenges that it represents.

The legal aspects proposed here are a kind of reference, points-beacons that can be used to form political, legal and program documents for smart cities. There is no doubt that these issues should be adequately reflected in them to ensure the necessary level of protection of individual rights and freedoms as well as the overall safety of technological solutions used in "digital twins".

The authors consider it promising to further study the issues of legal regulation of the use of the "digital twin" technology as an integrator technology in other aspects of public administration.

Funding. The reported study was funded by RFBR, project number 20-011-00584.

References

1. "Digital Kronstadt": MegaFon and St. Petersburg presented the "Digital twin of the city" 2019. Megafon, 27 May 2021. https://corp.megafon.ru/press/news/federalnye_novosti/201 90607-1332.html?utm_source=admitad&utm_medium=ag-perfo_partner_442763_banner_ cpa&utm_campaign=fed_flat_shop&admitad_uid=3265a0c85fc0863caee62568fd08ff30. Accessed 21 Oct 2021

2. "Digital twin" of Vladivostok from MTS will increase the efficiency of development of the entire region. Konkurent, 06 September 2019. https://konkurent.ru/article/24229. Accessed 21 Oct 2021

3. "Urban Planning Code of the Russian Federation" of 29.12.2004 # 190-FZ (rev. of 30.04.2021). http://pravo.gov.ru/proxy/ips/?docbody=&nd=102090643. Accessed 21 Oct 2021

4. Allam, Z., Jones, D.S.: Future (post-COVID) digital, smart and sustainable cities in the wake of 6G: digital twins, immersive realities and new urban economies. Land Use Policy **101**, 105201 (2021). https://doi.org/10.1016/j.landusepol.2020.105201

5. Assad Neto, A., Deschamps, F., Ribeiro da Silva, E., Pinheiro de Lima, E.: Digital twins in manufacturing: an assessment of drivers, enablers and barriers to implementation. Proc. CIRP **93**, 210–215 (2020). https://doi.org/10.1016/j.procir.2020.04.131

6. Baker, H., Olpherts-Forrester, J.: Digital twins and the Internet of Things (IoT): utilising data. Lexology, 24 January 2021. https://www.lexology.com/library/detail.aspx?g=a3d 08286-d0f3-4892-872e-44488fe5d282. Accessed 21 Oct 2021

7. Camili, R.: Legal implications of digital twins in the supply chain. Lexology, 10 November 2020. https://www.lexology.com/library/detail.aspx?g=55f86213-a6ff-404d-bfe7-d1b0bbbf1c86. Accessed 21 Oct 2021

8. Chernyavskaya, V.: Digital twins: how BIM technologies are changing urban development. Stroymos, 23 August 2019. https://stroi.mos.ru/articles/tsifrovyie-dvoiniki-kak-bim-tiekhn ologhii-mieniaiut-ghorodskuiu-zastroiku. Accessed 21 Oct 2021

9. Decree of the Government of the Russian Federation No. 1646 of 10.10.2020 "On Measures to Ensure the Effectiveness of Measures for the use of Information and Communication Technologies in the Activities of Federal Executive Bodies and Management Bodies of State Extra-Budgetary Funds". http://publication.pravo.gov.ru/Document/View/000120 2010140027. Accessed 21 Oct 2021

10. Decree of the Government of the Russian Federation No. 2101-r of 30.09.2018 "On the Approval of a Comprehensive plan for the modernization and expansion of the main infrastructure for the period up to 2024". http://static.government.ru/media/files/MUNhgWFddP3U fF9RJASDW9VxP8zwcB4Y.pdf. Accessed 21 Oct 2021

11. Deng, T., Zhang, K., Shen, J.: A systematic review of a digital twin city: a new pattern of urban governance toward smart cities. J. Manag. Sci. Eng. **6**(2), 125–134 (2021). https://doi. org/10.1016/j.jmse.2021.03.003

12. Digital Twin Market worth $48.2 billion by 2026. Markets&Markets. https://www.marketsan dmarkets.com/PressReleases/digital-twin.asp. Accessed 21 Oct 2021
13. Glaessgen, E., Stargel, D.: The digital twin paradigm for future NASA and U.S. air force vehicles. https://www.researchgate.net/publication/268478543_The_digital_twin_par adigm_for_future_NASA_and_US_air_force_vehicles/citation/download. Accessed 21 Oct 2021
14. Glover, J.: The challenges and legal implications of digital twins. Fenwick Elliot (2020). https://www.fenwickelliott.com/research-insight/annual-review/2020/challenges-legal-imp lications-digital-twins. Accessed 21 Oct 2021
15. Heaton, J., Parlikad, A.K.: Asset Information Model to support the adoption of a Digital Twin: West Cambridge case study. IFAC-Papers OnLine **53**(3), 366–371 (2020). https://doi.org/10. 1016/j.ifacol.2020.11.059
16. Jiang, Z., Guo, Y., Wang, Z.: Digital twin to improve the virtual-real integration of industrial IoT. J. Ind. Inf. Integr. **22**, 100196 (2021). https://doi.org/10.1016/j.jii.2020.100196
17. Liceras, P.: Singapore experiments with its digital twin to improve city life. Tomorrow Mag, 20 May 2019. https://www.smartcitylab.com/blog/digital-transformation/singapore-experiments-with-its-digital-twin-to-improve-city-life/. Accessed 21 Oct 2021
18. Millwater, H., Ocampo, J., Crosby, N.: Probabilistic methods for risk assessment of airframe digital twin structures. Eng. Fract. Mech. **221**, 106674 (2019). https://doi.org/10.1016/j.eng fracmech.2019.106674
19. Moscow is a Smart City 2030. https://2030.mos.ru/netcat_files/userfiles/documents_2030/str ategy.pdf. Accessed 21 Oct 2021
20. National Digital Twin Program, Centre for Digital Built Britain of Cambridge University. https://www.cdbb.cam.ac.uk/what-we-do/national-digital-twin-programme. Accessed 21 Oct 2021
21. Order of the Federal State Statistics Service of 30.07.2020 N 424 (rev. of 26.02.2021) "On Approval of the Forms of Federal Statistical Observation for the Organization of Federal Statistical Observation of Activities in the Field of Education, science, Innovation and Information Technology". http://www.consultant.ru/document/cons_doc_LAW_359374/. Accessed 21 Oct 2021
22. Order of the Ministry of Construction and Housing and Communal Services of the Russian Federation of 25.12.2020 N 866/pr "On approval of the Concept of the project of digitalization of urban economy Smart City". https://minstroyrf.gov.ru/upload/iblock/315/25.12. 2020_866_pr.pdf. Accessed 21 Oct 2021
23. Qi, Q., et al.: Enabling technologies and tools for digital twin. J. Manuf. Syst. **58**(B), 3–21 (2021). https://doi.org/10.1016/j.jmsy.2019.10.001
24. Rudskoy, A., Ilin, I., Prokhorov, A.: Digital twins in the intelligent transport systems. Transp. Res. Proc. **54**, 927–935 (2021). https://doi.org/10.1016/j.trpro.2021.02.152
25. Schradin, R.: The digital twin – a necessity for government facilities in a post-COVID world. GovDesignHub, 6 January 2021. https://govdesignhub.com/2021/01/06/the-digital-twin-a-necessity-for-government-facilities-in-a-post-covid-world/.YLa0YtWOE1J. Accessed 21 Oct 2021
26. Shpak, P.S., Sycheva, E.G., Merinskaya, E.E.: The concept of digital twins as a modern trend of digital economy. Herald of Omsk University. Ser. "Economics" **18**(1), 57–68 (2020). https://doi.org/10.24147/1812-3988.2020.18(1).57-68
27. The digital twin of the heat supply of Yekaterinburg interested the Ministry of Energy of Russia. Expert, 27 May 2021. http://www.acexpert.ru/articles/cifrovoy-dvoynik-teplosnabzhe niya-ekaterinburga-za.html. Accessed 21 Oct 2021
28. The Moscow project received the international ISOCARP Award 2020. Mos.ru, 10 November 2020. https://www.mos.ru/news/item/82365073/. Accessed 21 Oct 2021

29. Urquhart, L., McAuley, D.: Avoiding the internet of insecure industrial things. Comput. Law Secur. Rev. **34**(3), 450–466 (2018). https://doi.org/10.1016/j.clsr.2017.12.004
30. VanDerHorn, E., Mahadevan, S.: Digital Twin: generalization, characterization and implementation. Decis. Support Syst. **145**, 113524 (2021). https://doi.org/10.1016/j.dss.2021.113524
31. Weber, R.H.: Internet of things – need for a new legal environment? Comput. Law Secur. Rev. **25**(6), 522–527 (2009). https://doi.org/10.1016/j.clsr.2009.09.002
32. Zhao, Z., Shen, L., Yang, C., Wu, W., Zhang, M., Huang, G.Q.: IoT and digital twin enabled smart tracking for safety management. Comput. Oper. Res. **128**, 105183 (2021). https://doi.org/10.1016/j.cor.2020.105183
33. Zhuravleva, A.: Kronstadt has a "digital twin". RBC, 10 June 2019. https://spb.plus.rbc.ru/news/5cfa2b447a8aa9164b9903f2. Accessed 21 Oct 2021
34. Zong, X., Luan, Y., Wang, H., Li, S.: A multi-robot monitoring system based on digital twin. Proc. Comput. Sci. **183**, 94–99 (2021). https://doi.org/10.1016/j.procs.2021.02.035

Digital Society

Practices of Cumulative Deliberation:
A Meta-review of the Recent Research Findings

Svetlana S. Bodrunova(⊠) ⓘ

St. Petersburg State University, 7–9 Universitetskaya nab., St. Petersburg 199004, Russia
s.bodrunova@spbu.ru

Abstract. The paper suggests a new conceptualization of deliberation, namely cumulative deliberation, and makes a critical meta-review of the recent studies of cumulative deliberation made by a group of St.Petersburg scholars in 2019–2021. The concept is based on the idea of tug-of-war-like cumulation of opinion, mostly in online discussions; it aggregates cases of deliberative wins/losses under one umbrella and, i.a., insists that the 'spiral of silence' and silent majority theories are individual cases of cumulative deliberation. Our conceptualization allows for closer-to-life interpretations of the dynamics of deliberative online discussions due to a shift in normativity. Instead of demanding a high level of rationality and orientation to consensus from all (or major) discussion participants on social media, the new concept helps add value to micro-acts of deliberation and opinion cumulation, including likes, comments, and shares, whatever emotional, aggressive, or trivial they might be. To illustrate and operationalize the concept, we provide a review of the recent findings of our research group in the area of cumulative opinion formation and cumulative deliberative practices. This allows for grouping the results into four major research areas, which are cumulative patterns of discussion, structural impact of cumulation, relations between cumulation and discourse features, and relations between cumulative patterns and discussion context. We argue that cumulative deliberation may be viewed a dominant practice in polarized political discussions online.

Keywords: Deliberation · Social media · Online media · Online discussions · Opinion formation · Cumulative deliberation · Normativity

1 Introduction

In 2020, after a series of studies in online communication, the research group of the project 'Mediatized communication and the modern deliberative process' (Russian Science Foundation, 21-18-00454) has come up with a generalizing concept that can explain the logic of online discussions of current agendas. We have called this concept 'cumulative deliberation' [1, 2].

Studies of public deliberation have a long history; they have been spurred in the 20th century by development of mediatized public communication, as well as growth of importance of actors that aim at 'refeudalization' of the public space [3: 177–196]. These actors include commercial capitalist corporations, but also NGOs and the growing army

A. V. Chugunov et al. (Eds.): EGOSE 2021, CCIS 1529, pp. 89–104, 2022.
https://doi.org/10.1007/978-3-031-04238-6_8

of niche, single-issue and radical political parties and movements [4, 5] that challenge the public consensus (re-)established by the major parties and via their competition. Thus, the deliberative process was mostly accumulated within inter-institutional discussions and mainstream media discourse [6].

Most concerns of the international scholarship in terms of quality of deliberation process before the advent of social media were linked to normative dimensions of public communication, such as the levels of discursive rationality, equality and group inclusion in public dialogue, as well as the structural efficiency of public deliberative arenas [7, 8]. Beyond the works of Juergen Habermas himself, the scholars were relatively less concerned about the complex dynamics of opinion formation in the normatively described institutionalized and media-based public spheres. However, influential works such as those by Noelle-Neumann [9, 10] or Lassiter [11] that did not discuss public sphere and deliberation directly have anyway demonstrated that there were effects in opinion formation that could be called cumulative and that depended more on popular majority/minority formation than on institutional or media communication.

Fundamental changes to the public communication that were brought along by Internet and especially social media have already been acknowledged and studied extensively. They have put to light the nature of popular discussion that, previously, existed mostly in the form of rumors [12] and oral discussions in private spaces.

The impact of social media talk upon public deliberation and on how the scholars and deliberators see public spheres has been extensive. It has been assessed by the academe in a sinusoid way: from nearly utopian expectations on democratization including growth of equality and horizontality in representation of opinions [13] to extreme disillusionment in Internet's democratization capacities [14] and criticism towards the trivial nature of online communication [15], to gradual recognition of Internet in its growing reproduction the offline social divisions and disparities [16]. After 2016, with the botization of social media and the rise of 'computational propaganda' [17], Wikileaks revelations, and alleged intermingling of online forces into the US presidential elections, the negative perception of online communication as more a digital threat than a democratization tool for public deliberation has intensified [18].

Moreover, even if one treats social media as politically neutral spaces of personal-level dialogue, online media have brought along rapid growth of multi-dimensionality together with the rise of the level of white noise in public communication. Understanding of the modern public sphere as dissonant and disjointed [19] has spread around deliberation studies, demanding from ordinary users practically the same levels of normativity that were demanded from institutions and traditional media in the 20th century.

What is clear today is that theoretical descriptions of both the dynamics of opinion formation and its normativity might be outdated and missing the point in terms of nature of opinion formation online. We believe that the new concept unpacks the process of opinion formation online with greater accuracy and a lower degree of normativity than the previous models of consensual deliberation [20], public counter-spheres [21], competitive [22], agonistic/antagonistic [23], and dissonant public spheres [19]. These models describe a normative, rational, and dialogic round-robin consensus that must be oriented to exchange of ideas and to formation of enlightened opinion – and then criticize online communication for the lack of these theory-induced features.

To better capture the dynamics and normativity of user discussions, we suggest a generalizing concept of cumulative deliberation. It is not based on the desire for consensus, as users might have various motivations beyond reaching rational consensus. Rather, it is based on ongoing conflicts resolved not via dialogue but via accumulation and preponderance of supporters of a particular position, as in 'tug-of-war' games.

Conceptually, cumulative deliberation is another way of looking at the same online discussions, but with different normative lens which make each post, like, share, and comment *matter*. Tiny acts of user dialogue and participation [24] vary extremely in motivation, sentiment, and level of rational argument; and yet, they are critical in accumulating the mood of the crowd and then public opinion.

At the remainder of the paper, we follow the conceptual line for critical review papers, which implies defining a research area/research question, selecting and grouping the studies, assessing their quality and added value, and formulating generalizations. In our review, we highlight how cumulative patterns of deliberation are linked to polarization in discussions, the sentiment of user utterances, and context of discussions.

Section 2 sets the conceptual framework for cumulative deliberation studies. Section 3 assesses our previous research. Section 2 defines the areas in which our research findings contribute to the theory of public deliberation. Section 4 concludes the paper with establishing the research prospects for the studies of cumulative deliberation.

2 Cumulative Deliberation as a Concept

2.1 New Features of Hybrid Public Communication

As stated above, the recent studies of online discussions and of deliberation in mixed or hybrid online/offline environments has demonstrated some new and key features:

(1) the growth of complexity of public deliberation, which includes varying motivations of participants; multiple incoming options of issue resolution coming from multiple actors of various levels of institutionalization; and, thus, multiple directions of possible development of discussions, which implies lower predictability of consensus;

(2) the growing role of an individual user and his/her tiny acts of communication, including their political role, with the simultaneous decline of dialogical and round-table patterns of public discussion;
        while, at the same time,

(3) growing online reconstruction and reproduction of offline and pre-Internet social, cultural and political disparities and inequalities;

(4) the growth of emotional discourse, trivial posting, and white noise;

(5) the growth of digital threats, algorithmic participation, and relative failure of the idea of the 'earnest Internet' [25].

These features of hybrid public communication call for the idealistic view upon online discussions to be revised – from multiple viewpoints, but we will only focus on several of them. They call for the definition of deliberation and rediscussing its features.

2.2 Defining Cumulative Deliberation and Reviewing Its Features

Based on the idea of tiny user acts and their role in opinion formation, we call: (1) the process of accumulation, redistribution, and dissipation of public opinion by participation of users of various institutional status in online activity; and (2) the effects of accumulated opinion upon positions of institutional actors and discourses, including media and policymaking, the process of *cumulative deliberation*.

Cumulative deliberation critically differs from the institutions-based one, and we see several features that need to be reassessed.

The first is the dialogical and round-table nature of online deliberation. While institutional (including media-based) deliberation is built upon gradually approached consensus or conflict/antagonism, cumulative deliberation offers alternative ways of elaboration of opinion, influencing public opinion, and its overthrowing.

The second is the break between traditional normativity that is imposed by the society to the actors of deliberation, on one side, and the participants' acts, activities, or action, on the other. If we acknowledge that the latter cannot provide for the level of rationality and involvement expected from institutionalized and media-based communication, we need to redefine the normativity within cumulative opinion formation, which might, in many cases, be seen as normatively neutral group dynamics – but, in some cases, it should not. This, among the rest, implies a research focus upon non-deliberative nature of user expression vs. deliberative effects of aggregated opinion.

The third is the role of context in how cumulation is shaped and how the dominant opinion or mood is interpreted.

2.3 The Non-dialogical Nature of Online Discussions: Opinion Cumulation

The traditional (and idealistic, even if simplified here for better clarity of comparison) view of public deliberation implies that deliberation as a process possesses a recognizable order. This may include:

- a limited (even if large) and foreseeable (even if not exact) number of participants and parties involved;
- a certain order of speaking out, either formally established or informal;
- a hierarchy of importance of actors and, respectively, their contributions, which converts into stable or less stable impact of a given actor upon the dynamics of agreement;
- a shared understanding and agreement on the rules of reaching consensus (these may and need to be challenged by minority representatives), which also implies understanding on when the discussion stops or should stop;
- dialogical features of communication process, including 'question – response' patterns, argumentation, and rhetorical contributions;
- in many cases – pre-formed opinions and prepared arguments for public discussions by the major actors of public deliberation.

However, in today's socially-mediated discussions on online platforms, the number of participants may vary much less predictably; e.g. *ad hoc* conflictual discussions rapidly grow and dissipate [26–28] reaching millions of users.

Predicting popularity trends on social media is a growing area of research [29, 30], but scholars rarely ask whether exact numbers of participants in a given discussion matter and can be predicted. However, general systems theory suggests that, in dynamic systems, the number of units is critically important, and it forms thresholds for qualitative shifts and bifurcation points of low predictability. In such circumstances, we argue, traditional deliberative patterns lose relevance and influence.

Moreover, deliberative efforts of media and institutions get drowned in the multitude of comparably long and comparably potentially influential user posts. Public discussion online 'flattens' the importance of institutional actors vs. ordinary citizens. At the same time, Internet provides for new mechanisms of influencing, including the very appearance of influencers [31, 32].

Influencers are part of cumulative deliberation, not the traditional round-robin one, as they are 'made' by user support and are able to create detectable impact upon contents of online discussions. A bigger problem, though, is influencing life beyond the online realm: while consumer behavior is evidently and (rarely measured, but) measurably influenced by bloggers, measurably influencing traditional media, policing, and voting behavior remains next-to-matter of belief.

One more critical feature of cumulative nature is simultaneity of expression by an unlimited number of users, often from tens to thousands. This simultaneity, in the depths of which dominant opinions start to form, then grows into a 'bacterial culture' that adds more and more user utterances to the discussion bulk. The mass of user expressions is becoming structured by algorithmic recommendations, content filters, trending topics lists, or user-dependent instruments like hashtags; and yet, the moments of opinion formation remain elusive, while opinions move and fluctuate. The link between these fluctuations and policymaking remains unclear.

Thus, without abandoning the democratic vector in assessing the quality of the online public sphere, we believe that the classical understanding of deliberation does not correspond to the patterns of 'discussions' in social networks, generates unrealized expectations, and gradually loses its explanatory power. The very idea of a dialogical 'online discussion', whether consensual or dissonant, and the dilemma of 'coming online to either agree or to argue' [33], are scholarly illusions, which have become a key conceptual limitation for research on mediatized and networked public spheres. In contrast, the concept of cumulative deliberation is described as follows.

2.4 Neither to Agree Nor to Argue: Non-deliberative Expression of Views

In online communication, the principle of accumulation (cumulation) plays a basic role. The dialogue gives way to discrete personal statements caused by affect, desire of group belonging, wish to share experiences etc. Such motivations have little to do with the classical awareness of the need for social consensus, common political choice, and round-by-round discussion of future alternatives.

Deliberation online is cumulative in its motivation and emotion: it is built upon aggregation of opinions, polarizing and aggressive solidarization, following influential users, social grouping on the basis of 'friend or foe', shared experience, connective [34] and contributive [35] action.

Fragments of content express opinion, position, and attitudes to phenomena of the socio-political space. When such fragments assemble within a 'discussion', accumulation of opinion-bearing statements produces cumulative effects that are, supposedly, important for the dynamics of public opinion and political decision-making – and are truly understudied, as for today. The process of accumulation, redistribution, and dissipation of public opinion through users' participation in various online activities is called cumulative deliberation.

In such deliberation, it is crucial to accumulate a critical mass of statements. This opens a way to studying cumulative deliberative processes with the help of general systems theory and its branches (e.g. dissipative systems and dynamic systems theory).

2.5   (Re)assemblage of Opinion

The systems theory may be helpful in understanding an important feature of non-dialogical communication – its constant (re)assemblage. The concept of assemblage, as developed by Deleuze and Guattari [40], fits well if one considers how online discussions form and dissolve: the discussants stratify and 'territorialize' their discussion milieu by their efforts, and, in each new moment, any discussion is a new constellation of contributors; it remains a whole via topicality and its marking (like hashtagging).

In a pre-Internet era, one could be sure that actors of deliberation (authorities, media, NGOs, political movements) develop slowly enough to ensure continuity of participation and relatively high predictability of who can join. Today, though, discussions of similar topicality can see participants changed significantly and unpredictably within short time spans. This (re)assemblage is a new and important feature of cumulative deliberation that needs to be worked with.

2.6   From (Tiny) Acts to (Cumulative) Activity to (Political) Action

If cumulation is viewed as an underlying mechanism of opinion formation on social media, micro-practices of political and deliberative participation (most often likes, mentions, comments, and reposts) become a small but non-negligible part of the process of accumulating a society's vision upon an issue.

These tiny acts, as well as others, work on the level of an individual but may grow into practices of personal online presence (see below).

On an aggregate level, there are cumulation-based forms of deliberative and political participation. Online voting, flash mobs, petitions, online protest rallies, and other forms of political communication are directly based on the idea of aggregation of participation and opinion. It is the number of participants, as well as their contributions, allows the topic or issue attract attention of institutional actors, like media or authorities. The activity formed by individual acts turns into action (e.g. political action) when the surrounding community or wider society recognizes it as such, due to some unseen thresholds in public mind being overcome.

2.7 Eliminating Excessive Normativity in Public Deliberation Studies by Recognizing User Imperfection – and Creating New Norms

We see that cumulative deliberation, however neutral and non-purposeful on the level of tiny acts, may be recognized as political by both its own participants and outer audience. This, however, does not imply a demand to each single user to be perfectly deliberative – that is, rational, inclusive, and consensus-oriented.

Does that mean that such non-necessarily rational, inclusive, and consensus-oriented communication does not matter? No, it doesn't.

One of the early conclusions that stems from the aforementioned changes in the public spheres is that patterns of conflictual public discussions do not generate the expected substance of deliberation with high (or at least measurable) democratic quality.

Should they? – we ask.

We argue that, thanks to the lowered expectations towards individual participants of online discussions, the suggested concept of cumulative deliberation allows for assessing the achievement of consensus more accurately than the classical models of deliberation do, and saves the research of the public sphere from excessive normativity in several important aspects.

First, we argue that users have a right *not* to be deliberative – and not to even imagine they could ever be. We recognize their right *not* to aim for consensus and not to even have it in mind when talking online. Users have various motivations for expressing themselves, from vanity to compassion, and their non-consensual behavior forms the very fabric of online discussions. This, in its turn, implies that users' tiny acts first need to be viewed as 'normatively neutral' and not loaded with purpose or overarching goal – not because they aim at best practices in public deliberation and thus are politically neutral or inclusive but because most of their authors have no far-reaching normative aim of finding consensus or winning a dispute.

Third, we correct the treatment of user motivations. Within our concept, communication is initiated not by a wish for consensus in the future, but by its antipode: an existing conflict. The deliverance of the deliberative theory from normativity occurs due to the necessary refusal to attribute excessive subjectivity and responsibility in the course of the entire discussion to individual users.

Fourth, in the cumulative process, each tiny act matters. This goes against the dominant dismissal of online commenters as 'sofa critics' and 'slacktivists' [36]. In its turn, this implies that micro-motivations and emotions beyond the tiny acts influence the appearance of cumulative effects in socially-mediated communication. These effects might be, again, viewed as normatively neutral: that is, the linkage between the result of deliberation and an individual contribution is not direct, and the right of a user for non-rational, emotional, trivial, or even aggressive behavior is recognized.

Here, however, we need to acknowledge that, depriving public sphere studies of excessive expectations towards deliberative quality of individual contributions, the scholarship and policymakers gradually come to 'new normativity' of the *demand of civility online* and discuss uncivil online behavior, including deliberative effects of incivility and verbal aggression [37] like hate speech [38] and cyberbullying [39].

In response to this, we may propose to rethink and redraw the lines of normativity taking into consideration user intentions. Thus,

– emotional speech might be seen as a natural and legitimate part of online discussions, unlike in institutional deliberation, and the effects it casts upon the deliberative process need to be reassessed;

– verbal aggression within the boundaries of law, as well as unintentional misinformation, may be seen as a damaging structural bias that is present in most online discussions. It may play various roles, including positive ones (see below), for online discussions;

– intentional disinformation, e.g. computational propaganda, needs to be seen as an illegitimate practice, a subject to regulation; this is also true for hate speech and other types of speech prohibited by law (however, in non-democratic types of political regimes law may be used against freedom of speech –see below).

With the aforesaid in mind, the concept of cumulative deliberation, we argue, makes it possible to assess the achievement of consensus in online discussions more accurately than the classical models of deliberation, and saves the research of the public sphere from excessive normativity imposed by the society to institutionalized communication.

2.8 Neutrality of Judgment vs. Context-Bound Discussion Bulk

One of the most difficult questions in the study of cumulative deliberation is the question of taking context into account [41, 42]. Despite the 'mathematical' approach to users as free and rightful but somewhat faceless units of communicative activity, the theory of cumulative deliberation should be attentive to person, identity, and culture as parameters that determine the diversity of online communication and influence user motivations in communication acts.

Our approach allows us to pose questions: how do we evaluate the democratic quality and social utility of cumulative deliberation? And should we study its laws as a 'natural' and independent object, more 'mathematically', using the laws of systems theory and mass psychology, even if they are culturally conditioned? How exactly do we include contextual parameters into the studies of cumulative opinion formation and cumulative deliberation effects?

2.9 Previously Discovered Cumulative Patterns of Public Deliberation: The Spiral of Silence and the Silent Majority Concepts

It is not that we claim to be the first to see the cumulative processes in public opinion formation and deliberation as crucial. However, we argue that models of the formation of public opinion, such as the 'spiral of silence' [9] or 'silent majority' [11], are only individual manifestations of the cumulative process in opinion formation, even if discovered in pre-Internet communication and political choice.

As it has been reasonably argued for media effects studies, '[s]tudies on cultivation (Gerbner & Gross, 1976), agenda-setting (McCombs & Shaw, 1972), and the spiral of silence (Noelle-Neumann, 1974) all emerged from the idea of cumulative effects' [43: 2]; however, the 'differentiation between single and cumulative effects, simple and obvious as it might seem at first glance, has long been overlooked in media effects research' [43: 1]. The same may be stated for public opinion research where the 'umbrella' notion of cumulation has long been overlooked.

Here, though, we need to point out that, in media effects research, cumulative effects are understood as those created by continuous exposure to certain media content (or that with certain features like bias) [43, 44: 51], while the cumulative patterns in the very communication process, as well as effects of cumulative public opinion upon decision-making, depend on the multitude of individual (even if aggregated spatially, temporally, or topically) and diverse single-time contributions.

In the online realm, the 'spiral of silence' notion has transformed into echo chambering and filter bubbles research [45, 46], while the 'silent majority' and similar concepts are mostly used for technical detection of user sentiment [47]. Moreover, not only the 'spiral of silence' and 'silent majority' concepts but also the ideas of connective action [34] and contributive action [35] are built on cumulation, as certain thresholds are needed to be overcome for activity to turn into action (see above).

Thus, we argue, processes of cumulative deliberation are relevant for and may lay in the foundation of today's public opinion formation and its impact upon decision-making, political action, and social polarization.

3 Cumulative Deliberation Research: A Meta-review of the Works of 2019–2021

In Sect. 3, we critically overview the results of our previous research in the area of cumulative deliberation and suggest a systematization of research areas in cumulative deliberation based on four dimensions. We ground our logic on the work by Dahlberg [48] who has suggested three analytic dimensions for the public sphere perspective, as he defines it, namely the structural, the representational, and the interactional [48: 148].

To this, we add the contextual dimension, as based on the above-stated importance of contextual factors in public communication.

Below, we describe the findings represented in our papers of 2019 to 2021. As these findings are scattered around multiple papers and do not yet form a whole picture, by this meta-review, we hope to strengthen our argument and show that cumulative deliberation may be applied to varying areas of public sphere and online media studies.

3.1 Cumulation vs. Representation

User representations online, despite being seemingly distant from the idea of cumulation, play a role in cumulative patterns of opinion formation.

In our paper on the Russian political discussion on YouTube in 2019 [49], we have shown that aggressive user utterances were aggregately – and counter-intuitively – directed to expressing aggressive support and solidarity via condemnation, thus delineating the 'us – them' boundaries in political in- and out-groups in a polarized discussion. The utterances were non-deliberative and more phatic in their nature; users condemned one political camp without argumentation and, via this, supported the other. They were mostly not directed to dialogue with counterpart users but expressed discontent addressed *urbi et orbi* or support to the author of the video; taken on aggregate, they ensured the dominance of one or the other political position in discussions under the YouTube videos. In our another, forthcoming paper [50], we show that, for several influential users within discussion on Belarusian political YouTube channels in 2018, such phatic communication ('Well done!', 'Great!', 'I agree', 'Are you crazy?' etc.) forms a certain strategy of public presence.

Despite being absolutely non-deliberative in classic terms, this strategy allows such users to reach the center of discussions and influence perceptions of a given video by other users.

Another representational aspect shows up in activities like flash mobs based on visual material. In our paper on contributive action [35] we demonstrated how cumulative behavior of massive posting of World War II veteran portraits within an action called 'Immortal battalion online' allowed for re-appropriation of World War II memories back to people from the state. We have also shown how contributive acts within a flash mob become activity and then turn into political action when this practice gets public recognition and interpretation in traditional media.

Thus, representation practices may be cumulative. On the level of an individual, they are often linked to structural (e.g. polarization) and interactional (e.g. political action) aspects of cumulation.

3.2   User Interactions vs. Cumulation

In accordance with what is stated above, we have argued that online discussions are not 'discussions' – that is, they do not possess the expected micro-dialogue argumentative nature, to the extent that it becomes a structural feature of the online debate. Instead, the 'discussions' we studied were by 2/3 [51] or even more [49] constituted by user comments not linked to any other comment. This atomization of discussion structure on its lowest level, taken together with the simultaneity of posting, prevented the discussion as we know it, providing instead for the tug-of-war-like silencing practices.

However, the role of interaction in the cumulation of shared views differs depending on the platform and the contents of user posts. In another paper, we shave shown that Russian-speaking female Instagram users with migration background ('InstaMigrants') gradually created a shared space for politicized talk via sharing not opinions but their emigration and adaptation experience [52]. Within the new public that 'considers immigration experience and the realm of management of living worthwhile for a public discussion on a global scale' [52: 8], self-reflection and summarization of mundane experience has gradually grown into a fresh type of social critique.

3.3   Discussion Structure vs. Cumulation

Today, literally thousands of academic works are dedicated to structural aspects of cumulative deliberation, such as user polarization, discussion modularity and echo chambering, influencers' coming to the front stage of public debate, and the role of institutions like governments and traditional media in shaping online discussion.

Our contributions, however, have openly linked these aspects to cumulative patterns of user behavior. In particular, we have shown that user utterances provoke gradual latent polarization not detectable by user metadata or data on following, and polarization might be non-binary [53]. In this paper, we have suggested a methodology for detection of user grouping based of a quite complicated nature: it included revelation of influencers, manually coding their post conglomerates for support/opposition to several types of actors/realities, clustering of influencers based on the coding results, creation of vocabularies of unique words/tokens for the discovered influencers' groups, and applying these vocabularies to all the users in a discussion. Then the discussion of the users that 'belong' to particular clusters, as detected by vocabulary, may be reconstructed in time and/or space, to show when and where particular views accumulated.

We have also shown that verbal aggression is not unequivocally bad: its roles in socially-mediated discussions include fueling user interactions [49, 54], which helps opinion cumulation. In [54], we have shown how exactly the number of participants grows over a heated aggressive discussion center. However, it is necessary to continue these studies using experimental methodologies, as the variance of discussion intensity for different types of verbal aggression has remained unclear. It might also be useful to show in dynamics how echo chambers form around aggressive discussion centers.

In [49], we have detected a more complicated relationship between political aggressive speech, non-political aggressive speech, the volume of the discussion, and the type of discussion trigger (news/comments as a genre of YouTube video). We have shown that, as examples assessed qualitatively suggested, discussion under non-news videos depended on appearance of verbal aggression more than those under news videos; this demands statistical proof, though. Moreover, we have shown that, where dialogical patterns of user interaction emerge, aggression diminishes, thus slowing down formation of a particular opinion and giving floor to less dynamic but more substantial discussion.

As for the aforementioned discontinuity of the discussion structure and its (re)assemblage, our earlier works on influencers in conflictual discussions [32, 55] were complemented by the one on discontinued user presence, including influencers. In [56], we show that, in two topically identical discussions in German Twitter separated by two years, 95% of participants do not repeat, and among influencers this figure is even bigger. The only carcass that remained included several hybrid (online/offline) media. Unlike political actors whose presence in online discussion in democracies is unstable and often next-to-non-extant like in Russia [57] or unanimous like state bloggers in China, media presence seems to be more stable. This needs a lot of additional research, as well as on the new functional and normative roles of media in online debate [58].

Last but not least, our works point out to under-researched micro-effects of cumulative deliberation. We have already mentioned that aggression disappears from dialogical micro-spaces. Also, we have discovered micro-spirals of silence [2] and micro-shifts of agendas within discussions [59].

Micro-spirals of silence/silencing emerge when '[t]he aggressive-dialogical users enter discussion episodes and silence their opponents in skirmish-like communication' [2: 217]. We note that, due to micro-spirals, a bigger 'spiral of support' gradually forms.

Micro-shifts of agendas within quickly-growing *ad hoc* public discussions had not been a focus of scholarly research before we paid attention to the cross-cultural speed of agenda spread within such discussions. By using text summarizations for Twitter, we have hinted that the speed of the shift from retweeting news to discussing issues depends on the volume of a given discussion. We have also shown that micro-issues within the discussion are bound by local contexts.

3.4 Cumulation vs. Context

Context may shape discussions. Moreover, sometimes everything that researchers see in the data may be explained by local realities, without a chance for further generalization [41]. One needs to distinguish the context *of* the discussion from that *beyond* the discussion [42]; they are in interplay with cumulation of opinion or mood.

For the latter, we have shown that cumulative practices are linked to 'ghosts of the past' – historic traumas, social fears, resentment, national shame or, on the opposite, the moments of national pride [49]. Cumulative interpretation of issues (especially in a cross-cultural perspective), as well as the speed with which interpretations stabilize, remains a subject for future research.

4   Conclusion

In this paper, we have defined cumulative deliberation and discussed several of its crucial features. We have suggested four domains for rethinking of the cumulative practices and the democratic quality of the online debate, namely representational, interactional, structural, and contextual. In our reviewing of the research findings, we have shown how tightly these domains are linked and intertwined, when interactional or representational features shape the discussion structure.

The main disadvantage of many of the reviewed results is that they are based on scarce enough evidence and qualitative assessment of media content, without statistical proof. At the same time, combination of big data processing methods and qualitative interpretation has been fruitful for detecting micro-level cumulative phenomena.

The directions for future research lie, as we think, in the following. First, the concept of cumulative deliberation needs to be further elaborated and operationalized for empirical studies. It needs to be based on turning tiny acts of communication into tiny communicative actions, in accordance with Habermas's theory. Second, the dynamic systems theory needs to be applied to finding thresholds of opinion cumulation and its impact upon individual user. Cumulative processes of opinion formation may also need assessment with probabilistic methods of textual analysis. Third, normativity of online presence needs to be developed, and rightful user motivations, both rational and emotional, need to find their place in assessment of deliberative norms and deviations. Fourth, the linkage between opinion cumulation and policymaking needs to be established, however distant they seem from each other. Fifth, the roles of Internet technologies, especially platform affordances, in opinion cumulation need to be investigated. As platforms are milieus that foster formation of publics, including those in non-democratic states, affordances matter for community-bound, platform-wide, and cross-platform cumulation of views, and tech innovations may reshape deliberation in societies.

Acknowledgements. This research has been supported in full by the Russian Science Foundation, grant 21-18-00454 (2021–2023).

References

1. Bodrunova, S.: Cumulative deliberation: the lost ideal of rational consensus and new grounds for winning the public debate. In: Proceedings of the 12th International Media Readings in Moscow 'Mass Media and Communication 2020: De-Westernization of Media and Cultural Studies: New Discursive Practices in Digital World', p. 20. Lomonosov Moscow State University, Moscow (2020)
2. Bodrunova, S.S., Blekanov, I.S., Maksimov, A.: Public opinion dynamics in online discussions: cumulative commenting and micro-level spirals of silence. In: Meiselwitz, G. (ed.) HCII 2021. LNCS, vol. 12774, pp. 205–220. Springer, Cham (2021). https://doi.org/10.1007/978-3-030-77626-8_14
3. Habermas, J.: The Structural Transformation of the Public Sphere: An Inquiry into a Category of Bourgeois Society (Reprint). MIT Press, Boston (1991)
4. Leydet, D.: Ideological diversity, intelligibility and electoral design: a deliberative perspective. Representation **57**(3), 297–312 (2021)
5. Sintomer, Y.: From deliberative to radical democracy? Sortition and politics in the twenty-first century. Polit. Soc. **46**(3), 337–357 (2018)
6. Calhoun, C.J. (ed.): Habermas and the Public Sphere. MIT Press, Boston (1992)
7. Moe, H.: Dissemination and dialogue in the public sphere: a case for public service media online. Med. Cult. Soc. **30**(3), 319–336 (2008)
8. Dahlberg, L.: The Habermasian public sphere: taking difference seriously? Theory Soc. **34**(2), 111–136 (2005)
9. Noelle-Neumann, E.: The spiral of silence a theory of public opinion. J. Commun. **24**(2), 43–51 (1974)
10. Scheufele, D.A., Moy, P.: Twenty-five years of the spiral of silence: a conceptual review and empirical outlook. Int. J. Public Opin. Res. **12**(1), 3–28 (2000)
11. Lassiter, M.D.: The Silent Majority. Princeton University Press, New Jersey (2013)
12. Lake, P., Pincus, S.: Rethinking the public sphere in early modern England. J. Br. Stud. **45**(2), 270–292 (2006)
13. Haraway, D.: A manifesto for cyborgs: science, technology, and socialist feminism in the 1980s. Feminism/postmodernism 190–233 (1990)
14. Fossato, F., Lloyd, J., Verkhovsky, A.: The web that failed: how opposition politics and independent initiatives are failing on the internet in Russia. Reuters Institute for the Study of Journalism, University of Oxford (RISJ) (2008)
15. Trottier, D., Fuchs, C.: Theorising social media, politics and the state: an introduction. In: Social Media, Politics and the State, pp. 15–50. Routledge, London (2014)
16. Daniels, J.: Race and racism in Internet studies: a review and critique. New Med. Soc. **15**(5), 695–719 (2013)
17. Woolley, S.C., Howard, P.N. (eds.): Computational Propaganda: Political Parties, Politicians, and Political Manipulation on Social Media. Oxford University Press, Oxford (2018)
18. Miller, M.L., Vaccari, C.: Digital threats to democracy: comparative lessons and possible remedies. Int. J. Press/Polit. **25**(3), 333–356 (2020)
19. Pfetsch, B.: Dissonant and disconnected public spheres as challenge for political communication research. Javnost – Public **25**(1–2), 59–65 (2018)
20. Brown, J., Dillard, J.: Critical accounting and communicative action: on the limits of consensual deliberation. Crit. Perspect. Acc. **24**(3), 176–190 (2013)
21. Fenton, N., Downey, J.: Counter public spheres and global modernity. Javnost – Public **10**(1), 15–32 (2003)
22. Malina, A.: Perspectives on citizen democratisation and alienation in the virtual public sphere. In: Digital Democracy, pp. 37–52. Routledge, London (2005)

23. Mouffe, C.: Democracy as agonistic pluralism. In: Rewriting Democracy, pp. 35–45. Routledge, London (2017)
24. Margetts, H., John, P., Hale, S., Yasseri, T.: Political Turbulence: How Social Media Shape Collective Action. Princeton University Press, Princeton (2015)
25. Hedrick, A., Karpf, D., Kreiss, D.: The earnest Internet vs. the ambivalent Internet. Int. J. Commun. **12**, 1057–1064 (2018)
26. Papacharissi, Z.: Affective Publics: Sentiment, Technology, and Politics. Oxford University Press, Oxford (2015)
27. Bruns, A., Burgess, J.: The use of Twitter hashtags in the formation of *ad hoc* publics. In: Proceedings of the 6th ECPR General Conference. ECPR Conference Papers 2011, pp. 1–9 (2011). snurb.info/files/2015/Twitter%20Hashtags%20from%20Ad%20Hoc%20to%20Calc ulated%20Publics.pdf
28. Bodrunova, S.S., Litvinenko, A.A., Nigmatullina, K.R., Blekanov, I.S., Smolyarova, A.S.: Ad-hoc publics and influencers on the Russian Twitter: the case of discussion on migrants. In: Proceedings of 3rd International Multidisciplinary Scientific Conferences on Social Science and Arts (SGEM-2016), pp. 73–80. STEF92 Technologies, Albena (2016)
29. Zhang, P., Wang, X., Li, B.: On predicting Twitter trend: factors and models. In: Proceedings of the 2013 IEEE/ACM International Conference on Advances in Social Networks Analysis and Mining, pp. 1427–1429 (2013)
30. Krishna, A., Zambreno, J., Krishnan, S.: Polarity trend analysis of public sentiment on YouTube. In: Proceedings of the 19th International Conference on Management of Data, pp. 125–128 (2013)
31. Freberg, K., Graham, K., McGaughey, K., Freberg, L.A.: Who are the social media influencers? A study of public perceptions of personality. Public Relat. Rev. **37**(1), 90–92 (2011)
32. Bodrunova, S.S., Litvinenko, A.A., Blekanov, I.S.: Influencers on the Russian Twitter: institutions vs. people in the discussion on migrants. In: Proceedings of the International Conference on Electronic Governance and Open Society: Challenges in Eurasia, pp. 212–222, St. Petersburg (2016)
33. Yardi, S., Boyd, D.: Dynamic debates: an analysis of group polarization over time on Twitter. Bull. Sci. Technol. Soc. **30**(5), 316–327 (2010)
34. Bennett, W.L., Segerberg, A.: The logic of connective action: digital media and the personalization of contentious politics. Inf. Commun. Soc. **15**(5), 739–768 (2012)
35. Bodrunova, S.S.: <?covid19?> Contributive action: socially mediated activities of Russians during the COVID-19 lockdown. Med. Int. Aust. **177**(1), 139–143 (2020)
36. Rotman, D., et al.: From slacktivism to activism: participatory culture in the age of social media. In: CHI 2011 Extended Abstracts on Human Factors in Computing Systems, pp. 819–822 (2011)
37. Hwang, H., Kim, Y., Huh, C.U.: Seeing is believing: effects of uncivil online debate on political polarization and expectations of deliberation. J. Broadcast. Electron. Med. **58**(4), 621–633 (2014)
38. West, C.: Words that silence? Freedom of expression and racist hate speech. In: Maitra, I., McGowan, M.K. (eds.) Speech and Harm: Controversies over Free Speech, pp. 222–248. Oxford University Press, Oxford (2012)
39. Oswari, T., Prihantoro, E., Dunan, A., Mudjiyanto, B.: The political impact of cyberbullying and cyber victimization on social media against campaign patterns through reactive behavior in democratic elections in the era of society 5.0. Solid State Technol. **63**(6), 21539–21555 (2020)
40. Deleuze, G., Guattari, F.: A Thousand Plateaus. Capitalism and Schizophrenia, vol. 1. Viking Press, New York (1977)

41. Bodrunova, S.S.: When context matters. Analyzing conflicts with the use of big textual corpora from Russian and international social media. Partecipazione e conflitto **11**(2), 497–510 (2018)

42. Bodrunova, S.S.: The boundaries of context: contextual knowledge in research on networked discussions. In: Antonyuk, A., Basov, N. (eds.) Networks in the Global World V: Proceedings of NetGloW 2020, pp. 165–179. Springer, Cham (2021). https://doi.org/10.1007/978-3-030-64877-0_11

43. Koch, T., Arendt, F., Maximilian, L.: Media effects: cumulation and duration. In: International Encyclopedia of Media Effects, pp. 1–11 (2017)

44. Perse, E.M.: Media Effects and Society. Erlbaum Associates, Mahwah (2001)

45. Sunstein C.R.: Republic.com. Princeton University Press, Princeton (2001)

46. Bruns, A.: Are Filter Bubbles Real? Wiley, Hoboken (2019)

47. Venkataraman, M., Subbalakshmi, K.P., Chandramouli, R.: Measuring and quantifying the silent majority on the internet. In: Proceedings of the 35th IEEE Sarnoff Symposium, pp. 1–5. IEEE (2012)

48. Dahlgren, P.: The Internet, public spheres, and political communication: dispersion and deliberation. Polit. Commun. **22**(2), 147–162 (2005)

49. Bodrunova, S.S., Litvinenko, A., Blekanov, I., Nepiyushchikh, D.: Constructive aggression? Multiple roles of aggressive content in political discourse on Russian YouTube. Med. Commun. **9**, 181–194 (2021)

50. Bodrunova, S. S., Blekanov I. S.: A self-critical public: cumulation of opinion on Belarusian oppositional YouTube before the protests of 2020. Social Media + Society (2021)

51. Smoliarova, A., Bodrunova, S.S., Ivantey, E.: Commenting or discussing? Comment sections of German Russian-Speaking news media on Facebook. In: Meiselwitz, G. (ed.) HCII 2021. LNCS, vol. 12774, pp. 167–178. Springer, Cham (2021). https://doi.org/10.1007/978-3-030-77626-8_11

52. Smoliarova, A., Bodrunova, S.S.: InstaMigrants: global ties and mundane publics of Russian-speaking bloggers with migration background. Soc. Med. + Soc. **7**(3), 20563051211033809 (2021)

53. Bodrunova, S.S., Blekanov, I., Smoliarova, A., Litvinenko, A.: Beyond left and right: real-world political polarization in Twitter discussions on inter-ethnic conflicts. Med. Commun. **7**, 119–132 (2019)

54. Bodrunova, S.S., Nigmatullina, K., Blekanov, I.S., Smoliarova, A., Zhuravleva, N., Danilova, Y.: When emotions grow: cross-cultural differences in the role of emotions in the dynamics of conflictual discussions on social media. In: Meiselwitz, G. (ed.) International Conference on Human-Computer Interaction, pp. 433–441. Springer, Cham (2020). https://doi.org/10.1007/978-3-030-49570-1_30

55. Bodrunova, S.S., Litvinenko, A.A., Blekanov, I.S.: Comparing influencers: activity vs. connectivity measures in defining key actors in Twitter ad hoc discussions on migrants in Germany and Russia. In: Ciampaglia, G.L., Mashhadi, A., Yasseri, T. (eds.) Social Informatics, pp. 360–376. Springer, Cham (2017). https://doi.org/10.1007/978-3-319-67217-5_22

56. Smoliarova, A.S., Bodrunova, S.S., Blekanov, I.S., Maksimov, A.: Discontinued public spheres? Reproducibility of user structure in Twitter discussions on inter-ethnic conflicts. In: Stephanidis, C., Antona, M., Ntoa, S. (eds.) HCII 2020. CCIS, vol. 1293, pp. 262–269. Springer, Cham (2020). https://doi.org/10.1007/978-3-030-60700-5_34

57. Smoliarova, A.S., Bodrunova, S.S., Blekanov, I.S.: Politicians driving online discussions: are institutionalized influencers top Twitter users? In: Kompatsiaris, I., et al. (eds.) Internet Science, pp. 132–147. Springer, Cham (2017). https://doi.org/10.1007/978-3-319-70284-1_11

58. Bodrunova, S.S., Litvinenko, A.A., Blekanov, I.S.: Please follow us: media roles in Twitter discussions in the United States, Germany, France, and Russia. Journal. Pract. **12**(2), 177–203 (2018)
59. Bodrunova, S.S., Blekanov, I.S., Tarasov, N.: Global Agendas: detection of agenda shifts in cross-national discussions using neural-network text summarization for Twitter. In: Meiselwitz, G. (ed.) HCII 2021. LNCS, vol. 12774, pp. 221–239. Springer, Cham (2021). https://doi.org/10.1007/978-3-030-77626-8_15

Selecting the Right Software for Supporting Participatory Budgeting in Local Government – Reviewing Suitable Solutions

Achim Reiz[1]([⊠]) [iD], Michael Fellmann[1] [iD], Lotta-Maria Sinervo[2] [iD],
and Annukka Heinonen[3]

[1] Rostock University, 18051 Rostock, Germany
{achim.reiz,michael.fellmann}@uni-rostock.de
[2] Faculty of Management and Business, Tampere University, 33014 Tampere, Finland
lotta-maria.sinervo@tuni.fi
[3] LAB University of Applied Sciences, Lahti, Finland
annukka.heinonen@lab.fi

Abstract. Participatory Budgeting (PB) empowers the constituents to decide on how to spend a part of the public money. The citizens create proposals, which are then (if they are within the given rules of the PB) voted on by the public. It is believed that PBs strengthen democracy and increase the efficiency of public spending. Information and communication technology (ICT) can support these PB initiatives. There are several software solutions available for implementing a PB. However, picking the right solution is far from an easy task as the solutions are as diverse as the needs and possible requirements of administrations. This paper scrutinizes different solutions in aiming to provide support for aspiring municipalities in selecting the right PB software. The following work sheds light on the differences between the available software solutions. First, we shortly describe the applications and then lay out the tested capabilities of the software. Afterward, we show the fulfillment level of these capabilities and present an excel tool for making individual, informed decisions. The paper is concluded with a description of the tool selection process in two Finnish municipalities.

Keywords: Participatory budgeting · Software analysis · Review · ICT

1 Introduction

Participatory budgeting (PB) puts a part of the cities' budget in the responsibility of the constituents. This idea of PB as a democratic process which gives people real power over real money is crossing continents with various experiments and experiences from different parts of the world [1–3]. Since its origins in 1989 in Porto Alegre, Brazil, PB has spread to over 7,000 cities worldwide, and interest continues to grow [4]. In PB, the citizens can craft proposals for allocating the budget, and these proposals are later voted on by the whole community, with the proposals receiving the most votes getting implemented [5]. While a commonly accepted definition for a PB is missing, Sintomer et al. [2] defined five criteria for a PB:

© Springer Nature Switzerland AG 2022
A. V. Chugunov et al. (Eds.): EGOSE 2021, CCIS 1529, pp. 105–118, 2022.
https://doi.org/10.1007/978-3-031-04238-6_9

1. A PB is in its core concerned with questions on how a limited budget should be used.
2. The city level with some power over administration and resources has to be involved.
3. PB is not a one-time event but repeated over the years.
4. PB includes a form of public deliberation. A simple survey without a public forum is not deemed sufficient.
5. Accountability is a vital part of PB. Accepted projects get implemented, and the public must be informed regarding implementation progress.

In detail, a PB process could look like the following [4]: At first, citizens are informed on the rules of the upcoming PB and how to participate. In the following step, they are asked to create proposals on how and what to spend the money. If a given proposal passes a first check, where the city staff validates the eligibility criteria (meaning it conforms to the set PB rules and falls into the city's jurisdiction), it moves to the presentation stage, where all proposals are shown on a website. After the "request for proposal" stage closes, the city performs a final and very detailed feasibility check. The costs are checked carefully, as potential conflicts with other stakeholders. As soon as the final list of eligible and realistic proposals are crafted, these proposals are allowed to the public discussion and voting phase. After the voting is concluded and the constituents pick the best ideas, the realization follows, and the public is informed on the implementation progress.

The process depicted in Fig. 1 is just an example of a PB process. As a PB has to fit into the cultural and jurisdictional environment in which it is implemented, the process has to be adapted as well. Universally, however, it is believed that PB can strengthen democracy and improve state performance [6]. The former through citizens participation in open and public debates, which increases their understanding of public affairs. The latter through constraining the municipal government and their prerogatives and the increased opportunities for citizens to be engaged in public policy debates [7, 8].

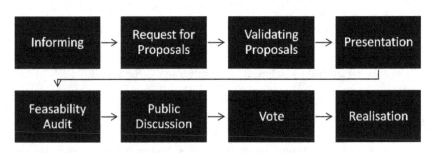

Fig. 1. Stereotypical PB process [9].

These processes can be strongly supported using information and communication technology (ICT) [10, 11]. As PB is a rising phenomenon worldwide, more applications for the electronic support of these participatory processes were developed. However, these software solutions differ widely in their functionality. This diversity can make the software selection for an administration difficult.

Moreover, the prior literature is limited in investigating PB processes from an ICT perspective. In 2011, IBM gathered examples for public engagement initiatives in a technical report [12]. While it also contains tool descriptions, it mainly outlines when to use which kind of engagement tactic. In 2016, the developer of AppCivist (a software solution that is also analyzed in this paper) examines a sample of currently available solutions for civic participation [13]. We fill the research and knowledge gap by focusing on the software solutions supporting the PB process. This study aims to provide a review of suitable software solutions for PB.

Consequently, we pose two research questions: (1) what the main features of suitable software solutions for PB are and (2) how those solutions can support successful implementation of the PB process in local governments. Research questions are answered by conducting a subsequent analysis and a review of software solutions. To illustrate the process of finding suitable solutions for PB, empirical case examples from Finland are provided and discussed. In a previous report [9], two of the authors presented a feature repository for PB applications. This feature repository is the foundation for the subsequent analysis of PB software presented here.

In total, we analyzed eleven PB solutions. The result is captured in an Excel-Sheet and available online [14]. In addition, the paper includes two empirical case examples of the ICT solutions in PB processes in Finnish municipalities. The first one, the city of Riihimäki, utilized the Decidim platform in their PB process. The second city, Lahti, utilized their existing ICT platforms not explicitly designed for PB, Maptionnaire, and Webropol. These empirical cases illustrate different approaches to ICT solutions in PB, showing that the PB process can benefit from ICT tools and that finding an ICT solution is a versatile issue. In both of these cases, empirical data is collected through semi-structured thematic interviews (8 interviews in Riihimäki, 17 interviews in Lahti) and surveys targeted for members of organization and citizens (in Riihimäki n = 75 in citizen survey and n = 30 respondents from members of organization citizens, in Lahti n = 243 and n = 39). The empirical data is analyzed with methods of content analysis.

The rest of this paper is structured as follows. The following section is concerned with a description of the analyzed PB software and the feature list the software is checked for. Section three presents the results of the analysis, followed by the Finnish case studies. Afterward, the research is concluded, and we give an outlook on future activities.

2 Analyzed Software and Features

2.1 Analyzed PB Software

The following section gives an overview of the analyzed PB software. It presents, in a short description, the different target groups and pricing models of the software. As not all software is also featured in academic literature, the list of analyzed tools is based on an internet search for software that supports public decision-making processes.

DemocracyOS.[1] Developed by Argentinian-based development team "democracia en red". They provide several democracy-related applications, e.g., PB, public consultation, crowd law-making, and goals tracking. All software is available open-source, though they provide an installation and customization service.

---

[1] shttps://democraciaos.org/en/.

OpenDCN.[2] Developed by Milano University (Italy). Integrated platform for PB, events, petitioning, and other e-democracy related use cases. Software is available ppen-source. Not regularly updated (last update from November 2018), parts of the description are just available in Italian.

AppCivist.[3] PB-suite by the University of California. Even though stated as opensource, commercial use is not permitted and requires permission. The tool is available as Software as a Service (SaaS[4]).

Placespeak.[5] Location-based consultation software. Developed by a private company in Vancouver (Canada). Provides the possibility to give feedback to local developments. Not a full-grown PB tool. Commercial, SaaS tool.

Polis.[6] Not a PB tool in the classical sense. Implements a system for gathering opinions based on the resonance of comments in a discussion. Developed by a nonprofit organization in Seattle, open-source.

Your Priorities.[7] A PB software that was made by the Islandic nonprofit "Citizens Foundation". Open-source, can be self-hosted or purchased as a SaaS service.

Loomio.[8] Loomio is a decision-making platform. It is targeted not only at governments but also at NGOs and private companies. The software is open-source, though a paid SaaS is offered.

Consider.it.[9] The application is not a PB, but a vote polling platform. The users can share an idea, and others can agree or disagree using a slider. U.S.-based; it is open source. SaaS and customization are available.

Consul.[10] Citizen participation software. It supports PB, collaborative legislation, debating, proposals and voting. It is developed by a European nonprofit organization. It is open-source; certified companies offer installation and development.

Decidim.[11] The Decidim software is a digital democracy platform that facilitates PB, citizen consultations, digital assemblies, communication, and strategic planning. It is an extensive software solution; PB is just one part of it. The software is open-source and managed by an NGO in Barcelona (Spain).

---

[2] http://www.opendcn.org.

[3] https://pb.appcivist.org/.

[4] In a Software as a Service (SaaS) delivery model, the hosting of the application is provided by the Vendor.

[5] https://www.placespeak.co.

[6] https://pol.is/home.

[7] https://citizens.is/.

[8] https://www.loomio.com.

[9] https://consider.it/.

[10] https://consulproject.org.

[11] https://decidim.org.

Citizenlab.[12] E-democracy platform. Offers a range of features like polls, survey, proposals, information and also PB. Source code is available but under a proprietary license. Offers SaaS. Developed by a private company in Brussels (Belgium).

Maptionnaire.[13] Not a PB-Tool, but developed for community engagement. Provides polling, surveys, and a form of gamified decision making. Developed by a for-profit company in Helsinki (Finland).

2.2 Checked Features

The following section presents the features that are the basis for the analysis of the software. These features are structured along the process shown in Fig. 1. Please note that these steps are not strictly subsequent but sometimes overlap.

Informing. The first phase captures how much information on PB is given on a software's website. It shall enable aspiring administration to see relevant use cases for a given application (Table 1).

Table 1. Analyzed features for process item "Informing".

Item	Description
Participation process	Provide information on how to participate in the PB process using the presented software
Goals for PB	Display the desired outcomes for a PB implementation on the software's web-page
Success stories	The web pages give examples for success stories of other municipalities

Request for Proposal. In this stage, the citizens are asked to hand in proposals to improve their city. The analyzed capabilities are, thus, related to the upload of proposals on the PBs website and the registration requirements.

Validating Proposals. Not every idea proposed by citizens is eligible. While the specific design of the proposal check is often highly customized, the chosen software has to provide the required assessment capabilities.

Presentation. As soon as a proposal passes the first check by the municipality, it is displayed on the PB's website. This stage comprises the capabilities for a user-friendly presentation of the data.

---

[12] https://www.citizenlab.co.
[13] https://maptionnaire.com.

Feasibility Audit and Public Discussion. The administration does a final feasibility check as soon as the "request for proposal" stage is closed. It also allows a discussion board for a general debate not only on specific proposals but on the PB in general. The latter, thus, is not bound to a specific timeline but can coexist throughout the whole PB timeline (Tables 2, 3, 4 and 5).

Table 2. Analyzed features for process item "Request for Proposals".

Item	Description
Mandatory registration	The software supports a mandatory registration before the handing in of proposals
Registration requirements	The software supports additional, formal registration requirements, e.g., issued code, citizen registration number
Predefined categories	To further structure the submitted proposals, they can be categorized (e.g., in "playground" or "landscaping")
Upload a file	The PB website implements a file storage. It is possible to upload a picture or a document smaller than 5 MB
Cost estimation	Citizens can include a cost estimation with their proposals
Locational data	The position of the proposal can be chosen and displayed on a map

Table 3. Analyzed features for process item "Validating Proposals".

Item	Description
Status management	Every submitted proposal is associated with a status representing the current state of the processing (e.g., "waiting for validation", "ready for voting")
Pre-moderation	The administration checks if a proposal fits into the given rules of the PB. It can also decline a proposal
Administrative feedback	The administration can write a short statement to the proposal. This statement is essential if a proposal is getting declined
Notification	Submitters are updated regarding comments and status updates of their proposals by e-mail

Table 4. Analyzed features for process item "Presentation".

Item	Description
Proposal list	The list of published proposals is shown on the web page
Search capability	The web page has a function to search the published list of proposals
List filtering	A user can filter the list for the predefined categories (e.g., implementation status, rating)
Export functionality	The list of published proposals can be downloaded (e.g., in an Excel or PowerPoint file)
Rating	Users can publicly rate a proposal (e.g., through "likes") These ratings are independent of the binding voting process
Comments in the reviewing process	Users of the platform can comment on each other's submitted and published proposals

Table 5. Analyzed features for process item "Feasibility Audit & Public Discussion".

Item	Description
Estimate costs	The list of published proposals is shown on the web page
Debate tool	Users of the platform can comment on each other's submitted and published proposals

Voting. With the list of eligible proposals finalized, the constituents now vote on the proposals they like best (Table 6).

Table 6. Analyzed features for process item "Voting".

Item	Description
Voting implementation	The PB software provides a voting capability
Voting codes	The voter eligibility is captured through the issue of a unique code

Realization. The realization stage accompanies the implementation of the voted proposals (Table 7).

Table 7. Analyzed features for process item "Realization".

Item	Description
Media involvement	The PB website informs citizens on the progress of the implementation of accepted proposals

Not all of these features are equally important regarding building a PB – while it might be possible to build a PB without filtering capabilities for the list of proposals, supporting a voting process is mandatory. [9] further categorizes these elements into "mandatory", "recommended", and "optional".

3 Analysis of the PB Software and Case Examples

3.1 Assessment Methodology

The evaluation builds upon the software's documentation. In cases where the documentation was insufficient, additional resources like reference implementations or blog posts were taken into account.

The assessment is translated into discrete "yes" or "no" values for the prevalence of capabilities. While one could argue that, for some of the assessed capabilities, a further breakdown of the assessment into gradual values enables the encoding of more information, the authors decided for a binary encoding to limit the influence of subjective perceiving and to circumvent possible scaling issues.

Possible dependencies between capability items were not considered. As these tools have to fit into an existing IT landscape, the possible dependency resolutions are manifold. For example, even though we can consider a voting capability mandatory, which heavily influences the rest of the PB software, a municipality might have such a system already in place that it wants to use. It, thus, is able to resolve the dependencies without the need for an individual capability. The selection of what is essential and what is not is, therefore, up to the user.

3.2 The Assessment Results

Figure 2 presents the assessment of the software using the capabilities presented in section 0. The specialized tools Maptionnaire and Polis fulfill the smallest amount of capabilities. This lack of functionality is explained by the fact that both do not focus on the PB use case but on gathering public opinions. The other tool that does not originate from a PB background is Consider.it. However, this application covers a surprising amount of PB capabilities.

The most extensive software is Decidim. It is shortly followed by Citizenlab and Placespeak. These software solutions cover a wide range of PB scenarios and are highly versatile in their possible application scenarios.

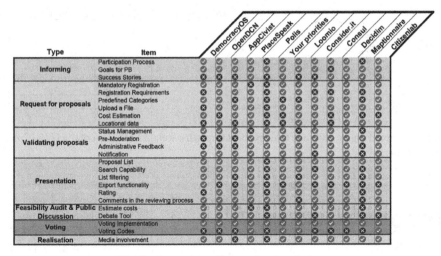

Fig. 2. Assessment of the software solutions.

3.3 Choosing the Right Tool

Choosing the right software tool is far from a trivial task. Not all functionalities have the same relevance for an administration. Also, the needs and capabilities of citizens vary. To assist municipalities in selecting the right software, the authors developed a tool to help them make an informed choice.

It incorporates a rating based on the multi-attribute decision theory and implements a weighted sum model to calculate the best-fitted software [15].

The user provides weights to the importance of each capability item, and the tool calculates the PB software that best fits the needs in a given situation. A weight can be any number between 0 and 100 (thus, it is also possible to use percentage values). The software then evaluates the PB-tools by multiplying the capability rating with the weights (thus, summing up the weights for the capabilities that the software provides). At the last step, the summed up values are normalized to a percentage value, and a rank is created. The program is based on Microsoft Excel and is available online [14].

To use the tool, the user should provide a weight for each capability item and state if it must be fulfilled or not. The range of the weights is up to the user. The weights shall represent the individual assessment of the importance of each item in comparison to the others. They can be assigned any number above zero. A weight of zero constitutes that a capability is not considered in the ranking of the software (Fig. 3).

While some capabilities are nice to have and optional, others are mandatory. These mandatory categories can be filtered using the column "Must-Criteria". If a capability is set to be a "Must-Criteria", all items that do not fulfill this criterion are not further considered in the ranking. If such filtering occurs, the cell fills red.

An example of the ranking is shown in Fig. 4. As – in this fictive example – DemocracyOS does not fulfill a Must-Criteria; it is not further considered in the comparison of the available tools.

Item	Description	Weight	Must-Criteria	DemocracyOS	OpenDCN	AppCivist
Participation Process	Provide information on how to participate in the PB-process using the presented software.	0	No	Yes	Yes	Yes
Goals for PB	Display the desired outcomes for a PB implementation on the web-page.	0	No	Yes	Yes	Yes
Success Stories	The web-pages give examples for success stories of other municipalities.	1	No	No	No	No
Mandatory Registration	The software supports a mandatory registration before the handing in of proposals.	3	No	Yes	Yes	Yes
Registration Requirements	The software supports additional, formal registration requirements, e.g., issued code, citizen registration number.	0	Yes	No	Yes	Yes
Predefined Categories	To further structure the submitted proposals, they can be categorized (e.g., in "playground" or "landscaping").	2	No	Yes	Yes	No
Upload a File	The PB-website implements an object storage. It is possible to upload a picture smaller than 5 MB.	2	No	No	Yes	Yes

Fig. 3. Excerpt of online tool for PB assessment (top half): weight and must-criteria [14]. (Color figure online)

Debate Tool	Users of the platform can comment not only on each submitted and published proposal, but also in a general forum for discussion on a broader perspective (not only related to proposals).	3	Yes	Yes	Yes	Yes
Voting Implementation	The PB software provides a voting capability.	5	Yes	Yes	Yes	Yes
Voting Codes	The voter eligibility is captured through the issue of a unique code.	3	No	No	No	No
Media Involvement	The PB-website informs citizens on the progress of the implementation of accepted proposals.	2	No	Yes	Yes	No
				0%	84%	71%
				7	5	6

Fig. 4. Excerpt of online tool for PB assessment (bottom half): calculated ranking of the tools based on the provided weights and must-criteria [14].

While the fulfillment level of the selected capabilities is a valid criterion for the nomination of a tool, one should not be overly concerned with the prevalence of additional capabilities. Simply selecting the tool with the most extensive set of capabilities available might create a bulky overhead regarding implementation and maintenance.

Rather than looking for a tool that fits as many capabilities as possible, it is likely better to look for the tool that best fits one's individual needs. Furthermore, besides the hard factors of the fulfillment level, soft factors should also influence the tool selection process.

Depending on the size and utilization of the local IT department, a government might choose a SaaS tool or run the applications themselves. Municipalities from smaller countries might face obstacles in the availability of language packs. Moreover, as PB initiatives happen in a highly local environment and are often bound to local laws, selecting a tool from a vendor who has experience with the local cultural and jurisdictional environment might also prove helpful, especially if there are already existing relationships between the vendor and the municipality, as the next section will show.

4   Case Examples from Finland

Participatory budgeting has sparked broad interest in Finland, especially in local government, ever since 2012 (e.g., [6]). Finnish municipalities are active in promoting PB as a method of strengthening citizen participation. Municipalities are not obligated to run PB, but it is mentioned as a suggestion of one method of participation in the Finnish Local Government Act. Both of the Finnish empirical case examples have run their first rounds of city-level PBs. The data was collected after the first round of PB in Lahti in November-December 2020 and after a second round of PB in Riihimäki in February-March 2021. In addition, in Lahti, a first citizen survey was conducted before the first round of PB in September–October 2019. As our case examples illustrate, each pilot process is as unique as are the IT tools used in them.

A citizen survey conducted in 2019 in the city of Lahti – the first EmPaci PB pilot in Finland - showed an interest in PB and especially taking part by using electronic services. Lahti ran their first city-level PB process in 2020 and used existing ICT platforms for the process. Ideas were gathered using Maptionnaire – a map-based platform previously mainly used in city planning. Voting was conducted using Webropol. There was a strong political will to try out PB in Lahti, but the same will was not shared in the city organization. Also, Lahti was simultaneously making difficult cutback management decisions which affected the resources for PB. There were no financial resources available for investing in a separate participatory ICT platform. Also, the financial resources to be allocated through PB were taken from the operational resources of the department responsible for coordinating PB. This created difficulties in the adequacy of resources for service operations and affected the interest and attitudes to try out PB.

The Maptionnaire platform provided a possibility to put ones' idea on the map and then clarify it with text and by adding documents. It was also used to gather background information on those leaving ideas such as age, gender, or household income level. This type of data is important for process evaluation purposes, even though collecting it can raise questions among citizens. The end-use and necessity need to be well communicated to avoid misunderstandings that can hinder participation. A downside of this platform was that the ideas were not publicly on show during the process.

This resulted in overlapping ideas that needed to be processed by the city personnel in the pre-checking phase and took up citizens' time, possibly affecting their satisfaction with the process.

In the citizen survey conducted after the PB, respondents were relatively satisfied with the use of the tools. The tools were seen as easy to use. Feedback from the city PB personnel was also positive. The map-based solution received positive responses. The main criticism was addressed to the fact that ideas were not on public display. Only those ideas that passed the pre-check phase and moved on to voting were published. This limited the transparency of the process, leaving citizens unaware of the result of their submitted idea. Also, using two different platforms received criticism. While both platforms were relatively easy to use, this created unnecessary hindrances for the agility and transparency of the process. It is also essential to recognize that different citizen groups find using ICT tools convenient or difficult. As an example, the majority of the citizens involved in PB, in this case, were working-aged women.

The second Finnish PB pilot, the city of Riihimäki, had begun their PB in 2019. They had decided to invest in a separate platform: A Decidim based solution, a rather popular choice among Finnish benchmark municipalities of different sizes such as Tuusula and the capital city Helsinki. It was also used in the second run in 2020, although some changes were made to the first model after feedback received from citizens and staff on the first round. Similar to Lahti, also local politicians in Riihimäki supported the implementation of PB. However, the starting point for PB in Riihimäki was different than in Lahti. As the city council decided to implement PB, they allocated financial resources of 1 million euros for PB into a fund that was established specifically for PB and to be used in multiple years to come. Simultaneously, they decided to invest in a new, customized PB software - Decidim.

This platform offers necessary functionalities and can be easily altered to suit individual needs but with extra cost for tailoring. The Riihimäki platform hosted the entire process from leaving ideas to voting, providing a transparent process as citizens had access to each other's ideas. To leave an idea or vote, one had to register on the platform, but data about the individuals were not gathered. This meant that process evaluation could not be conducted at the same level as, for example, in the Lahti case. This is also something municipalities should take into consideration when choosing and using a platform. One of the changes the city made after the first process was to include a Like-function in their process. For an idea to make it through to the final voting, it had to gather at least 10 Likes on the platform. This was done to activate citizens and encourage them to visit between leaving ideas and voting.

Citizen feedback on the use of the platform was divided as nearly 50% of respondents found leaving their ideas poor or satisfactory in the citizen survey. The newly introduced Like-system also raised questions as the process was somewhat unclear to many respondents. All in all, here, like in Lahti, the most active participants were working-aged women. The respondents of the surveys were concerned that the IT platform does not reach all citizen groups – for instance, the elderly were seen to be left out.

City personnel, in turn, pointed out some technical difficulties they had encountered in the platform and hoped for improvements on it to make it easier to use/clearer and make voting more see-through for future processes.

Also, the platform did not support the collection of user data. This created difficulties in contacting citizens that submitted their idea. Many of the ideas were drafts that needed clarifications in order to be evaluated by the city personnel.

In both of the case examples, PB was run during the outbreak of the COVID-19 pandemic. The role of ICT solutions became more evident than it was initially expected. Face-to-face meetings and campaigns were canceled, and PB was promoted mainly by using social media. Especially in Riihimäki, the second round of PB laid heavily on the Decidim platform. Due to the change in staff but also to the impact of the COVID-19 pandemic on city personnel, PB was caught in the middle. However, Lahti chose a different approach and focused on still offering something positive for citizens during the volatile times in the form of PB even though their initial plans would have focused more on live meetings, not a separate platform. Thus, in Lahti, the PB process was considered a success with 713 ideas and 3896 votes. While in Riihimäki, interviewees regarded the PB process "a technical implementation" of PB without the live meetings and face-to-face promotions of the first round of PB. The turnout of the second round of PB in Riihimäki was fewer ideas and votes than the first round of PB.

Based on the findings in the analysis of the empirical data, it can be said that different ICT models and tools can work even if a municipality cannot choose an ideal tool due to, for example, financial, availability, or timeline constraints. Some tools take more financial commitment, others are more labor-intensive, but each PB is different, as are the municipalities running them and the citizens taking part. It is worth keeping in mind that PB should be an ever-evolving process by nature. Bold trials and continuous development have a place also in finding the right tools. Another noteworthy point is that the process of PB cannot merely rest on the ICT tool. As the Riihimäki case illustrates, PB cannot solely be run with the ICT platform. It needs human and financial resources. While an ICT platform is designed for PB, there might still appear during the PB such needs that the platform cannot meet, which might create hindrances for PB process and limit the successful turnout of PB. ICT tools can support the process at its best, but it cannot be the whole process.

5 Conclusion and Outlook

The presented paper compared various available software solutions for supporting participatory budgeting. A PB process can take various shapes, thus differ the requirements of a PB software tool. The analyzed data and evaluation framework can help cities that aspire to implement a PB to pick the right tool that best fits their individual PB process.

However, as seen by the case examples, there is more to selecting software than a mere list of features. Equally important are "soft" factors like previous usage experience, the will and knowledge (or not) to adapt and develop open-source software, or the willingness to pay a commercial vendor. Choosing a more extensive software with more supported features might, on the one hand, provide enough reserve for future extensions. On the other hand, this extensive range of functions also brings a higher level of complexity. Thus, the tool's strategy should fit into the strategy of the city.

We believe that the proposed evaluation methodology helps municipalities select the right software for their specific needs. The presented case examples already brought insights into the selection processes of PB software. However, there is room for further studies on how cities select PB software and what they might need to make better-informed decisions.

Acknowledgments. We thank the students Egor Nikitin and Kirill Kashtanov for their support in collecting the underlying data for the analyzed tools. The authors and the cities Lahti and Riihimäki are part of the EU-funded EmPaci project (Empowering Participatory Budgeting in the Baltic Sea Region). This project is part of the European Regional Development Fund.

References

1. Sintomer, Y., Herzberg, C., Röcke, A.: Participatory budgeting in Europe: potentials and challenges. Int. J. Urban Reg. Res. **32**, 164–178 (2008). https://doi.org/10.1111/j.1468-2427. 2008.00777.x
2. Sintomer, Y., Herzberg, C., Röcke, A., Allegretti, G.: Transnational models of citizen participation: the case of participatory budgeting. J. Public Deliberation **14**, 70–116 (2012). https://doi.org/10.16997/jdd.141
3. Pinnington, E., Lerner, J., Schugurensky, D.: Participatory budgeting in North America: the case of Guelph, Canada. J. Public Budgeting Account. Financ. Manag. **21**, 455–484 (2009). https://doi.org/10.1108/JPBAFM-21-03-2009-B005
4. Dias, N., Enrìquez, S., Júlio, S. (eds.): Participatory Budgeting World Atlas, Portugal (2019)
5. Ebdon, C., Franklin, A.L.: Citizen participation in budgeting theory. Public Adm. Rev. **66**, 437–447 (2006). https://doi.org/10.1111/J.1540-6210.2006.00600.X

6. Lehtonen, P.: Shifting the Power to People: opening the practices of governance with participatory budgeting. Nordicom Inf. **40**, 63–69 (2018)
7. Shah, A.: Participatory budgeting. Public sector governance and accountability series. World Bank, Washington D.C. (2007)
8. Lerner, J.: Conclusion: time for participatory budgeting to grow up. New Polit. Sci. **39**, 156–160 (2017). https://doi.org/10.1080/07393148.2017.1278860
9. Rostock University: Feature Repository & Recommendations. Group of activities 4.1: Output 3. Project: "Empowering Participatory Budgeting in the Baltic Sea Region – EmPac", Rostock, Germany (2020). http://empaci.eu/photo/Files/Empaci%20-%20Output%204.1.3.pdf. Accessed 30 July 2021
10. Rose, J., Rios, J., Lippa, B.: Technology support for participatory budgeting. IJEG **3**, 3–24 (2010). https://doi.org/10.1504/IJEG.2010.032728
11. Kapoor, K.K., Omar, A., Sivarajah, U.: Enabling multichannel participation through ICT adaptation. Int. J. Electron. Gov. Res. **13**, 66–80 (2017). https://doi.org/10.4018/IJEGR.201 7040104
12. Leighninger, M.: Using Online Tools to Engage – and be Engaged by – The Public. IBM (2011)
13. Holston, J., Issarny, V., Parra, C.: Engineering software assemblies for participatory democracy. In: Dillon, L., Visser, W., Williams, L. (eds.) Proceedings of the 38th International Conference on Software Engineering Companion. ICSE 2016: 38th International Conference on Software Engineering, Austin, Texas, 14 May 2016–22 May 2016, pp. 573–582. ACM, New York (2016). https://doi.org/10.1145/2889160.2889221
14. Rostock University: PB Comparison Table (2021). Excel Spreadsheet. https://github.com/Uni-Rostock-Win/PB-Software-Evaluation
15. Ishizaka, A., Nemery, P.: Multi-criteria Decision Analysis. Methods and Software. Wiley, Chichester (2013)

Influence of Media Type on Political E-Discourse: Analysis of Russian and American Discussions on Social Media

Daniil Volkovskii[(✉)] and Olga Filatova

St. Petersburg State University, 7 Universitetskaya Emb., 199004 St. Petersburg, Russia
daniil.volkovskii@yandex.ru

Abstract. The article presents the results of discourse analysis where authors define how media identity influences character and quality of online discussions on actual socio-political themes. The research is carried out in terms of theory of J. Habermas and methodology of Misnikov who develops the conception of German philosopher. The empirical data comprises Russian and American cases: A. Navalny's court sentence and D. Trump's second impeachment are analyzed. Russian media platforms are divided by political affiliation into independent, pro-state and neutral while American ones are represented by democratic, republican and central media sources. The authors use such parameters of deliberative standard to assess quality and character of online deliberation as distribution of positions, argumentation, culture of communication, interactivity and dialogicity. As a result, investigators come to conclusion that media type has an impact on the way opinions are polarized in online discussions; quality and amount of argumentation; communication culture towards object of discussion and participants of interaction both in Russian and American political e-discourse.

Keywords: Social media · Online discussion · Online deliberation · Political discourse · E-discourse

1 First Introduction

In recent years, social networks have assumed a special role in such interaction which have taken on promising in the political context functions correlating with active development of the processes of political participation and democracy [1, 13, 17, 18, 22]. Moreover, there is a growing quantity of evidence that social media fosters group identity and informal activism [6, 23, 24].

In the research that will be presented below, we decided to focus on social media networks because there can be massive public discussions and active social polarization of opinions. Each media has a role model that partly sets a tone for their political orientation and activities in online space. As scientific research shows, digital platforms force us to rethink these roles based on study of media behavior in a communicative online environment and structural limitations of platforms [2–4]. To understand specifics of media, we examined several models of their online behavior.

© Springer Nature Switzerland AG 2022
A. V. Chugunov et al. (Eds.): EGOSE 2021, CCIS 1529, pp. 119–131, 2022.
https://doi.org/10.1007/978-3-031-04238-6_10

The concept of public media identity is understood as a real or perceived image of particular media [8]. In addressing issues of public policy and expression of will, the endless proliferation of media resources allowing to debate publicly requires greater clarity about impact of their political commitment on discourse outcomes. It is assumed that a process of political participation requires acceptance of someone's side and, thus, a formation (joining) of certain solidarities between participants. Membership in a political party or any other organized group with specific social goals usually means solidarity with like-minded people, especially when meeting personally. However, engaging in online discourses (often anonymous) is a different type of social and personal experience that provides more flexibility in choosing a preferred discussion community. This was partially investigated by us earlier [8].

The purpose of research presented in this article is to identify how media type on the Internet platforms of which various discussions take place affects the quality of Internet discourse.

In the empirical part of our research we will analyze social media discussions of various media types in Russia and the United States.

RQ1. Does nature and quality of online discussion depend on the type of media in Russian Internet discourse?

RQ2. Does nature and quality of online discussion depend on the type of media in foreign Internet discourse?

2   Research Approach and Data

The research is in line with the concept of Habermas. When a participant formulates a similar opinion about something that has already been expressed by someone else, he or she joins in virtual "solidarity" with that participant at that point in discourse. This is what J. Habermas defines within the framework of his theory of discourse ethics "intersubjective solidarity" [14], built to share common values expressed in the public sphere. Habermas's approach can rightly be called discursive since public sphere is formed in the free discourse of citizens, free discussion, i.e. deliberation [5]. It is important that the philosopher institutionalizes public sphere and communication as a space for application of communicative action, making it one of the structural parts of political system.

Literature review dedicated to methods of discourse analysis can be divided into several analytically discernable areas.

The first area, the functional linguistic analysis, deals with language as a system and studies mechanisms of its functioning. The Michael Halliday's systemic functional linguistics is an example of this approach, when the language is considered as a separate paradigm that allows its native speakers to choose different linguistic forms to express thoughts. The role and context of discourse, as well as its participants' intentions, exist but matters little. An exception is the transformational generative grammar by Noam Chomsky, who studied syntax as a set of rules, pointing at interrelation of limited deep language structures to the limitless possible grammatically correct variants of their expression, i.e. sentences in the common language [7].

Social discourse analysis prioritizes cultural and political practices as forms of public discourse through the lens of which a meaning of texts and images are defined. The prominent theory here is the critical discourse analysis by Norman Fairclough, who argues that discourse is the indispensable part of social practice [11, 12]. By analyzing changes in discourses by studying intertextuallity it is possible to reveal the transformation of the sociocultural practices themselves. The formal rules of the language and the computer processing of the content is in this case the supplementary procedure to facilitate the analysis.

Research on online civic activism and e-participation are related to a broader domain of cyberspace sociology. In this area web-demographic and behavioral explorations of the Internet are produced. Communications via the Internet are viewed as a means of unification and mobilization of people bearing common culture and public views, sharing common rules of good behavior. Such works actively use visualization methods to describe communication in social networks [10]. Content-analysis and discourse-analysis are also widespread [21].

The research was carried out on the basis of discourse analysis technique developed and described by Yu. Misnikov [9, 15, 16, 19]. The scholar developed "Deliberative Standard to Assess Discourse Quality" [19] and described seven thematically different discourse parameters corresponding to specific research questions for guiding the process of coding messages of Internet discussions: participatory equality, argumentation, communication culture (civility), validity of statements, interactivity, dialogicity, thematic diversity. It should be noted that Misnikov was the first to do this since at the time of his dissertation publication there were no direct analogs in the scientific literature. One of strong sides of this methodological approach is that each parameter contains a set of specific empirical characteristics designed to reflect certain discursive qualities and determine nature of discussion. In addition, a method is not difficult to use and all counting can be done and analyzed in Excel program. For more accurate analysis a few decoders of messages are needed to compare results. This is a limitation of our research as one person decoded comments.

To study online deliberation as a form of public dialogue we took several parameters presented in the deliberative standard. As a result, Russian and American online discussions on political topics were analyzed according to such parameters as distribution of positions, argumentation, culture of communication, interactivity and dialogicity. You can read more about the technique used in our other publications [8, 16]. We analyzed positions, participants, their argumentation, culture of communication, interactivity and dialogicity in discussions since this is the necessary minimum of important parameters to determine nature and quality of discourse. Perfectly, it is better to analyze a full range of parameters with addition of modified parameter (the degree of dialogue) for a more detailed description of deliberation. Positions For/Against were analyzed by determination of participant's opinions towards problematic. For doing it, every message was read and analyzed without usage of linguistic processing. Argumentation and communication culture forms were analyzed according to developed and described criteria of Misnikov.

To determine interactivity, it is needed to divide number of participants' requests to each other's posts, mentions of each other by total number of posts in discussion. To define dialogicity is almost the same as defining interactivity but only mentions by participant's names are counted and divided by total number of posts.

Table 1. List of online discussions on media pages on VKontakte social network.

Sources	Rain	Meduza	Channel One	KP.RU	TASS
Media type	Independent		Pro-state		Neutral
Article title, material	The suspended sentence was replaced with a real one for Navalny. Taking into account the time spent under house arrest, Navalny will spend two years and eight months in the colony	Will Navalny be replaced with a real one? We follow what is happening in the court - and around it	The Moscow City Court sentenced Alexei Navalny to 3.5 years in prison and a fine of 500 thousand rubles	The court sentenced Alexei Navalny to 3.5 years in prison in a general regime colony	Navalny's lawyer said that her client will spend about 2 years and 8 months in the colony
Post time	02.02.2021 (20:46)	02.02.2021 (18:34)	04.02.2021 (14:03)	02.02.2021 (21:24)	02.02.2021 (21:20)
Num. of comments	602	155	160	148	100

Table 2. Online discussions of the second impeachment of D. Trump on the pages of media on Facebook social network.

Sources	MSNBC	The New York Times	The Washington Times	Fox News	The Wall Street Journal
Media type	Democratic		Republican		Neutral
Article title, material	As House votes to impeach him, Trump's focus shifts to brand rehabilitation	Impeached, Again	Impeachment trial won't begin until after Trump leaves office	House meets to debate article of impeachment against President Donald Trump	Opinion I This Time, Trump's Impeachment Is Warranted
Post time	14.01.2021 (3:12)	14.01.2021 (16:50)	13.01.2021 (22:15)	13.01.2021	14.01.2021 (4:31)
Num. of comments	504	654	281	904	588

The empirical base was formed by Russian online discussions on the sentence of A. Navalny on VKontakte social network (see Table 1) and American online discussions on the second impeachment of D. Trump on Facebook social network (see Table 2).

3   Research Results

We analyzed online discussions on the topic of A. Navalny's sentence on the pages of five media outlets on VKontakte social network according to such parameters as distribution of positions, argumentation, communication culture, interactivity, dialogicity. Media were divided by political affiliation into independent, pro-state and neutral as we tried to identify how public identity of media affects a discussion. It was found that media type affects the level of argumentation and how positions in the discussion are distributed. Comparing discussions on the pages of independent and pro-state media, we came to the following conclusions.

For a more accurate study, we decided to analyze the media with clearly subjective rhetoric and compare them with those media whose rhetoric is more or less objective. State media have a clearly positive rhetoric towards the ruling political class, while private media, so-called opposition or liberal ones, are clearly directed against authorities. Therefore, we decided to analyze such media as Channel One and Komsomolskaya Pravda on the one hand, and Dozhd and Meduza on the other. The news agency (TASS) was chosen as media whose rhetoric should be conditionally objective. The limitation of study is that media sample needs further improvement.

1. In discussions on pro-state sources the most negative attitude towards politician A. Navalny as he is an oppositionist to the current government, therefore, the overwhelming majority of participants in the discussions support the court verdict and support the appointment of a longer term. The total percentage of positions "Against" was 85.2%, "For" - 14.8%. In online discussions of all five media at least 2/3 of users spoke out against Navalny supporting the court's verdict, although some people disagreed with him claiming that the term was insufficient but they still supported the actions of authorities. The highest percentage of negative attitude towards politician was illustrated in online discussions of pro-state media (92.75%), the lowest on platforms of independent media (75.35%); neutral TASS is in the middle: the percentage of "Against" positions was 87.5%. Considering each source separately we note that the largest share of negativity towards A. Navalny was recorded on the Vkontakte pages of Komsomolskaya Pravda (93.8%) and Channel One (91.7%). Participants of online deliberation on the Rain page (32.6%) were most positive about politician. Need to add that that data may not be entirely accurate as some user's comments have been removed. In addition, in the discussions of some media there were few opinions about the stated problems which to a certain extent limits the representativeness of results. Moreover, some participants in the course of online discussions indicated on presence of bots and trolls which could leave an imprint on data obtained and discussion in general due to the fact that the bots were difficult to identify.

2. The general level of argumentation in discussions on independent media is higher than in discussions on the pages of pro-state media (see Table 3).

3. The general level of communication culture in discussions on independent media is higher than in discussions on pro-state media (see Table 4).
4. In discussions on independent media the largest number of posts was recorded: a) personal and abstract from the topic character, b) rough culture of communication in relation to the participant while the largest percentage of rough culture of communication in relation to the topic, object of discussion is in discussions on pro-state media (see Table 4).
5. Discussions on independent media are more interactive (66,2%) and dialogical (62,2%) than discussions on pro-state media (58% and 56,7% respectively).

Examples of comments:
«Freedom to Navalny!»
«Also, Navalny has got a fine 500 thousands of rubles which will be paid by the West»

Table 3. Analysis of argumentation in Russian online discussions (results in percent).

Media type	Independent		Pro-state		Neutral
	Rain	Meduza	Channel One	KP.RU	TASS
Facts and numerical indicators of factual nature	8,3	8,2	2	5,3	2,9
Numeric data	1,1	3,3	2	1,1	5,7
Examples, cases, comparisons, events, citations	0,8	0	0	2,1	2,9
References to political figures	31	44,3	35,3	31,9	28,5
Conclusions, generalizations	53,6	42,6	58,7	56,4	60
Recommendation, suggestions, calls to action	2,3	0	2	3,2	0
Links on various online sources	2,9	1,6	0	0	0
General % of argumentation	63,8	39,4	31,9	63,5	35
General	51,6		47,7		

We analyzed online discussions on the topic of D. Trump's second impeachment on the pages of five leading American media outlets on Facebook social network according to the same parameters as Russian discussions. Media were divided by political affiliation into democratic, republican and neutral as we tried to identify how public identity of media influences the discussion. A similar situation was noted as in the analysis of Russian online discussions: media type affects distribution of positions in the discussion including the level of argumentation. Comparing discussions on the pages of democratic and republican media, the following differences were revealed.

1) In the discussions on the pages of the republican media the majority of users does not agree with the second impeachment of D. Trump and support the US President while in the discussions on the pages of democratic media more people agree with impeachment and do not support Trump; discussion on centrist media is represented by two polarized camps of opinions in approximately equal proportions.

   According to the aggregate analysis of all media, 53.5% of users are against Trump and for his impeachment while 46.5% are for Trump and against his impeachment (excluding bots' posts). If we take into account the posts of bots, then the data is 55.8% and 44.2%, respectively, which to a small extent but gives an advantage to demos and supporters of the opinion about Trump's removal from the presidency. Bots could be identified manually as a) they were pointed out by some users to whom these bots responded to the comment with their message; moreover, users went to the Facebook pages from which bots responded to the comment and indicated on the lack of information about users; b) the messages of bots were constantly duplicated and without changing the text which immediately prompts the idea of them. Based on the analysis of all positions, we can see that the American society is split into two camps in almost equal proportions.

2) The general level of argumentation in discussions on democratic media is higher than in discussions on the pages of republican media (see Table 5).

3) The general level of communication culture in discussions on democratic media is higher than in discussions on republican ones (see Table 6).

4) The general level of rude culture of communication both in relation to the participant and object of discussion is higher in discussions on the pages of democratic media. It means that participants in "republican" discussions are more polite than participants in "democratic" ones, although in the discussion on neutral source the level of intolerance culture of communication is the lowest (see Table 6).

5) Discussions on republican media are more interactive (28,5%) and dialogical (28,5%) than discussions on democratic media (24% and 24% respectively).

Examples of comments:

«Being impeached twice is something i doubt Trump will brag about. If anything will he most possible be angry if that get mentioned near him after he is out of office»

«He should have been removed from office when the Senate had the chance. We wouldn't be in this mess if they had»

Table 4. Analysis of culture of communication in Russian online discussions (in percent).

Media type	Independent		Pro-state		Neutral
	Rain	Meduza	Channel One	KP.RU	TASS
Thematically empty posts with participant name's mention, only interpersonal communication	50	41,9	42,8	22,3	37
Posts with participant name' mention, discussion on topic, but rude towards participant	9,1	4,5	2,5	2	0
Posts with participant name's mention, discussion on topic, but rude towards object of discussion	0,7	0,7	3,1	2	2
Posts with participant name's mention, discussion on topic in a polite, tolerant way	0	0	0	0,7	1
Posts without participant name's mention, with discussion on topic, but rude to-wards participant	0,3	1,9	1,3	0,7	0
Posts without participant name's mention, with discussion on topic, but rude towards object of discussion	1,8	1,9	1,3	4,7	1
Posts without participant name's mention, with discussion on topic in a polite way	0	0	0	0	0
Total % of negative civility towards participant	9,4	6,4	3,8	2,7	0
Total % of negative civility towards object of discussion	2,5	2,6	4,4	6,7	3

(*continued*)

Table 4. (*continued*)

Media type	Independent		Pro-state		Neutral
	Rain	Meduza	Channel One	KP.RU	TASS
Total % of civility	61,9	50,9	51	32,4	41

Table 5. Analysis of argumentation in American online discussions (in percent).

Media type	Democratic		Republican		Neutral
	MSNBC	The New York Times	The Washington Times	Fox News	The Wall Street Journal
Facts and Numerical Indicators of Factual Nature	6,5	2,8	2,5	2	6,6
Numeric Data	3,2	0,7	2	1	2,8
Examples, Cases, Comparisons, Events, Citations	1,7	1	1	0,8	2,5
References to Political Figures	23,3	31,2	30,6	38,9	31,6
Conclusions, Generalizations	60,6	58,9	55,8	50,1	45,2
Recommendation, Suggestions, Calls to Action	1,5	0,7	2,5	4,8	1,3
Links on Various Online Sources	3,2	4,7	5,6	2,4	10
General % of Argumentation	92	65	70	60	80
General % of Argumentation	78,5		65		

Table 6. Analysis of communication culture in American online discussions (in percent)

Media type	Democratic		Republican		Neutral
	MSNBC	The NYT	The WT	Fox News	The WSJl
Thematically empty posts with participant name's mention, only interpersonal communication	0	0,1	0	0,8	0
Posts with participant name's mention, discussion on topic, but rude towards participant	0	0,8	0,75	0,2	0,5
Posts with participant name's mention, discussion on topic, but rude towards object of discussion	0,2	1,2	0,75	0,8	1,9
Posts with participant name's mention, discussion on topic in a polite, tolerant way	0,6	0,1	0	0	0
Posts without participant name's mention, with discussion on topic, but rude towards participant	0	0	0	0,2	0
Posts without participant name's mention, with discussion on topic, but rude towards object of discussion	7,1	4,4	2,8	7,2	1,4
Posts without participant name's mention, with discussion on topic in a polite way	0	0,1	0	0	0,1
Negative civility towards participant	0	0,8	0,75	0,4	0,5
Negative civility towards object of discussion	7,3	5,6	3,55	8	2,3
Average negative civility in dependence of parties	6,85		6,35		2,8
Total civility	7,9	6,7	4,3	9,2	3,9

4 Discussion

Our research has demonstrated a clear difference between discussions on platforms of different media types in terms of such indicators as distribution of positions, argumentation, culture of communication, interactivity and dialogicity. Media identity influences the quality and nature of online discussion. No doubt, for the most part it depends on people who come to these platforms to discuss. Nevertheless, media identity makes it possible to gather more supporters, fans of these media where they can meet the same ones and communicate with them on common topic, and these people have similar views. It is about a consolidating role if we consider the example of American discussions. The question of expression and opinion freedom of expression is also important. This was clearly demonstrated on the platforms of Russian media, especially in the discussions on the platforms of independent media. Moreover, comments of participants in the discussions in groups of independent media were not removed or moderated which cannot be said about state media.

However, we cannot say with certainty why media type so noticeably affects the quality of Internet discourse. Definitely, it requires further research. Key political preferences, biases and motivations do not change quickly. Nevertheless, ideally, the virtual environment of online communication can apparently help citizens compare differences, clarify established positions and completely change them as a result of Internet communication.

5   Conclusion

To sum up, we got positive answers to both the first and the second research question. Does nature and quality of online discussion depend on the type of media in both Russian and foreign Internet discourse?

In Russian online discussions participants in discussions on independent media platforms support A. Navalny more, speak less negatively towards the object of discussion but more negatively towards each other than participants in pro-state ones. Discussions on the platforms of independent media are more reasoned, interactive and dialogical (RQ1).

As for American discussions, on social networks of republican media, the majority of users does not agree with the second impeachment of D. Trump and support the politician while on democratic social networks more people agree with the impeachment and do not support Trump. In democratic media groups participants speak more negatively in relation to the object of discussion, and in general their culture of communication is more intolerant than those of participants in discussions on the platforms of republican media. Discussions on democratic platforms are more argumentative than on republican ones, but less interactive and dialogical (RQ2).

In the future more in-depth studies of the quality of Internet discussions on various media platforms and in different cultural contexts are needed.

Acknowledgment. This work was supported by the Russian Science Foundation, project No. 21-18-00454.

Referencess

1. Bächle, M.: Social Software, Informatik-Spektrum, pp. 121–124 (2006)
2. Bodrunova, S., Blekanov, I., Maksimov, A.: Measuring influencers in Twitter Ad-hoc discussions: active users vs. internal networks in the discourse on Biryuliovo bashings in 2013. In: Proceedings of the AINL FRUCT 2016 Conference, St. Petersburg, Russia (2017)
3. Bodrunova, S., Litvinenko, A., Blekanov, I.: Influencers on the Russian Twitter: institutions vs. people in the discussion on migrants. In: Proceedings of ACM conference "Electronic governance and open society: challenges in Eurasia", St. Petersburg, Russia, pp. 212–222 (2016)

4. Bodrunova, S.S., Litvinenko, A.A., Blekanov, I.S.: Please follow us. Journal. Pract. 177–203 (2018). https://doi.org/10.1080/17512786.2017.1394208
5. Bodrunova, S.S.: Mediacracy: media and power in modern democratic societies: Ph.D. thesis. SPb (2015)
6. Boulianne, S.: Social media use and participation: a meta-analysis of current research. Inf. Commun. Soc. **18**(5), 524–538 (2015)
7. Chomsky, N.: Aspects of the Theory of Syntax. MIT Press. ISBN 0-262-53007-4 (1965)
8. Chugunov, A., Filatova, O., Misnikov, Y.: Citizens' deliberation online as will-formation: the impact of media identity on policy discourse outcomes in Russia. In: 8th International Conference on Electronic Participation (ePart), September 2016, Guimarães, Portugal, pp. 67–82 (2016)
9. Chugunov, A.V., Kabanov, Y., Misnikov, Y.: Citizens versus the government or citizens with the government: a tale of two e-participation portals in one city – a case study of St. Petersburg, Russia. In: ACM International Conference Proceeding Series. 10. CEP. "Proceedings of the 10th International Conference on Theory and Practice of Electronic Governance, ICEGOV 2017", pp. 70–77 (2017)
10. Dodge, M., Kitchin, R.: Code/Space. Software and Everyday Life. MIT Press, Cambridge (2011)
11. Fairclough, N.: Analysing Discourse: Textual Analysis for Social Research. Routledge, London and New York (2003)
12. Fairclough, N.: Discourse and Social Change. Polity Press, Cambridge (1992)
13. Green, D.T., Pearson, J.M.: Social software and cyber networks: ties that bind or weak associations within the political organization? In: Proceedings of the 38th Hawaii International Conference on System Sciences (2005)
14. Habermas, J.: Moral Consciousness and Communicative Action. Polity Press, Cambridge (1992)
15. Filatova, O., Kabanov, Y., Misnikov, Y.: Public deliberation in Russia: deliberative quality, rationality and interactivity of the online media discussions. Media Commun. **7**(3), 133–144 (2019)
16. Filatova, O., Volkovskii, D.: Key parameters of internet discussions: testing the methodology of discourse analysis. In: Chugunov, A.V. et al. (ed.) Digital Transformation and Global Society (DTGS 2020). Proceedings of the 5th International Conference, St. Petersburg, pp. 32–46 (2021)
17. Lovari, A., Valentini, C.: Public sector communication and social media: opportunities and limits of current policies, activities, and practices. In: The Handbook of Public Sector Communication, pp. 315–328 (2020)
18. Misnikov, Y.: Democratisating the Eastern partnership in the digital age: challenges and opportunities of political association beyond the language of official texts. In: Political and Legal Perspectives of the EU Eastern Partnership Policy, pp. 59–79 (2016)
19. Misnikov, Y.: Public Activism Online in Russia: Citizens' Participation in Webbased Interactive Political Debate in the Context of Civil Society. Development and Transition to Democracy: Ph.D. thesis … Ph. D./Leeds (2011)
20. Oliveira, C.: Proposed solutions to citizen engagement in virtual environments of social participation: a systematic review. Int. J. Electron. Gov. **12**(1), 76–91 (2020)
21. Papacharissi, Z.: A Networked Self: Identity, Community and Culture on Social Network Sites. Taylor & Francis, New York (2011)
22. Stieglitz, S., Dang-Xuan, L.: Impact and diffusion of sentiment in political communication. In: An Empirical Analysis of Public Political Facebook Pages, Proceedings of the 20th European Conference on Information Systems (ECIS) (2012)

23. Valenzuela, S.: Unpacking the use of social media for protest behavior: the roles of information, opinion expression, and activism. Am. Behav. Sci. **57**(7), 920–942 (2013)
24. Warren, A.M., Sulaiman, A., Jaafar, N.I.: Understanding civic engagement behaviour on Facebook from a social capital theory perspective. Behav. Inf. Technol. **34**(2), 163–175 (2015)

Mobilization of Protest Activism on «TikTok»: Scale, Features and Threats

Elena V. Brodovskaya(✉) ⓘ, Vladimir A. Lukushin ⓘ, and Maria A. Davydova ⓘ

Financial University under the Government of the Russian Federation, Moscow, Russia
brodovskaya@inbox.ru

Abstract. The article presents the results of an applied political research on the use of the digital service "TikTok" as a tool of protest mobilization on the example of mass actions that took place in Russian cities in the winter 2021. The aim of the study was to determine the distinctive characteristics of the platform that make it possible to effectively use it for organizing, coordinating and providing information support for protests. The scale of user involvement in the protest agenda, the demographic profile of the audience involved, key discourses and protest triggers were revealed through the use of a hybrid strategy that includes social media analysis, event analysis, and cognitive mapping of digital content. According to the results of the study, it can be concluded that the service is highly politicized, combined with a wide user reach. The multimedia and informal nature of political content correlates with a high level of emotionality and opposition. At the same time, the study showed the practice of using a number of mobilization technologies and psychological triggers targeted at different social groups. The authors are convinced that the prevailing opinion in the media about the dominance of children and young people in the general age structure of the service is outdated, which is confirmed by the empirical data obtained. The authors identified the risks of further use of "TikTok" to mobilize mass civil actions, which requires the development of comprehensive measures, taking into account the declared characteristics of the service.

Keywords: Tiktok · Civic activism · Protest mobilization · Social media · Digital environment · Social media analysis · Information flows

1 Introduction

Modern research demonstrates an increase in the use of social media as the main source of information. According to sociologists, the share of Russians receiving daily news from social networks has doubled over the past 5 years [1]. Researchers note the dynamically increasing demand for large social media and the highest level of trust in them on the part of young people [2]. However, the COVID-19 pandemic has changed not only real life, but also the digital space. The Chinese entertainment service "TikTok" gained the greatest popularity in Russia with the beginning of large-scale epidemiological restrictions.

The service attracts with developed recommendation systems, a high degree of adaptability to the interests of each user, as well as providing a wide space for self-expression.

© Springer Nature Switzerland AG 2022
A. V. Chugunov et al. (Eds.): EGOSE 2021, CCIS 1529, pp. 132–144, 2022.
https://doi.org/10.1007/978-3-031-04238-6_11

Since 2019, the platform has managed to increase its own base of domestic users by more than 7 times. The active influx of users made it possible to form of 25 million audience two years later, surpassing such popular platforms as Facebook and Twitter in this indicator.

Simultaneously with the rapid growth of the audience, the subject of the content is expanding, specific thematic blocks appear, primarily of a political nature. The emergence of such materials has contributed to the actualization of "TikTok" as a potential political tool. One of the first examples of the use of "TikTok" as a digital protest instrument can be considered the regional protests in Khabarovsk, which began in the summer of 2020 and had a significant impact on the protest moods of Russians [3]. During the same period, "TikTok" created the basis for prolonged protests in Belarus, replicating manipulative discourses about the illegitimacy of the authorities, violent actions of representatives of power structures, heroizing representatives of the opposition [4]. These events can be interpreted as testing the political potential of the platform.

The political situation in Russia in the winter 2021 was characterized as rather tense. The factors of domestic policy tension can be considered the onset of the electoral cycle associated with the election of deputies to the State Duma; economic downturn associated primarily with the negative consequences of the pandemic; social uncertainty due to the rise in new cases of COVID-19. In this context, the return of the Russian opposition leader Alexei Navalny becomes another trigger, which is complemented by his arrest. During the protests in January–February 2021, "TikTok" became a powerful tool for organizing and coordinating protests. The service provided a full-fledged informational support of the actions. In this regard, a number of research areas are being updated: analysis of the role of service in the formation of protest moods; identification of technologies and mechanisms for converting protests from online to offline, from conventional to non-conventional; defining the key characteristics of the service as a tool for mobilizing protest actions.

The main research questions of applied research: what is the specificity of "TikTok" as a tool for the protest mobilization of Russian Internet users? How the structure of the protest information flow in "TikTok" is related to the involvement of Russian users in the protest agenda of winter 2021. The structure of the article includes the following sections: theoretical and methodological basis of the research; key findings – characteristics of the information flow and the involved users; conclusion, discussion and research prospects.

2   Literature Review

Current research on civic engagement increasingly focuses on the analysis of digital communications and the role of social media in organizing, coordinating and converting protests. The information agenda in the digital space determines the level of public tension and creates conditions for the mobilization or demobilization of protest activity [5]. The largest digital platforms (Facebook, Twitter and others) aim at the formation of political participation, including protest, their functionality makes it possible to facilitate the exchange of information, emotional and motivational attitudes [6]. It should be borne in mind that social networks have a positive effect on engagement in civic activity and political participation, which allows us to speak of a direct relationship between social media support of protest activity and the involvement of users [7]. Social media is increasing the involvement of young users in political issues (both conventional and non-conventional) [8]. Social media have become a platform for informing and mobilizing various disunited groups, while they are of the greatest importance for mobilizing and moderating the activity of members of the organization [9]. For a long time, social media have been an organizational platform for mobilizing and managing protests [10, 11].

The growing popularity of "TikTok" and the actualization of the questions raised has led to a number of studies. There are several options for modern scientific works. The first group is devoted to the analysis of political confrontation in individual service segments [12, 13]. It is noted that at the beginning of the US presidential race in 2020, "TikTok" uses its role in exacerbating political competition between candidates and their supporters. This is a factually capable ramified network structure, the ability to build wide information branches created through reactions to videos of other users ("duets"), as well as a set of internal political hashtags of the opposing sides.

The second group of works determines the dependencies between the technological features of the service and the practice of using the tool of political mobilization [14, 15]. According to the researchers, "TikTok" has a multi-level gaming architecture that defines the horizontal and informal nature of communication between users, which serves as a promising model of engagement. The attractive features for new users are high-speed content update services, multimedia, lack of media and politicians. These characteristics form a special environment favorable for the political self-organization of users. Among other things, the researchers note an increase in users' trust in each other and a decrease in various barriers (language, geographical, value etc.)

The central theme for the third group of works is the increased popularity of the service among Gen Z and the underlying system of young microinfluencers, characterized by high density and dynamism [16–19]. A separate group of works is made up of studies of virtual and real threats emanating from the service. This direction has gained popularity among Russian authors, who argue about the significant risks of using "TikTok" as a means of spreading socially dangerous phenomena – the ideologies of terrorism and extremism, as well as the need to develop new approaches to counter these processes in conditions of low efficiency of political actors [20].

3   Methodology

The research is based on a hybrid strategy, embodied in the use of classical and modern theories and concepts. G. Le Bon, who considered collective behavior, pointed to the existence of a "collective mind" acting as a unifying factor and embracing all members of the crowd [21]. G. Reingold introduces the concept of "smart crowd", characterized by a high level of cohesion and solidarity, which form the possibility of using new digital platforms for the spontaneous and operational organization of mass actions [22]. M. Castells points out that the process of modern communications is based on the principles of network interaction, where each individual is represented as a separate network node. According to the author, the active dissemination of digital technologies has significantly enhanced the development of network communications that form new types of political participation and mobilization [23]. E. Katz and P. Lazarsfeld, within the framework of the concept of opinion leaders, substantiate a two-stage mechanism for the perception of information by a wide audience through people who have the greatest influence on the addressee [24]. Meanwhile, "slacktivism" theory emphasizes the special nature of political participation in the digital environment, where most of the users do not show real activity, confining themselves to the mechanisms provided by the virtual environment [25]. In turn, R.K. Garrett notes that with the dominance of social media in the modern information space, civic activism has undergone radical changes. The researcher identifies digital activism as an autonomous model of social action [26]. Much attention in the study of modern digital platforms as tools for mobilizing civic engagement is paid to recommender systems and special algorithms focused on meeting the interests of specific users [27]. This scientific direction is especially relevant in the course of researching modern digital platforms built on recommendation algorithms.

The study is based on a combination of methodological approaches: 1) network approach – the use of which in this study is associated with the study of the features of the interaction of actors in the modern network space [28]; 2) cognitive approach – associated with the search for patterns in the development of user reactions to digital political content and the characteristics of its perception [29]; 3) post-behaviorism – taking into account the influence of information factors on the formation of strategies of political behavior of Internet users [30]. In addition, the research methodology is based on the general principles of social media predictive analytics, which includes the implementation of an intelligent search for markers of digital activity of political actors through the use of automated tools for collecting and processing big data, further scenario and forecasting of sociopolitical processes based on the collected data sets [31].

A complex of modern methods and tools was used to implement the set tasks. At the first stage, cognitive mapping of digital video content presented in the main segment of the "TikTok" service was carried out. The sample included 300 of the most popular videos. The analysis made it possible to establish the content characteristics of the published materials, the dominant protest triggers and discourses, the mobilization technologies used, and also to compile a search query dictionary consisting of key protest hashtags. At the second stage, social media analysis (SMA) was carried out by combining the capabilities of two automated tools ("Popsters" & "Pentos"), allowing to determine the quantitative characteristics of content through a group of selected thematic hashtags, as well as the characteristics of the audience involved. The collected dataset amounted to 20 000 videos relevant to the research topic in January–February 2021. The use of these tools made it possible to evaluate the following digital markers: the number of videos, the number of views, the number of likes, the number of reposts, the number of comments.

To deepen and interpret the data obtained, an event analysis was carried out using the web analytics tools "Google Trends" and "Yandex.Wordstat", which made it possible to compare quantitative values with the main political events.

4 Findings

4.1 Content and Functional Characteristics of the Protest Information Flow

At the initial stage of the study, cognitive mapping of popular protest videos posted on the service was carried out. During the analysis, key hashtags were identified, dedicated to both specific protest actions and the general situation with politician and activist Alexey Navalny (#23January, #31January, #2February, #freenavalny, #wearenavalny, #livenavalny etc.[1]). It should be noted that hashtags are understandable and intuitive, contributing to their mass replication and attracting the attention of users in the feed of most popular videos ('for you page'). The recommended algorithms are structured in such a way that the content that instantly attracts the mechanism has additional opportunities to reach a wider audience.

The identified protest triggers are combined into 4 thematic groups, for each of which the representation in the total volume of the protest information flow is determined: 1) irremovability of power (32%), 2) violent actions by law enforcement agencies and mass detentions (29%), 3) injustice in relation to Navalny's team, criticism of law enforcement agencies and the judicial system (23%), 4) corruption (16%). A high degree of their intersection and joint use was also recorded in most of the analyzed materials. The distribution of triggers by topic shows the orientation of the protest towards criticism of the current political regime, and not towards the demands for the release of Alexey Navalny and his supporters.

Cognitive mapping made it possible to identify several important content characteristics of protest content. First, this is a high degree of unconventionality and opposition, expressed in the use of direct calls for the use of violent actions against law enforcement agencies, direct insults to Russian politicians and law enforcement officials. The most radical content with direct appeals is emotionally charged. At the same time, in the general array of videos, instructions and explanations for the protesters are highlighted, made in a purely rational style. During the analysis, the authors recorded the use of various manipulative techniques. These include dehumanization – in relation to the security forces, primitivization, stereotyping and juxtaposition – in relation to Russian politicians. The obtained data show that the main subject of manipulative influence is law enforcement officers (Fig. 1). The data obtained show that the main subjects of manipulative influence are law enforcement officers. The media strike associated with attempts to discredit the law system in order to increase the motivation and readiness of the protesters is directed at them.

Separately, it is worth mentioning the use of the latest multimedia mechanisms that form a special type of content through filters, neural networks, branded short audio (dance/entertainment trends that have developed into "protest anthems"), multi-user challenges that penetrate the political sphere and significantly increase the coverage and influence of the declared discourses. These mechanisms are similar to viral ones and are based on infection technology that is rapidly spreading in other social networks, repeatedly duplicated and sent to users personally. In this regard, it is worth returning to the branch-like structure of the service associated with the ability to record the reactions of other users' videos, increasing the speed of content distribution. The research

---

[1] Hereinafter, hashtags are translated into English.

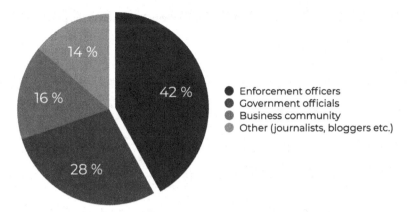

Fig. 1. Subjects of manipulation in the protest information flow.

experience of the author's team associated with the analysis of the political segment of Russian social media shows a significant difference in the speed and number of links with other digital platforms.

4.2   The Scale and Dynamics of Protest Information Flows

The statistical indicators collected based on the results of the study demonstrate a wide scale of the protest agenda and a high level of user activity (Table 1). The average number of likes on one protest video is 10000, reposts – 300, comments – 200. In addition, a uniform distribution of videos by days of the week and time of day is recorded, which ensures their uninterrupted feed to the recommendation feed. The absence of long breaks in the publication of protest videos may also be due to their external administration.

The frequent use of comments as a form of user reaction to sensitive and topical topics is a distinctive feature of the platform, which forms a free space for citizens' self-expression. While on other social media the comment block does not attract significant user attention, on "TikTok", comments are an integral part of the content. Commentaries on popular political videos are turning into a platform for fierce political disputes and discussions. Individual comments, which often get more user reactions than original videos, have their own opportunities to influence the audience.

Despite the lack of content moderation capabilities for the authors of videos, they can mark comments themselves, which will be shown to users in the first place. This technical capability is actively used as a manipulation tool. Thus, at the top of the list of comments, only those opinions remain that are beneficial to the authors of the content. This mechanism is similar to the concept of the "spiral of silence" [32] and is highly effective both in the process of imposing specific political views on the audience and in the course of their political mobilization.

At the next stage of the study, an event analysis was carried out with the aim of additional interpretation of the results obtained in the course of SMA. As a result, the dynamics of publication activity for the selected hashtags was correlated with the main political events (Fig. 2). The first peak falls on January 17 – the date of Navalny's

Table 1. Aggregate indicators of user activity by protest hashtags.

Hashtag	Likes	Reposts	Comments
#23January	58,683,354	1,736,222	1,368,718
#31January	8,436,988	264,068	220,481
#2February	1,037,583	50,486	46,002
#FreeNavalny	94,837,740	2,205,102	1,769,779
#LiveNavalny	1,199,833	58,766	22,849
#WeAreNavalny	3,150,400	70,94	93,421

return to Moscow, after a long stay in Germany. In addition to the fact that the return of Navalny itself is becoming a major informational occasion, additional attention is drawn to the situation with the redirection of the plane with Navalny to another airport and his immediate arrest by law enforcement agencies. These events are becoming a catalyst for not only political, but also entertainment content on "TikTok", spawning a number of humorous videos from major bloggers. At the same time, several hashtags were launched in the service in support of the oppositionist, and the first proposals for holding single pickets and mass actions appeared. An additional trigger that actualized the protest mood was the court session, which chose a measure of restraint for the oppositionist.

The release of a new investigation by opposition about the alleged residence of President Putin, which attracted a lot of public attention, is becoming a central topic for the political segment of "TikTok". The topic of corruption is added to the discourses of injustice and illegality of Navalny's detention. Against this background, "TikTok" is launching a number of new trends and challenge. It is worth paying attention to the material characteristics of the protest content – a variety of protest artifacts, which were specially counted on in the investigation in the context of the creation of many political memes and their rapid distribution ("disco", "mud warehouse", "wineries" etc.).

With the film's growing popularity and major opinion leaders joining its coverage, there are calls for massive unsanctioned actions across the country, the first of which took place on 23 January. "TikTok" has become a means of active campaigning, organization and information support of civil actions in both large and small cities. Despite the peaceful and sparse nature of many of the protests, they launched a new group of triggers, including reactions to mass arrests and targeted use of force against protesters. We also note the absence of a sharp drop in the number of publications after the promotion. Thematic hashtags were smoothly replacing each other, and videos for a long time summed up the results of protest events both in Moscow and in the regions.

Further actions on January 31 attracted less attention from the audience, primarily due to the narrowing of the geography of the protests. Added to the protest triggers are demands to release the protesters detained a week earlier. An important component is the level of protest moderation, which became a reason for discussion and attracting public attention. The last peak can be considered on February 2, when the next hearing on the Navalny case takes place, which also gathers a number of his supporters near the court, and then near the place of his detention. During this action, which had a

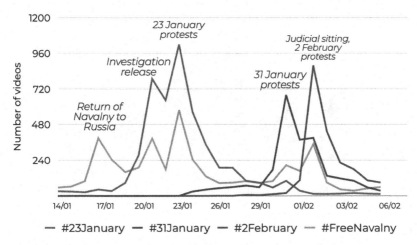

Fig. 2. Time distribution of videos by popular protest hashtags.

predominantly spontaneous nature, the service demonstrated technological flexibility and the ability to adapt to the current political situation, which was actively used by the organizers of the protests. A significant role in drawing attention to the events of the protest days was played by the demonstrative disregard of the rallies by regional and federal authorities, traditional media and even some social media. The lack of effective opposition to unconventional protest activity in the information field has led to the transition of the audience to new digital platforms.

4.3   Characteristics of the Audience of Protest Information Flows

Combining the results of SMA and cognitive mapping made it possible to determine the age core of the protest information flow in "TikTok" (Fig. 3). Contrary to the opinion widespread in the media about the dominance of school-age children and their corresponding content, the analysis showed the predominance of the age groups of 26–35 and 36–45 years old. It can be assumed that the further development of the service and the influx of a new audience will only increase the increase in the share of the adult audience in its age structure. In addition, the study showed the growth of a group of dissatisfied with the excessive politicization of the service, which is formed mainly at the expense of an adult deideologized audience. This fact can lead to the fragmentation of the service into two large segments in terms of the level of involvement in the current political agenda and readiness for public discussion of sociopolitical processes.

The distribution of the protest triggers described earlier by age groups demonstrates significant intergenerational differences, the reasons for which are changes in political requests and attitudes (Fig. 4).

For young people, the most significant problems are the irremovability of power and the preservation of the political system. With an increase in age characteristics, priorities change – socioeconomic problems become more important, the perception of corruption changes. It can be assumed that the formation of such gaps in the digital space is only increasing. This can be influenced by intelligent recommendation mechanisms

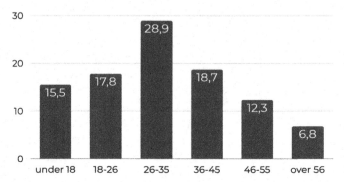

Fig. 3. Distribution of involved users by age, %.

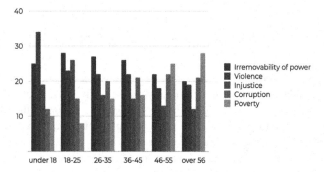

Fig. 4. Distribution of protest topics by age groups, %.

and microtargeting systems that understand the current requests and moods of users, combining them into groups, including by age.

5   Conclusion, Discussion and Prospects

The following conclusions can be drawn from the results of the applied research. First, the political content on "TikTok" is characterized by a wide reach and level of user activity, which is confirmed by the downloaded statistics. Secondly, the publication activity on the service is situational and flexible, adjusting to the current political situation more quickly than other platforms. Thirdly, the published thematic content is distinguished by its unconventionality and opposition, which creates significant risks and requires the development of a set of measures to counter these processes. Fourthly, the process of protest mobilization in "TikTok" is accompanied by the use of a complex of psychological triggers, as well as various mechanisms for manipulating the audience, which increases its effectiveness. Fifth, the core of the protest agenda in the service is made up of adult users, who are targeted by the bulk of the disseminated political materials. Sixth, protest triggers are adapted to the age of users and take into account their values, political sentiments and expectations.

The strategy used in the presented research has a number of limitations. The tools of automated SMA show the greatest efficiency in the "here and now" mode. Carrying out the main stage of the research at the end of the most important protest events narrows the research opportunities. It is also necessary to take into account the peculiarities of the Internet services and the limitations imposed by the platforms under study. In addition, any data obtained from such an analysis must be validated and verified through multiple iterations.

Given the high prevalence of manipulative information in "TikTok" and other social media aimed at misinforming the mass audience and violating social stability, the problem of countering the development of destructive information remains urgent. An increasing number of researchers from various scientific fields are paying attention to the problem of the formation and transformation of fake news in the post-truth era [33].

In particular, it mentions the complication of fakes in the digital era, an increase in the number of conspiracy theories and disinformation operations in the political sphere. The organization, mobilization and coordination of mass protest actions is only one of the directions of the development of digital manipulation tools. It is noteworthy that a popular technology for the implementation of these processes is deepfakes – products of the synthesis of images and videos using modern neural network technologies. In the course of the current study, the use of a number of high-quality deepfakes was recorded, dedicated to calls for unconventional forms of civic engagement and the popularization of protest in general.

It is assumed that the multimedia nature of "TikTok" provides huge opportunities for the distribution of deepfakes, along with other manipulation technologies. At the same time, media researchers note that the perception of deepfakes in the online space is subject to broad segments of the audiences [34]. These facts form the risks of misleading the mass audience, as well as the formation of a stable public opinion based on non-existent phenomena.

In the conditions of high volatility of political processes in the modern world, such an impact of digital technologies on public consciousness poses a serious threat to society and the state. At the same time, it is necessary to understand that new digital platforms provide significant opportunities for self-organization, the development of civil society institutions, which can be used as a tool for building a constructive dialogue between the state and citizens. According to experts, the positive experience of working with social media should be expressed in the desire, opportunities and availability of suffi- cient competencies of government representatives in the process of building sustainable digital communications with citizens in various areas [35]. The dysfunctionality of the authorities and other political forces in the online environment will continue to contribute to the spread of destructive ideas and phenomena that pose a serious danger. Researchers are attracted by the latest technological innovations used by states as a tool for building systemic interaction with society. For example, the concept of e-government is actively complemented by the Internet of Things (IoT) and blockchain technology in the devel- opment of various areas: combatting ecological challenges, improvement of the global healthcare system, e-voting. We are more often faced with attempts to automate social and political relations in a digital environment that make life easier for citizens [36, 37].

The use of new formats of interaction with users and the multimedia nature of content form promising areas of current research related to the analysis of political memes, entertainment videos, relevant audio materials, the practice of using neural network technologies and augmented reality. This study proves the fact that the study of modern processes of civic activity that take place mainly online is impossible without the use of modern interdisciplinary tools. One of the methods for solving new research problems can be considered the evaluation of protest visual content using portable eye trackers and cardiometers. The use of such an oculometric/cardiometric analysis will allow us to analyze the unconscious reactions of users and significantly deepen the data obtained during the research of the social media [38]. Recent applied research in the field of oculometry demonstrates the wide possibilities of this technique for assessing the personal security in the digital space [39]. The results of such interdisciplinary studies can form the basis of new recommendations for public authorities on building a digital communication system and limiting the negative effects of mobilizing mass political protests.

Acknowledgments. The study was supported by a grant from the Russian Science Foundation (project No. 20-18-00274), National Research University Higher School of Economics.

References

1. Social networks in Russia 2021 by Yuri Levada Analytical Center (in Russian). https://www.levada.ru/2021/02/23/sotsialnye-seti-v-rossii/. Accessed 26 July 2021
2. Popova, O.V.: Online political communication of youth from Russian megapolicies. Galact. Media J. Media Stud. **3**(2), 28–54 (2021). https://doi.org/10.46539/gmd.v3i2.157. (in Russian)
3. Brodovskaya, E.V., Davydova, M.A., Eremin, E.A.: Prolonged political protests in Russia and the Republic of Belarus in summer-autumn 2020: reference of the Russian social media audience. Humanities and social sciences. Bull. Financ. Univ. **11**(1), 6–13 (2021). https://doi.org/10.26794/2226-7867-2021-11-1-6-13. (in Russian)
4. Brodovskaya, E.V., Davydova, M.A., Nikulin, E.R.: Mass political protests in the Republic of Belarus in summer-autumn 2020: causes, social base, digital infrastructure. J. Polit. Stud. **5**(1), 23–35 (2021). https://doi.org/10.12737/2587-6295-2021-5-1-23-35. (in Russian)
5. Oskooii, K.A.R., Lajevardi, N., Collingwood, L.: Opinion shift and stability: the information environment and long-lasting opposition to Trump's Muslim ban. Polit. Behav. **43**(1), 301–337 (2019). https://doi.org/10.1007/s11109-019-09555-8
6. Jost, J.T., et al.: How social media facilitates political protest: information, motivation, and social networks. Polit. Psychol. **39**, 85–118 (2018). https://doi.org/10.1111/pops.12478
7. Skoric, M., Zhu, Q., Goh, D., Pang, N.: Social media and citizen engagement: a meta-analytic review. New Media Soc. **18**, 1817–1839 (2016). https://doi.org/10.1177/1461444815616221
8. Boulianne, S., Theocharis, Y.: Young people, digital media, and engagement: a meta-analysis of research. Soc. Sci. Comput. Rev. **38**(2), 111–127 (2020). https://doi.org/10.1177/0894439318814190
9. Anderson, A.: "Networked" revolutions? ICTs and protest mobilization in non-democratic regimes. Polit. Res. Q. (2020). https://doi.org/10.1177/1065912920958071
10. Breuer, A., Groshek, J.: Online media and offline empowerment in post-rebellion Tunisia: an analysis of internet use during democratic transition. J. Inform. Tech. Polit. **11**(1), 25–44 (2014). https://doi.org/10.1080/19331681.2013.850464
11. Clarke, K., Kocak, K.: Launching revolution: social media and the egyptian uprising's first movers. Br. J. Polit. Sci. **50**(3), 1025–1045 (2018). https://doi.org/10.1017/S000712341800194

12. Epp, J.: #SocialismSucks: Trump' TikTok teens. Dissent **67**(2), 16–20 (2020)
13. Serrano, J.C.M., Papakyriakopoulos, O., Hegelich, S.: Dancing to the partisan beat: a first analysis of political communication on TikTok. In: Southampton 2020: 12th ACM Conference on Web Science. ACM, New York (2020). https://doi.org/10.1145/1122445.1122456
14. Vijay, D., Gekker, A.: Playing Politics: How Sabarimala Played Out on TikTok. Am. Behav. Sci. **65**(5), 712–734 (2021). https://doi.org/10.1177/0002764221989769
15. Bronnikov, I.A.: Self-organization of citizens in the age of digital communications. Outlines Glob. Transf. polit. Econ. Law **13**(2), 269–285 (2020). https://doi.org/10.23932/2542-0240-2020-13-2-14. (in Russian)
16. Bossen, B.C., Kottasz, R.: Uses and gratifications sought by pre-adolescent and adolescent TikTok consumers. Young Consum. **21**(4) (2020). https://doi.org/10.1108/YC-07-2020-1186
17. Kennedy, M.: If the rise of the TikTok dance and e-girl aesthetic has taught us anything, it's that teenage girls rule the internet right now: TikTok celebrity, girls and the Coronavirus crisis. Eur. J. Cult. Stud. **23**(6), 1069–1076 (2020). https://doi.org/10.1177/1367549420945341
18. Haenlein, M., Anadol, E., Farnsworth, T., Hugo, H., Hunichen, J., Welte, D.: Navigating the new era of influencer marketing: how to be successful on Instagram, TikTok, & Co. Calif. Manag. Rev. **63**(1), 5–25 (2020). https://doi.org/10.1177/0008125620958166
19. Jaffar, B.A., Riaz, S., Mushtaq, A.: Living in a moment: impact of TicTok on influencing younger generation into micro-fame. J. Content Commun. Commun. **10**(5), 187–194 (2019). https://doi.org/10.31620/JCCC.12.19/19
20. Gaetkulov, E.N.: Political protest in the digital era: major patterns of citizens' self-organization. Soc. Polit. Econ. Law **7**(96), 27–30 (2021). https://doi.org/10.24158/pep.202 1.7.4. (in Russian)
21. Le Bon, G.: Psychology of Crowds. Sparkling Books, London (2009)
22. Rheingold, H.: Smart Mobs: The Next Social Revolution. Basic Books, New York (2003)
23. Castells, M.: The Rise of the Network Society, The Information Age: Economy, Society and Culture, vol. I. Blackwell, Oxford (1996)
24. Katz, E., Lazarsfeld, P.F.: Personal Influence. The Free Press, New York (1955)
25. Bauman, Z.: The Individualized Society. Polity, Cambridge (2000)
26. Garrett, R.K.: Protest in an Information society: a review of literature on social movements and new ICTs. Inf. Commun. Soc. **9**(2), 202–224 (2006)
27. Adomaviciu, G., Tuzhilin, A.: Toward the next generation of recommender systems: a survey of the state-of-the-art and possible extensions. IEEE Trans. Knowl. Data Eng. **17**(6), 734–749 (2005)
28. Emirbayer, M., Goodwin, J.: Network analysis, culture and the problem of agency. Am. J. Sociol. **99**(6), 1411–1454 (1994)
29. Dunleavy, P.: Mass political behaviour: is there more to learn? Polit. Stud. **38**(3), 453–469 (1990)
30. Easton, D.: The new revolution in political science. Am. Polit. Sci. Rev. **63**, 1051–1061 (1969)
31. Brodovskaya, E.V., Dombrovskaya, A.Yu., Karzubov, D.N., Sinyakov, A.V.: Developing methodology for "smart" search for political process markers in social media. Monit. Public Opin.: Econ. Soc. Changes **5**(141), 79–104 (2017). https://doi.org/10.14515/monitoring. 2017.5.06. (in Russian)
32. Noelle-Neumann, E.: The spiral of silence a theory of public opinion. J. Commun. **24**, 43–51 (1974)
33. Kassen, M.: Blockchain and e-government innovation: automation of public information processes. Inf. Syst. **103** (2022). https://doi.org/10.1016/j.is.2021.101862
34. Malodia, S., Dhir, A., Mishra, M., Bhatti, Z.A.: Future of e-government: an integrated conceptual framework. Technol. Forecast. Soc. Change **173**, 121102 (2021). https://doi.org/10. 1016/j.techfore.2021.121102

35. Horne, C.L.: Internet governance in the "post-truth era": analyzing key topics in "fake news" discussions at IGF. Telecommun. Policy **45**(6), 102150 (2021). https://doi.org/10.1016/j.telpol.2021.102150

36. Ahmed, S.: Who inadvertently shares deepfakes? Analyzing the role of political interest, cognitive ability, and social network size. Telemat. Inf. **57**, 101508 (2021). https://doi.org/10.1016/j.tele.2020.101508

37. Osipova, O.S., Bagdasarova, R.A., Lukushin, V.A.: Modern media as a tool for improving the dialogue between government and society. Humanities and social sciences. Bull. Financ. Univ. **11**(1), 20–28 (2021). https://doi.org/10.26794/2226-7867-2021-11-1-20-28. (in Russian)

38. Ognev, A.S.: Cardio-oculometric (cardio-oculographic) detection of functional states in a human individual. Cardiometry **14**, 104–105 (2019)

39. Brodovskaya, E., et al.: Intelligent search for strategies to minimize the risks of internet communication of teens and youth. In: Yang, X.-S., Sherratt, R.S., Dey, N., Joshi, A. (eds.) ICICT 2020. AISC, vol. 1183, pp. 261–268. Springer, Singapore (2021). https://doi.org/10.1007/978-981-15-5856-6_26

Exploring Citizens' Awareness of E-Services and Attitude Towards Smart City: A Comparative Analysis of the Cases of St. Petersburg and Tomsk

Lyudmila Vidiasova[1]([envelope]) [iD], Nataliia Kolodii[2] [iD], Natalia Goncharova[2] [iD], Andrei Chugunov[1] [iD], and Rodoflo Baggio[3] [iD]

[1] ITMO University, Saint Petersburg, Russia
`bershadskaya.lyudmila@gmail.com`, `chugunov@itmo.ru`
[2] National Research Tomsk Polytechnic University, Tomsk, Russia
`{kolna,natg}@tpu.ru`
[3] Bocconi University, Milan, Italy
`rodolfo.baggio@unibocconi.it`

Abstract. Smart city phenomenon has been rapidly developed over part 15 years. In an attempt to overcome technological determinism, and focus on the citizens-centric approach, the paper presents a comparative study of 2 Russian cities that develop smart city concept: Saint Petersburg and Tomsk. A comparative research was conducted on the base of social constructivism approach. A total number of 878 respondents were interviewed in both cities with the use of online service Anketolog. The 2 waves of survey revealed citizens' attitudes toward city problems, as well as the ways to solve them and online services being presented in the studied areas. According to the survey results, the citizens have demonstrated quite high awareness of services and technologies, as well as some steps towards participation in social not political city life.

Keywords: Electronic services · Smart city · Regional administration · Opinion poll · Citizens

1 Introduction

Smart city phenomenon has been rapidly developed over part 15 years in many countries and territories. If at the dawn of its appearance the phenomenon of "smart city" was shrouded in an aura of abstractness (and one might even say it was mythologized in a certain sense [1]), now this category is sufficiently conceptualized, and considerable experience of its application has been accumulated in research practice.

For quite a long period, a "smart city" was subject to technological determinism, and its measurements mainly took into account the issues of using various IT applications, as well as organizational issues [2]. However, then the focus of attention began to shift towards social factors affecting the success of the development of a smart city [3]. The

© Springer Nature Switzerland AG 2022
A. V. Chugunov et al. (Eds.): EGOSE 2021, CCIS 1529, pp. 145–158, 2022.
https://doi.org/10.1007/978-3-031-04238-6_12

study of citizens' attitudes, their preferences and assessments of the authorities' actions began to form a serious layer of scientific work [4, 5].

It should be noted that most of the studies are case studies describing the development of a concept within one urban area. The use of different approaches in the implementation of the principles of "smart city", as well as the lack of comprehensive assessment methods, lead to the difficulty of comparing achievements and failures in different territories.

One of the attempts to move towards comparable comparisons is standardization. In 2020, the Ministry of Construction in Russia adopted a Standard that defines the involvement of citizens in addressing issues of urban development [6]. At the same time, the existing accumulated experience in the construction of "smart cities" makes it possible to raise the question of the importance of "smart cities" comparative analysis with a focus on the needs of residents living in these cities.

This article is devoted to the development of a methodology and a comparative study of the use of electronic services of the "smart city" in two large Russian cities, St. Petersburg and Tomsk.

The structure of this paper is composed of the following elements. The literature review demonstrates trends in research on electronic services of interaction between government and citizens. The Methodology section describes a unified comparative study approach, procedures for conducting two field studies, and algorithms for working with data. The Results section shows comparisons of e-services usage in the studied cities. Finally, the section Concluding discussion reveals the prospects for using the results obtained and the horizons for research directions.

2 Literature Review

The very first mentions of settlements we call cities dates back to the very origins of civilization, after the Neolithic revolution. The advent of agriculture and the decline of hunter-gathering activities encouraged people to leave nomadic regimes and to come together in enclosed areas. Since then, cities have attracted more and more inhabitants. It is only in the early 20th century, however, that urbanism emerges as a significant phenomenon, mainly due to the rise of centralized manufacturing and a convergence of a whole pleiad of factors [7]. In 2014 the United Nations pronounced data that 54% of world inhabitant are the urban citizens, and that the proportion will rise to 66% by 2050, and the largest 600 cities generate about 60% of global GDP.

Information and communication computerized technologies (ICTs) come into practical being in the second half of 1950s, with the introduction of the first commercial electronic computers [8]. In the last part of last century, a set of hardware and software technologies, collectively known as the Internet were assembled make information exchange better and more efficient. They powerfully emerged, and in very few years became so widely diffused that they induced profound and radical modifications in most of our economic and social life [9].

It is no surprise then, the realization that the two fields - city planning and modern ICTs - have much in common so that a joint venture surfaced. Although dating back to the first uses of computers in the late 1960s early 1970s, the idea of smart city emerges around the end of the 20th century and has a strong impulse in the last years.

No agreed or shared definitions exist of what a smart city is. But the beginning of one of the first important contributions to the field expresses what can be taken as a common view [10] emphasizing the close interconnection of technological components to achieve the goal of building a safe city, comfortable for life.

Over time, we can note an increasing number of studies in this subject area. driven by the numerous projects that have been designed and implemented in many parts of the World [11, 12]. Some authors used different naming, including "creative city" as a complex of multi-level relations between all government layers [13] (Boren et al.).

Verrest and colleagues emphasize the importance of moving away from technological determinism towards the three most important dimensions in the study of smart cities: socio-economic, cultural and political characteristics and environment, interconnection of urban problems and implemented solutions, expanding the perception of the urban as going beyond the administrative boundaries [14].

Many problems associated with planning a smart city are proposed to be solved according to the principle of participation (participation of all city audiences), which is a key element for successful development. Participatory planning is considered as one of the possibilities for coordinating the opinions of all participants and preventing conflicts between the opposing sides. In addition, it allows the involvement of marginalized groups that would otherwise not be able to participate in the planning process [15].

Research has already provided evidence that direct participation by people in city planning adjusts them appropriately to develop and effectively implement urban projects [16]. And the government and government bodies note a higher level of cooperation when citizens are in close partnerships.

In general, the civic orientation regarding the prioritization of citizens' requirements when developing and characterizing the stages of providing smart services, when implementing smart projects of various sizes, was comprehended thanks to the approach developed by researchers [17, 18]. Cardullo and colleagues talk about new new aspects of the development of a smart city through the prism of expressing civil rights (political will, as well as the rights to participate in urban governance) [19].

The centrality of smart city dwellers has been understood through the development of ideas by Castelnovo [20]. Citizens are no longer silent adherents of new technologies, they are full-fledged participants in the construction and management of a smart city.

A fairly systematic view of the variation in the roles of citizens is presented in the work of Malek et al. [21]. Table 1 presents two slices: smart city services in their diversity, and the roles that residents play.

The issues of why developers of smart city technologies underestimate the significant citizens' role was substantiated through the use of empirical research methodology in the works of some researchers [17, 20–23]. The results helped to comprehend the activity of townspeople in modern conditions; as well as barriers that arise along the way. Independence as a necessary attribute of modern citizens in the digital city has been helped to explore by such authors as [9, 23].

Awareness and awareness as instrumental values that are assessed as most important in modern human experience were understood and operationalized thanks to the approach of [19, 23, 27]. Such category as citizens' learning was developed in research by [25,26,28]. Another important aspect is connected with participation in public life

Table 1. Smart city services and citizens' roles. Analysis results for works of Malek et al., 2021, Lim et al., 2021. Source: [21, 22].

Smart city services	Citizens' roles
Models and applications	Leaders—"lead local authorities to make decisions"
System architecture	Local champion—"takes the initiative"
Energy management	Co-producers—work together
Connected vehicles	Entrepreneurs—bring economic innovation
Service management	Solution proposers—advise and propose
Environmental and sensing monitor	Human sensors—supply data, reports, or complaints
Traffic management	Volunteers—contribute time and energy
Video surveillance	Experts—share competencies or experience
Water management	
Parking management	
Waste management	
Citizens governance	
Planning and development	

and creative space. This topic was reflected and operationalized as key concepts of our general research thanks to the works of [19,23,24,29].

The literature review shows a gap in development of a systematic methodology for a smart city evaluation focusing on a human-driven method application towards investigation of smart city. In the research the authors tried to shed a light on detection citizens needs and attitudes toward smart city building.

3   Research Design

A key research question was to determine the extent to which residents are ready and willing to implement a smart city. The study solved the problem of developing a methodology that allows one to assess a set of parameters that characterize the attitude of residents and their willingness to participate city life through new proposed channels. A social constructivism approach was chosen as a methodological research base. According to the approach the smart city development could be determined by the actions of citizens, their previous experience and attitudes towards new technologies.

The objects of the study were residents of two large Russian cities that are not the capital: St. Petersburg and Tomsk. The choice of cities in order to conduct the study was dictated by several considerations. Both Saint Petersburg and Tomsk are the cities that have a pronounced cultural specificity. Both these cities have a long, centuries-old history, which has been and remains to this day an important factor in the organization of social and cultural life.

Both cities embody models of spatial development that are typical of Russia: Saint Petersburg – as the second capital of Russia, Tomsk – as the city of the so-called second echelon of smart development.

The cities of the second echelon include large administrative-territorial units of the regional level that perform metropolitan functions. They accumulate the main resources of the development of the region and they are included in national projects. These cities possess high potential, development prospects and capacity to absorb new resources, but these opportunities are less powerful than those of capitals and megalopolises.

Tomsk and Saint Petersburg are the cities that form quite similar images of the future of the Russian cities. The map of the future of Saint Petersburg and the concept of "Big city/Big university" in Tomsk bear evidence of the community of ideals of the City of Tomorrow. The Smart City concept is closely related with the Strategy of Social and Economic Development of Saint Petersburg until 2035.

Both cities demonstrate a combination of traditions and innovations in education. The charter of Tomsk states that academic organizations are a city-forming complex (there are no other such precedents in Russia), which makes Tomsk the oldest-standing scientific center in the east of Russia.

Both Saint Petersburg and Tomsk are distinguished by a variety of smart-activity arenas (integrated platforms such as "Building Together. Tomsk 3D"), a common philosophy of involving citizens in co-design (the "Living laboratory" in Tomsk, the Interuniversity campus in Tomsk, and the ITMO campus in Saint Petersburg), the formation of practices for creating smart streets, smart neighborhoods (interaction with neighborhoods). Table 2 shows the comparative characteristics of these cities, describing important socio-economic indicators.

Table 2. Comparison of socio-economic characteristics: Saint Petersburg and Tomsk

Parameter	Saint Petersburg	Tomsk
Population	5,398 mln	0,589 mln
Size	1439 km^2	295,1 km^2
Demographic load ratio (estimate at the end of the year; there are people of disabled age per 1000 people of working age)	736	740
Migration growth rate (per 10,000 people)	27	3,3
Average per capita monetary income of the population, per month	47169 roubles	28381 roubles
Employment rate of the population	66,4%	49,17%

In both cities, the study was carried out using a questionnaire method provided by service Anketolog.

For the survey in St.Petersburg a representative sample was used. The survey was performed online due to persisting limitations. 548 respondents participated in the study according to the sample. The respondents were divided into 6 age groups, respectively: 13% were respondents aged 18–25 years, 21% - 26–35 years old, 18% - 36–45 years old, 20% - 46–55 years old, 16% -56- 65 years old and 11% are over 65. Among the respondents, 80% have a higher education, 16% have a special secondary education, and 4% have an incomplete secondary education. The distribution of the sample by areas of employment is determined as follows: employees/specialists (45%), businessmen (5%), managers (11%), workers, security guards, drivers (8%), non-working pensioners (13%), temporarily unemployed (8%), housewives (3%), and others (4%). Survey was conducted in 2021.

In Tomsk, an online survey was conducted on a representative sample using the online panel of respondents who have filled in the questionnaire. A total of 330 people were interviewed with the following distribution of respondents by age: 18–25 years old (27%), 26–40 years old (27%), 40–65 years old (30%), over 65 years old (16%). Among the respondents, 59% have a higher education, 26% have a special secondary education, and 3% have an incomplete secondary education. The distribution of the sample by areas of employment is determined as follows: employees/specialists (23%), businessmen (4%), managers (10%), workers, security guards, drivers (12%), non-working pensioners (26%), temporarily unemployed (6%), housewives (6%), and others (13%). Survey was conducted in April-May 2021.

4 Research Results

4.1 Case of Saint Petersburg

In 2018, the Smart St. Petersburg program was adopted, the main goal of which is to improve the life quality level in the city. The program included broad areas for the implementation of IT solutions and new city services.

A project-based approach is actively used in the above mentioned program. Priorities determine the effective communication between all stakeholders, as well as to increase the motivation of users of new services and services. At the federal level, there are also relevant programs in the country, and St. Petersburg's plans are closely related to federal KPIs as well.

The surveyed citizens are active Internet users: 52% are online almost all the time, 44% go online at least once a day, and about 4% are among those survey participants who use the Internet less often.

The study assessed e-city services, which literally permeate the smart city. In the first block of questions, the respondents were asked what services, in their opinion, would be in demand in the city. According to the respondents, the most demanded services are services in the field of health care, security and transportation (Fig. 1).

The study assessed the parameter of awareness of residents of St. Petersburg about the availability of certain services that allow them to take part in city management. According to the survey, 94% know about the portal of public services, 53% of the portal for solving urban problems "Our Petersburg", the unified portal of appeals of citizens of the city 49%, the portal "Your budget" 12%, the portal for filing petitions "Russian Public Initiative" 24%, Petition Portal Change.org 58%, Regional Governance Center 14%, Feedback Platform 12%.

According to the study, most often city residents use e-mail to contact authorities (45%), services of multifunctional centers (36%), as well as feedback forms on official websites (26%).

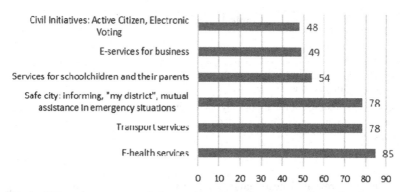

Fig. 1. Citizens' assessment of city services demand among residents, % of answers

According to the study, at the moment the most popular subject for citizens' appeal are issues in the field of housing and communal services (51%), health care and landscaping (45%) and city improvement (28%).

According to the survey, in general, 42% trust the interaction with representatives of the authorities in the network. More than half of the respondents (56%) generally note that online interaction with authorities has become easier than through personal visits. At the same time, only every fourth respondent believes that the authorities in St. Petersburg are effectively coping with their tasks.

Emphasizing the convenience of personal use of online services, respondents are less enthusiastic about the potential of the Internet in the fight against corruption in government (19%), as well as in the field of control over the activities of officials (25%).

In general, the study recorded a positive trend: 46% of the respondents believe that, in general, city residents are focused on a constructive dialogue with the authorities. At the same time, 43% believe that city dwellers in general are focused on solving their personal problems to a greater extent than on solving the general problems of the region. Only 28% agree with the statement that city residents offer useful ideas to improve city life (Table 3).

Table 3. Distribution of the respondents' agreement/disagreement with the statement "In their current state, online tools for interaction between citizens and authorities increase the efficiency of decisions by taking into account citizens' opinions", % distribution by types of respondents' income

Parameter	Disagree	Do not decide	Agree
Very low income (sufficient primarily to purchase food and/or pay utility bills)	1,3	1,8	1,5
Low income (enough to buy food, pay utility bills, but even buying clothes can sometimes be difficult)	4,6	3,7	2,2
Average income (enough to buy food and clothing, pay utility bills, but buying a TV, refrigerator, etc. is difficult)	15,6	17,3	15,2

(*continued*)

Table 3. (*continued*)

Parameter	Disagree	Do not decide	Agree
High incomes (not enough just to make large spending, such as buying a home, car, and expensive vacations)	10,1	13,6	12,1
Very high incomes (sufficient for almost any spending, including paying for an expensive vacation, an expensive car, or housing	0,2	0,4	0,4

Thus, the study revealed the demand for electronic city services, and a low willingness to express citizenship and participate in urban governance.

4.2 Case of Tomsk

Since 2010 it is possible to record the research attention of Tomsk universities to smart cities and sustainable development, and the Tomsk Oblast Administration to the effects of governance, large corporations (Rosatom, Rostelecom) to the creation of digital platforms for interacting with citizens. In the Tomsk Region, the Smart City program line emerged from the housing and utilities sector - through participation in the federal program "Formation of a Comfortable Urban Environment". In 2018, in accordance with the general line of the Ministry of Construction, the Center of Competence on the Urban Environment and Implementation of the "Smart City" project (hereinafter - the Center of Competencies) was created in Tomsk.

The study in Tomsk was devoted to clarifying the attitude Tomsk's residents: to the smart city model; to technologies and services for a sustainable smart growth and solutions to the problems that residents face in their daily lives. One of the objectives of the study was to identify citizens' assessments of the usefulness and effectiveness of "smart support" for everyday life, to study the awareness of Tomsk residents about the presence of certain digital platforms and services that allow them to take part in urban design and planning.

When residents choose the most suitable smart city model, acceptable specifically for Tomsk, then this is a model focused on creating a united, compact, connected city (79.6%). Moreover, among the technologies through which sustainable smart development is carried out, residents single out green technologies (14%); services that enable smart growth; technologies that do not harm the ecology of the city (27%), information and communication technologies and platforms (22%) (Fig. 2).

The survey respondents are most concerned with what will help them in solving their problems. Among which the key ones are transport problems (which is a significant problem for every fourth respondent - 21%), traffic jams (20% of respondents noted this problem), the inability to quickly implement labor (11%) and leisure mobility (9%). At the same time, every second respondent prefers to have information about the means to solve the problems in real time.

But it should be noted that the more significant problems for residents, if we bear in mind the everyday life, which, as they see it, is not connected with smartization, are the

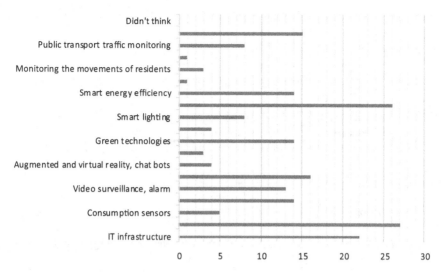

Fig. 2. The smart city shaped by the technologies (%)

issues related to the increase in prices for housing and public utilities and the quality of medical services; more than half of the respondents are worried about them.

When faced with certain difficulties: for example, one in five respondents try to contact the authorities, 18% speak on the Internet, but the majority (64%) of respondents admitted that they express their opinion to their relatives, and one third of respondents did nothing at all.

When solving problems, city residents pay more attention to make demands to the authorities. In fact, they believe in the effectiveness of traditional forms and methods (protest, rally, collective petitions), but the entire system of online communications with the authorities is also gaining weight.

At the same time, the choice of residents in the priority of smart technologies that provide problem solutions is quite definite - these are digital services, thanks to which interaction with the authorities takes place. 22% of respondents marked the information and communication technologies are among the important and significant for smart growth. For a city that claims to be smart, that is not a lot. This is due mainly to the fact that not all residents are clearly aware that ICT and digital services today are the basis for the functioning of a digital city (Fig. 3).

To the question: do you think that modern technologies and services are currently being effectively used to improve life in Tomsk, the answer was affirmative for 7% of respondents, negatively - 63% and 30% - have not decided on their opinion. But people have heard a lot about smart city technologies, they are able to build value hierarchies, identifying as strategically important for a smart city those that ensure sustainability and environmental friendliness (34%), and those that, in their opinion, guarantee an increase in living standards (36%).

The study assessed the parameter of awareness of the residents of Tomsk about the availability of certain digital services aimed at improving the daily life of the towns-people and ensuring decision-making taking into account the citizens' opinion. In 2020,

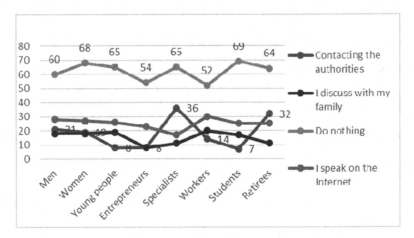

Fig. 3. Respondents' actions when faced with problems (% by groups).

residents of the Tomsk region began to use the "Public Services Portal of the Russian Federation" more often. Thus, during 2020, 2.3 million applications from Tomsk residents were registered - 600 thousand more than in the previous year. In 2020, the level of satisfaction of Tomsk residents with the quality of state and municipal services reached 94.7%. The electronic service "Active Citizen of the Tomsk Region", although it stopped functioning due to the transmitting of all messages and appeals of citizens to the Feedback Platform based on the "Public Services Portal of the Russian Federation", also contributed to the practice of using digital services has been more diversified and more responsive to their needs. But every second respondent noted that online tools for C2G communication in that case increase the efficiency of decision-making if platforms and services are functioning stable, without failures, forming "habits" (citizens do not distinguish between the services "Active Resident", "Active Citizen").

Out of 11 digital services, the development of which were associated with a smart city, and which were used actively, residents more often singled out online registration services in government institutions (36%), electronic administration services (13%). Residents monitored the functioning of such a service as a public transport arrival board (accuracy of timing). Attention to its functioning was shown by 28% of the respondents.

This part of the respondents made very specific proposals for improving this service, noting that the presence of different owners responsible for the maintenance of stop complexes worsens not only the digital service itself, but also the creation of a full-fledged integrated infrastructure of the city. This only confirms the idea that a citizenship mode, if it has also formed outside the electoral system, functions like any other mode (for example, participatory, visual) as a type of structuring and interaction of a certain set of cultural and social codes, techniques, and practices. participation and activism, coexisting in a single cultural space, historically mobile and flexible.

The majority of the respondents, not coincidentally, preferred to participate as data collecting volunteers, who, thanks to sensors, sensor devices, together with managers, would create a database about the city in real time. Residents trust such data more, such data strengthens and improves environmental monitoring of a smart city - this was the opinion of 22% of respondents, such data consolidation allows for increased personal security (13%), smart support for everyday life (16%).

5 Concluding Discussion

The study in two cities allowed us to look at the smart city implementation through the eyes of citizens of these territories. The data obtained may be interesting for the purposes of improving urban management. The survey recorded positive trends in the perception of smart city technologies and new services.

However, the situation is much more complicated with the real participation in city administration and decision-making. Choosing "Do nothing" as a response to urban problems shows a very serious failure in possible smart city vision.

According to the VCIOM data [30], since 2007, among those who do not participate in the social and political life of the country, by 13 percentage points, the share of those who do not believe that his participation will change something has decreased (from 29% to 16% in 2021). It is worth emphasizing that over the past 14 years, the lowest estimate of the population's political indifference was recorded at 15%. These data, together with the identified trends in the demand for electronic public services and services, allow to talk about positive prospects from the proper smart city view.

The study limitations are associated with its online mode, which could cause a distortion of the sample in favor of Internet users living in St. Petersburg and Tomsk. At the same time, the realities of the global pandemic should not be canceled, which significantly complicate the conduct of face-to-face surveys among residents. Another limitation is associated with the lack of a unified methodological basis at the time of its conduct. The study compared similar positions and issues of smart city development measured in St. Petersburg and Tomsk. Further research should be carried out using a single methodology.

The residents' attitude under study to the services and technologies of a smart city always results in the assessment of the potential of participatory methodologies, identification of the ways people would be involved in city management issues and other joint activities.

In this way, according to Tomsk results, it is possible to conclude that every third respondent admits the fact that citizens are not active participants in the smart development of Tomsk, and 54% believe that smart solutions are not always meant to meet their needs, necessities. A majority of the respondents (18%) think that smart technologies are not used efficiently in the development of Tomsk and that this should be in the areas that influence their daily life.

Most of the respondents admit that a differentiated approach is required when implementing smart solutions, especially for new (rural-urban outskirts) and old city districts (with a dense layer of cultural, historical, and architectural sights), taking into account different experience of various demographic groups involving smart communities.

The mobility of citizens (interpreted in a multi-vector manner, but representing a holistic phenomenon) within the framework of existing smart solutions has entailed the maximum number of complaints and, at the same time, recommendations of the residents.

Connected city formation is a second area for citizen science and its experts. The development of social solidarity is also a subject that is of interest for the respondents of the survey. Needless to say, "we-prospect" disappears from many practices of life, but the need for cooperation at the levels of local communities and neighborhoods is recognized by the residents. In the opinion of their leaders, it is the communities that form the ideal behaviors of citizens of smart cities (active, independent, aware, educated, and participation in public life).

However, for the time being citizens may act as leaders of local community organizations, in which they make decisions, distribute resources such as funding and human capital, as well as mediate between public organizations and individuals.

In Tomsk, there is also a threat of a "no change" scenario of spatial development, conditioned by the stippling of installations of smart solutions in the infrastructure and management of the city. In addition, in some smart projects, it is possible to reveal the staging of the activity of citizens, which is specially noted by social media. That is to say, the activity of residents, involvement in smart-development processes, according to experts, could change the pace and quality of smart city growth.

The emerging regime of citizenship (outside the electoral system) requires additional research, especially in the context of the emergence of communities/crowds, grouping around bloggers-urbanists, participants in hackathons, "Living Laboratories" etc. [31]. The crisis of confidence in traditional collective identities, the loss of a common social horizon, the rejection of "we" as a strategy for manifesting a common vision of the development goal, and "an emerging trend towards "nonrepresentational democracy"" [32] create a more complex outline of the citizenship regime [33].

The authors associate further areas of research with the construction of multifactor models that explain the smart city scenarios on changes in the social, political, economic and migration activity of citizens and involving statistical models and functions.

According to the authors, the development of pilot comparative studies in large cities of different types on the topic "Development of a smart city" will allow transferring this experience to interstate studies.

Currently, there is a need for such research as part of the "Digital Agenda of the Eurasian Economic Union" implementation. Naturally, when scaling this research practice to the interstate level, it is necessary to refer to the experience of similar projects and programs of the European Union, using the data obtained by research centers from the EU countries.

Acknowledgements. Kolodii N., Goncharova N. and Baggio R. also acknowledge the support in part from the Erasmus+ Programme of the European Union in the framework of Jean Monnet project "Co-creation of EU Human Smart Cities" (project number 600426-EPP-1-2018-1-RU-EPPJMO-PROJECT), and in part from the Ministry of Education and Science of the Russian Federation in the framework of Competitiveness Enhancement Program of TPU. The publication reflects only the views of the authors, and the European Commission cannot be held responsible for any use which may be made of the information contained therein.

References

1. Soupizet, J.: The smart city: myth and reality. Futuribles **434**, 49–65 (2020). https://doi.org/10.3917/futur.434.0049
2. Jucevicius, R., Patasiene, I., Patasius, M.: Digital dimension of smart city: critical analysis. Proc. Soc. Behav. Sci. **156**, 146–150 (2014)
3. Monfaredzadeh, T., Krueger, R.: Investigating Social Factors of Sustainability in a Smart City. Proc. Eng. **18**, 1112–1118 (2015)
4. Meijer, A.J., Gil-Garcia, J.R., Bolívar, M.P.R.: Smart city research: contextual conditions, governance models, and public value assessment. Soc. Sci. Comput. Rev. **34**(6), 647–656 (2016). https://doi.org/10.1177/0894439315618890
5. Vidiasova, L., Cronemberger, F.: Discrepancies in perceptions of smart city initiatives in Saint Petersburg, Russia. Sustain. Cities Soc. **59**, 102158 (2020)
6. Citizens' Involvement Standard in Addressing Urban Development Issues. Ministry of the Construction (2020). https://100gorodov.ru/standart
7. Morris, A.E.J.: History of Urban form Before the Industrial Revolution, 3rd edn., Kindle Edition, 457 p. Routledge, London, New York (2013)
8. Campbell-Kelly, M., et al.: Computer. A History of the Information Machine, 378p. Routledge, New York (2014)
9. Dholakia, N., et al.: Internet diffusion. Prepared for The Internet Encyclopedia, edited by Hossein Bidgoli. Wiley, New York (2003)
10. Hall, R., Bowerman, B., Braverman, J., Taylor, J., Todosow, H., Wimmersperg, U.: The vision of a smart city. 2nd Int. Life (2000)
11. Allwinkle, S., Cruickshank, P.: Creating smarter cities: an overview. J. Urban Technol. **18**, 1–16 (2011)
12. Cocchia, A.: Smart and digital city: a systematic literature review. In: Dameri, R., Rosenthal-Sabroux, C. (eds.) Smart City, pp. 13–43. Springer, Cham (2014). https://doi.org/10.1007/978-3-319-06160-3_2
13. Borén, T., Grzyś, P., Young, C.: Intra-urban connectedness, policy mobilities and creative city-making: national conservatism vs. urban (neo)liberalism. Eur. Urban Regional Stud. **27**(3), 246–258 (2020). https://doi.org/10.1177/0969776420913096
14. Verrest, H., Pfeffer, K.: Elaborating the urbanism in smart urbanism: distilling relevant dimensions for a comprehensive analysis of smart city approaches. Inf. Commun. Soc. **22**(9), 1328–1342 (2019). https://doi.org/10.1080/1369118X.2018.1424921
15. Van Waart, P., et al.: A participatory approach for envisioning a smart city. Soc. Sci. Comput. Rev. **34**(6), 708–723 (2016). https://doi.org/10.1177/0894439315611099
16. Grant, J., Manuel, P., Joudrey, D.: A framework for planning sustainable residential landscapes. J. Am. Plann. Assoc. **62**, 331–345 (1996)
17. Berntzen, L.: Citizen-centric eGovernment services: use of indicators to measure degree of user involvement in eGovernment service development. In: Proceedings of the 6th International Conference on Advances in Human-oriented and Personalized Mechanisms, Technologies, and Services (CENTRIC), Venice, Italy, 27 October–1 November 2013, pp. 132–136. IARIA, Barcelona (2013)
18. Kamalia Azma, K., Nor Laila, M.N.: Citizen-centric demand model for transformational government systems. In: Proceedings of the 21st Pacific Asia Conference on Information Systems (PACIS), Langkawi, Malaysia, 16–20 July 2017, Paper No. 139. AISeL, Milan (2017)
19. Cardullo, P., Kitchin, R.: Smart urbanism and smart citizenship: the neoliberal logic of 'citizen-focused' smart cities in Europe. Environ. Plann. C: Polit. Space **37**(5), 813–830 (2019). https://doi.org/10.1177/0263774X18806508

20. Castelnovo, W.: Citizens as sensors/information providers in the co-production of smart city services. In: Proceedings of the 12th Italian Chapter of the Association for Information Systems (IT AIS), Carisolo, TN, Italy, 10–13 February 2016, pp. 51–62 (2016)
21. Malek, J.A., Lim, S.B., Yigitcanlar, T.: Social inclusion indicators for building citizens-centric smart cities: a systematic literature review. Sustainability **13**, 376 (2021). https://doi.org/10.3390/su13010376
22. Lim, C., Chi, G., Kim, J.: Understanding the linkages of smart-city technologies and applications: key lessons from a text mining approach and a call for future research. Technol. Forecast. Soc. Chang. **170**, 120893 (2021). https://doi.org/10.1016/j.techfore.2021.120893
23. Giffinger, R., Fertner, C., Kramar, H., Kalasek, R., Pichler, N., Meijers, E.: Smart cities: ranking of European medium-sized cities. TU Vienna, Wien (2007)
24. Caragliu, A., Bo, C.D., Nijkamp, P.: Smart cities in Europe. In: Proceedings of the 3rd Central European Conference in Regional Science (CERS), Technical University of Košice, Košice, Slovak Republic, 7–9 October 2009, pp. 45–59 (2009)
25. Cardullo, P., Di Feliciantonio, C., Kitchin, R.: The Right to the Smart City. Bingley, Emerald (2019)
26. Vanolo, A.: Is there anybody out there? The place and role of citizens in tomorrow's smart cities. Futures **82**, 26–36 (2016)
27. Garcia Alonso, R., Lippez-De Castro, S.: Technology helps, people make: a smart city governance framework grounded in deliberative democracy. In: Gil-Garcia, J.R., Pardo, T.A., Nam, T. (eds.) Smarter as the New Urban Agenda. PAIT, vol. 11, pp. 333–347. Springer, Cham (2016). https://doi.org/10.1007/978-3-319-17620-8_18
28. Winters, J.V.: Why are smart cities growing? Who moves and who stays. J. Reg. Sci. **51**, 253–270 (2011)
29. Nam, T.; Pardo, T.: Conceptualizing smart city with dimensions of technology, people & institutions. In: Proceedings of the 12th Annual International Conference on Digital Government Research, College Park, MD, USA, 12–15 June 2011, pp. 282–291 (2011)
30. Social and political activity of the Russian citizens: monitoring results. VCIOM. August 2021 (2021). https://wciom.ru/analytical-reviews/analiticheskii-obzor/socialnaja-i-politicheskaja-aktivnost-rossijan-monitoring
31. Joss, S., Cook, M., Dayot, Y.: Smart cities: Towards a new citizenship regime? A discourse analysis of the British smart city standard. J. Urban Technol. **24**(4), 29–49 (2017)
32. Usmanova, A.: "Coarse knowledge": production and dissemination of knowledge in conditions of the digital turning-point Topos. **1–2**, 7–27 (2017)
33. Jenson, J.: Redesigning citizenship regimes after neoliberalism: moving towards social investment. In: What Future for Social Investment?, pp. 27–44. Institute for Future Studies, Stockholm (2009)

Smart Culture in Russia Pre-COVID: Development and Online Presence of Cultural Organizations

Galina Kurcheeva and Maxim Bakaev[✉]

Novosibirsk State Technical University, Novosibirsk, Russia
bakaev@corp.nstu.ru

Abstract. The pandemic-related restrictions on visiting theaters, museums, libraries, etc., as well as on organization of cultural events, had provided a boost to online forms of culture. The paper considers digitalization of culture and analyzes and assesses the development of "smart culture" within the framework of smart cities. First we aggregate the statistical data on attendance and digitalization of libraries and museums per the 8 Federal Okrugs of Russia in the Pre-COVID period of 2014–2019. We forecast that the growth of offline attendance during the timeframe of the National Project "Culture" will amount to 29%, which is considerably higher than the 15% required by the respective goal of the Project. Our results demonstrate uneven pace of digitalization for different types of cultural organizations and different regions of Russia. For instance, 50% of theaters in Moscow had websites by 2006, whereas the same threshold for the rest of Russia was only achieved around 2012. We expect that aiding people's involvement with the culture-related ICT can provide social, economic and technical effects. At the same time, our findings might be useful for policy-makers engaged in e-culture and e-government development.

Keywords: Digital culture · Smart city · Information society

1 Introduction

The COVID-19 pandemic and the related imposed restrictions have caused psychological problems in citizens and led to increased social anxiety in many regions of the world [1, 2]. Besides the purely health-related concerns, the people were struck by sharp impoverishment of social and cultural life, as they have to remain isolated for considerable periods of time. In this situation, access to online communication tools and robust digital content become crucially important for sustaining the societies. Particularly, in our paper we consider the resources of digital culture and the overall "smart culture" development in the Russian Federation.

The National Project "Culture", which is a part of the Russian program "On National Goal and Strategic Tasks for Development of the Russian Federation till 2024", includes several key performance indexes (KPIs) that need to be achieved by 2024:

© Springer Nature Switzerland AG 2022
A. V. Chugunov et al. (Eds.): EGOSE 2021, CCIS 1529, pp. 159–173, 2022.
https://doi.org/10.1007/978-3-031-04238-6_13

– Increase the attendance of cultural organizations by 15% (from 877.9 million people in 2017 to 1,009.3 million people in 2024).
– Increase the number of visits for the culture-related digital resources – virtual concert halls, digital libraries, online translations, augmented reality guided tours, etc. – by 5 times, that is from 16 million people in 2018 to 80 million in 2024 [3].

To achieve the goals and fulfill the above KPIs, several more detailed tasks have been developed, which are provisional for the Russian regions and cities. For example, to improve staffing, increase the number of theaters, stage performances, and so on. The transformation of cultural organizations to smart culture should imply both implementation of ICT and a positive trend in the cultural organizations' main activities. Further we consider the KPIs of the three major types of cultural organizations: theaters, museums and libraries. The dynamics of the indicators presented in Table 1 are based on the data regularly provided by the Federal State Statistics Service of Russia[1] [4] (the data for Crimea and Sevastopol are not included for the sake of consistency).

Table 1. Dynamics for the main KPIs of cultural organizations in Russia (2014–2019).

	2014	2015	2016	2017	2018	2019
Population of Russia, millions people	143.7	146.3	146.5	146.8	146.9	146.9
Number of public libraries, thousands	51.2	46.1	38.2	37.4	37.1	41.8
Registered users of libraries, millions people	59.6	55.9	51.5	50.5	50.7	50.7
Items in libraries, billions	1027	923	831	818	810	810
Library items accessible via Internet, billions records	10.8	14.7	15.4	17.2	18.4	18.4
Share of libraries with Internet access, %	61.5	66.6	70.2	75.8	81.6	84.0
Number of museums	2047	2578	2742	2742	2809	2809
Museum visitors, millions people	73.2	81	123.6	117.4	113.8	155.0
Share of museums that have a website, %	65.8	72.8	76	80.4	82.8	82.8
Digitalization of the museum items (share of all items), %	38.9	40.3	44.5	47.8	49	49
Number of professional theaters	547	604	651	649	657	647
Theater visitors, millions people	30.8	31	38.9	39.6	40.8	51.8
Visitors per 1000 population	210	217	265	269	278	353
Share of theaters that have a website, %	95.3	96.8	97.4	98	98	99

The data presented in Table 1 suggest that in 2017–2019 the average increase in the attendance for the three considered types of cultural organizations – libraries (+0.4%), museums (+32.0%) and theaters (+30.8%) – was +21.1%, which is already higher than

---

[1] Several relevant links are collected e.g. at https://nangs.org/analytics/rosstat-rossiya-v-tsifrakh.

the +15% planned in the National Project "Culture" until 2024. As for the second goal of the Project, however, it is clear that the required 5-times increase in the virtual attendance cannot be purely expansive, i.e. resulting from the growth in the offline attendance. So, the cultural organizations would need to prioritize the advancement and promotion of digital resources to enhance the respective KPIs.

These are currently unevenly developed between the three types: for instance, the share of museums with a website lags behind the one for theaters, although the digitalization of the items far exceeds the one for libraries and approaches 50%.

Meanwhile, although the successful outcome of the National Project "Culture" appeared very promising already in 2019, the pandemic seemingly had put it at risk. Despite the speculations that lock-outs should have intensified the development of digitals forms of culture, there were little to no official reports on this. The Russian Ministry of Culture seems to be reluctant to disclose the aggregated statistics in the year of the pandemic, as currently (Oct 2021) its open data for 2020 is not available for most of the cultural institutions, unlike attendance and digitalization data for 2019, which was published rather rapidly after the end of that year. Some data has been published for libraries (but even these are without the number of registered users), but not for museums or theaters.

So, the problem addressed in our study is the development of smart culture in Russia and its comparison to the goals set by the relevant National Project "Culture" pre-COVID. The rest of the paper is structured as follows. In Sect. 2 we provide overview of related work and describe the methods and data collection procedures we use in our study. In Sect. 3, we present and analyze statistical data aggregated by the authors for libraries and museums per the 8 Federal Okrugs of Russia (2014–2019). Section 4 is dedicated to more in-depth analysis of digitalization for theaters, with the focus on their online presence and the functionality that might contribute to increasing online attendance. Finally, we provide conclusions and discuss our findings.

2 Methods and Related Work

2.1 Smart Culture in Smart Cities

In our work, we focus on digitalization of the cultural sphere, which means the instrumental use of technical capabilities to create a new cultural environment "in which a person anchors", and to create new opportunities for studying and introducing cultural values. The culture digitalization considered in this context can be conditionally divided into five main directions. The first three directions are associated with the processes of study, preservation, creation, dissemination and consumption of cultural values and cultural goods, that is, directly with cultural activities. Moreover, it is not always possible to clearly separate the digitalization processes in these three areas. The fourth area concerns the use of digital technologies to improve organizational, economic and financial processes in the activities of cultural organizations. Within the framework of the fifth direction, specialized information systems are being created that allow keeping records of cultural objects and cultural values.

Since the National Project "Culture" was developed on the basis of the principles of accelerated introduction of digital technologies in the economy and social sphere, it can be considered as a direction of smart or digital city development that had been gaining momentum throughout the world and in our country [5, 6]. Its development areas include "smart transport", "smart environment", "smart medicine" and others. So, the area of "smart culture" can be defined in a similar manner, originating from the concepts of smart city and culture. At the moment, there appears to be no accurate definition of the "smart culture" – e.g., a related term "digitalization of cultural heritage" [7] that is often used in European documents clearly covers only a part of the whole cultural sphere development. The latter, in the professional sense, is a sphere of human activities in which cultural values and norms are realized, and where cultural institutions function, i.e. cultural organizations, cultural governing bodies, etc.

Thus, we can understand "smart culture" as an innovative approach to the cultural sphere, which uses information and communication technologies (ICT), as well as other technological advances, to improve the quality of life for the people, contribute to their spiritual growth by preserving and providing access to the accumulated achievements of mankind (writing, religion, morality, ethical teachings, works of art, languages, educational methods, traditions, rituals, etc.). Accordingly, the analysis and assessment of the smart culture development factors is necessary for the goal-oriented management and the increasing the quality of life in a digital city. Although we approach the digital culture development via e-government's perspective, we are not concerned about funding (monetary or material resources) in our study. Citizens need to internalize the new forms of interaction with the culture, so consideration of people's engagement (particularly, attendance of cultural organizations) is crucial.

A very recent conceptual review of the effect of digital transformation on the citizens' well-being can be found in [8]. The authors note that the digital revolution has already affected communication, transportation, education and certain other areas of activity within cities, and the transformation of culture into smart culture is about to follow. They found positive correlation between cultural digitization and cultural participation, which suggests that involving citizens into activities of cultural organizations, particularly via their online representatives, may be crucial. They also note that the culture digitalization requires significant resources, particularly specialized staff and digital platforms. At the same time, in [9] the authors note the certain shortage of history and culture-related applications in smart cities.

2.2 The Major Cultural Organizations

As for specific types of cultural organizations, an overview of smart city platforms and their translation into innovations in digital culture, with a particular focus on museums, is provided in [10]. The authors highlight that the future smart museums will have presence no longer in a particular physical space, but in virtual environment. The transformation of traditional public libraries in the context of smart cities and their reactions to modern technologies were explored in [11]. The outcome is that the libraries increasingly position themselves as the "hubs" and co-located centers for social gatherings and learning. Libraries are also somehow distinct from theaters and museums in the sense that the former are not so dependent of the number of tickets sold, but since we do not focus on culture funding or material resources, we believe the analysis of attendance in these different cultural organizations is justified.

So, in the first part of our analysis we consider the data reflecting the development of libraries and museums in different regions (FOs) of Russia in 2014–2019.

Since theaters historically play a large cultural role in Russia and at the same time show the highest degree of digitalization, with nearly 100% of them having websites, we chose this type of cultural organizations for more in-depth analysis.

2.3 Online Presence of Theaters

In our analysis of the theaters' digitalization, we relied on such indicators as "availability of a website" and the "services provided by the website". We have considered the 8 Federal Okrugs (Districts) of Russia and the 13 Russian cities with the population over 1 million people (the city of Krasnodar that had just recently earned the megapolis status was not included). Moscow and St. Petersburg, which are very different from the other Russian cities, were considered separately. For the sake of consistency, theaters of the Crimea region and Sevastopol were not included.

We also manually explored the websites of 10 professional theaters of Novosibirsk, which we have personal experience with. We only covered the functional features that were missing in at least one website – i.e. for instance the repertoire information that is present in each and every theater's website is not shown. The number of website visitors (last year) was estimated with Alexa service.

The data was collected as of March 2021. In the collection and aggregation of the data, the authors also relied on the help of student volunteers from our crowd-intelligence lab. In total, 28 undergraduate students took part in this project, of whom 20 were female and 8 were male.

To define the date of a website launch for each theater, we mostly relied on the initial domain registration date. However, this approach only worked for 2nd level domains, but not for 3rd level domains, e.g. novat.nsk.ru. So, the domain creation date was checked against the legacy information provided by the *Internet Archive* service at http://web.archive.org, where we relied on the first date the theater's website was saved in the archive. In some cases, we also cross-checked the information with the one supplied by https://www.similarweb.com and https://www.alexa.com/siteinfo/ services, which also provided the current estimation for the numbers of websites visitors. Unfortunately, they cannot provide historical data, which is rather problematic to obtain if one is not the owner of the website.

3   The Regional Analysis

3.1   The Libraries and Museums Digitalizaton Development

The development of the cultural organizations in the context of smart culture is uneven per the different Russian regions. In Tables 2, 3, 4, 5, 6, 7, 8 and 9, we present the data on libraries and museums in the 8 Federal Okrugs (FOs) of Russia, in the order of their population in 2019. The corresponding statistics is not readily available, so the data presented in the tables were aggregated by the authors from the data per cities and towns belonging to the respective FOs provided by the Russian Ministry of Culture[2].

---

[2] https://opendata.mkrf.ru/item/statistics.

The dynamics of the main indicators in the Central FO (Table 2) is generally positive from the standpoint of digitalization; particularly the volume of library items accessible via the Internet reported an impressive growth of +51.7% over the five years. At the same time, although the total number of libraries has grown by about +15%, the number of their registered users has diminished, which can actually also be explained by the rapid digitalization. The share of museums that have a website is already over 90%, and the number of visitors is growing as well. This can be partially explained with the overall increase of the population in the Central FO (+1.5%), and the popularity of Moscow and some other cities of the FO with tourists and transit travelers.

Table 2. Dynamics of some cultural organizations' indicators in the Central FO (2014–2019).

	2014	2015	2016	2017	2018	2019
FO population, millions people	38.8	39.0	39.1	39.2	39.3	39.4
Number of public libraries	8188	8864	9419	9565	9415	9371
Registered users of libraries, millions people	12.7	12.4	12.2	11.8	11.6	11.7
Library items accessible via Internet, millions records	3239	3714	4105	4505	4960	4915
Share of libraries with Internet access, %	57.3	64.4	68.4	75.5	83.5	86.0
Number of museums	638	636	635	635	637	644
Museum visitors, millions people	33.6	42.6	35.7	37.5	35.1	43.3
Share of museums that have a website, %	74.1	78.7	79.5	85.7	87.6	90.2

The Near-Volga FO (Table 3) is even more advanced than the Central FO in terms of library items accessible via the Internet (the record growth of +118% over the five years), but is lagging behind in other indicators of libraries and museums digitalization. Despite the decreasing population (−1%), the number of libraries has increased (+4.8%), and the number of registered users remains stable. The number of museums has also shown a notable growth (+6.6%), unlike in the Central FO.

The population statistics for the Siberian FO (Table 4) report a certain twist in 2019, so we analyze the values for the four years (2014–2018). Unfortunately, both the number of libraries (−2.9%) and of their users (−11.4%) demonstrate a decline, as well as the number of museums (−11.3%) and of their visitors (−12.2%). Although the digitalization indicators for the Siberian FO are respectable, we might conclude that this is a particularly problematic FO with respect to smart culture, as the absolute indicators decline or grow relatively slowly (e.g., the number of library items accessible via the Internet).

Analyzing the absolute numbers for the Southern FO (Table 5) is somehow problematic, due to the merger with the Crimea FO in 2016. Still, we decided to keep the data, since the relative values do allow making certain highlights regarding the digitalization of cultural organizations. First of all, the share of museums that have a website has demonstrated a very rapid growth (+70.2% during the 5 years) and achieved the record 92.8%, i.e. higher than in any other FO. The share of libraries with Internet access is second only to Ural FO, and this might be actually also due to the significant investments made into renovation of infrastructure in Crimea.

Table 3. Dynamics of some cultural organizations' indicators in the Near-Volga FO (2014–2019).

	2014	2015	2016	2017	2018	2019
FO population, millions people	29.7	29.7	29.7	29.6	29.5	29.4
Number of public libraries	10054	9801	10778	10711	10602	10539
Registered users of libraries, millions people	12.3	12.1	12.0	11.9	11.9	12.4
Library items accessible via Internet, millions records	14133	18059	21910	24609	27906	30765
Share of libraries with Internet access, %	61.4	67.8	68.0	72.8	79.1	79.9
Number of museums	591	594	608	608	623	630
Museum visitors, millions people	12.9	14.3	16.1	16.0	14.9	15.7
Share of museums that have a website, %	67.3	75.2	77.5	78.9	79.4	80.9

Table 4. Dynamics of some cultural organizations' indicators in the Siberian FO (2014–2019).

	2014	2015	2016	2017	2018	2019
FO population, millions people	19.3	19.3	19.3	19.3	19.3	17.2
Number of public libraries	6132	5731	5778	5766	5953	6000
Registered users of libraries, millions people	7.0	7.3	7.2	6.8	6.2	7.1
Library items accessible via Internet, millions records	17820	32627	24028	25282	27821	29868
Share of libraries with Internet access, %	56.8	60.4	64	73.4	82	77.7
Number of museums	388	390	382	382	344	349
Museum visitors, millions people	7.4	7.5	7.4	7.5	6.5	7.1
Share of museums that have a website, %	64.4	72.6	72.9	80.6	84.1	84.3

Although the number of libraries in the North-Western FO (Table 6) suffered a notable decrease (−11.8%), this did not affect the number of registered users, which remained rather stable. The libraries' digitalization indicators have demonstrated steady even though not very remarkable growth.

This can be also said about the increase in the number of museums (+4.9%), although the number of their visitors did increase more rapidly (+22.3%), which is to be expected for the FO that includes the city of St Petersburg. At the same time, the share of museums that have a website (90.6%) is even higher than in the Central FO and is second only to the Ural FO.

Table 5. Dynamics of some cultural organizations' indicators in the Southern FO (2014–2019).

	2014	2015	2016	2017[a]	2018	2019
FO population, millions people	14.0	14.0	14.0	16.4	16.4	16.5
Number of public libraries	3340	3365	3945	3978	3960	3934
Registered users of libraries, millions people	4.7	4.6	5.2	5.1	5.1	5.5
Library items accessible via Internet, millions records	6353	8561	9926	11032	11608	12655
Share of libraries with Internet access, %	69.9	75.1	72.4	77.2	87.2	88.8
Number of museums	172	173	211	214	214	214
Museum visitors, millions people	7.6	7.4	11.9	11.8	12.3	12.5
Share of museums that have a website, %	54.4	58.4	75.5	83.6	87.7	92.8

[a] From 2017, the data includes the Crimean FO that joined the Southern FO.

Table 6. Dynamics of some cultural organizations' indicators in the North-Western FO (2014–2019).

	2014	2015	2016	2017	2018	2019
FO population, millions people	13.8	13.8	13.9	13.9	14.0	14.0
Number of public libraries	2753	2730	2750	2760	2731	2428
Registered users of libraries, millions people	4.6	4.8	4.6	4.7	4.7	4.8
Library items accessible via Internet, millions records	20044	28761	29406	33089	33900	36698
Share of libraries with Internet access, %	75.3	70.8	80.4	82.6	89.9	89.9
Number of museums	263	258	261	258	269	276
Museum visitors, millions people	28.7	30.7	31.8	32.0	31.7	35.1
Share of museums that have a website, %	78.3	85.9	88.3	90.6	92.9	90.6

While the number of libraries in the Ural FO (Table 7) saw a notable decrease (−6.0%), the number of registered users has still increased (+19.5%). While the growth in the number of library items accessible via the Internet was not very remarkable (+91.9%), this FO boasts the highest share of digitized libraries (99.7%), which might be due to relatively high level of urbanization. As for the museums, both their number and digitalization demonstrate steady increases.

The North-Caucasian FO (Table 8) has shown the highest growth in the number of libraries (+74.2%), which can be probably partially explained by the effect of low base.

Table 7. Dynamics of some cultural organizations' indicators in the Ural FO (2014–2019)

	2014	2015	2016	2017	2018	2019
FO population, millions people	12.2	12.2	12.3	12.3	12.4	12.4
Number of public libraries	3128	3137	3066	3003	2910	2941
Registered users of libraries, millions people	4.1	4.5	4.5	4.6	4.7	4.9
Library items accessible via Internet, millions records	9849	13446	16710	18583	17782	18905
Share of libraries with Internet access, %	87.1	92.7	95.3	95.8	99.7	99.7
Number of museums	223	222	221	223	234	239
Museum visitors, millions people	3.9	4.2	4.2	4.3	4.2	5.3
Share of museums that have a website, %	60.9	77.0	81.5	79.5	85.8	83.8

So far, the number of registered users is relatively lagging behind (+13.8%), and is rather consistent with the general increase of the population (+3.1%). At the same time, the digitalization of libraries and museums is the lowest, with just about 60% of the museums having a website. Still, the number of library items accessible via the Internet is growing quickly (+107%) and is on par with the other more digitalized FOs.

Table 8. Dynamics of some cultural organizations' indicators in the North-Caucasian FO (2014–2019).

	2014	2015	2016	2017	2018	2019
FO population, millions people	9.6	9.7	9.7	9.8	9.8	9.9
Number of public libraries	1345	1341	2379	2391	2329	2343
Registered users of libraries, millions people	2.9	3.0	3.0	2.9	3.0	3.3
Library items accessible via Internet, millions records	2225	2639	3369	4275	4188	4608
Share of libraries with Internet access, %	39.9	46.0	56.5	61.4	56.1	69.7
Number of museums	128	131	133	134	134	136
Museum visitors, millions people	1.8	2.1	2.0	2.3	2.2	2.3
Share of museums that have a website, %	46.9	51.1	55.2	58.5	58.8	59.4

The Far Eastern FO (Table 9) has extremely stable number of libraries, which can be probably explained by the lack of dynamic megapolises and general remoteness of settlements. This probably also is the reason behind the record growth in the number of registered users (+43.4%). The libraries also report rapid digitalization with the +101%

increase in the number of items accessible via the Internet, and the share of the Internet access being higher than even in the Central FO. The museums show more moderate digitalization (only 75% have a website), but the growth in their number is very high (+27.2%), which is probably partially explained by the effect of low base.

Table 9. Dynamics of some cultural organizations' indicators in the Far Eastern FO (2014–2019).

	2014	2015	2016	2017	2018	2019
FO population, millions people	6.2	6.2	6.2	6.2	6.2	8.2
Number of public libraries	2975	2975	2975	2975	2975	2975
Registered users of libraries, millions people	2.3	2.3	2.4	2.4	3.1	3.3
Library items accessible via Internet, millions records	5674	5887	7696	7696	10798	11403
Share of libraries with Internet access, %	61.5	66.6	70.2	75.8	81.6	82.9
Number of museums	187	187	186	187	232	238
Museum visitors, millions people	2.5	2.5	2.3	2.2	2.6	2.8
Share of museums that have a website, %	44.6	49	56.6	64.6	69.8	75.2

In Table 10 we summarize the previous data for the numbers of cultural organizations ("num."), their attendance ("att.") and digitalization indicators ("dig."). All values are growth rates between 2014 and 2019, expressed in percentages. The open data on theaters was available only in the aggregated form.

Table 10. The growth rates for cultural organizations in the Federal Okrugs of Russia (2014–2019).

FO	Libraries			Museums			Theaters		
	num.	att.	dig.	num.	att.	dig.	num.	att.	dig.
Central	14.4	−7.9	50.1	0.9	28.9	21.7	–	–	–
Near-Volga	4.8	0.8	30.1	6.6	21.7	20.2	–	–	–
Siberian*	−2.9	−11.4	44.4	−11.3	−12.2	30.6	–	–	–
Southern	17.8	17.0	27.0	24.4	64.5	70.6	–	–	–
North-Western	−11.8	4.3	19.4	4.9	22.3	15.7	–	–	–
Ural	−6.0	19.5	14.5	7.2	35.9	37.6	–	–	–
North-Caucasian	74.2	13.8	74.7	6.3	27.8	26.7	–	–	–
Far Eastern	0.0	43.5	34.8	27.3	12.0	68.6	–	–	–
Avg. per year	**1.3**	**0.6**	**6.2**	**1.0**	**4.6**	**5.3**	**3.7**	**5.8**	**0.6**

* The growth for the Siberian FO is for 2014–2018, due to the reasons noted previously

Linear extrapolation (1) suggests that if the current trends are maintained, the average attendance growth ($Growth_{Att}$) for the 3 considered types of cultural organizations during the 7 subsequent years covered by the National Project "Culture" will amount to about +29%:

$$Growth_{Att} = ((Lib_{Att} + Mus_{Att} + Th_{Att})/3 + 1)^7 - 1, \qquad (1)$$

where $Lib_{Att} = 0.6$ is average annual attendance growth for libraries in 2014–2019, $Mus_{Att} = 4.6$ is the growth for museums and $Th_{Att} = 5.8$ is the growth of theaters.

Since +29% is nearly 2 times as high as the attendance increase required by the Project, we can conclude there is a good chance that this goal will be achieved. However, the development of digitalization relevant for the second goal of the Project deserves a separate analysis, which we subsequently perform for theaters.

3.2 The Theaters Digitalization Analysis

Theaters were chosen for the detailed analysis of the digitalization both because they seem to be underexplored in the literature and because their number is the smallest one among the cultural organizations, thus facilitating "hand-made" close examination. In our analysis of the online presence, we were able to find the corresponding data for 293 websites of theaters, which corresponds to about half of all professional theaters existing in Russia. Of them, Moscow had 118 websites (a lion's share of 40.3%), St. Petersburg had 47 (16.0%), while the 13 major cities in total had 88 (30.0%), and all the other cities had 40 (13.7%).

Table 11. The shares of Russian cities and population for which theaters are not available.

FO	Total population, mln. people	Total number of cities	Number of cities without theaters	Population of the cities without theaters, mln. people
Central	39.4	304	237 (78%)	4.1 (10%)
Near-Volga	29.4	200	109 (55%)	2.0 (7%)
Siberian	17.2	114	89 (78%)	2.9 (17%)
Southern	16.5	96	73 (76%)	3.0 (18%)
North-Western	14.0	148	143 (97%)	3.5 (25%)
Ural	12.4	115	89 (77%)	3.3 (27%)
North-Caucasian	9.9	58	51 (88%)	2.4 (24%)
Far Eastern	8.2	82	68 (83%)	1.4 (18%)
Total	**146.8**	**1117**	**859 (77%)**	**22.6 (15%)**

First, in line with one of the goals of the National Project "Culture", we sought to estimate the whole pool of the Russian population that can be potential visitors of the theaters' websites. For that end, we assessed the availability of theaters, operationalized as their presence in cities of Russia (Table 11). So, more than ¾ of Russian cities do not have a theater, although the population of such cities is only 15% of total population in the 8 FOs.

Interestingly, the Ural FO and the North-Western FO, despite their high level of urbanization, have high shares of population in the cities without theaters – 27% and 25% respectively. The clear leader in the availability of theaters is the Near-Volga FO (7%), followed closely by the Central FO (10%).

Second, we mapped the theaters' websites by the creation date, for the 8 FOs (Fig. 1) and for the 13 major cities (Fig. 2) of Russia. To measure the speed of the digitalization for this group of cultural organizations, we calculated the years in which the cumulative value of 50% had been reached. In Moscow, 50% of the considered websites have been already launched by 2006, in St. Petersburg by 2008, in the 13 major cities by 2010, in all FOs (that exclude Moscow and St. Petersburg but include smaller cities) by 2012. This indeed reflects the uneven speed of the culture digitalization in various Russian regions.

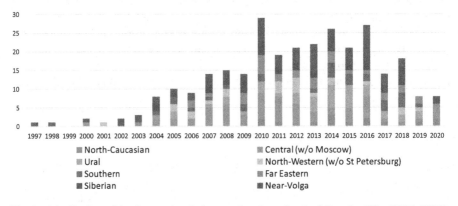

Fig. 1. Distribution of the theaters' website creation dates for the 8 Russian FOs (1997–2020).

Third, we mapped the functionality of the theaters' websites and explored its effect on the number of people visiting the websites. Although the sample size was only 10, we performed regression analysis, for the sake of identifying the significant factors and the direction of their influence. Currently there is no standard template for a theater's website, but commonly it includes the following features or chapters (the 5 dummy variables that we used in the regression are specified in brackets):

– Theater-related information: about us/history, troupe/actors, virtual tours (*VT*), contact information, etc.;
– Events-related information: news, repertoire, particular performances pages, virtual performances (*VP*);
– Communication: feedback form (*FF*), guestbook/forum, links to social networks, etc.;
– Ticket purchase: through the website (*TW*) or via an external service (*TE*).

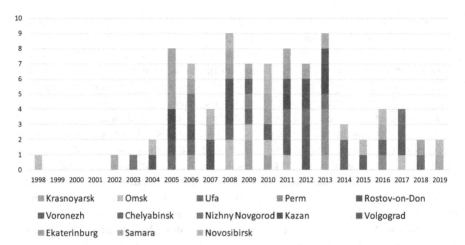

Fig. 2. Distribution of the theaters' website creation dates for the 13 Russian major cities (1998–2019).

The linear regression model (2) constructed using the backwards variable selection method was significant ($F_{2,7} = 20.3$; $p = 0.001$; $R^2 = 0.853$) and included 2 significant factors: *FF* ($p < 0.001$; Beta $= 0.967$) and *VP* ($p = 0.019$; Beta $= 0.467$):

$$Visitors = 386400 - 356703 \times FF + 103436 \times VP, \tag{2}$$

4   Discussion and Conclusions

The improvement in citizens' quality of life and social welfare is linked to the development of cultural environment, creativity-promoting events, etc., as well as to the distribution of the related content through up-to-date digital channels [12]. In our current paper, we considered whether the ongoing advancement of smart culture in Russia, which we see as one of smart city development directions, is on par with the goals imposed in the National Project "Culture". The latter relates to all existing types of cultural organizations, whereas our sample included their 3 most widespread types: libraries, museums and theaters. We believe that our study is essential particularly in the context of the pandemic, when the government seemingly became more reluctant to report unfavorable statistical information and the national projects' KPIs. Since the infrastructural development of Russia and its funding are quite uneven between the country's regions, in our analysis we purposefully considered different Federal Okrugs (FOs) and cities.

The aggregated statistics presented in Sect. 2 and summarized in Table 10 suggests that the Siberian FO is the most problematic region in terms of extensive growth of libraries and museums. Their numbers and attendance levels have suffered a notable decrease during the considered period (2014–2018). The country-wide increase in the attendance of the considered cultural organizations, however, is projected to achieve +29%, which is well over the +15% increase required by the National Project. Still, it is worth noting that the KPIs for libraries, unlike for museums and theaters, are close to stagnation, which can be partially explained by the growing share of the items accessible in electronic form. Also, about 70% of libraries in Russia are located in the countryside [13], and thus get less attention and resources from the government. A policy advice might be to preserve library items and intensify the conversion of older paper books into digital forms. E.g., many Soviet-times library items are still indispensable for technical specialist and do not have alternative versions accessible over the WWW.

The KPIs related to the digitalization of libraries and museums demonstrated even faster increase during the considered period, at +6.2% and +5.3% annual growth respectively. However, as they approach the "ceiling" of 100%, the growth is naturally slowing down – as the digitalization of theaters demonstrates, with its mere +0.6% annual increase. Thus, intensive development of smart culture is needed in order to attain the second goal of the National Project "Culture" that implies 5-times increase in online attendance. From the theaters' websites data we collected and partially presented in Fig. 1 and Fig. 2, we can note that the speed of the culture digitalization across Russia, i.e., in Moscow and smaller cities, is very uneven.

Our detailed study of 10 professional theaters of Novosibirsk (the city that is sometimes called the "Theatrical Capital of Siberia") revealed that their websites have varied functionality and profoundly different numbers of visitors. The regression analysis suggests that the presence of Virtual performances (*VP*) functionality (found in only 50% of the websites in the sample) have statistically significant positive effect on a website's online attendance. The significant negative effect of the Feedback form (*FF*) is likely just an analysis artifact that emerged due to relatively high number of visitors for the *Novosibirsk State Academic Opera and Ballet Theater*, whose website alone did not have this functionality. Policy-wise, we believe that the Ministry of Culture might want to publish official guidelines and best practices for implementation of theaters' websites.

The limitations of our study include consideration of only 3 popular types of the cultural organizations, while there are others. Also, in our analysis of the dynamics (Tables 2, 3, 4, 5, 6, 7, 8 and 9) we did not consider the values per 1000 population. However, since the populations in the FOs remained largely stable, we consider this to be a minor deficiency at most. The dramatic changes of the population observed in the Southern and Siberian FOs were considered as outliers and minded in the analysis. Finally, the statistics on the cultural organizations is incomplete and spread between different sources, not all of which might be entirely reliable. Most importantly, the Ministry of Culture in the unprecedented situation caused by COVID-19, which likely have lead to unnatural decrease in many KPIs, stopped publishing the related open data at https://opendata.mkrf.ru/item/statistics. Correspondingly, in our study we only consider the data until 2019, i.e. not covering the period after the start of the pandemic.

Overall, we believe that the results of our study might be useful both for setting the goals in smart culture management and for implementing concrete development measures. The ICT have already made culture more accessible to the people and added to its preservation and augmentation. With the presented trends we demonstrate that there is the potential for further enhancement of smart culture in Russia, which can contribute to achieving the key indicators of social policy and increasing the citizens' quality of life.

Acknowledgment. The reported study was supported by Novosibirsk State Technical University's research grant TP-ASU-3_21.

References

1. Tso, I.F., Park, S.: Alarming levels of psychiatric symptoms and the role of loneliness during the COVID-19 epidemic: a case study of Hong Kong. Psychiatry Res. **293**, 113423 (2020)
2. Bartusevicius, H., Bor, A., Jørgensen, F.J., Petersen, M.B.: The psychological burden of the COVID-19 pandemic drives anti-systemic attitudes and political violence. PsyArxiv (2020). (preprint)
3. Ministry of Culture of Russia. Order #229 of 01.03.2019 "On accepting the plan for actions of the Ministry of Culture of the Russian Federation in 2019–2024" (in Russian). http://www.consultant.ru/document/cons_doc_LAW_319630/. Accessed 03 March 2021
4. Sabelnikova, M.A.: Information society in the Russian Federation. 2019. Statistical collection. Federal Service of State Statistics. HSE, Moscow (2019). (in Russian)
5. Dameri, R.P.: Searching for smart city definition: a comprehensive proposal. Int. J. Comput. Technol. **11**(5), 2544–2551 (2013)
6. Bogatinoska, D.C., Malekian, R., Trengoska, J., Nyako, W.A.: Advanced sensing and internet of things in smart cities. In: Proceedings of IEEE 39th International Convention on Information and Communication Technology, Electronics and Microelectronics (MIPRO), pp. 632–637 (2016)
7. Kurcheeva, G.I., et al.: Digital city: the characteristics of development indicators of new technologies. Jo. Phys. Conf. Ser. Inf. Technol. Bus. Ind. **1333**, Art. 072013 (2019)
8. Fanea-Ivanovici, M., Pană, M.C.: From culture to smart culture. How digital transformations enhance citizens' well-being through better cultural accessibility and inclusion. IEEE Access **8**, 37988–38000 (2020)
9. Allam, Z., Newman, P.: Redefining the smart city: culture, metabolism and governance. Smart Cities **1**(1), 4–25 (2018)
10. Borda, A., Bowen, J.P.: Smart cities and digital culture: models of innovation. In: Giannini, T., Bowen, J.P. (eds.) Museums and Digital Culture. SSCC, pp. 523–549. Springer, Cham (2019). https://doi.org/10.1007/978-3-319-97457-6_27
11. Leorke, D., Wyatt, D., McQuire, S.: "More than just a library": public libraries in the 'smart city. City Cult. Soc. **15**, 37–44 (2018)
12. Kurcheeva, G.I., Bakaev, M., Klochkov, G.A.: Analysis of tools and data sources for assessment of digital city development. In: Journal of Physics: Conference Series, vol. 1661, no. 1, p. 012179. IOP Publishing (2020)
13. TASS. Ministry of Culture of the Russian Federation: Every year about thousand libraries close in Russia (in Russian) (2020). https://tass.ru/kultura/3328627. Accessed 20 Feb 2021

Problems of Migration Management in the Conditions of Global Digitalization of Society

Olga B. Skorodumova[1]([⊠]) [iD], Ibragim M. Melikov[1] [iD], and Rufat S. Tabasaranskiy[2] [iD]

[1] Russian State Social University, St. Wilhelm Pick, Building 4, p. 1, Moscow, Russia
{skorodumovaob,MelikovIM}@rgsu.net
[2] Representative Office of the Heydar Aliyev Foundation in the Russian Federation, Maly Golovin Per., 12, Moscow, Russia

Abstract. Intensive processes of digitalization of society, which allow us to talk about the onset of a new digital era, have a significant impact on the structures of modern society, its organizational forms and processes. Migration as an emerging new social institution affecting many aspects of social life is being transformed under the influence of digitalization. This gives rise to the need for a socio-philosophical analysis of changes and innovations in migration management processes. The purpose of the article is to investigate the consequences of global digitalization on organizational forms of migration and migration management processes. The purpose of the article is to investigate the consequences of global digitalization on organizational forms of migration and migration management processes. The contradictory nature of the digitalization process makes it necessary to analyze both the achievements of digitalization aimed at personal development, and the socio-anthropological risks associated with its development. Analysis of emerging risks allows us to propose strategies aimed at reducing them. During the research, statistical materials and theoretical conclusions were used from such policy documents as "World Migration Report 2020" and the UN analytical report "The Age of Digital Interdependence". Based on the dialectical approach, the authors analyzed the contradictions associated with the intensification of digitalization and its impact on management processes. Comparative methods of analysis made it possible to identify the differences between the current state of the information society and its development at earlier stages. In the course of the analysis, special attention was paid to such an organizational form of migration as the diaspora, also its role and significance in the context of digitalization were considered.

Keywords: Migration · Digitalization · Socio-anthropological risks · Management · Diaspora

1 Introduction

The second decade of the twentieth century is characterized by a new qualitative stage in the development of information technology. While digital technology has evolved over

© Springer Nature Switzerland AG 2022
A. V. Chugunov et al. (Eds.): EGOSE 2021, CCIS 1529, pp. 174–185, 2022.
https://doi.org/10.1007/978-3-031-04238-6_14

the years, in the past decade, its cumulative impact has become so profound that it has allowed experts to talk about the onset of the digital age. Digital technologies and, above all, the so-called new social networking technologies such as big data, blockchain, crowd-sourcing, new achievements in the development of artificial intelligence (the emergence of emotional artificial intelligence, virtual voice assistants based on computer neural networks), are rapidly transforming society, while providing unprecedented progress and generating new social and anthropological risks. Migration processes, its organizational structures and migrants themselves are influenced by these trends, which leads to new factors, the registration and analysis of which is extremely necessary.

Diaspora, using new digital technologies, becomes a link between countries of origin and receiving migrants. It carries out not only economic functions of supporting migrants and their families, but also social, cultural and political ones. The Diaspora, under the influence of digitalization, is becoming a social organization actively participating in political processes. In the struggle for the electorate and geopolitical influence, the migration factor is acquiring a significant role. The purpose of this work is to consider the impact of digitalization on the structures and forms of migration management. As a hypothesis of the study, there are provisions, which say that digitalization affects the deep basis of migration, changing the nature of economic ties, which become transnational, introducing innovative changes in communication processes, which lead to an increase in the role of the diaspora as an organizational structure of migration, a number of new socio-anthropological risks arise. Related to threats of criminalization, manipulation of consciousness and political mythologization.

2 Literature Review

The processes of digitalization and their impact on modern society, including migration processes, are considered both in expert reviews [1, 2] and in a number of monographs and articles [3–5, 28, 32]. The works analyze a wide range of influences of digitalization, leading to the transformation of personality, the formation of mosaic consciousness, the transformation of value attitudes.

The latest digital technologies, first of all, new social network technologies: crowd-sourcing, blockchain, big data, the latest achievements in the field of artificial intelligence studied in the works of both domestic [33, 34] and foreign authors [6–9]. They lead to a revolution in communication interactions [8, 24, 29, 30, 31], which makes it possible for migrants, being at a considerable distance from their homeland, to maintain close ties with it both economically and spiritually. This, in turn, creates favorable opportunities for maintaining and strengthening the national, cultural and religious identity associated with the country of origin and hinders integration into the host community.

Considerable factual and statistical material has been accumulated, based on surveys of migrants, analysis of their stories in the media, stories of friends and eyewitnesses of migrants' lives in social networks, etc., presented in the analytical report of the International Organization for Migration (IOM) [10]. The analysis of the transformations of migration models in the USA is presented in the work of S. Huntington's [14], in which he explores the basic ideas and principles of the "melting pot" and "salad bowl" models, the conditions and factors that determine the transition and maintenance of cultural diversity. Particular attention is paid to the ideas of multiculturalism and their impact on the differentiation and fragmentation of society, the closure of migrants within Diasporas. Stating and justifying the acceleration of migration processes as an objective regularity of the modern world, P. Collier [11] believes that migration can lead to a conflict of values.

Analyzing the situation in Europe, due to historical specifics, he is wary of all manifestations of nationalism, at the same time he draws attention to the importance of the culture and values of the indigenous population, stating the existence of risks of infringement of their rights under the pressure of the influx of migrants. The paradoxical nature and conflict potential of migration on the basis of many examples and specific stories is also discussed in the work of A. El-Mafaalani [12]. Paying special attention to political correctness, multiculturalism, subjective mistakes of specific politicians in the development and implementation of migration policy, the authors of the research pay insufficient attention to objective factors determining the specifics of modern migration processes, in particular, such as digitalization, which stimulated the choice of the object of our research. In the research literature, considerable attention is paid to the analysis of the diaspora as a social education, the features of its historical development and the current state are considered [14–17].

At that time, the patterns of transformation of the diaspora under the influence of the processes of civilization, transformation into a new social community, claiming to replace the nation and accumulating values and national identity in a global sense, linking their carriers into a single whole in all countries of the world, were practically not investigated. When analyzing the risks generated by digitalization [35−37, 39], the main emphasis is on the economic component [20–23]. Threats associated with socio-anthropological risks are analyzed, but mainly in the context of the imperfection of the legal system [18, 19], while the socio-cultural foundations of these risks have not been sufficiently investigated.

The analysis of the available literature allows us to conclude that considerable factual material has been accumulated concerning migration and digitalization as social phenomena, which requires its generalization at the level of interdisciplinary and socio-philosophical analysis, which is carried out in this work.

3   Methodology

The availability of extensive concrete material on various aspects of both migration processes and digitalization makes it relevant to study and detect common trends and relationships at the level of meta-analysis, which makes the use of interdisciplinary methods and approaches, the implementation of socio-philosophical analysis. The empirical basis was the data contained in the reports of the International Organization for Migration (IOM) and reports of the United Nations (UN). Based on inductive methods, specific situations and stories of migrants related to their activity in the digital age are summarized and analyzed. Specific examples were used to illustrate the identified trends and patterns.

The nonlinearity of social processes, which leads to the emergence of dissipative structures in society that can both increase the level of organization and reduce its manageability, makes the use of a synergetic approach, which was used in the analysis of transformations of the diaspora, changes in its functions, in demand. The comparative method made it possible to consider the transformations of the diaspora in its historical development, to identify the differences of modern models in comparison with the previous ones.

The inconsistency of the digital age and the migration processes characteristic of it also makes the use of a dialectical approach in demand, which allows us to identify and analyze the opposite trends. It is the intensification of migrants' activities leading to the enrichment and development of their personality and the emergence of socio-anthropological risks associated with the impact of the latest manipulative technologies, the widespread introduction of which is due to the intensification of digitalization.

4 Results and Discussion

4.1 The Digital Economy and New Opportunities for Migrants

The concept of "digital economy" dates back to 1994. Don Tapscot in his book "Digital Society" [3], defining it as an economy based on the use of computer technology. Subsequently, the development of the digital economy led to the emergence of a new business model covering all spheres of human activity [21] and focused on personal service for the majority of the population anywhere and at any time.

According to the forecasts of UN experts, an inclusive digital economy and society have practically taken shape [1]. A digital environment has formed, covering almost all states and allowing various types of activities to be carried out using smartphones [22]. According to experts, 52% of the world's population has access to the Internet; in 2019, there were more than 1.5 billion smartphones with certain applications, which allow users to carry out the necessary operations with a minimum level of digital literacy. The speed of transactions has also significantly increased, allowing you to interact quickly with the whole world. The development of the Internet of Things [4], which unites technical devices, medical, energy and agricultural networks, numbering more than 22 billion devices, into a single system in real time, makes it possible to create high-tech platforms. They can be used in a variety of activities, from e-commerce to renting an apartment or buying tickets [23]. The COVID-19 epidemic has intensified digitalization processes. The need for control in connection with the Covid-19 epidemic has led to the legitimization of surveillance of citizens, with profound social implications [24]. Communication interactions have an impact on the structuring of society, the redistribution of power, increasing the role and importance of public institutions [5].

Migration as an emerging new social institution [25], in the digital age is experiencing qualitatively new changes in organizational and management processes The development of the digital economy creates opportunities for the active participation of small businesses in it, which is very important for migrants who do not have significant start-up capital to start their own business.

In the event that high-tech e-commerce platforms create a level playing field for small entrepreneurs to conduct business, favorable conditions are created for people starting a business. This allows them to go beyond their region and creates new opportunities for promoting their proposals to entrepreneurs from socially disadvantaged groups: disabled people, women, etc. [1, p. 31] Migrants are also among weakly protected groups, especially for illegal migrants.

The most important condition for running such a business is trust both in the manufacturer of goods and services and in the consumer. The use of new-networked social technologies, in particular blockchain, allows increasing the degree of trust, which is very important for migrants.

The blockchain is based on the transparency of all operations carried out, which excludes fraud and dishonesty, which often threatens small entrepreneurs. The technology is designed in such a way that it allows protecting authorship and entrepreneurial initiative. Lack of hierarchy, implementation of free identification, extreme democracy, since there is no ranking within the framework of status differences, protection from changes and distortions of information favorably affect the formation of trust between the participants in interactions [6].

In 2015, The Economist magazine published an article "The trust machine" [26], which argued that blockchain technology could fundamentally change economic relations in the direction of building trust.

Mobile money technologies are the most important tools for the development of entrepreneurial activity of migrants and strengthening their financial position. One of the most famous examples of mobile money is Kenyan M-Pesa and China's Alipay. M-Pesa was originally designed to microfinance transfers from one individual to another. Its feature is that you can make transfers in the absence of a bank account [27]. This is especially important for illegal migrants, who often need to have a stable source of income to undergo naturalization. According to UN experts, more than a billion people in the world do not have the opportunity to identify officially and confirm their identity, to obtain the necessary documents that are required to open a bank account and conduct business [1, p. 10]. Research by experts from the International Organization for Migration (IOM) shows that in 2013, 93% of Kenyans were registered on M-Pesa services. The M-Pesa platform facilitated the creation of small businesses and about 20 million Kenyans, including those with very low incomes, had access to financial services. Their income has more than tripled in three years [1, p. 172].

Another promising technology that can be used to involve migrants in active creative activities is crowdsourcing. Crowdsourcing enables anyone to participate via the Internet in solving non-standard tasks. There are no restrictions on status, age and education in crowdsourcing projects, which is attractive for migrants. The range of problems solved with the help of crowdsourcing is quite wide, from artistic activities to the search for missing people [7]. In Europe, crowdsourcing companies have developed and are using regulatory codes of conduct. For example, in Germany, the Crowdsourcing Code of Conduct states principles of fair remuneration, reasonable terms for receiving remuneration are fixed, data protection is provided for employees of Internet platforms [1, p. 13]. Employees are involved in collective areas of activity on the basis of crowdsourcing digital platforms [28].

Analysis of the impact of digitalization on the economic opportunities of migrants suggests that they have expanded significantly. Migrants not only affect the economy of the host country, but also have a significant impact on the country of origin. There is a diversification of opportunities associated with better conditions for doing small business and the manifestation of creative initiative.

4.2 Communication Processes in the Era of Total Digitalization

The availability of digital content is one of the significant public goods of modern society. In recent years, significant transformations have taken place in the development of transnational communication, which has led to an increase of opportunities for access to information in different countries of the world. Now you can enter into communication contacts with virtually no restrictions. Social media provides an opportunity to express your point of view, organize a group of interests and attract attention. M. Castells believes that we can talk about a communication revolution based on the development of digital technologies. Defining communication as "the collective use of meanings in the exchange of information" [21], M. Castells notes the fundamental innovations that characterize the communication processes in the modern world. The technical component based on the widespread digitalization of information flows is of great importance. Media commercialization and networking are also taking place. Much attention is being paid to audience segmentation and its cultural identity.

Technological innovations in the field of communication interactions are significant for migrants. On the one hand, they help not to lose touch with the country of origin, maintaining relationships between abandoned friends and relatives, helping to provide quickly material assistance to the remaining family members. On the other hand, maintain regular contact with members of the diaspora, who may be located in different cities and countries of the world. Such contacts are very important for using the skills and experience of fellow citizens who have migrated before. A good example is making an app available for Android and iOS as the video game Survival. Developed in cooperation with migrants with the participation of the UN Civilization Alliance and Omnium Lab Studios, it allows you to virtually walk the path of a migrant, get acquainted with the difficulties that may be encountered along the way, and learn social integration skills in a playful way [1, p. 204]. This helps refugees to be more independent from intermediaries, among whom there is a large number of criminalized structures.

With all the positive aspects of these processes, there are also serious costs associated with uncontrolled flows of information on the Internet. One of the surveys of Internet users in England showed that up to 40% of young people state the presence of online content containing information of a racist nature, attempts at extortion, sadistic treatment of children [30]. Children with a still fragile psyche are at particular risk. Statistical studies confirm that a third of them under the age of 18 have been exposed to contacts propagating violence and hatred while communicating on the Internet [31].

Another significant problem is the spread of disinformation. In the context of total digitalization, it can spread very quickly using algorithms that can be created by various commercial and political forces [32]. Artificial intelligence systems make it possible to create high-quality fakes of audio and visual content that imitate real people and their activity, which cannot be distinguished from real events without special procedures [33].

Migrants, many of whom are among the most vulnerable, are also vulnerable to online aggression. Research using big data technologies in 2015–2016 revealed a significant amount of destructive information on Twitter. About 7.5 million tweets were analyzed.

As a result, it was found that there is a pronounced tendency to portray refugees and other migrants in a negative way without relying on facts. On social media, there is an active struggle between content creators who treat refugees from a humanistic perspective and their opponents. The aggravation of this struggle and the growth of information humiliating refugees are also associated with political processes in Europe and the United States, when the migration factor becomes one of the most important in the political struggle. The situation is complicated by the fact that, as the study showed, Twitter itself is not neutral, but serves certain political interests, in particular the extreme right, which are characterized by pronounced anti-migrant sentiments [1, p. 181].

The spread and widespread introduction of the latest artificial intelligence systems is also dual in its social consequences. The development of the latest artificial intelligence systems open up boundless possibilities for a person, since they are able to adapt to the needs of each individual person. Based on the analysis of the user's psychoemotional reactions (emotional artificial intelligence) [9], they can structure the presentation of information, determine the rate of presentation of the material, its visual saturation, etc. It becomes possible to analyze the degree of user's attention, to reveal his preferences. If we are talking about training, this creates conditions for the construction of individual programs and algorithms, taking into account the specifics of the individual [34].

At the same time, one cannot ignore the dangers associated with the development of these technologies. According to experts, intelligent computer systems can increase discrimination against certain segments of the population, since the prejudices and orientations of the programmers who created them can be embedded in the algorithms [35]. The proliferation of intelligent systems based on computer neural networks requires their training. The problem is what data will be selected for this kind of training. There are certain difficulties in identifying potential opportunities for the system to discriminate, but when making responsible decisions, these qualities of the system can be critical [36].

For migrant children, who often have limited job choices, developing skills that are in demand in the digital age, such as creativity, collaboration and critical thinking are especially relevant. Studies show that professions that require these skills are difficult to automate and, therefore, will be in demand in the future. The boundaries between work and learning are becoming blurry, which necessitates lifelong learning. To do this, it is necessary to combine the efforts of both government agencies and public organizations.

The analysis of the development of communication interactions in the conditions of a total civilization made it possible to identify extremely contradictory processes. On the one hand, the quality of the transmitted information has sharply increased, which leads to a deeper and more comprehensive impact on the person. Migrants now have the opportunity to model the situation even before the start of migration, to familiarize themselves with the possibility of problems arising in a playful virtual form, which is very important for developing a rational strategy of behavior. On the other hand, the number of destructive content related to violence and disinformation is on the rise. Migration issues are becoming an arena of political struggle, which leads to a sharp increase in fake messages discrediting migrants.

4.3 Digital Technologies and Security Issues

At the same time, the widespread adoption of the latest digital technologies can create significant threats. The use of the blockchain and the cryptocurrencies created on its basis, the most famous of which is bitcoin, allows anonymous transactions, which can contribute to the development of crime [20]. A dual situation arises for migrants: on the one hand, they can be involved in criminal activities such as selling drugs. Human trafficking, terrorist attacks, etc., but, on the other hand, they themselves become victims of criminal acts carried out using digital technologies. Crowdsourcing platforms can be used to combat discrimination against migrants, to prevent threats and violence. The African Migration Center, with the support of the university community, has created the Xenowatch platform, which allows you to track and monitor threats based on SMS messages and e-mail [1, R.288]. Such platforms play an important role in crises, allowing migrants to receive the information they need to decision making. For example, during a flood in Thailand and only thanks to crowdsourcing platforms, a large number of illegal migrants who did not speak Thai well were able to receive timely information about the flood, which allowed them to make timely decisions and avoid death [1, p. 296].

The use of big data technologies allows comprehensive monitoring and analysis of various aspects of migrants' activities: their position and attitudes towards society, various aspects of family life, educational level and interest in receiving additional education, dynamics of wages and employment, legal status, gender orientations, political and ideological preferences [1, p. 324].

Research using big data technologies, conducted by French experts in 2016, revealed that the second generation of migrants from North Africa did not consider the ideas of Islam and the identity based on them incompatible with the French identity. They considered themselves as French as everyone else. This conclusion was very useful for solving controversial issues about migrants in the formation of European migration policy [1, p. 325].

At the same time, big data technologies carry serious risks for migrants. The collected and processed information can be used to manipulate consciousness, suggest certain ideas and preferences. Nadj technologies are indicative in this respect [8]. Based on the analysis of big data, it is possible to identify certain stereotypes that can push a person to make certain decisions [37]. External control of behavior is possible by creating special situations when a person will rely on habits and stereotypes in his actions. To identify them, it is necessary to analyze and summarize a large amount of data about this person: where he went, how he has fun, with whom he communicates, what he enjoys, etc. Big data technologies allow receiving and analyzing this array of information. The most striking example of the application of these technologies in politics was the use of the Palantir system in Trump's election campaign in 2016. With the help of this system, "pain points" were identified, influencing which the conservatives managed to attract voters to their side [8]. Cambridge Analytica made a significant contribution to the development of algorithms for influencing voters, based on information obtained from Palantir and another similar system, Quid. The company, acquiring databases from such large corporations as Facebook, Twitter, Google, WhatsApp, etc. possesses an asset of information about more than a billion people from different countries of the world according to 150 parameters [37, p. 74]. All attempts by the Russian Roskomnadzor to localize the databases of Russians on servers located in Russia were unsuccessful [38]. Considering that migrants are actively involved in the political struggle by competing political groups on their side, their manipulation based on nadj technologies becomes especially urgent. The United States is an example. Natives of the countries of South America - Mexico, Guatemala, Honduras and El Salvador represent the vast majority of illegal migrants who have crossed or seek to cross the US borders. The so-called "migrant caravan" in 2018 has sparked a fierce political debate. If the conservatives led by Trump were sharply negative about the reception of migrants, then the Democrats, on the contrary, sought to attract them to their side and further legalize, thereby contributing to the replenishment of their electorate [1, p. 104]. If we take into account that only Mexican migrants, according to the data of 2019, numbered more than 11 million people [1, p. 109], then attracting them to your side within the framework of the election campaign becomes a significant factor in guaranteeing victory in the elections.

Digitalization leads to the emergence of recruiting structures associated with the criminal migration business and carrying out extensive advertising activities via the Internet. They are interested in women and children, who are mostly defenseless, but can bring significant potential profits.

The dominant forms of exploitation in Asia, Africa and especially America are sexual exploitation, forced marriage, organ harvesting, slavery, etc., from which women are the first to suffer.

In Europe, slave dependence takes on forms that are more sophisticated and are better disguised as legal activity, but nonetheless exists. The legislation of England allows the import of domestic servants, the further fate of which is not controlled in any way. Most of the servants do not speak English, are completely powerless and dependent on their masters. The story of the girl Lakshmi Swami, which became public [39], testifies to the extreme cruelty and arbitrariness that the owners commit towards their servants.

As noted by K. Bailes [39], veiled forms of slavery are widespread - "contract slavery". His research shows that a "contracted worker" is "… a slave who is threatened with violence, is deprived of freedom of movement and is not paid anything. This form of slavery is currently the second largest and growing fastest" [39].

According to the IOM, trafficking in persons remains a serious problem in Europe, and the region is witnessing an increase in trafficking in persons for labor and sexual exploitation. Human trafficking for sexual exploitation remains the predominant form of human trafficking in Europe (56%) [1, p. 95].

The situation with the migration of children is also very difficult. IOM notes that in 2015, 31% of refugees arriving in the European Union by sea were children, and at the beginning of 2016, the proportion of children among those arriving at sea in Greece was approximately 40% [1, p. 246]. The scale of child migration is increasing. The latest estimate of the total number of migrant children in the world is approximately 31 million [1, p. 236]. Child and adolescent migration is increasing as a result of climate change, the impact of information technology, increasing global inequality, the activation of criminal gangs, extremist religious organizations that control migration flows. Child victims are taken out of their homes by slave traders, religious orders, and field commanders. etc. With the increase in homosexual families in Europe and the United States, the interest of the guardianship authorities in the removal of children during the deportation of parents for transferring them to foster families is growing. The number of unaccompanied refugee children is growing.

Overcoming this negative trend could be facilitated by the activities of the diaspora, which is an adaptation mechanism for people moving to a permanent place of residence in a foreign country. The most important feature of the diaspora is the residence of an ethnic community outside the country of origin in a different ethnic environment. Despite the separation from the historical homeland, the diaspora retains its national identity, preserves traditional attitudes, supports them and introduces them into everyday culture. The revitalization of the diaspora's work is significant for the fight against criminal migration schemes.

As a result, I would like to note that digitalization, along with the previously described constructive capabilities, also creates a number of significant risks and threats. The shadow Internet, the ability to use anonymous transactions in electronic currency by criminal structures, sophisticated recruitment activities in social networks and manipulation of consciousness pose significant threats to migrants, as an insufficiently protected part of society. The growing importance and role of the diaspora in social governance processes could mitigate the emerging risks.

5   Conclusions

The results of the study show the contradictory nature of total digitalization and its impact on migration. On the one hand, opportunities for a more intensive and comprehensive development of the migrant's personality are created, the processes of social management of migration are closely linked with the development of the diaspora, which is an organizational structure that supports and guides the life of a migrant. On the other hand, digitalization exacerbates the problems associated with more sophisticated ways of manipulating migrants; both by criminal structures and by political entities in the struggle for the electorate. The growth of destructive information about migrants makes them close within the diaspora, creates the prerequisites for the idealization of the country of origin and hinders integration into the host society. Diaspora, being a transnational center that preserves traditional values for migrants, on which trust is based, can serve as the basis for reducing socio-anthropological risks arising under the influence of digitalization. At the same time, it is necessary to activate government structures of both national states and international organizations to control the digital environment and actively interact with diasporas. In conclusion, I would like to note that, given the increasing role of the diaspora, the processes of its interaction with state structures remain insufficiently studied: both with the governments of the host countries and with the country of origin. The accumulated experience of such interaction, characteristic of China, Armenia and other countries, requires further research and understanding.

The structure and functions of the diaspora are changing. If in previous eras, the diaspora was localized within one country, then in the digital era it acquires a global character, linking migrants in many countries of the world with the country of origin into a single whole. To a certain extent, the modern diaspora claims to be a nation, preserving values, national and cultural identity. There is a close interaction of the Diaspora with the country of origin in economic, political and spiritual terms. The activity of the diaspora in lobbying for the interests of the country of origin is increasing.

References

1. The Age of Digital Interdependence|the age of digital interdependence. Report of the UN Secretary-General's High-level Panel on Digital Cooperatio (2019). https://www.un.org/en/pdfs/DigitalCooperation-report-for%20web.pdf. Accessed 21 Nov 2016
2. Schwab, K., Mallere, T.: COVID-19: The Great Reset The Great Reset. Forum Publishing House, Geneva (2020)
3. Tapscott, D.: Digital Society: Pros and Cons of the Age of Network Intelligence. ITN Press, Relf-Book, Kiev-Moscow (1999)
4. Gringard, S.: Internet of Things: The Future is Here. Alpina Digital, Moscow (2016)
5. Schmidt, K., Cohen J.: New Digital World. Mann, Ivanov and Ferber, Moscow (2013)
6. Tapscott, A.: Blockchain Technology is What Drives the Financial Revolution Today. Bombora, Moscow (2018)
7. Howe, J.: Crowdsourcing: Collective Intelligence as a Tool for Business Development. Alpina Pabliche, Moscow (2012)
8. Larina, E. Nadzh: from information wars to behavioral ones. Izborsk club. Russian Strategies **3**(59), 68–71 (2018)
9. Goleman, D.: Emotional Intelligence in Business. Mann, Ivanov and Ferber, Moscow (2013)
10. World Migration Report (2020). https://publications.iom.int/system/files/pdf/wmr_2020.pdf. Accessed 21 Nov 2016
11. Collier, P.K.: Exodus: How Migration is Changing Our World. Publishing house of the Gaidar Institute, Moscow (2016)
12. El-Mafaalani, A.: The paradox of integration. Why the successful adaptation of migrants leads to new conflicts. New Literary Review, Moscow (2020)
13. Shevchenko, K.D., Sillaste, G.G., Galas, M.L.: Migration in the context of the crisis development of the world community and its risks in Russia. Prometheus, Moscow (2020)
14. Huntington, S.: Who are we?: Challenges of the American national identity. LLC "Publishing House ACT", LLC "Transitkniga", Moscow (2004)
15. Loshkarev, I.D.: The role of the Polish diaspora in modern world politics (on the example of the United States). Dissertation for the degree of candidate of political science. Moscow (2019)
16. Toshchenko, Zh.T., Chaptykova, T.I.: Diaspora as an object of sociological research. Sotsis **12**, 33–42 (1996)
17. Shain, Y., Barth, A.: Diasporas and international relations theory. Int. Organ. **57**(3), 449–479 (2003)
18. Kiyutin, V.G., Kschyrov, T.L.: Illegal immigration in the European Union: challenges and answers. Ilimpoz, Bishkek (2005)
19. Bales, K.: Disposable people. The new slavery in the global economy. Novy Chronograph, Moscow (2006)
20. Revenkov, P. V.: Cybersecurity in the conditions of electronic banking. Prometheus, Moscow (2020)
21. Kushnir, E.A.; Telegina, L.A.: The confrontation of the XXI century: in 2 volumes, vol. 1. FSUE "RFYATSVNIIEF", Sarov (2019)
22. Choudary, S.P.: Platform scale: how an emerging business model helps startups build large empires with minimum investment. Platform Thinking Labs, Boston, Massachusetts (2015)
23. Parker, G.G., Van Alstyne, M.W., Choudary, S.P.: Platform Revolution: How Networked Markets Are Transforming the Economy-and How to Make Them Work for You. Kindle Edition. Amason (2012)
24. Zizek, S.: The will to ignorance. Logos **31**(2), 63–76 (2021)

25. Skorodumova, O.B., Tabasaransky, R.S.: Migration as a factor of transformation of modern society. Manuscript **14**(6), 1180–1184 (2021)
26. The trust machine: The technology behind bitcoin could transform how the economy works. In: The Economist, 31 October 2015. https://www.economist.com/leaders/2015/10/31/the-trust-machine. Accessed 21 Nov 2016
27. Why does Kenya lead the world in mobile money? In: The Economist, 02 March 2015. https://www.economist.com/the-economist-explains/2015/03/02/why-does-kenya-lead-the-world-in-mobile-money. Accessed 21 Nov 2016
28. Schoemann, K.: Digital technology to support the trade union movement. In: Open Journal of Social Sciences, Vol. 06, 01 (2018). https://file.scirp.org/Html/5-1761684_81823.htm. Accessed 21 Nov 2016
29. Castells, M.: The Power of Communication. Ed. House of the Higher School of Economics, Moscow (2016)
30. Internet users' experience of harm online: summary of survey research. In: Ofcom and UK Information Commissioner's Office, July 2018. https://www.ofcom.org.uk/data/assets/pdf_file/0018/120852/Internet-harm-research-2018-report.pdf. Accessed 21 Nov 2016
31. NSPCC, Net Aware report 2017: Freedom to express myself safely, 04 September 2018. https://learning.nspcc.org.uk/research-resources/2017/net-aware-report-2017-freedom-to-express-myself-safely. Accessed 21 Nov 2016
32. Ving, P.: Democracy in the Digital Age, 22 February 2018. https://ec.europa.eu/epsc/sites/epsc/files/epsc_-_report_-_hearing_on_preserving_democracy_in_the_digital_age.pdf. Accessed 21 Nov 2016
33. Skorodumova, O., Matronina, L., Skorodumov, B.: Social network technologies as a transformation factor in modern vocational education [Las redes sociales como factor de transformación en la educación profesional moderna]. Opcion **20**, 213–232 (2019)
34. Melikov, I., Skorodumova, O.: Philosophy as a methodology of understanding in the educational process IEEHGIP 2020: integrating engineering education and humanities for global intercultural perspectives, pp. 1015–1023 (2020)
35. Noble, U.: Algorithms of oppression – how search engines reinforce racism, 08 January 2018. https://nyupress.org/9781479837243/algorithms-of-oppression/. Accessed 2 Nov 2016
36. Eubanks, V.: Automating Inequality: How High-Tech Tools Profile, Police, and Punish the Poor. St. Martin's Press (2018). https://us.macmillan.com/excerpt?isbn=9781250074317. Accessed 21 Nov 2016
37. Thaler, R.H., Sunstein, C.R.: Nudge: Improving Decisions About Health, Wealth, and Happiness. Yale University Press (2008)
38. WhatsApp, Facebook and Twitter were fined 36 million rubles for refusing to localize data. In: Kommersant, 26 August 2021. https://www.kommersant.ru/doc/4958170. Accessed 21 Nov 2016
39. Britain's Secret Slaves: Investigation into the Plight of Overseas Domestic Workers in the United Kingdom (Human Rights). Anti-Slavery International (1993)

Assessing Public Value of Urban Green Zones Through Their Public Representation in Social Media

Alexandra Nenko$^{(\boxtimes)}$, Marina Kurilova, and Maria Podkorytova

ITMO University, Saint Petersburg, Russia
al.nenko@itmo.ru

Abstract. Assessing the potential of the cultural ecosystem services of green areas (values, images and behaviors that green areas offer to their visitors) is one of the tasks of the systemic development of natural ecosystems in the city. The article shows how data from geolocated social media, namely Instagram supplemented with Google Places and Strava, is used to analyze the representation of green areas in the perception of users as well as their actual use practices. In the study of Voronezh 33 topical green zones represented in Instagram posts are defined and the categories of public value of the green zones are constructed based on the hashtags. Three varying cases of urban green are analyzed in detail and compared to demonstrate the ability of the VGI to reveal differences in their public value. It is shown how different VGI sources supplement each other and give a more nuanced picture of the public value profile of the park.

Keywords: Green zones · Urban green · Cultural ecosystem services · Volunteered geographical data · Social media

1 Introduction

The value users ascribe to the urban landscape, green zones in particular, might differ from the objective parameters of their quality, such as size, density, height of trees or monetary turnover of the paid services. The public value depends on the perceived characteristics of the green zones, in other words, on how people evaluate the opportunities in the parks or urban gardens in satisfying their needs.

The urban green has been lately considered not through a given set of functions regulated by the urban plan of the city, however through an ecosystem concept. This concept derives from the system theory and highlights the complex nature of a green zone as well as its active role in influencing surrounding environment and human beings, converting its concept as a passive non-acting domain (Andersson et al. 2014). According to this vision, green city zones as ecosystems provide citizens with different services: from supporting natural processes, such as water turnover, to providing cultural inspiration through nature aesthetics.

Viewing urban green through ecosystem services is a relatively new approach in urban planning and is still paving its way. One of the obstacles for the spread of this

© Springer Nature Switzerland AG 2022
A. V. Chugunov et al. (Eds.): EGOSE 2021, CCIS 1529, pp. 186–200, 2022.
https://doi.org/10.1007/978-3-031-04238-6_15

systematic vision is a lack of developed methods to estimate the provided services. To assess the capacity of urban green in regulating the quality of air or in supporting life of different species in the city GIS analytical approaches are increasingly used (Coutts et al. 2010, Guo et al. 2019). However, appreciation of cultural services of the green zones is not yet developed and acquires researchers' attention. Cultural ecosystem services represent the ways the green zones provide space and affordances for the recreation, spiritual life, aesthetic experience, leisure and sports activities of the citizens. Assessment of cultural ecosystem services is possible based on data on social demand for green zones. It is important that evaluation of the green zones comes directly from the users. Researchers state that cultural ecosystem services have been assessed marginally if compared to other types of services (Schaich et al. 2010).

In this paper the possibilities of user generated geolocated data for exploring the public value of the green zones are presented. In the case study of the city of Voronezh, Russia, data from Instagram is applied to define the representations of public parks, squares and gardens users share. The act of sharing a post with a photograph and accompanying text (hashtags) is considered here as an act of evaluating a certain green place and expressing an opinion on its personally important features.

2 Literature Review

The concept of "ecosystem" has been applied to describe nature's functional complexity and its components (plants, animals, microorganisms, water, air etc.) as well as the interactions between these components (Millennium Ecosystem assessment 2005). Functioning ecosystems are the foundation of human wellbeing and economic activity, because almost every resource that humankind utilizes on a day-to-day basis relies directly or indirectly on nature. The benefits that humans derive from nature are known as ecosystem services of four types:

1. provisioning services - material or energy resources of ecosystems,
2. regulating services - the services that ecosystems provide by regulating air and soil quality or ensuring the fight against floods and diseases, etc.,
3. supporting services - ecosystems provide living space for plants and animals and maintain their diversity,
4. cultural services - intangible benefits from contact with ecosystems, aesthetic, spiritual and psychological values (TEEB Foundations 2010).

Cultural ecosystem services consist of the following groups: (a) recreation, mental and physical health, (b) tourism, (c) aesthetic value and inspiration for culture, art and design, (d) spiritual experience and a sense of place (TEEB Foundations 2010). CESs are dependent on their perceived public value or features and affordances people ascribe to them.

Cultural ecosystem services connect nature to human values and behaviour and can act as gateways for improving urban sustainability (Andersson et al. 2015). CESs are also seen as tangible and intangible cultural heritage, including not only historical objects or landscape features, but also stories, knowledge systems and traditions. CESs maintain meanings and a sense of collective identity, emphasising the intimate linkage between cultural heritage and identity (Tengberg et al. 2012, 17), (Breuste et al. 2013). In urban studies green zones are usually considered as a source of citizens' well-being (Gómez-Baggethun 2013). A sociological survey in Mexico City also shows how the physical parameters of the park affect the well-being of residents (Ayala-Azcárraga 2019). Studying public representation of green zones and interaction with users through social networks is extremely significant for sustainable management of the green zones, while dialogue between park management and local communities may boost thoughtful patterns of recreation (Arni and Khairil 2013). The link between happiness levels in Seoul and access to parks (Kim et al. 2018). Comprehension of the public value of the green zones might advance the development of the city master-plan and the natural carcasses in the city (BenDor et al. 2017).

One of the major issues in the studies on cultural ecosystem services is the question of the rigorous methodological approach and insightful data sources. In the classical studies on urban green perception the methods of sociology, anthropology and environmental psychology were usually employed. Qualitative sociological studies, based on individual and group interviews, have shown the different needs people satisfy in the urban green, such as socialization, leisure activities, psychological recovery (Burgess et al. 1988). Quantitative sociological surveys have explored gender, age and ethnical inequalities in assessing green areas and in using them for leisure, socialization and recreation (Jorgensen and Anthopoulou 2007). These sociological studies, though providing thorough investigation of the social indicators, are lacking the geographical dimension and do not show a comparative picture of the urban green cultural services in a certain territory. Meanwhile, the geographical research was focused on calculating availability and accessibility of the green areas using quantitative measures (Kabisch et al. 2015). However some authors highlight the lack of social component in the geographical research on urban green (Langemeyer and Connolly 2020).

COVID-19 pandemic highlighted the significance of urban parks as places of safe social interaction. Xie et al. studied the interconnection between social interaction, physical well-being and visiting parks in Chengdu during pandemic. They employed online questionnaire, asking people among other things about their activities in the parks. It turned out that basic physical activities, like walking, are most common during pandemic. Unfortunately, authors did not make a comparison of activities between different parks (Xie et al. 2020).

Moreover, analysis of cultural ecosystem services is often conducted as an expert-led activity focused on mapping and categorizing mainly the tangible values of the environment (Olsson 2008). However, the bottom-up construction of the popular landscape meanings is needed, while memories linked to places and objects are creating cultural value at a local level (Ashworth et al. 2007). Recent studies have argued that there is a lack of methodological approach that addresses the social importance of cultural ecosystem services for regional planning based on analysis of spatial distribution of public perceptions (Pastur et al. 2016).

To address this methodological gap this paper is based on the analysis of one of the current sources of abundant data on public representation of the urban green - Volunteered Geographic Information (VGI). VGI is geolocated data created and disseminated by the users through a range of technologies (Goodchild 2007) and includes geolocated social media, such as Instagram or twitter. VGI as datasource has several advantages, which make it useful to understand the cultural aspects of human-environment interaction: richness of data with subjective perceptions, locational preciseness due to geotags, volumnosity due to the number of people posting, and scalability due to the coverage of different territories. However VGI has been seldomly used for analyzing the system of ecosystem services, in particular, cultural ones. One of the exceptional cases is the study by Guerrero et al. (2016) on the Instagram data collected with a hashtag #sharingcph, created by the City of Copenhagen in 2014. This study focuses on the spatial distribution and categorization of users' images, however its sample is limited to the abovementioned hashtag and the categorization was limited to 6 types of urban nature without revealing specificity of user practices in green zones. In this paper we are paving the way further and show how Instagram data could be used to illustrate different environmental values people ascribe to the green zones and how this information could be supplemented with other VGI to give a clearer picture on the cultural ecosystem services.

3 Study Case and Methodological Approach

The case-study of this paper is the city of Voronezh, Russia. The choice of this case is argued by a number of reasons: the city is a typical example of the largest cities in the Russian Federation (with population over 1 million people) and is quite compact in terms of urban planning structure. Moreover Voronezh has an articulated policy of becoming the 'city of gardens' and promoting the development of the green zones inside and outside of the city.

With a population slightly over 1 million people Voronezh is among 15 largest Russian Cities and situated in the South of the Central Federal District (Federal State Statistics Service). The Voronezh agglomeration is the biggest after the Moscow agglomeration in the district and makes up more than 1, 3 mlln people. The city was founded in the XVI century, though the most significant sprawl and population increase took place during the Soviet period (Historical Materials Website). Consequently, the major part of urban space has been designed in the Soviet era and reveals the values of the Soviet state. In Soviet urban planning greenery was observed as a "hygienic infrastructure", aiming to support physical and mental health of workers (Pervushina 2012; Meerovich 2018). Green zones as many other urban spaces were designed mostly identical, without any attention to unique local features. Exclusion was made for a small number of symbolic green zones, like Victory Parks. During the post-Soviet period Soviet urban space is "recycled": new meanings imbue stereotype and symbolic spaces (Gerlach and Kinossian 2016; Golubchikov 2016).

The actual volume of green zones in Voronezh is quite high compared to other cities-millionaires in Russia. Figure 1 represents the spatial distribution of the green zones, including forests and clusters of trees, with the exception of forestry and hunting areas, based on the data from Open Street Map source retrieved in August 2020 (Fig. 1).

However the objective volume of green zones does not necessarily correspond to the subjectively important ones. We assume that social media representation can be considered as a criterion of the subjective importance of a green zone in the mental image of the citizens. To grasp the subjective representation of Voronezh green areas, Instagram was chosen as an online mobile application focused on sharing photographs in a moment of experiencing a certain mood or practice. Instagram enables its users to share pictures taken with a smartphone camera publicly with a hashtag (#), if the user wishes. Instagram is owned by Facebook© and is forming a global community that shares more than 60 million photos every day (Instagram 2021). Instagram is one of the most representative social media within Russian Internet users.

Fig. 1. A map of Voronezh green zones based on Open Street Map data. (Color figure online)

We consider Instagram data as a source for defining the public value of green areas the following way. From one side, spatial distribution of the Instagram posts allows to define social demand on the green zones, their media represented popularity. In other words, the distribution of the geolocated posts in the green zones shows the preferences of the users towards different green zones, which combines their actual practice of visitations as well as their willingness to present these visits publically online. From another side, Instagram hashtags can be used to define the subjective functional profile of each of the green zones, in other words, the ways the parks and gardens are used by the citizens. Creation of the hashtag is an act of organic bottom-up classification of the functional load of a green zone by a user. Therefore a hashtag is a trace of a social value associated with a green zone. For example, if the posts about the park are tagged as #sports', #doing sports, #outdoractivity, this park is associated with doing sports and its value for the user is being a good place for physical activity. Below we are demonstrating these two steps of processing the Instagram data for Voronezh green areas. Data visualization was carried out in the QGIS software with the Pseudo-Mercator coordinate system.

3.1 Defining Topical Green Zones in the Public Image of the City

On the first step, the allocation of the city green zones presented in the posts of Instagram users was conducted. The green areas were selected based on hashtag sampling of Instagram data. A pool of hashtags was chosen related to the concept of a green zone:

'park', 'garden', 'green square', and 'embankment'. All Instagram images were retrieved via its API (Instagram 2021) and stored in a PostGIS geodatabase (Obe and Hsu 2015). The data set includes links to the images stored on Instagram, their text, the date they were taken and their geographical locations.

82,076 Instagram images posted in the period from 01 June 2018 till 31 Jul 2020 were retrieved for Voronezh green areas within the actual borders of green zones represented in Fig. 1. In total 33 green zones which are posted about in Instagram were allocated. Figure 2 shows the mapped representation of those green areas.

Fig. 2. Voronezh green zones presented in the instagram data. (Color figure online)

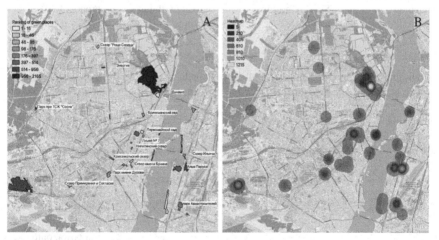

Fig. 3. (A) Ranking of the popularity of the green zones based on the Instagram data, (B) heat map representation of the ranking. (Color figure online)

Based on the quantity of the posts associated with the green areas the media popularity was defined. Figure 3(a, b) illustrates the ranking of the green areas popularity in two modes - as a discrete distribution of the so called 'votes' (i.e. users' posts in the green zones) and their aggregate in the form of a heatmap. The latter shows in a more pronounced way a triangle of the most popular green zones in the city, with two edges situated on the banks of the Voronezh river and its reservoir (the Central Park for Culture and Recreation and the Scarlet Sails Park) almost opposite each other and the third edge - to the South-West of the city (the Optimist Park).

Table 1. Grouping of the hashtags to the posts on the green zones, Instagram.

#Sports	#Recreation	#Beauty	#Family
onsport, sport, fitness, streetworkout, sportisoureverything, instafitness, dayofsport, fitbabe, activerecreation, exercices	walks, walking, weekendwalk, hotdrink, recreating, myfriends, weekendwithbeloved, funwalks, walkbyfoot, vacation	model, vsco, cute, vscocam, photography, beautyphoto, girlsbeauty, beautiful, instafashion, familyphoto	momfortwo, cutebabies, goingoutwithkids, specialmom, momforbestkids, outkids, specialkids, husband_wife, favouritekids, momandson
#Food	#Time	#Animals	#Hobby
instacoffee, homemadebread, coffee, fruit, milk, easteregg, instafood, icecream, wine, vegetables	summer, snow, winter, lastdayofwinter, spring2020, momentsinthesun, springhilidays, Sundaymorning, suninface, summertime	dogfriend, kitten, corgiworld, squirrel, moodypuppy, hedgehoginfog, parrot, happydog, walkingwithdog, starlings	fishing, handmade, art, drawing, artprocess, huntingfishing, waterclorslandscap, hiphop, hobby, creative, colors
#Places	#Events	#Mood	#Nature
greentheatre, zoo, citypark, urbangarden, embankment, park, summercamp, leftbank, nativeplaces, freshair	studentday, wedding, happymamafest, victoryday, happynewyear, fireworks, Easter, motherday, flowerexhibition, happyvalentine	happiness, dreamsbecometrue, smile, breathin, springmood, goodsense, thereisagoal, lovelife, summerinsoul, beautifulday	tree, weather, sun, sea, freshair, bloom, geranium, pelargonium, clouds, snow, hail, rain, heat, cold, frost, plant, nature, landscape, sky, bush, foliage, water, inthevillage, plants, hike, herringbone, rainbows, outdoors, flower, green, roses, snowdrop

3.2 Defining Represented Value of a Green Zone

On the second step, the hashtags for Voronezh green zones were semi-manually grouped into twelve categories: sports, recreation, beauty, family, food, time, animals, hobby, places, events, mood and nature (Table 1).

Firstly the initial coding of the hashtags was run manually, based on the principle of axial coding, and the conceptual categories were defined. Secondly, the automatic grouping procedure was run in Python based on the library of synonyms for the words defined at the first stage. Summing up the contents of the defined groups several tendencies in the public perception of the green zones become evident: (a) importance of the green zones as natural spots with different dynamics in time, having variety of natural places and animal world, (b) affordances of the green zones in terms of social activities: their ability to become background for the family leisure, sports activities, beauty lifestyle, recreation, and hobby, (c) affordances of the green zones in terms of infrastructure, such as food and events, (d) affordances of the green zones in terms of emotional and spiritual needs - the variety of moods they support.

In Table 1 the most popular 10 hashtags for each of the groups are given. The number of the hashtags in each group varies from 20 up to 50.

The generalized diagram (Fig. 4) of the hashtag groups shows how the values applied to the green zones of Voronezh are distributed. The most important value is, not surprisingly, being in nature and contact with nature, the second most important is good physical and emotional state and the third most important is the beauty lifestyle, which can take place in the natural setting.

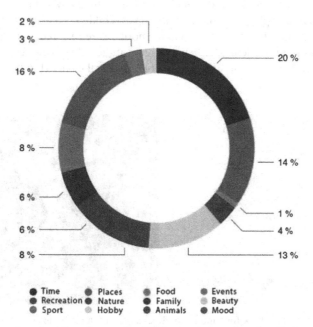

Fig. 4. Categories of public value ascribed to the green zones based on Instagram hashtags.

4 Results: Comparing Perceived Values of the Three Voronezh Parks

In this section we are considering the three parks, which came out to be the most represented in Instagram. These are the Central Park for Culture and Recreation, Optimist Park and Scarlet Sales Park. All three parks are among specially protected natural areas, consequently, some kinds of activities like barbeques, dog walking, irrigation and landscape transformation are forbidden there (Information System "Specially protected natural areas"). Those spaces are managed and regulated by local governments. To have a more detailed image of the perceived value of those parks and practices of their usage we supplement Instagram data with Google Places and Strava data. Google Places shows the user rating for a place and the popularity of a place based on the number of votes (Google Places 2021). Strava is an open source mobile application for sports and active leisure activities and its data shows the actual routes of physical activity for a territory (Strava 2021).

The Central Park for Culture and Recreation (CPCR) is a landscape type of an 'ideal' green zone in Soviet urban planning. The CPCRs were considered to be exemplary in terms of functional load and events, as well as landscape design. They used to be places for the major open-air cultural activities and 'civil' leisure. These green areas most often have a history much longer than that of the soviet parks, and are often filled with different architectural forms, historical monuments and statues. Voronezh CPCR is situated on the left bank of Voronezh River, constitutes 100 hectares and is the largest urban recreation area in the city. It was launched as a parking zone over 170 years ago, and in the 1960s received its status as CPCR (Voronezh Central Park Official Website 2021). In 2015–2016 the park was completely reconstructed and new children's and sports grounds were created, green theater, fountain, pond and memorial were restored, and new trees and perennial plants were planted. After a major renovation, exhibitions, festivals, cultural, sports and recreation events are intensively organized in the park (Fig. 5).

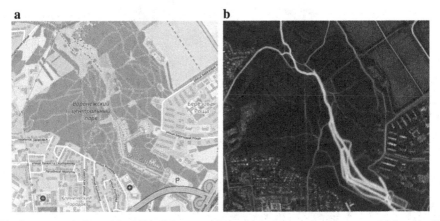

Fig. 5. Voronezh Central Park for Culture and Recreation: (a) area in the context of the city, (b) intensity of physical activity in the park based on Strava data.

The number of Instagram posts with hashtags for the park is the biggest in the sample and makes up 13056. CPCR rating in Google Places is also high - 4.9, the highest for the analyzed green zones. Distribution of the hashtag categories for Central Park shows the prevalence of the following perceived values: places, time and mood (Fig. 6). This can be interpreted the way that Central Park is valued for its activity intensity and possibility to spend time differently and in a variety of spots.

The exemplary post with a hashtag #autumntime and an autumn-mood photograph shows the autumn activity in the park. There is a contradiction in social media data: though Strava data reflects quite a high intensity of the park usage for active leisure, the Instagram hashtags of 'sports' group are low in number. This might be explained by a difference in these media audiences. The comparison of data gives a mode detailed account on the public usage of the park and gives evidence that the Central Park is good for different kinds of activities in users' view.

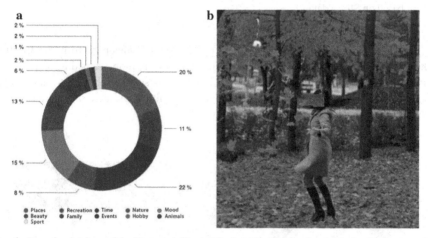

Fig. 6. Perceived values of the Voronezh Central Park (a) by distribution of the hashtag categories, (b) exemplary photograph from Instagram with representation of #autumntime.

The second case is a newly built Scarlet Sales Park which represents a typical example of a relatively novel green landscape development as well as a recent project of public space design. The functional and business model of the park is oriented towards commercial activities. However, according to the official description, Scarlet Sales park was created in 2016 in order to propagate ideas of environment protection (Specially protected natural areas 2021). Currently it is second in rating of green zones in Google Places with 4.7 points, revealing its popularity as a place of interest. The number of Instagram posts with hashtags in this park is 4058, which is less than in the Central Park and is conditioned by the novelty of this place.

The main value of this park defined through the hashtags is mood. Scarlet Sales presents a number of opportunities for people to enjoy good views, interactive activities and contact with nature and water.

Other important values are time, beauty and places. The park is not used for sports, as seen at Fig. 7b as well as in the small share of the sports hashtags in the diagram

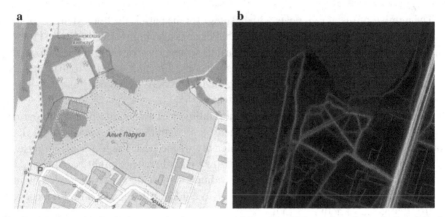

Fig. 7. Scarlet Sales Park: (a) area in the context of the city, (b) intensity of physical activity in the park based on Strava data.

Fig. 8a. The difference of the public image of the Scarlet Sales park from the Central Park becomes evident from social media data: the latter is more valued as a space for beautiful emotions. The Scarlet Sales park has been designed recently, so landscape architects might keep in mind contemporary digital culture and give more attention to photography itself as a type of leisure.

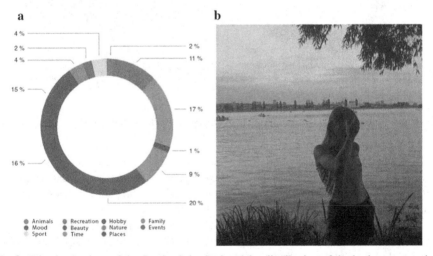

Fig. 8. Perceived values of the Scarlet Sales Park: (a) by distribution of the hashtag categories, (b) exemplary photograph from Instagram with representation of #mood.

The third case is the Optimist Forest Park, situated more remotely from the city centre, compared to the previous two cases, on the left bank of Voronezh river. It was founded in 1946 and represents another type of a green zone - an area for preservation of the wildlife and for human-nature interaction in the city.

According to the official documents, the focus of the park is on nature conservation. Initially it was designed to prevent wind erosion, which is significant in the Voronezh region (Specially protected natural areas 2021). Its square is bigger than that of the Scarlet Sales Park and comparable to the Central Park. The rating in Google Places is lower than the first two cases and makes up only 4, 5 points. The number of Instagram posts with hashtags in this park is 9329, which is bigger than in the Scarlet Sales Park, but lower than in the Central Park.

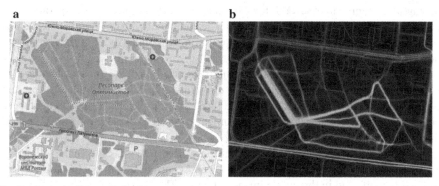

Fig. 9. Optimist Forest Park: (a) area in the context of the city, (b) intensity of physical activity in the park based on Strava data.

According to the hashtag groups the main perceived value of the Optimist forest park is its different manifestations in time. Moreover, the category of animals is important. In combination this makes the park a place it was meant to be - for human-nature interaction. The lower rating of the park in Google Places rating could be explained by the fact that there are less cultural and leisure activities here. Strava data (Fig. 9b) shows that the park is quite often used for sports and physical activity, however the representation of sports activities in Instagram hashtags of the park is the lowest (together with the 'events' category) (Fig. 10).

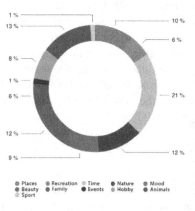

Fig. 10

5 Conclusions

The importance of analysis of the public value of the green zones should not be under-estimated in the context of the global ecological crisis and rapid development of the cities.

The geolocated social media data proves to be a valuable and illustrative source for analyzing public representation of the values of the green zones. The data source used in this paper for a detailed overview of the perceived characteristics of the urban green is Instagram, which unites several items of data combined in the analysis - geolocation, hashtag and a photograph. Instagram data can be compared with other social media, e.g. Google Places and Strava data, to receive proof on the popularity of a green zone and insights about actual practices of its usage.

The categories defined based on the organic classification of the important features of the green zones and human-park interaction through hashtags in Instagram posts present a clear classification of affordances parks provide to their users. The distribution of these categories for each case is illustrative and might be used to explore the parks' 'public value profile'.

Comparison of the perceived values of the three urban parks has shown the following. Firstly, the initial landscape planning type as well as current functional load of the park are clearly manifested in the public images of them. The Scarlet Sales Park is the most 'moody' park and has the newest landscape design, the Optimist Park as a forest park zone is mostly valued for seasonal changes, animals, and nature, the Central Park as an 'ideal park' type is valued for seasonal changes, different leisure possibilities as well as variety of places. These manifestations should not be regarded as given truth, while social evaluations often differ from the designs input by the landscape planners. Secondly, VGI data shows the strong features of each of the parks, and at the same time analysis illustrates the 'missing' values, for example, low position of the animal world in the Scarlet Sales Park.

Comparing detected categories of the green zones values based on hashtags with the typology of the ecosystem services of the green zones one could see a clear intersec-tion. Users as lay experts dwell more upon the class of cultural ecosystem services and consider the emotional experiences, recreation potential, aesthetical value of the green zones. However users are also partly receptive to the consideration of the supportive ecosystem services, when they pay attention to the animal and plant variety in the park.

The public value profiles of the parks and other green areas can be used for the purposes of urban green management and marketing: understanding the main public values managers could create proper event programs, promote certain park features, find a balance between the wild and the civilized parts of the park, create infrastructure to support public needs (e.g. instaspots for making beauty photos for Instagram).

6 Discussion

There appear to be discrepancies in the Instagram data representation of the public good and in Strava data showing actual usage of a green zone for active leisure. Most evidently this contradiction revealed itself in the case of the Optimist forest park, which is used for physical activity according to Strava, however this is not supported by Instagram data. These types of inconsistencies should be explored further. However this also proves the necessity to compare different VGI sources to receive a more nuanced picture on the public perception of a park.

Further steps of this research are in visual analysis of the Instagram photographs, consequent definition of symbolically important items of the green zones and further correlation analysis between visual and textual categories of perceived values received from the hashtags. Further comparative analysis of the whole sample of Voronezh green zones is planned with the aim to understand the correlation between the planning and functional characteristics of the green area and its perceived value.

Acknowledgement. This paper was supported by Russian Foundation for Basic Research grant № 20–013-00891 A "Emotional perception of urban environment as a factor for urban resilience".

References

Andersson, E., et al.: Reconnecting cities to the biosphere: stewardship of green infrastructure and urban ecosystem services. Ambio **43**(4), 445–453 (2014)

Andersson, E., Tengö, M., McPhearson, T., Kremer, P.: Cultural ecosystem services as a gateway for improving urban sustainability. Ecosyst. Serv. **12**, 165–168 (2015)

Arni, A.G., Khairil, W.A.: Promoting collaboration between local community and park management towards sustainable outdoor recreation. Procedia Soc. Behav. Sci. **91**, 57–65 (2013)

Ashworth, G., Graham, B., Tunbridge, J.: Pluralising Pasts: Heritage, Identity and Place in Multicultural Societies. Pluto Press, London (2007)

Ayala-Azcárraga, C., Diaz, D., Zambrano, L.: Characteristics of urban parks and their relation to user well-being. Landsc. Urban Plan. **189**, 27–35 (2019)

BenDor, T.K., Spurlock, D., Woodruff, S.C., Olander, L.: A research agenda for ecosystem services in American environmental and land use planning. Cities **60**(part A), 260–271 (2017)

Breuste, J., Qureshi, S., Li, J.: Scaling down the ecosystem services at local level for urban parks of three megacities. Hercynia-Ökologie und Umwelt in Mitteleuropa **46**(1), 1–20 (2013)

Burgess, J., Harrison, C.M., Limb, M.: People, parks and the urban green: a study of popular meanings and values for open spaces in the city. Urban Stud. **25**(6), 455–473 (1988)

Central Park for Culture and Recreation Voronezh (2021). https://centralniy-parkvrn.ru/

Coutts, C., Horner, M., Chapin, T.: Using GIS to model the effects of green space accessibility on mortality in Florida. Geocarto Int. **25**, 471–484 (2010)

Federal State Statistics Service. Russian Regions: Major Socio-Economic indicator for Cities (2021). https://rosstat.gov.ru/folder/210/document/13206

Guerrero, P., Møller, M.S., Olafsson, A.S., Snizek, B.: Revealing cultural ecosystem services through instagram images: the potential of social media volunteered geographic information for urban green infrastructure planning and governance. Urban Plan. **1**(2), 1–17 (2016)

Guo, S., et al.: Analysis of factors affecting urban park service area in Beijing: perspectives from multi-source geographic data. Landsc. Urban Plan. **181**, 103–117 (2019)

Gerlach, J., Kinossian, N.: Cultural landscape of the Arctic: 'recycling' of soviet imagery in the Russian settlement of Barentsburg, Svalbard (Norway). Polar Geogr. **39**(1), 1–19 (2016)

Golubchikov, O.: The urbanization of transition: ideology and the urban experience. Eur. Geogr. Econ. **57**(4–5), 607–623 (2016)

Gómez-Baggethun, E., et al.: Urban ecosystem services. In: Elmqvist, T., et al. (eds.) Urbanization, Biodiversity and Ecosystem Services: Challenges and Opportunities, pp. 175–251. Springer, Dordrecht (2013). https://doi.org/10.1007/978-94-007-7088-1_11

Goodchild, M.F.: Citizens as sensors: the world of volunteered geography. GeoJournal **69**(4), 211–221 (2007)

Google Maps Platform.: Places. Google Maps Platform (2021). https://cloud.google.com/maps-platform/places

Historical Materials Website. http://istmat.info/node/21343, Accessed 21 Sept 2021

Instagram.: About us. Instagram (2021). https://www.instagram.com/about/us

Jorgensen, A., Anthopoulou, A.: Enjoyment and fear in urban woodlands – does age make a difference? Urban Forest. Urban Green. **6**(4), 267–278 (2007)

Kabisch, N., Qureshi, S., Haase, D.: Human-environment interactions in urban green spaces: a systematic review of contemporary issues and prospects for future research. Environ. Impact Assess. Rev. **50**, 25–34 (2015)

Kim, D., Jin, J.: Does happiness data say urban parks are worth it? Landsc. Urban Plan. **178**, 1–11 (2018)

Langemeyer, J., Connolly, J.J.: Weaving notions of justice into urban ecosystem services research and practice. Environ. Sci. Policy **109**, 1–14 (2020)

MacKay, K.J., Couldwell, C.M.: Using visitor-employed photography to investigate destination image. J. Travel Res. **42**(4), 390–396 (2004)

Meerovich, M.: Urban planning policy in USSR 1917–1929: from city-garden to departmental workers' village. [Gradostroitelnaia politika v SSSR 1917–1929: ot goroda-sada k vedomsvennomu rabochemu poselku]. New Literature Review, Moscow (2018)

Millennium Ecosystem Assessment.: Ecosystems and Human Well-being: Biodiversity Synthesis. World Resources Institute, Washington, DC (2005)

Obe, R.O., Hsu, L.S.: PostGIS in action. Manning Publications Co (2015)

Olsson, K.: Citizen input in urban heritage management and planning: a quantitative approach to citizen participation. Town Plan. Rev. **79**(4), 373–394 (2008)

Martínez Pastur, G., Peri, P.L., Lencinas, M.V., García-Llorente, M., Martín-López, B.: Spatial patterns of cultural ecosystem services provision in Southern Patagonia. Landscape Ecol. **31**(2), 383–399 (2015). https://doi.org/10.1007/s10980-015-0254-9

Pervushina, E.: Leningrad utopia. Avangard in architecture of the Nothern capital. [Leningradskaya utopiia. Avangard v architekture Severnoi stolitsy]. Tsentrpoligraph, Moscow (2012)

Schaich, H., Bieling, C., Plieninger, T.: Linking ecosystem services with cultural landscape research. Gaia-Ecol. Perspect. Sci. Soc. **19**(4), 269–277 (2010)

Specially Protected Natural Areas, Russia (2021). http://oopt.aari.ru/oopt

Strava.: Strava heatmap. Strava (2021). https://www.strava.com/heatmap#7.00/-120.90000/38.36000/hot/all

Tengberg, A., Susanne Fredholm, S., Eliasson, I., Knez, I., Saltzman, K., Wetterberg, O.: Cultural ecosystem services provided by landscapes: assessment of heritage values and identity. Ecosyst. Serv. **2**, 14–26 (2012)

Tahroodi, F., Ujang, N.: Engaging in social interaction: relationships between the accessibility of path structure and intensity of passive social interaction in urban parks. Archnet-IJAR Int. J. Arch. Res. (2021)

TEEB. The Economics of Ecosystems and Biodiversity for Local and Regional Policy Makers (2010). www.teebweb.org

Voronezh Central Park Official Website (2021). https://centralniy-parkvrn.ru/park/history/

Xie, J., Luo, S., Furuya, K., Sun, D.L.: Urban parks as green buffers during the COVID-19 pandemic. Sustainability **12**, 6751–6768 (2020)

Citizens' Involvement in Participatory Budgeting on Municipal Level: The Case of Yuzhno-Primorskiy Municipality of St. Petersburg (Russia)

Anastasia A. Golubeva ⓘ, Daria A. Bakalets ⓘ, and Evgenii V. Gilenko$^{(\boxtimes)}$ ⓘ

St. Petersburg State University, 3 Volkhovskiy Per., St. Petersburg 199004, Russia
e.gilenko@gsom.spbu.ru

Abstract. This study focuses on the factors influencing the intention of citizens to be involved in participatory budgeting (PB) on the municipal level via different electronic communication channels. Having classified such factors based on a literature review, we construct a comprehensive model of citizens' participation in electronic PB (e-PB) which comprises the following three blocks of factors: (1) citizens' attitude towards electronic communication with public authorities; (2) citizens' social capital (as related to their municipality); (3) citizens' motivation to participate in e-PB. To empirically verify interconnections and influence of different factors on citizens' involvement in e-PB, we conducted a survey. To this end, we developed a questionnaire to poll the inhabitants of the Yuzhno-Primorskiy municipality of St. Petersburg. Using the collected information on 259 respondents, the developed model was estimated using the partial least squares structural equation modeling approach (PLS-SEM). We demonstrate that citizens' motivation has the highest, statistically significant influence on the intention of people to be involved in PB. The found mediation effects allowed to confirm the influence of social capital and attitude towards electronic communication on citizens' motivation to participate in e-PB. Based on the obtained results, we provide relevant recommendations for the administration of the Yuzhno-Primorskiy municipality, which are expected to help the authorities more actively involve the citizens of the municipality in participatory budgeting.

Keywords: Participatory budgeting · Electronic communication · Local government · Partial least squares · Structural equation modeling

1 Introduction

Involvement of citizens in the budgetary process is a worldwide trend that reflects the transparency and openness of the information on public budgets, the increasing number of public discussions of budgets on different levels, as well as the active introduction of innovative management approaches aimed at developing both greater involvement

A. V. Chugunov et al. (Eds.): EGOSE 2021, CCIS 1529, pp. 201–215, 2022.
https://doi.org/10.1007/978-3-031-04238-6_16

of citizens in solving the local (municipal) issues and their greater trust in the authorities by providing the citizens with the opportunity of direct participation in public budget allocation – the participatory budgeting (hereafter, PB).

In the literature, there is no single, generally accepted definition of PB. Broadly speaking, PB is a form of public participation in state and municipal management. The principal criteria for considering a public participation to be PB are the following: (1) citizens setting priorities in public budget allocation; (2) local authorities participating in the process; (3) implementation on a constant basis; (4) regular public discussions within specially organized meetings, commissions, web-platforms; (5) public reporting events.

The global experience of PB development has clearly been showing a wide range of positive effects and outcomes of PB implementation. Among them are: higher efficiency of public finance use; overall increase of the quality of public administration; higher trust in authorities; better formation of community's social capital; positive changes in the electoral behavior of citizens, in particular, higher voting rate.

Since 2007, PB has been actively developing in Russia. While first PB projects were initiated within various international programs, nowadays, PB procedures are being readily incorporated in government programs of different Russian regions. PB has become a key point in the main document of national strategical planning – the "The main activities of the Government of the Russian Federation for the period up to 2024" – as one of the principal ways for implementing mechanisms of citizens' participation in socioeconomic development of Russian territories. This document explicitly states the need for Russian citizens to participate in resolving local (municipal) issues by using the practices of PB. For instance, it is expected that, by 2024, the number of Russian regions to implement PB practices in their development programs will be 62 [1]. In 2019, the principal directions of PB development were included by the Russian government in the "Concept of efficiency of budget expenditures in 2019–2024" document.

Over the past few years, the rate of implementation of PB practices on the local (municipal) level has increased substantially. In particular, there has been much more PB initiatives that imply initiation and financing of projects proposed by citizens exclusively at the expense of local budgets [1]. According to the Russian Ministry of Finance, in 2018, there were 91 practices implemented on the local level, while in 2019 this number rose to 147.

Municipal PB practices are characterized by significant independence and a variety of applied methodologies, in contrast to conservative regional PB programs. Municipalities are readily experimenting with various PB participation procedures, while actively introducing the online format (for example, in the procedures for proposing initiatives, discussing projects and voting on them); implementing new public forms of participation; providing multi-channel participation opportunities [1].

On January 1, 2021, Federal Law No. 236-FZ "On Amendments to the Federal Law «On General Principles of Organization of Local Self-Government in the Russian Federation»" came into force, creating a legal basis for application of PB on the municipal level. This Federal Law is aimed at implementing the List of Instruction of the President of the Russian Federation No. 354 (dated March 1, 2020) on increasing the share of distribution of local budgets with the participation of the population to 5% over the forthcoming three years. Thus, in connection with the declared implementation of PB practices, Russian local government entities (hereinafter, LGEs) have been facing the question of the prospects and strategies for involving citizens in the budgetary process.

But, despite of a wide range of benefits for citizens, many PB projects suffer from low citizens' involvement, thus questioning the very functioning of such projects. There is a whole bunch of reasons – both internal (related to the attitude of citizens) and external (concerning the organization of a PB process) – capable of lowering citizens' motivation to participate. For example, citizens' low awareness of the PB process is one of such reasons being an obstacle for a wide implementation of PB. Surveys of citizens conducted in various countries demonstrate that people wanted to be involved in PB – they just were not aware of such option [2]. Other obstacles are: accessibility issues; complexity of the PB process; lack of interest; under-development of communication channels with population; low trust in authorities; and some other [3].

With citizens' show-up rate at municipal elections in St. Petersburg (Russia) remaining very low – for example, according to the data on the elections of deputies of the Municipal Council of the sixth convocation of the Yuzhno-Primorskiy municipality on September 8, 2019, the show-up rate was only 19.8%, – the problem of citizens' motivation for participation is the key for implementation of PB projects on the local level, forming a strong topicality of studying it further.

The purpose of the current research is to reveal the factors influencing the intention of citizens to take part in PB projects and to provide relevant recommendations for LGEs on how to appropriately increase citizens' involvement in PB.

To this end, we studied the opinions of citizens of the Yuzhno-Primorskiy municipality of St. Petersburg (Russia). Taking into account the freedom that the municipality has in selecting the ways of PB implementation, we decided to focus on analyzing the application of electronic means of PB implementation (e.g., web-portals). Thus, in this study we consider what is called electronic participatory budgeting (hereafter, e-PB), in which the corresponding process is organized in the online format (using electronic communication channels).

The rest of the paper is organized as follows. Section 2 illustrates the theoretical model and the research methodology for the current study, while Sect. 3 gives the obtained empirical results and discussion. In Sect. 4, based on the obtained calculation results, the relevant recommendations are provided. Section 5 concludes.

2 Research Methodology

In this section, we provide details on construction of the theoretical framework underlying the current research and development of the corresponding research hypotheses (Stage 1), as well as on the sample collection process (Stage 2).

2.1 Development of the Theoretical Framework and Research Hypotheses (Stage 1)

Literature Review

At the first stage of our analysis, based on an extended literature review, we identified and grouped the important factors of citizens' participation in PB. Actually, there is a number of publications concerning these questions and proposing different theories and models in various fields – economics, political science, sociology, and some other (see Table 1).

Model of Factors of Citizens' Participation in PB

Taking into account the theoretical approaches used in the literature, as well as their limitations, in this research we propose a conceptual theoretical model of citizens' participation in PB via electronic channels (see Fig. 1). The *dependent* variable in the model is the intention of a citizens to be involved in e-PB (hereafter, *Intention*). The *independent* variables are split into *three* principal blocks: *social capital in the local community (municipality)* (hereafter, *Social capital*), *motivation to participate in e-PB* (hereafter, *Motivation*), and *attitude towards e-communication* with authorities and LGEs (hereafter, *Attitude*). The rest are control variables.

The "Social Capital" Block

The three key aspects of social capital that are widely discussed in the literature [5, 8] are: trust, social networks and civic norms. These three constitute the basis for measuring *Social capital* (latent variable) in our model. The corresponding manifest variables are: trust in local government, social trust in the local community, identification with the local community and the territory of inhabitance, interaction in the local community, commitment to the local community, and collective efficacy.

The "Motivation" Block

This block of factors is given as a pyramid which reflects different levels of citizens' motivation to participate in PB. This hierarchical structure allows to allocate the factors identified in the literature – from the basic awareness up to the high-level motivators (such as civic duty, desire to influence local government's decisions, and common good orientation).

The "Attitude" Block

This group of factors comprises the following: attitude, effort expectancy, performance expectancy, social influence, facilitating conditions (such as user-friendliness of the graphical user interface), perceived risk.

Control Variables

The model includes such control variables (attributes of the respondent) as gender, age, children, marital status, education level, income level, economic activity, NGO membership, interest in politics, election participation, attitude towards costs of participation in civil activities.

Table 1. Factors of citizens' participation in PB.

Group of factors	Factors	Sources
Attitude towards the authorities	• Support of current political system (state and local level) • Trust in government; trust in public authorities taking part in PB • Satisfaction with budgetary policy/democracy • External political efficacy • Probability of PB-initiatives (projects) realization	[4–6]
Civic attitudes	• Norm for participation (citizens should have a possibility to take part in important local decisions), including: - Civic duty - Attitude towards participation – to be more politically active in order to control and influence decisions of those governing	[5, 7, 8]
Individual motivators	• Internal political efficacy • Personal concern, private needs/benefits • Information and control, access to government decision-making • Reputation, social status • Altruism	[5, 8, 9]
Social factors	• Social capital • Social influence • Sense of community • Trust in people in community • Sense of place • Desire to help their communities, empathy to the needs of others	[4, 7–9],
Organization of participation process in PB	• Knowledge, awareness of the opportunity to participate in PB • Accessibility • Costs of participation (cognitive costs, time and money expenditures, e.g., transport costs)	[2, 5]
Attitude towards electronic communication with public authorities	• Performance expectancy • Effort expectancy • Attitude towards e-participation • Social influence • Facilitating conditions, internet access, computer literacy • Perceived risk, confidentiality of personal information	[2, 6, 9, 10]

(*continued*)

Table 1. (*continued*)

Group of factors	Factors	Sources
Control variables (incl. socio-demographic characteristic)	• Gender, age, income, social class, education, years of living in the municipality, political participation (incl. voter participation), interest in politics, civic engagement, NGO membership	[4, 6–10]

2.2 Research Hypotheses

The constructed theoretical framework (see Fig. 1) allowed to formulate the following research hypotheses.

RH1. The greater the citizen's motivation to participate in e-PB, the greater their intention to participate in e-PB. It is anticipated that the factors of motivation towards participation in PB together (as a set of motivators in the pyramid in Fig. 1) will positively influence the citizen's intention to engage in e-PB. These factors are found in the literature as potentially influential to stimulate citizens to take part in PB.

RH2. The citizen's social capital in the local community has a positive influence on the citizen's intention to participate in e-PB. Based on previous studies, it can be assumed that citizens with higher level of social capital in the local community, who have significant social recourses in there (e.g., they communicate with other residents regularly) and already participate in the community's events, etc., are characterized by a greater intention to participate in e-PB.

RH3. The citizen's social capital in the local community has a positive influence on the citizen's motivation to participate in e-PB. Residents with higher level of social capital in their community are most likely to have greater incentives to participate in e-PB due to their increased sense of responsibility for the community, higher level of their commitment to their community, deeper trust in effectiveness of collective actions, etc., which, in turn, strengthens their motivation to engage in PB.

RH4. The citizen's social capital in the local community has a positive influence on the citizen's attitude towards electronic communication with public authorities. Since one of the items measuring attitude towards e-communication with public authorities is the citizen's attitude towards organization of PB through e-channels, and social capital encompasses citizens' trust in the local government, the following can be assumed: citizens with a greater level of social capital in the local community most probably will trust these e-channels and, as a consequence, will have a more positive attitude towards the electronic format of participation in PB.

RH5. The citizen's attitude towards electronic communication with public authorities has a positive influence on the citizen's intention to participate in e-PB. The citizen may be so keen on the idea to participate in e-PB (as well as, generally, to use electronic communication with public authorities), that they will readily be involved in e-PB.

RH6. The citizen's attitude towards electronic communication with public authorities has a positive influence on the citizen's motivation to participate in e-PB. Organization of the PB process via electronic communication channels can spur the citizen's motivation to be involved in PB because of the ease of use, reduction of transaction costs, etc. If citizens are fascinated by the electronic format of participation, they are likely to be more stimulated to engage in the e-PB practice.

RH7. Facilitating conditions have a positive influence on the citizen's intention to participate in e-PB. As showed in previous research on e-PB, the citizen's confidence in their skills necessary to use online participation channels, easy access to such electronic devices as smartphones and computers, as well as other conditions, will increase their intention to participate in e-PB.

RH8. Facilitating conditions have a positive influence on the citizen's motivation to participate in e-PB. Facilitating conditions (as a set of resources needed to effectively use a certain technology) can boost the citizen's motivation: without the required skills and infrastructure, there is no possibility to achieve the desired outcomes of participation in e-PB.

2.3   Sample Collection and Description (Stage 2)

At this stage of the research, based on the constructed theoretical framework, we developed our own questionnaire which consisted of 5 principal parts and included questions directly related to both the principal blocks of the theoretical model, and socio-demographic characteristics of the respondent. It total, there were more than 50 questions in the questionnaire.

Experiment Design
The survey was conducted in spring 2021. Due to the COVID-19 situation, the survey was run *online* via the popular Russian social network "VKontakte" (vk.com). The coverage was 9 different VK-groups related to the Yuzhno-Primorskiy municipality.

In total, we collected 278 responses[1]. After running an exploratory data analysis (which included removing outliers and observations with missing values from the sample), the final sample size was 259. It should be noted that, currently, sample size of more than 250 observations is considered tolerable to obtain reliable results of estimation, in particular, by PLS-SEM (see [11]).

Sample Description
Below, we provide the description of the sample as related to both the socio-demographic traits of the respondents, and their opinions on the subject matter.

Socio-demographic Characteristics of the Respondents
The information on the corresponding characteristics is given in Table 2. To give it in brief, in the sample, 78% are female respondents; the major age groups are two – ranged 23–35 years (38.2%) and 36–45 years (35.1%). More than three quarters (76.4%) of the respondents have a higher education, and the total majority of them living with a partner (87.3%) and have at least one child (72.2%). More than two thirds of the people (69.5%)

---

[1] As of January 1, 2021, the official population size of the Yuzhno-Primorskiy municipality was 91,319 people. With the chosen 5% margin of error and 90% confidence level, the corresponding representative sample size is 272.

are currently employed and more than half of the respondents estimate their level of income as middle (55.2%).

Other Characteristics of the Respondents

We now switch to some descriptive statistics on the key questions of citizens' motivation and participation in the municipality's activities and PB. To begin with, 30.9% of the respondents took part in the last municipal council elections – which, majorly, is in line with the official rate (19.8%) of voting participation in the Yuzhno-Primorskiy municipality.

Table 2. Socio-demographic characteristics of the respondents.

Characteristic	Group	%
Age (years)	16–22	4.6
	23–35	38.2
	36–45	35.1
	46–59	16.6
	>60	5.4
Gender	Male	22
	Female	78
Education	Secondary school	0.8
	High school	5.8
	Vocational education	12.7
	Incomplete higher education	4.2
	Higher education	76.4
Occupation	Studying (college, university)	4.2
	Unemployed	6.6
	Employed	69.5
	Housekeeper	12.7
	Pensioner/retired	6.9
Income	Very low income	2.3
	Low income	11.6
	Middle level of income	55.2
	High income	28.6
	Very high income	2.3
Household	Lives alone	12.7
	Lives with a partner	87.3
Children	Has children	72.2
	No children	27.8

Regarding public attitudes to local government, approximately 45% of the respondents didn't trust LGEs, while 41% of them had a neutral position. These results practically coincide with the level of the respondents' satisfaction with the quality of performance of the LGEs. Almost the same figures were obtained in terms of the citizens' satisfaction with the informational transparency of public entities: roughly a half (45%) of the people questioned said that local public authorities didn't provide enough information about their activities to the society, and, moreover, more than a half of them (55.2%) emphasized that the authorities didn't take into account the opinions of the local community.

Looking at the respondents' participation in local activities (their commitment to community), only 12.3% of the people specified that they actively took part in community events, as opposed to 45.9% of those who said they didn't participate at all. Nevertheless, in terms of the collective efficacy, just under three-quarters (70%) of the respondents were willing to participate in collective actions on the municipality's territory development, and around 80% of them believed that participation of the community in the local public decision-making was really necessarily.

Considering the electronic format of participation in PB, it is noteworthy that over three quarters of the respondents (79.2%) regularly used e-channels to communicate with different public authorities (for instance, via the St. Petersburg portal of public services or the 'Our St. Petersburg' e-participation platform, and some other). This number is close to the figure on the residents' responses on their preferences of the electronic communication channels over the traditional ones – 72.6% of the surveyed people said they preferred electronic channels over the traditional ones when dealing with a specific problem (with 51% of them always used e-communication and 21.6% – almost in each case). Moreover, the idea of online PB participation (via a mobile app and/or a web-platform) was supported by over three-quarters (75.7%) of the citizens. In general, the given statistics highlight the fact that the citizens are ready for participation by the electronic means.

The obtained results on the residents' willingness to participate in PB were quite optimistic: 78% of the surveyed people intended to engage in this practice, and, beyond that, 65.6% of respondents expressed their readiness to initiate proposals of projects to be implemented via PB (with 80% of them feeling that they were ready to take part in voting on PB-projects). Overall, it can be concluded that the PB practice has a strong potential to be demanded by the inhabitants of the municipality. Meanwhile, a comparatively small gap between the figures on the two key forms of participation in PB – project's initiation and voting – can be a sign that citizens are interested to be actively involved in the whole PB process.

3   Results and Discussion

Based on the collected sample, we empirically estimated the developed theoretical model using the partial least squares structural equation modeling (PLS-SEM). This technique is a method of structural equation modeling which allows estimating complex cause-effect relationship models with latent variables. It is now widely applied in many social science disciplines. Application of PLS-SEM in the modern studies is very appealing as it allows to estimate complex models with many constructs, indicator variables and structural paths without imposing distributional assumptions on the data [12]. In this study, we used the semPLS R-package [13] to obtain the estimates for the coefficients of our model.

3.1 Estimation Results

The results of model estimation are given in Fig. 1. According to them, the model explains 52% of the variance of *Attitude*; 53% of the variance of *Motivation*; 55% of the variance of *Intention*. Also, in Fig. 1, only the values of coefficients that are statistically significant at least at the 10% level are provided. Correspondingly, positive and statistically significant influences are given in red; positive, but not significant – in yellow; negative and insignificant – in blue.

3.2 Results of the Research Hypotheses Testing

The obtained results allow to make conclusions on the formulated research hypotheses.

RH1 (*The greater the citizen's motivation to participate in e-PB, the greater their intention to participate in e-PB*) found its support. Moreover, it is *Motivation* that has the highest impact on *Intention*. The corresponding path coefficient is +0.62, which also reflects the highest impact of motivation on intention. The other latent variables also influence the intention to participate in e-PB, but this influence is indirect (via motivation).

RH2 (*The citizen's social capital in the local community has a positive influence on the citizen's intention to participate in e-PB*) is not supported by the calculations, while RH3 (*The citizen's social capital in the local community has a positive influence on the citizen's motivation to participate in e-PB*) found an empirical support. The corresponding path coefficient for RH3 is positive and statistically significant (+0.47), while the coefficient for RH2 turned out to be negative and insignificant. These findings reflect an important full mediation effect – the independent variable (*Social capital*) significantly influences the mediator (*Motivation*) which, in turn, has a significant impact on the dependent variable (*Intention*). This finding allows to conclude that those citizens who have higher *Motivation* and, as a result, higher *Intention*, are also characterized by a higher level of *Social capital*.

The influence of *Social capital* on *Attitude*, although positive, appeared to be statistically insignificant, so RH4 (*The citizen's social capital in the local community has a positive influence on the citizen's attitude towards electronic communication with public authorities*) is rejected.

Speaking about RH6 (*The citizen's attitude towards electronic communication with public authorities has a positive influence on the citizen's motivation to participate in e-PB*), we can see that the corresponding coefficient is positive and statistically significant (+0.35), while the coefficient related to RH5 (*The citizen's attitude towards electronic communication with public authorities has a positive influence on the citizen's intention to participate in e-PB*) almost twice as smaller in its size (+0.16), although still positive and statistically significant. This speaks in favor of the presence of a partial mediation effect of *Motivation* on the connection between *Attitude* and *Intention*.

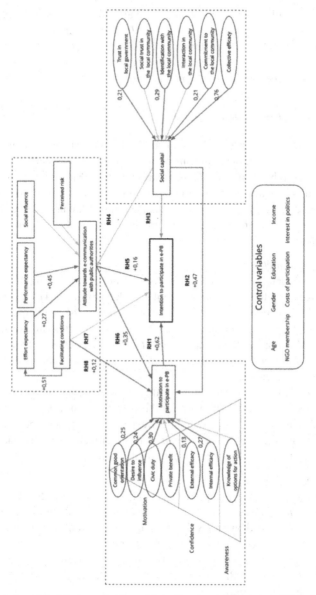

Fig. 1. Estimated model of factors of citizens' intention to participate in e-PB (only values of the coefficients that are statistically significant at least at the 10% level are given in the figure).

Speaking about *Facilitating conditions* – RH7 (*Facilitating conditions have a positive influence on the citizen's intention to participate in e-PB*) and RH8 (*Facilitating conditions have a positive influence on the citizen's motivation to participate in e-PB*) – we can say that only RH8 is supported by the calculations (RH7 is rejected). This reflects the presence of yet another full mediation effect between *Facilitating conditions* and *Intention*, where, again, the mediator is the *Motivation* variable.

These results already allow to make an important conclusion that the *Motivation* block is the key hub in our theoretical framework. This finding will be used later when discussing the developed policy recommendations.

3.3 Components of the Latent Variables

The results of previous studies show that usually the biggest category of citizens who actively use different electronic platforms of public participation, particularly in PB, are those who are driven by their personal (egoistic) interests [8].

But our results revealed another, more powerful type of citizens' motivation. In this subsection, we describe the components of the estimated latent variables as related to the corresponding blocks in our theoretical model (see Fig. 1) – *Motivation*, *Attitude*, and *Social capital*.

The "Motivation" Block
The *Motivation* is determined, to the greatest extent, by such components as[2]: civic duty (0.30), desire to influence local government's decisions, (0.24), and common good orientation (0.25), meaning the intention to participate in the municipality's development. At the same time, such component as "Private benefit" virtually has no influence on *Motivation*. This implies that, when extending PB practices in this municipality, the authorities should appeal to the desire of people to create a common good – not just to meet their personal interests.

This is especially true because the significant value of the weight of the external efficacy (0.13) means that it is important for the citizens to know that their participation will matter and bring to the desired outcome. Besides, the weight of the internal efficacy (0.27, second biggest in this block) signals that the citizens feel a special need to be competent (have enough knowledge) to participate in this kind of activities.

The "Social Capital" Block
Analysis of influence of the components in this block showed that *Social trust* and *Interaction in the local community* do not significantly contribute to the *Social capital* latent variable (as estimated on the level of an individual citizen). This result may indicate that in the local community the citizens just do not actively interact in person. For instance, after coming home from work (let us recall that 69.5% of the respondents are employed), the citizen will most likely interact with neighbors in social networks (online), rather than in person.

At the same time, collective efficacy (0.76), identification (0.29) with the local community and the territory of inhabitance and commitment (0.21) to the local community, and trust in local government (0.21) are the most influential in forming the *Social capital* latent variable. As it was discussed above, the influence of social capital of the citizens on their intention to participate in e-PB is mediated by *Motivation*.

So, the key component in forming *Social capital* is *Collective efficacy*. This means that those citizens who consider important and most efficient the collective way of

---

[2] The corresponding component weights are given in parentheses.

participation, overall, they are more ready to take collective actions to achieve a common goal and, as a result, are more motivated to be involved in PB.

The next important component here is *Identification with the local community and the territory of inhabitance*. The higher is the level of such identification, the higher the level of *Social capital* will be, thus, increasing *Motivation*.

The next in line is *Commitment to the local community*. Those citizens who have higher level of social capital and more actively participate in local public events, tend to have more incentives to be involved in PB.

Finally, as to the *Trust in local government* component, it also, along with other components, ultimately positively influences *Motivation*. It is worth noting that, as well-known, trust in authorities increases, in particular, when the people are well informed about their activities – the corresponding information is available and transparent.

The "Attitude" Block

In this block, which is about the attitude of citizens towards electronic communication with the authorities (via, for example, web-portals for public services and other channels of online participation), we also identified certain important connections. For the correspondent latent variable of crucial importance are *Performance expectancy* (0.45) and *Effort expectancy* (0.27).

The highest weight of *Performance expectancy* implies that if the citizens perceive the electronic communication channels as those that will help in achieving the desired results of communication, then using of the corresponding communication system will be of value to the citizens and, ultimately, these people will be more loyal to participation in e-PB via such channels. Moreover, if the citizens also consider using the electronic communication channels easy (*Effort expectancy*), this fact will also encourage people to have better attitude to the electronic communication.

4 Recommendations

The conducted analysis allows to conclude that in order to increase involvement of people in e-PB, the authorities of the Yuzhno-Primorskiy municipality should work in two directions simultaneously. First, the benefits that the citizens get by participating in e-PB should be promoted and explained on a regular basis. Second, the transaction costs of being involved in e-PB should be minimized.

A good solution here would be development of a *specialized mobile application* for citizens' participation in e-PB. This recommendation is supported by the fact that, as mentioned above, *Performance expectancy* is one of the most significant component in the *Attitude* block, thus, the electronic ways of communication and interaction with citizens should be more effective and efficient from this perspective (as compared to the offline ways).

To elaborate on this, we recommend to take into account that in such mobile application the presence of the following attributes should be organized:

- *a friendly graphical user interface* (GUI) – to create the most comfortable environment for the user's work with the application;

- *means for communication* (common chats) between citizens can contribute to the full implementation of the PB practice, which involves not only organizing voting opportunities, but also creating a platform for citizens to communicate with each other and exchange opinions;
- *means for co-working* of citizens to promote cooperation within local communities, enhancing collective efficacy;
- *statistical information* on citizens' participation in PB (available to all users) to highlight the collective efforts and make them more transparent;
- *PB-project presentations and push notifications* can significantly improve the perceived effort expectancy of citizens;
- *means for feedback provision* to the local authorities can have a significant impact on a whole range of factors influencing the motivation of citizens to participate in PB;
- *a crowdfunding mechanism* since co-financing of PB projects by the citizens is allowed (as one of the mechanisms for co-participation of citizens in the PB practices).

The presence of the above-specified attributes in the mobile application (to allow for provision of reports on the work progress on the projects selected by citizens, on the results of completed projects, on statistics of PB participation) can not only increase the trust in the authorities, but also stimulate other significant motivational factors.

Of course, the use of electronic means of communication will depend on the degree to which the citizen is convinced that he or she is a confident user of these means. In this regard, local authorities must work on increasing social inclusiveness of citizens in order to avoid the digital divide.

From this perspective, it is difficult to imagine an increase in the involvement of citizens in PB practices without ensuring *multichannel access* to such activities, for example, by installing electronic terminals in socially accessible places.

5 Conclusion

The practice of participatory budgeting (PB) is ultimately aimed at forming the civil initiative, strengthening local communities, and creating an effective environment for collaboration of citizens and local authorities. But, of course, this approach cannot be forcedly introduced and implemented "from the top" (by the government) – for the positive outcomes to occur, the citizens themselves should be ready.

The results of empirical validation of the proposed theoretical framework clearly demonstrated that the factors of citizens' e-PB involvement, which are related to the *Motivation* block, have the highest power in explaining citizens' intention to participate in e-PB. As ranked by their relative weights, these factors are: civic duty, internal efficacy, common good orientation, desire to influence, and external efficacy.

Achieving of the desired results of PB via more active citizens' participation is impossible without a thoughtful organization of all of the steps in this practice, starting from creating and promoting of PB projects and ending with obtaining the relevant feedback on the results of their implementation. And all these steps should be based on the principal of minimization of citizens' costs with simultaneous widening of the range of their benefits. The results obtained in this research (even taking into account its certain limitations) allow to shed light on the mechanisms of creation of citizens' motivation to participate in PB.

Ultimately, successful implementation of e-PB will help increase trust in authorities, which, in turn, will help wider realization of (electronic) public services [14], more actively propelling the national economy from different crisis situations [15].

References

1. Romanov, S., et al.: The report on the best practices of participatory budgeting development in the regions of the Russian Federation and municipalities. The Ministry of Finance of the Russian Federation, Moscow (2020)
2. Zepic, R., Dapp, M., Krcmar, H.: Participatory budgeting without participants: identifying barriers on accessibility and usage of German participatory budgeting. In: Conference for E-Democracy and Open Government (CeDEM), Krems, pp. 26–35 (2017)
3. Golubeva, A.A., Gilenko, E.V.: Communication channels in public policy development and implementation: online or offline? (the case of separate waste collection in St. Petersburg). In: Chugunov, A., Khodachek, I., Misnikov, Y., Trutnev, D. (eds.) EGOSE 2020. CCIS, vol. 1349, pp. 172–183. Springer, Cham (2020). https://doi.org/10.1007/978-3-030-67238-6_12
4. Švaljek, S., Rašić Bakarić, I., Sumpor, M.: Citizens and the city: the case for participatory budgeting in the City of Zagreb. Public Sect. Econ. **43**(1), 21–48 (2019)
5. Schneider, S.H.: Bürgerhaushalte in Deutschland. Individuelle und kontextuelle Einflussfaktoren der Beteiligung. Politische Vierteljahresschrift. **60**(4), 827-828 (2018). https://doi.org/10.1007/s11615-019-00192-8
6. Choi, J.-C., Song, C.: Factors explaining why some citizens engage in e-participation, while others do not. Gov. Inf. Q. **37**, 101524 (2020)
7. Porten-Cheé, P., Frieß, D.: What do participants take away from local eparticipation?: Analyzing the success of local eParticipation initiatives from a democratic citizens' perspective. Anal. Kritik **40**(1), 1–30 (2018)
8. Montambeault, F.: Participatory citizenship in the making? The multiple citizenship trajectories of participatory budgeting participants in Brazil. J. Civ. Soc. **12**(3), 282–298 (2016)
9. Naranjo-Zolotov, M., et al.: Examining social capital and individual motivators to explain the adoption of online citizen participation. Future Gener. Comput. Syst. **92**, 302–311 (2019)
10. Naranjo-Zolotov, M., Oliveira, T., Casteleyn, S.: Citizens' intention to use and recommend e-participation: drawing upon UTAUT and citizen empowerment. Inf. Technol. People **32**(2), 364–386 (2019)
11. Rosseel, Y.: Small sample solutions for structural equation modeling. In: van de Schoot, R., Milica, M. (eds.) Small Sample Size Solutions: A Guide for Applied Researchers and Practitioners. Routledge, Taylor & Francis Group, London/New York (2020)
12. Hair, J.F., Risher, J.J., Sarstedt, M., Ringle, C.M.: When to use and how to report the results of PLS-SEM. Eur. Bus. Rev. **31**(1), 2–24 (2019). https://doi.org/10.1108/EBR-11-2018-0203
13. Monecke, A., Leisch, F.: semPLS: structural equation modeling using partial least squares. J. Stat. Softw. **48**(3), 1–32 (2012)
14. Golubeva, A.A., Gilenko, E.V.: Creating public value through public e-services development: the case of landscaping and public amenities in St. Petersburg. In: Chugunov, A., Misnikov, Y., Roshchin, E., Trutnev, D. (eds.) EGOSE 2018. CCIS, vol. 947, pp. 249–264. Springer, Cham (2019). https://doi.org/10.1007/978-3-030-13283-5_19
15. Gilenko, E.V.: The sudden transition to the free floating exchange rate regime in Russia in 2014. J. Rev. Global Econ. **6**, 181–192 (2017)

Where Security Meets Accessibility: Mobile Research Ecosystem

Radka Nacheva[(⊠)] [iD], Snezhana Sulova[iD], and Bonimir Penchev[iD]

University of Economics – Varna, Varna, Bulgaria
{r.nacheva,ssulova,b.penchev}@ue-varna.bg

Abstract. User-oriented approaches help teams develop digital products that will not only be functional, but will also help to enhance the emotional experience. The specifics of human beings, that are placed at the centre of the development, are determining the entire interaction flow with digital devices and software products. One of the topics that researchers' study in the field of human-computer interaction is accessibility. It is associated with the ability of a person to use barrier-free products or services. Accessibility, in turn, is also related to the user security such as attacks and vulnerabilities that often lead to a lack of access to digital devices. In this regard, the aim of our paper is to define a mobile research ecosystem for testing and evaluating secure and accessible mobile multi-device environments. The ecosystem should simultaneously implement the basic principles of accessibility and security of mobile applications. Thus defined aim determines the objectives of the paper, which are: to study the main problems of mobile applications' accessibility; to study mobile security frameworks; to test mobile accessibility and security. Design-thinking process flow is implemented in our approach. The accessibility and security of mobile operating systems Android and iOS are tested.

Keywords: Mobile accessibility · Mobile security · Research ecosystem · User experience

1 Introduction

The topic of cybersecurity is one of the leading in the last five years, along with others like artificial intelligence, machine learning, the Internet of Things, automation, automotive autonomy. In particular, privacy and confidential computing are enshrined in the Regulation (EU) 2016/679 General Data Protection Regulation (GDPR). Chapter 5 of the document regulates the terms of transfers of personal data to third countries or international organizations, including articles on: the general principle for transfers, transfers on the basis of an adequacy decision, transfers subject to appropriate safeguards, binding corporate rules, transfers or disclosures not authorized by union law, derogations for specific situations and international cooperation for the protection of personal data [1]. The document regulates the conditions under which personal data must be processed by the so-called data processor, ensuring the ongoing confidentiality, integrity, availability and resilience of processing systems and services, as well as the encryption of personal data [1].

© Springer Nature Switzerland AG 2022
A. V. Chugunov et al. (Eds.): EGOSE 2021, CCIS 1529, pp. 216–231, 2022.
https://doi.org/10.1007/978-3-031-04238-6_17

Despite the efforts of cybersecurity experts, malicious individuals discover security vulnerabilities in software products and take advantage of them when committing illegal acts. This is also proved by the statistical data. A McAfee report from the beginning of 2021 shows that the pandemic situation has had a negative impact on cyber security. In 2020, the most affected are scientific and educational institutions, public administrations and IT companies. The most common security issues were vulnerabilities, targeted attacks, malware and account hijacking [2]. According to McAfee data, publicly disclosed incidents surged 100% in Europe from Q3 to Q4 2020. Incidents in Asia increased by 84% and those in North America rose by 36% [2]. There are approximately 3.1 million external attacks on cloud accounts from more than 30 million users worldwide during Q4 of 2020 [2]. There has been a significant increase in attacks on all families of operating systems from Q3 to Q4 of 2020: PowerShell threats grew to 208%; MacOS malware increases by 420%; Linux malware increased to 6%.

Another company, Norton, also provides a complete picture of cybersecurity globally. According to statistics published by the company, for 2020 over 75% of cyberattacks are launched via email [3]. Last year, the FBI received 15,421 internet crime complaints from 60 countries around the world. The first half of 2021 saw a 102% increase in ransomware attacks compared to the same period in 2020 [3]. Norton also confirmed that the COVID-19 pandemic had a negative impact on cybersecurity, stating that the FBI had reported a 300% increase in reported cybercrimes [3]. Users report an increase in fraudulent emails, spam, and phishing attacks from their corporate email.

Mobile users are also affected by cyberattacks. According to the statistical portal Statista.com for the last quarter of 2020 the number of malicious installation packages was over 2,106 million, which is over one million compared to the first quarter of 2020 and over 600 thousand more than the first quarter of 2021 [4]. In comparison, many malicious installation packages reported in 2019 equal those reported in Q4 of 2020. iOS users are less affected by malware than those of Android [5]. It is reported that mobile malware worldwide in 2020 were AdWare (57,26%), RiskTool (21,34%), trojan (4,46%), backdoor (1,49%), etc. [6]. Kaspersky shares 2020 statistics according to which 87% of Android mobile phones are exposed to security risks [7]. According to the company, the most common types of malwares faced by Android users are banking malware, mobile ransomware, mobile spyware, MMS malware, mobile adware and SMS trojans. To them, for 2021 open WiFi, phishing attacks, spyware, poor password security can be added [8].

As can be seen from the cited sources, the pandemic situation has significantly affected the committed cybercrimes. A breach of the security of individual and corporate users is reported. On the other hand, the problems that these cyberattacks create for people with special needs must also be taken into account. This is mainly due to their inability to access or make full use of digital devices. The consequences of disrupted cybersecurity are also at odds with the policies and strategies for people with disabilities developed by global organizations such as United Nations and the World Health Organization (WHO), as well as the European Union.

The WHO said the pandemic has led to an urgent need for scale up disability services, including healthcare. According to the organization, people with disabilities are unable to use different services due to prohibitive costs and inadequate skills and knowledge of the people who offer these services [9]. The facts reported by WHO are worrying - the percentage of people with some kind of disability is growing. This is about 10% of the world's population, and the share of young people is even higher - 30% [10]. The United Nations has an even higher share - 15% of the world's population lives with some form of disability, with 80% of people living in developing countries where their care is extremely low [11]. WHO cites UNESCO as saying that 9% of children in low-income countries do not attend school [10]. The United Nations has set 7 targets of the Sustainable Development Goals entirely aimed at people with disabilities [11]. These focus on: no poverty (Goal 1), zero hunger (Goal 2), good health and well-being (Goal 3), quality education (Goal 4), gender equality (Goal 5), reduced inequalities (Goal 10), peace, justice and strong institutions. (Goal 16) [12]. The 2030 Agenda for Sustainable Development was adopted in 2015 by all members of the United Nations [12]. It is an act of partnership between nations around the world to share common goals and strategies to reduce inequalities between people, improve health and education, and spur economic growth. In this regard, technological progress should be helpful in achieving the United Nations Sustainable Development Goals. Researchers are working on problems related to the practical application of business intelligence in education [13], the impact of social media [14] and e-learning methods [15] in education, the methods and tools for processing big data [16], the Internet of Things [17], the programming and database issues of web and mobile applications' development [18–20], the human resource management practical aspects [21–23]. All these topics are part of the overall view of providing quality digital products through which to achieve end-user satisfaction with the services they use [24].

The presented facts give us a reason to direct the **aim of this paper** as defining a mobile research ecosystem for testing and evaluating secure and accessible mobile multi-device environments. The ecosystem should simultaneously implement the basic principles of accessibility and security of mobile applications.

Based on the goal we can formulate the following research questions:

- (RQ1) What are the standards and good practices for bettering the mobile accessibility and security?
- (RQ2) What tools can be used to test the accessibility and security of mobile applications?

To answer research questions, the paper should meet the following objectives:

- to study the main issues of mobile applications' accessibility;
- to study mobile security frameworks;
- to examine mobile accessibility and security.

2 Related Work

To answer the RQ1, we must explore the international standards about accessibility and security. In addition, researches related on these problems should be explored too. In order to find the intersection between the major topics of security and accessibility, it is necessary to look for the unifying link between them – human beings. The ways in which people use digital devices and machines are explored by the scientific field human-computer interaction. The efforts of specialists and scientists who work in that area are aimed mainly at minimizing the barriers between people's mental models in terms of fulfilling their goals and technological support of their tasks. Device access and information processing are essential for building multi-channel consistency within multi-device environments.

In the last two decades, the philosophy of user-centered design (UCD), also known as human-centered design (HCD), has emerged. According to ISO 13407: 1999 - now it is recognized by ISO 9241-210:2019(en), UCD is defined as an approach to developing interactive systems that focuses on creation of usable systems [25]. HCD is described as a multidisciplinary activity that includes human factors and ergonomics, techniques to increase efficiency and productivity, to improve human well-being, user satisfaction, accessibility and sustainability, the working conditions of people with a system and neutralize the possible adverse effects of its use on human health, safety and productivity [26]. Accessibility is one of the areas defined by the standard for expanding the digital inclusion of a wide range of people with specific needs, characteristics and capabilities to achieve the goals in a particular context of use [26].

The standard provides guidance for the UCD throughout the life cycle of developing computer-based interactive systems, which is divided into four parts: rationale, principles, planning and activities. Our interest is targeted to the setting of its principles and activities. The principles of user-oriented design are four:

– active participation of the users of the system and clear understanding of the tasks they should perform;
– appropriate distribution of functions between users and technology;
– re-use of design solutions;
– multidisciplinary design.

The UCD process is built by four activities (Fig. 1):

– Specifying the context of use: this includes getting to know the user, the environment of use, as well as the targeted tasks.
– Specifying the user and organizational requirements: it includes determining the criteria for the success of the usability of the product in relation to user tasks, such as how quickly a typical user must be able to complete a task with the product. This includes setting design guidelines and imposing various restrictions.
– Developing of product design solutions: taking into account the knowledge of human-computer interaction (e.g., visual design, interaction design, usability), a variety of design solutions are created.
– Evaluation of designs in accordance with the imposed requirements: the usability of the designs is evaluated according to user tasks.

On the other hand, HCD is closely related to the so-called "design thinking". It is considered as an iterative process in which user needs should be understood and, on this basis, problem solving could lead to innovation and competitive advantage [27, 28].

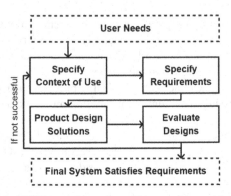

Fig. 1. UCD's activities adapted in accordance with [25].

The flow of the design-thinking framework is consisted of understanding, exploring, and materializing segments [27]. Within them five or six phases could be conducted. According to [28], these are: Empathize, Define, Ideate, Prototype, Test. [27] adds to them Implement stage. [27] states that the process starts with research about what users do, say, think, and feel. After that all observations are combined and problems are defined. These two stages are part of the understanding stage of the design-thinking framework flow. Next part of the flow – Explore, is formed by ideating and creating a prototype. Their task is to generate creative ideas and, on their basis, to build up tactile visual representations. The last part of the flow – Materialize, is related to collecting end user feedback and materializing user visions.

The most important factors that play significant role in building human-oriented technologies are: the audience, the context of use, the defined system requirements both by users and by the organization. Compliance with these criteria should lead to the creation of design solutions tailored to all levels' requirements.

Meeting the standards ensures quality development of UCD digital products. They can be related to any aspect of human-computer interaction, including accessibility. In terms of this paper's purpose, we are focusing on mobile accessibility standards.

Within the Web Accessibility Initiative (WAI) World Wide Web Consortium (W3C) supports the standard for application of Web Content Accessibility Guidelines (WCAG) to mobile. It's applicable to mobile web content, mobile web apps, native apps, and hybrid apps using web components inside native apps [29]. It provides only an informative guidance, but not any technical details that are useful for mobile development. The document includes four main principles as WCAG. Under the Perceivable principal guides related to user interface (UI) elements manipulations are formalized. The Operable principle defines recommendations for keyboard control, touch target size and spacing and touchscreen gestures. The Understandable principle is related to screen orientation, consistent layout and positioning important UI elements. The last one – Robust, is targeted to providing guides for using easy methods for data entry and supporting the characteristic properties of the platform. All the developer techniques that apply to mobile are summarised in another W3C document [30]. It includes an example code that visualizes the realization of WCAG to mobile.

Another international institution – the European Telecommunications Standards Institute (ETSI), supports accessibility standard EN 301 549 v2.1.2, that is applicable to mobile applications and "their compliance with the essential requirements of perceivability, operability, understandability and robustness defined in the Web and Mobile Accessibility Directive" [31]. It contains functional requirements and provides a reference document that can be followed by different stakeholders (e.g., managers, developers, UI designers, etc.). It includes WCAG recommendations too. The standard is based on the Directive (EU) 2016/2102 issued by the European parliament and the Council. The last one is targeted to accessibility of websites and mobile applications of public sector bodies [32]. It provides principles for digital inclusion of people with disabilities, but an example code is not included. Another European Union document that mentions mobile accessibility is Directive (EU) 2019/882. It is related to [30] and its purpose is more general – to document accessibility requirements for products and services and to contribute the proper functioning of the internal market by approximating laws, regulations and administrative provisions of the Member States [33].

There are national standards and guidelines. For example, Section 508, The Americans with Disabilities Act, New Zealand Web Accessibility Standard 1.1, etc. Some of them are also based on WCAG.

On the other hand, mobile operating systems' companies also form accessibility guidelines that are followed up by the developers. The most used are Google Android [34] and Apple iOS guidelines [35]. Companies provide complete guides for both designers and programmers, including principles, user interface elements patterns, programming code, and testing tools. They also have rapidly adopted the design thinking approach.

The combination of platform-specific standards and guidelines provides opportunities to fully address mobile accessibility issues. Closely related to the availability of digital devices and services is their security, which often predetermines the possibilities for their trouble-free use.

Unlike design thinking and user-centred design process, mobile device security research depends on the specifics of the platform. The development focus is not only on the interaction, but also on the approaches and standards for delivering better functionalities. Open Web Application Security Project (OWASP) Foundation works to improve the software security through various projects. It offers a Security Knowledge Framework, which is an expert system for applying the principles of secure coding in various programming languages [36]. It is based on the OWASP Application Security Verification Standard. It implements 4 phases of security research: defining the requirements for the project, defining security acceptance criteria, coding according to the established good security practices, testing according to the established requirements [36]. The testing is based on established security metrics and is conducted with the help of a wider range of specialists working on the project.

Similar to the W3C WCAG, OWASP defines a standard for mobile applications' security [37] and guidelines for testing mobile security [38]. Like WCAG, the OWASP mobile security standard sets out guidelines and principles for developing secure mobile applications. They are formed in two security verification levels and a set of reverse engineering resiliency requirements (RERR). The first level contains generic security requirements that are recommended for all mobile applications. Level two is aimed at applying principles for handling highly sensitive data. RERR covers additional protection mechanisms that can be applied in the prevention of threats. Security verification is most fully accomplished when combining both levels with RERR. This ensures the security resiliency of the project.

The OWASP Mobile Security Guidelines are divided into three main sections: general guidelines, Android guidelines, iOS guidelines. The general guidelines provide explanations for the place of security testing in the life cycle of software development. Depending on the development methodology, different methods for testing the security of applications are applied. It can be performed sequentially or iteratively; in both cases a risk assessment must be performed for the individual components of the applications as well as for the entire applications. The application of security techniques accompanies the entire life cycle - from defining the requirements to testing and implementation. OWASP takes into account the importance of human resources, seeing them as one of the weak links of security [38]. We can find similarities with the sources cited above, which put human beings at the centre of development and take into account their individual characteristics. [38] also offers specific coding techniques to follow when developing Android and iOS applications.

The major developers of mobile operating systems Google and Apple also offer complete guides for creating secure mobile applications that take into account the specifics of their platforms. They summarize good practices, principles and a sample code that can be put into practice in real mobile projects. Apple offers a security framework that implements different levels of security (Fig. 2).

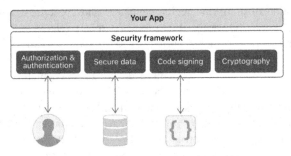

Fig. 2. iOS security framework by [39].

Authorization and Authentication, Secure Data, Secure Code, Cryptography and Result Codes [39]. They provide sample codes that can be used in iOS applications to increase security levels when performing: logging in, session management, network data exchange, malicious code isolation, encryption of user personal data, application security assessment.

Google's best practices for developing secure Android applications are similar to those of Apple. They are related to the security of user personal data, secure transmission over the Internet and storage of local devices, application of cryptographic techniques, user authentication, protection against malware [40].

Individual scientists and author teams study security in a specific context. Such are the developments in the field of m-learning [41, 42], finance [43], healthcare [44], military training [45], machine learning [46], etc. Some also define frameworks [47] and general-purpose ecosystems [48]. Most of them are based on OWASP's mobile security projects and/or Apple's and Google's security guides. The ways of interaction with mobile devices, prevention of cyber-attacks and increase of security in data exchange are taken into account.

Based on the above mentioned, the main direction of the practical application of all frameworks, ecosystems, principles and standards can be outlined: user-oriented, a barrier-free digital experience, personal security.

3 Method

3.1 Material

Our research is aimed at defining a mobile research ecosystem for testing and evaluating secure and accessible mobile multi-device environments. In this regard, it is necessary to choose appropriate platforms for approbation of our approach. In particular, we used Android and iOS ones (Table 1).

Table 1. Specification of targeted mobile devices and platforms.

Characteristics	Device 1	Device 2
Operating System	iOS 14.7.1	Android 11
Device Brand	iPhone 12	Redmi Xiaomi Note 9
Year	2020	2020
CPU	Apple A14 Bionic six-core	Octa-core Max 2 GHz
RAM	4 GB	4 GB
Communication	Wi-Fi, Bluetooth, GPS, NFC, USB	Wi-Fi, Bluetooth, GPS, NFC, USB

Source: own elaboration

We would like to compare two different mobile platforms and the limitations that each of them imposes. On the first place, both devices were manufactured in 2020 with the same RAM capacity and the same hardware communication components. By specification, the main difference between the two stems from the technology used to develop the processor, which strongly affects the performance of the devices. According to tests, devices with Apple A14 Bionic processor are significantly more productive. According to some benchmark tests, Apple's CPU performance is much higher than Xiaomi's one – 93 overall scores versus 61 [49, 50]. Our research explored both platforms for passing the security and accessibility tests, including the overall performance point of view.

On the other hand, because of the platform-specific features each device security and accessibility were tested by different applications. Android accessibility is tested through Google Accessibility Scanner. As for the iOS accessibility testing, we used the Accessibility third-party tool. Security testing was performed by the following applications: MyTop Mobile Security (iOS) and WOT Security (Android).

The limitations of this paper are related to the versions of operating systems and hardware configurations of the devices used, as well as the accessibility and security testing software. We do not claim to be exhaustive of the types of devices and platforms. Our goal is put in practice the testing procedure described in Sect. 3.3.

3.2 Design

The study observes the following main factors: speed of testing; the number of security errors and the number of accessibility errors. These are the dependent variables. The independent variables are the mobile operating system of the devices and their hardware specifications.

3.3 Procedure

Based on the frameworks outlined in the previous two sections, we choose to follow an iterative procedure of exploring the security and availability of mobile applications. The procedure we followed consists of 5 phases: Define, Design, Test, Analysis and Implement (Fig. 3). They summarize the experiences of [25, 27, 28, 36]. We can define it as benchmarking approach too.

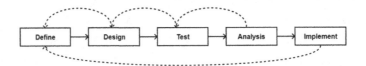

Fig. 3. Proposed benchmarking approach. Source: own elaboration.

- In the first phase - Define, the research of the project requirements is carried out, the peculiarities of the mobile platforms and the users who will use them are defined.
- In the second phase – Design, the project is planned, research questions, the metrics for success and milestones (if necessary) are determined. Possible metrics in accordance with the aim of the approach are: non-human traffic; mean time between failures; mean time to detect; mean time to acknowledge; mean time to contain identified attack vectors; mean time to resolve issue; mean time to recovery from error; security policy compliance; accessibility policy compliance; accessibility validation errors, etc. depending on the aim of the research. A weight of each of the metrics could be given to measure the overall accessibility and security level of mobile applications.
- In the third phase – Test, the testing of the security and accessibility of mobile platforms is performed according to the plan prepared at the previous stage.
- In the fourth phase – Analysis, an in-depth analysis of the test results is performed, a report with recommendations for improving security is formed.
- In the last phase – Implement, the recommendations from the report are put into practice.

If the recommendations cannot be implemented, the cycle is repeated until the recommendations are fully implemented in order to eliminate the weaknesses of the mobile platforms. The approach can be applied both at the application level and at the mobile platform level.

4 Results

In order to respond to RQ2, it is necessary to approbate our benchmark approach. Following the procedure described above, in the first phase, we determined that we would use Device 1 and Device 2 to perform our tests.

In the second phase of the research procedure, we defined the following metrics for test success: test speed, number of accessibility errors, number of security vulnerabilities. In the third phase of the procedure, we perform the tests of security and accessibility of the selected devices and platforms. More in-depth research should be done if specific problems are defined. Possible examples include: access by people with visual impairments to a specific mobile operating system or application; improving the security of banking mobile applications for people with visual or hearing impairments. In these situations, metrics and tests are adapted to the specifics of the problems. That is why in this paper the author's team only gives guidelines for performing a benchmark procedure without claiming to cover a wide range of cases.

Device 1 showed the following accessibility issues (Fig. 4).

Fig. 4. Device 1 accessibilities issues. Source: own elaboration.

There are mainly problems with the color scheme, contrast, size and thickening of the texts, sound alternatives to the interface elements for people with visual impairments; video alternatives for people with hearing impairments; assistive touch problems for people with motor disabilities.

Testing of Device 2 shows that it would create mainly problems for people with visual and motor impairments (Fig. 5). The problems with it are also with the colour scheme, text sizes, sound matching, touch and rotation problems, switch access.

Device 1 security testing shows that mainly network security and identity protection issues have been found (Fig. 6, on the left-hand side is MyTop Mobile Security). Only

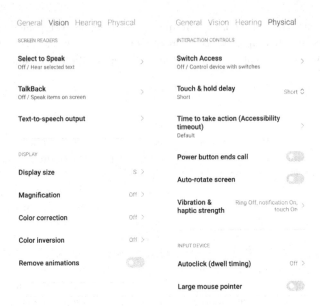

Fig. 5. Device 2 accessibilities issues. Source: own elaboration

one problem was found with Device 2 – Internet browsing protection (Fig. 6, on the right-hand side is WOT Security).

The test speed for both devices is fast:

- Device 1 accessibility test – 1 s.
- Device 2 accessibility test – 3 s.
- Device 1 security test – 10 s.
- Device 2 security test – 9 s.

As a result of the tests of the fourth phase of our proposed research procedure, an analysis of the accessibility and security of mobile applications or platforms is performed. It is also related to monitoring the success of the tests. The planned metrics are also taken into account. We observe the following results in terms of:

- Test speed: Device 1 is faster in performing accessibility tests, while Device 2 is faster in security testing. The differences are not significant, but it should be noted that the software used is different. This is also a prerequisite for the results of the speed of the tests to be accepted as conditional;
- Number of accessibility errors - 16 possible accessibility problems were found on both devices. In both types of tests, the software allows additional adjustments to be made to eliminate the detected problems. Both operating systems feature a wide range of settings for people with visual, hearing, motor and cognitive impairments. The specific features of the users also predetermine the settings of the accessibility of mobile devices;

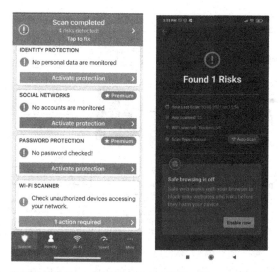

Fig. 6. Security issue of both devices. Source: own elaboration.

– Number of security vulnerabilities - in Device 1 4 security vulnerabilities were detected, while in Device 2 there is only one. As can be seen from Fig. 6, these are problems that can be solved by the user after raising awareness regarding cyber threats that may violate his privacy. Purely technical security breaches are established by testing the stability of the code to check for non-compliance with coding techniques.

5   Discussion

In view of the current paper's goal and the tests performed, we propose to unite the user expectations and experiences in a complete mobile research ecosystem for testing and evaluating secure and accessible mobile multi-device environments. It should meet some of the basic requirements set by the principles of user-oriented design [25], namely the active user participation and a functional design that meets their expectations. Activities related to the specification of: context of use, user and organizational requirements, the tools for developing product design solutions and the methods for evaluation of designs should also be defined. On the other hand, the security research phases proposed by the OWASP Application Security Verification Standard [36] should also be considered.

The study conducted in this paper gives us reason to propose a mobile research ecosystem (Fig. 7) that implements the procedure described in Sect. 3.3 and the features of mobile communication described in [48]. We need to keep in mind that there are limitations of interacting with individual devices in mobile contexts related to mobile multi-device environments [51]. These environments are a set of interacting devices that coordinate with each other. As stated in [52], more should be taken into account when defining such ecosystems: end-user privacy controls, self-regulation by platforms, legal regulation.

As a result of the first phase of the process, a summary report is generated for the individual characteristics of the users and the features of the tested platforms. For

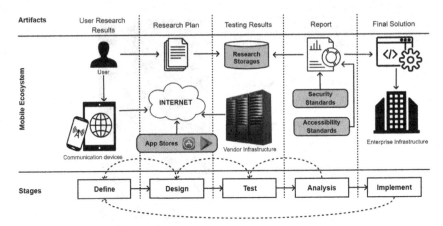

Fig. 7. Proposed mobile research ecosystem. Source: own elaboration.

example, type of disability, operating system. They provide a basis for preparing a study plan that provides guidance for conducting the design phase. As a result of the study of mobile accessibility and security, quantitative results are generated. For example, number of errors, internet speed and mobile connection. The result of the fourth phase is a report with recommendations for improving accessibility and security, and in the last phase - a working solution.

An important condition for the preparation of the reports is to comply with the standards for accessibility and security, which are formed by international organizations. Full coverage of the problems aims to achieve a better user experience.

6   Conclusions

As the capacity of mobile devices to process increasingly complex information increases, so do the requirements for the applications designed for them. As [53] points out, the mobile OS market is divided between Google Android and Apple iOS with respective market shares of roughly 70% and 30%. These two platforms also impose rules for the development of mobile applications, as well as much of the mobile ecosystem, including standards and applications. Development teams create a new generation of software in which users are placed at the centre of projects, and the products themselves must comply with the physical limitations imposed by devices and the specifics of the context of use, which changes frequently.

As a result of the research conducted in this paper, we can conclude that:

- accessibility is a context-sensitive concept that is determined by the individual needs of users;
- security issues are a prerequisite for restricting the personal freedom of people;
- availability and security testing of mobile platforms should be performed periodically in order to troubleshoot.

As a result of the experiments conducted in terms of security and accessibility of mobile platforms, as well as the definition of a mobile research system, we believe that we meet the goal of this paper. The need to apply the standards for accessibility and security, considered in the theoretical part, is taken into account. It is reflected that consumers are actively involved in the study of human-computer interaction in order to implement the principles of user-oriented design and development of digital technologies to help people.

We believe that in the future we can improve our proposed research procedure, which we can adapt to the specific needs of people with visual, hearing or motor impairments.

Acknowledgment. The study was supported by project NPI-36/2019 "Contemporary Approaches to The Integration of Mobile Technologies in Higher Education".

References

1. General Data Protection Regulation. https://gdpr-info.eu. Accessed 24 Aug 2021
2. McAfee ATR Threats Report. https://www.mcafee.com/enterprise/en-us/lp/threats-reports/apr-2021.html. Accessed 24 Aug 2021
3. Cybersecurity statistics and trends you need to know in 2021. https://us.norton.com/internetsecurity-emerging-threats-cyberthreat-trends-cybersecurity-threat-review.html. Accessed 24 Aug 2021
4. Number of detected malicious installation packages on mobile devices worldwide from 4th quarter 2015 to 1st quarter 2021. https://www.statista.com/statistics/653680/volume-of-detected-mobile-malware-packages. Accessed 24 Aug 2021
5. What systems have you seen infected by ransomware? https://www.statista.com/statistics/701020/major-operating-systems-targeted-by-ransomwar. Accessed 24 Aug 2021
6. Distribution of new mobile malware worldwide in 2020, by type. https://www.statista.com/statistics/653688/distribution-of-mobile-malware-type. Accessed 24 Aug 2021
7. Android Mobile Security Threats. https://www.kaspersky.com/resource-center/threats/mobile. Accessed 24 Aug 2021
8. Top Security Threats of Smartphones (2021). https://www.rd.com/article/mobile-security-threats/. Accessed 24 Aug 2021
9. Disability and health. https://www.who.int/en/news-room/fact-sheets/detail/disability-and-health. Accessed 24 Aug 2021
10. Fact sheet on Persons with Disabilities. https://www.un.org/disabilities/documents/toolaction/pwdfs.pdf. Accessed 24 Aug 2021
11. United Nation Inclusion Strategy. https://www.un.org/en/content/disabilitystrategy, Accessed 24 Aug 2021
12. The 17 Goals. https://sdgs.un.org/goals. Accessed 24 Aug 2021
13. Marinova, O.: Business intelligence and data warehouse programs in higher education institutions: current status and recommendations for improvement. Electron. J. Econ. Comput. Sci. **5**, 17–25 (2016)
14. Parusheva, S., Aleksandrova, Y., Petrov, P.: A study of the use of social media in higher education institutions in Bulgaria. In: 4th International Multidisciplinary Scientific Conferences on Social Sciences and Arts, SGEM 2017, Albena, vol. 1, pp. 19–26 (2017)
15. Todoranova, L.: E-learning at the University of Economics - Varna. In: Proceedings of Scientific Conference: TechCo - Lovech 2019, vol. 2, pp. 244–248 (2019)

16. Stoyanova, M., Vasilev, J., Cristescu, M.: Big data in property management. Applications of mathematics in engineering and economics. In: Proceedings of the 46th Conference on Applications of Mathematics in Engineering and Economics (AMEE 2020), vol. 2333, no. 1, pp. 070001-1–070001-7. American Institute of Physics (2021)

17. Armiyanova, M.: IoT problems and design patterns which are appropriate to solve them. In: Proceedings of the International Conference Information and Communication Technologies in Business and Education, pp. 291–305 (2019)

18. Bankov, B.: Software evaluation of PHP MVC web applications. In: Proceedings of 19 International Multidisciplinary Scientific Geoconference, SGEM 2019, vol. 19, no. 2.1, pp. 603–610 (2019)

19. Sulov, V.: Iteration vs recursion in introduction to programming classes: an empirical study. Cybern. Inf. Technol. **16**(4), 63–72 (2016)

20. Kuyumdzhiev, I.: Comparing backup and restore efficiency in MySQL, MS SQL server and MongoDB. In: Proceedings of 19 International Multidisciplinary Scientific Geoconference, SGEM, vol. 19, no. 2.1, pp. 167–174 (2019)

21. Antonova, K., Ivanova, P.: Emerging or changing occupational hazards at the workplace. In: International Academic Conferences: Proceedings of IAC 2018 in Vienna Management, Economics and Marketing (IAC-MEM 2018), pp. 350–355. Czech Technical University, Prague (2018)

22. Veleva, M.: Best practices as opportunities for leadership soft skills improvement in human resource management in Bulgarian tourism organizations the four-season hotels example. Izvestia J. Union Sci. Varna Econ. Sci. Ser. **9**(3), 63–71 (2020)

23. Koleva, V.: Labor needs of IT specialists in Bulgaria. East. Acad. J. **1**, 51–62 (2018)

24. Sirendi, R., Taveter, K.: Bringing service design thinking into the public sector to create proactive and user-friendly public services. In: Nah, F.F.-H., Tan, C.-H. (eds.) HCIBGO 2016, Part II. LNCS, vol. 9752, pp. 221–230. Springer, Cham (2016). https://doi.org/10.1007/978-3-319-39399-5_21

25. International Organization for Standardization. Human-centred design processes for interactive systems (ISO 13407:1999(en)). https://www.iso.org/obp/ui/#iso:std:iso:13407:ed-1:v1:en. Accessed 24 Aug 2021

26. International Organization for Standardization. Ergonomics of human-system interaction — Part 210: Human-centred design for interactive systems (ISO 9241-210:2019(en)). https://www.iso.org/obp/ui/#iso:std:iso:9241:-210:ed-2:v1:en. Accessed 24 Aug 2021

27. Design Thinking 101. https://www.nngroup.com/articles/design-thinking/. Accessed 24 Aug 2021

28. Design Thinking. https://www.interaction-design.org/literature/topics/design-thinking. Accessed 29 Aug 2021

29. Mobile Accessibility: How WCAG 2.0 and Other W3C/WAI Guidelines Apply to Mobile. https://www.w3.org/TR/mobile-accessibility-mapping/. Accessed 29 Aug 2021

30. WCAG 2.0 Techniques that Apply to Mobile. https://www.w3.org/WAI/GL/mobile-a11y-tf/MobileTechniques/. Accessed 29 Aug 2021

31. ETSI. Accessibility requirements for ICT products and services (EN 301 549 v2.1.2). https://www.etsi.org/deliver/etsi_en/301500_301599/301549/02.01.02_60/en_301 549v020102p.pdf. Accessed 29 Aug 2021

32. Directive (EU) 2016/2102 of the European Parliament and of the Council of 26 October 2016 on the accessibility of the websites and mobile applications of public sector bodies. https://eur-lex.europa.eu/legal-content/EN/TXT/PDF/?uri=CELEX:32016L2102&from=en. Accessed 29 Aug 2021

33. Directive (EU) 2019/882 of the European Parliament and of the Council of 17 April 2019 on the accessibility requirements for products and services. https://eur-lex.europa.eu/legal-content/EN/TXT/PDF/?uri=CELEX:32019L0882&from=EN. Accessed 29 Aug 2021

34. Developing for Accessibility. https://www.google.ca/accessibility/for-developers/. Accessed 29 Aug 2021
35. Accessibility on iOS. https://developer.apple.com/accessibility/ios/. Accessed 29 Aug 2021
36. OWASP Security Knowledge Framework. https://owasp.org/www-project-security-knowledge-framework/. Accessed 29 Aug 2021
37. Holguera, C., et al.: OWASP Mobile Application Security Verification Standard. OWASP Foundation (2021)
38. Mueller, B., et al.: OWASP Mobile Security Testing Guide. OWASP Foundation (2021)
39. iOS Security Framework. https://developer.apple.com/documentation/security. Accessed 29 Aug 2021
40. Android Developers Guides: Security. https://developer.android.com/topic/security/best-practices. Accessed 29 Aug 2021
41. Shonola, S., Joy, M.: Security framework for mobile learning environments. In: Proceedings of ICERI2014 Conference, pp. 3333–3342 (2014)
42. Mahalingam, S., et al.: Learners' ensemble based security conceptual model for m-learning system in Malaysian Higher Learning Institution. In: Proceedings of 10th International Conference Mobile Learning, pp. 335–338 (2014)
43. Ambore, S., et al.: A resilient cybersecurity framework for Mobile Financial Services (MFS). J. Cyber Secur. Technol. 1(3–4), 202–224 (2017)
44. Srivastava, M., Thamilarasu, G.: MSF: a comprehensive security framework for mHealth applications. In: 2019 7th International Conference on Future Internet of Things and Cloud Workshops (FiCloudW), pp. 70–75 (2019)
45. Hatzivasilis, G., et al.: Modern aspects of cyber-security training and continuous adaptation of programmes to trainees. Appl. Sci. 10, 5702 (2020)
46. Sagar, R., et al.: Applications in security and evasions in machine learning: a survey. Electronics 9, 97 (2020)
47. Ding, C., et al.: A hybrid analysis-based approach to android malware family classification. Entropy 23, 1009 (2021)
48. Mitrea, T., Borda, M.: Mobile security threats: a survey on protection and mitigation strategies. In: Proceedings of International Conference Knowledge-Based Organization, vol. 16, no. 3, pp. 131–135 (2020)
49. Apple A14 Bionic. https://nanoreview.net/en/soc/apple-a14-bionic. Accessed 23 Oct 2021
50. Xiaomi Redmi Note 9. https://nanoreview.net/en/phone/xiaomi-redmi-note-9. Accessed 23 Oct 2021
51. Grubert, J., et al.: Challenges in mobile multi-device ecosystems. mUX: J. Mob. User. Exp. 5, 5 (2016)
52. Binns, R., et al.: Third party tracking in the mobile ecosystem. In: Proceedings of the 10th ACM Conference on Web Science, pp. 23–31 (2018)
53. Kim, J., et al.: The Value of Technology Releases in the Mobile App Ecosystem. The Economic Impact of Software Developer Kits. Data Catalyst (2021)

E-participation Portals in the E-Governance Institutional Structure of the EAEU Countries: A Trend Study

Andrei Chugunov[1] ⓘ, Vladislav Belyi[1] ⓘ, Georgy Panfilov[1],
and Radomir Bolgov[2](✉) ⓘ

[1] ITMO University, Birzhevaya line 14, 199034 Saint Petersburg, Russia
[2] Saint Petersburg State University, Universitetskaya emb. 7-9, 199034 Saint Petersburg, Russia
r.bolgov@spbu.ru

Abstract. The authors attempt to identify general patterns in the development of e-portals for interaction between citizens and authorities in the Eurasian Economic Union (EAEU) countries, as well as to find common methods for assessing the effectiveness of the portals functioning. The research team presenting the preliminary results in this paper suggests using the experience that has been successfully tested on the Russian Federation case to develop such a technique. Below we demonstrate the results of e-participation systems monitoring study in Russia, that was conducted by e-Governance Center of ITMO University in January-February 2021. The monitoring is a continuation of a study started in 2020, as well as pilot studies of 2017–2019. The first represented study made an attempt to design a basic model which describes the functioning of various channels for e-interaction between the citizens and authorities, determine the specifics of each channel, develop an assessment system and monitor online platforms that ensure the functioning of one or more channels of e-participation. The study was conducted using the same methodology as the 2020 study. Participation channels were assessed according to five criteria: (1) "Openness", (2) "Availability", (3) "Decision Making", (4) "Quality of feedback" and (5) "Special requirements", each of which includes 3 indicators (totally 15 indicators). The methodology is focused on assessing the development of six main e-participation channels: (1) open budget, (2) participatory budgeting, (3) complaint mechanisms, (4) e-initiatives, (5) e-voting, (6) crowdsourcing. The proposed methodology attempts to solve this complex problem and evaluate several e-participation channels that are currently developing in Russia at regional and local levels. The second monitoring trend study uses the United Nations E-Participation Index methodology. The e-services portals of the EAEU countries were explored with an interval of 5 years (2016 and 2021).

Keywords: E-Participation · E-Governance · EAEU · Post-Soviet countries

1 Introduction

The Eurasian Economic Union (EAEU) is an international organization which consists of five post-Soviet countries (Armenia, Belarus, Kazakhstan, Kyrgyzstan, and Russian

A. V. Chugunov et al. (Eds.): EGOSE 2021, CCIS 1529, pp. 232–243, 2022.
https://doi.org/10.1007/978-3-031-04238-6_18

Federation). ICT is the key area of cooperation between the member states. [1] There is a Draft of Digital Agenda, as well as a lot of normative documents (https://docs.eaeuni on.org). The aim is to create a common Digital Space until 2025.

E-governance technologies may be used for successful integration in specific fields, for instance, in customs and migration coordination. Thus, we explore the national specific features of e-services implementation and then identify general patterns. We focus on the e-services which provide the interaction between citizens and authorities in electronic form.

2 Scope of Research

When we analyze the development of e-Government institutions, including e-participation in the EAEU countries, we consider it appropriate to rely on the approach to the analysis of these phenomena proposed by Tolbert and Mossberger, who suggested [2] two basic paradigms in the relationship between government and citizens in the context of e-interaction:

1) The Entrepreneurial Approach, where the focus is on high-quality services and the effectiveness of interaction within the state.
2) The Participatory Approach, where the focus is on increasing the trust to the government by means of direct democratic participation, building dialogue, establishing of government accountability and transparency.

Earlier, it was already indicated that the EAEU countries are currently only beginning to introduce certain elements of the e-Governance and e-Participation approach. [3] Therefore, in this study, we proceed from the entrepreneurial approach, aimed at creating sustainable and effective connections among the member countries of the organization. The legal and regulatory framework for e-participation and comparative analysis of e-government implementation in the EAEU countries was previously presented in [4]. The key problems of e-governance in the EAEU countries were revealed low levels of economic development and democracy, the desire of national elites to maintain control and mechanisms of influence on ongoing processes.

We attempt to reveal general patterns in the development of e-portals for established channels through which citizens can interact with authorities in electronic form in the EAEU countries, as well as to find common methods for evaluating the results of the work of these electronic resources.

We pose the following research questions:

RQ1: Is there a realistic prospect of joint approaches to e-services within the EAEU, to the integration of e-services through public service portals?
RQ2: If yes, is it possible to integrate legislation and institutions of e-Governance?

As part of our response to RQ2, we start from the provisions of the neo-functionalist theory, according to which the countries' similarity of institutional and legal framework in specific areas, in particular, the e-Governance, results in its political regulation in the framework of international organizations, and, consequently, in the political integration [5].

To do this, it is necessary to analyze the similarities and differences of legislation and institutions. That is, are there common entry points for electronic services in the EAEU? Comparison of monitoring results from portals and ratings without studying the internal situation with institution sand legislation does not make sense.

3   E-Participation Evaluation: International Experience

Recently, the channels of electronic participation have often been created at the initiative of regional and local authorities, and differ significantly from each other. This leads to the problem of the lack of a universal methodology capable of assessing the level of development of e-participation channels in a certain territory. [6] Sometimes the researchers focus on certain e-participation instruments, such as government portals [7] or social media accounts [8]. So it is crucial to provide unified parameters for evaluation.

Moreover, the assessment should focus not only on the readiness of e-portals but also on the results of citizen participation in politics and decision-making. Chugunov and Kabanov demonstrate the "institutionalization" effects on electronic participation [9].

There is also the problem of the national specifics of each country. The researchers focus on various institutional and policy effects on the e-government and e-participation, including "the level of decentralization in e-tools implementation" [10].

The UN assessment of the level of e-government and e-participation in the EAEU countries allows us to speak, in general, of the high ranking positions of this countries. [11] EGDI ranking is a combination of three important dimensions: the provision of online services, the level of access to portals and human potential.

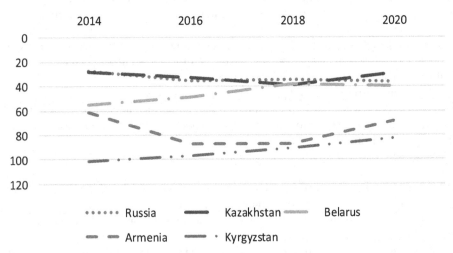

Fig. 1. Evolution of the EAEU countries positions in the UN Electronic Government Index

In 2014, Russia and Kazakhstan ranked 27th and 28th. In 2020, they dropped to 36th and 29th places, respectively (see Fig. 1).

Armenia, in comparison with 2014, moved from 61 to 68, and Belarus moved from 55 in 2014 to 38 in 2018, although it was on 40th position in 2020. Only Kyrgyzstan has a stable positive trend in the period under review. Since 2014 and 101 places in the ranking Kyrgyzstan smoothly moved to 83rd position in 2020.

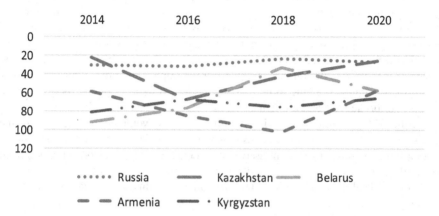

Fig. 2. Evolution of the EAEU countries positions in the UN Electronic Participation Index

A comparable picture is observed in the UN e-participation ranking (see Fig. 2). The indicator of this ranking demonstrates the access of citizens to information, public services and the possibility of citizens' participation in making government decisions that affect the society. The leaders of the ranking in the electronic participation index among the Eurasian Economic Union countries are also Russia and Kazakhstan, but compared to 2014, both countries worsened their positions in the ranking.

The modern state policy for the development of the digital space in the Russian Federation is aimed at expanding and including as many life situations as possible between the authorities, business and citizens in the functionality of e-services. The development strategy of services assumes their centralization, proactivity, availability (including free access), interdepartmental orientation in the light of digital transformation.

Earlier, the use of e-interaction services in St. Petersburg was analyzed using a survey of citizens on a representative sample. [12] So, it was found that most often citizens use the Internet to interact with authorities on issues of obtaining public services (more than 80%), for appeals to authorities related to solving problems of housing (more than 60%), requests for information from authorities (55%) and for complaints about actions of authorities (more than 50%).

Also, during the study, the most demanded services were determined. It is connected with the provision of the population with services in health care, security, urgent problems of city residents. The results showed that the most active citizens used e-services related to health and safety for solving problems of interaction with district police officers and ensuring the safety of citizens, as well as services in the field of public and personal transport. [13] It can be assumed that a similar structure of the most relevant portals and the logic of their development, as well as the structure of citizens' requests, will be observed for the portals of e-interaction of the EAEU countries. Respectively, government decisions will develop in the indicated vector.

Indeed, according to the State Program "Digital Development of Belarus" for 2021–2025, the Republic of Belarus is expected to accelerate the development of digital transformation and portals of interaction between citizens and authorities. This document proclaims a strategy for the introduction of new information systems, simplification of information interaction between citizens, business and the state using only electronic interaction. Also, work is being done in Belarus to centralize the e-health system to transfer citizens lifecycle processes in digital format, to address the city problems (for example, the portal "Maya Respublika"). In general, the Belarus government proclaimed a program to develop a digital infrastructure for the implementation of interdepartmental information interaction, the formation of a modern system for public services on the principles of proactivity and multichannel.

For the EAEU countries, there is a common line of development of state electronic portals. However, the level of e-services in Russia is sufficient to include services in the existing functionality for resolving issues of foreigners, primarily labor migrants from the EAEU countries. For example, a database of digital profiles of foreigners arriving in the country is already being created. It is assumed that this service will provide labor migrants with the opportunity to use the "State Services" portal and receive a wide range of government e-services.

A similar model of e-services development makes possible an introducing of a unified system for assessing of the e-interaction portals in the EAEU space. Thus, the Prime Minister of the Russian Federation called the delay in digitalization of customs administration in the EAEU a direct threat, and the absence of common digital platforms and systems, in his opinion, will force the EAEU countries to return to control measures on the internal border. Thus, the position of Russia within the EAEU sounds the following way: further integration is strongly related to the promotion of a joint digital agenda and e-services.

4   Research Design and Findings

The research team which presents the preliminary results in this paper suggests the use of the experience that has been successfully tested on the Russian case to develop a monitoring technique according to a unified method.

Below are the results of a monitoring study of e-participation systems in Russia, conducted by e-Governance Center of ITMO University in January-February 2021. The monitoring is a continuation of a study started in 2020 [12], as well as pilot studies of 2017–2019 [14].

Although at the moment there are a large number of approaches to assessing e-participation systems at the international [15, 16] and Russian [9, 17] levels, most studies are focused on analyzing only certain channels of participation, for example, e-petition portals [18, 19] or government websites [7, 20]. At the same time, the variety of channels and technologies of e-participation is rapidly expanding [21], in connection with which there is a need for a comprehensive assessment of all available tools and the contribution of each of them to e-participation.

The first represented study made an attempt to design a basic model which describes the functioning of various channels for electronic interaction between the authorities and citizens, determine the specifics of each channel, develop an assessment system and monitor online platforms that ensure the functioning of one or more channels of e-participation.

The research methodology is based on a system approach in political science (D. Easton, 1957), according to which the political system consists of the following basic elements: (1) System per se ("Black box"), (2) "Entrance" ("requirements" and "support" from citizens), (3) "Exit" (decisions and actions of the authorities), (4) Feedback (correspondence between "Entry" and "Exit").

The study was conducted using the same methodology as the 2020 study. Participation channels were assessed according to five criteria: (1) "Openness", (2) "Availability", (3) "Decision Making", (4) "Quality of feedback" and (5) "Special requirements", each of which includes 3 indicators (total - 15 indicators). A detailed version of the methodology was presented in a 2020 article [14].

The methodology is focused on assessing the development of six main e-participation channels: (1) open budget, (2) participatory budgeting, (3) complaint mechanisms, (4) e-initiatives, (5) e-voting, (6) crowdsourcing.

The proposed methodology attempts to solve this complex problem and evaluate several channels of e-participation that are currently developing in Russia. The methodology was applied to assess the e-participation channels created by regional and municipal authorities in cities that are regional capitals.

Table 1. General results of monitoring.

Resource type	Number of resources		Coverage of regions[a]	
	Regional	Municipal	Qty	%
Open budget	84 (+1)	80 (+3)	85 (0)	100% (0)
E-complaints	37 (+7)	19 (−1)	47 (+4)	55 (+4)
Initiative budgeting	38 (−13)	16 (−9)	43 (−17)	51 (−20)
E-voting	24 (+11)	17 (−3)	34 (+6)	40 (+7)
E-petitions	12 (+2)	10 (+4)	21 (+4)	25 (+5)
Crowdsourcing	12 (+3)	6 (+1)	17 (+4)	20 (+5)
Total	209 (+11)	148 (−7)	41 (0)	48 (0)

[a]The column "Coverage of regions" shows the number of regions in which there is at least one resource supervised by any level of government.

The monitoring made it possible to record the dynamics in the number and quality of the channels under consideration. The generalized monitoring results in relation to the dynamics in relation to the previous year are presented in Table 1.

As in the first stage, significant disparities were revealed in the development of the channels, both at the regional and municipal levels.

The number of regional channels increased from 198 to 209, and the number of municipal channels, on the contrary, decreased from 155 to 148. The overall score at the regional level was from 85 to 0 points, and at the municipal level - from 53 to 0 points. Many regions and cities have changed their positions in the ranking due to the emergence of new resources, revision of old ones, or, on the contrary, their closure or not updating.

The most widespread channel of e-participation remained resources for informing about the budget process of the Open Budget type. Problem reporting channels have improved their positions in quantitative and qualitative terms. In contrast, the number of resources for proactive budgeting has decreased. E-initiatives, e-voting and crowd-sourcing are still fewer common channels and have not significantly changed their positions.

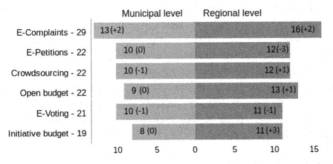

Fig. 3. Average score of regional and municipal e-participation channels for 2021.

The average scores by each of the e-participation channels are shown in Fig. 3. The values in brackets depict the dynamics of the 2021 result in relation to the 2020 result level than the municipal one. This difference is most noticeable in the budget channels and problem reporting channels.

The results obtained can be associated with institutional changes caused by the state policy of Russia regarding e-participation.

Stimulation of changes occurred primarily as a result of the signing by the President of the Russian Federation of a list of instructions following the meeting of the Council for the Development of Local Self-Government, which took place on January 30, 2020 [22].

The instructions meant the creation of a unified Feedback Platform, within which it is supposed to interact through such channels of e-participation as reporting problems, polls, voting and public discussions. The platform will operate on the basis of the Unified Portal of State and Municipal Services. As of February 2021, the list of regions, to the executive authorities, local governments and subordinate organizations of which you can send applications has already amounted to 74 regions. [23] For this purpose, special widgets were published on the official websites of the Governments of the regions, allowing to submit appeals.

Another important innovation is also related to the already cited instructions of the President of Russia. By December 31, 2020, the process of developing a network of

Regional Management Centers was completed. The key task of the Centers was to ensure effective interdepartmental and inter-level interaction of authorities and organizations in solving problems received from citizens in appeals and voiced in social media. The Regional Management Centers are supposed to use the Feedback Platform as the most significant sources of information on incoming requests [24].

These measures of the authorities should be considered as a step towards unification and streamlining of regional e-participation resources and data processed through them. It should be noted that as a result of such centralization, many regions that have created their own channels of e-participation with well-built logistics for processing citizens' appeals have faced the problem of the need to ensure information interaction between regional systems and the federal one, were forced to abandon their own systems and completely switch to the federal platform. For example, this happened in the Leningrad region, where in January 2021 it was announced that the Narodnaya Expertise portal was closed and that it was completely switched to the federal Feedback Platform [25].

However, in a number of cases, regional resources for participation were retained and integrated with the Feedback Platform, due to which requests received through the regional portal were redirected to the federal one.

Table 2. Analysis of the EAEU countries e-Government portals [26].

Examined issues	E-government portals in EAEU countries									
	Armenia		Belarus		Kazakhstan		Kyrgyzstan		Russia	
	2016	2021	2016	2021	2016	2021	2016	2021	2016	2021
Archive information and data bases	+	+	+	+	+	+	−	+	+	+
Social networks functions	−	−	−	−	+	+	−	−	−	−
E-consultation mechanisms	+	+	−	+	+	+	+	+	+	+
Public opinion instrument	−	+	−	−	+	+	+	+	−	+
E-decision making instruments	−	−	−	−	−	−	−	−	−	−

The second monitoring trend uses the United Nations E-Participation Index methodology. The Eurasian Economic Union countries e-services portals were explored with an interval of 5 years (2016 and 2021): "Public Services Portal of Russian Federation" (https://www.gosuslugi.ru/), "Common Portal of E-Services" (http://portal.gov.by – Belarus), "Public Services and Online Information" (http://egov.kz/wps/portal/index?lan

g=ru – Kazakhstan), "Electronic Government of the Republic of Armenia" (e-gov.am), and "E-Petition Portal of Kyrgyzstan" (http://www.kattar.kg/)[1].

We selected for analysis a set of parameters (see Table 2) [26].

However, most sites do not have direct tools for interacting with authorities. Nevertheless, e-participation tools are aimed at "provision the e-interaction between citizens and state". According to experts, the functioning of some portals and services for receiving electronic services does not correspond to the stated objectives. In particular, there are portals for electronic voting and petition, for example, the portal "Russian Public Initiative" [26].

5   Conclusion and Further Steps

According to experts, today the electronic government development in the EAEU countries implies an increase in public administration efficiency, as well as the development of communication between the authorities and citizens, adaptation of public services to the population needs, free access to information about government and social programs. Also, E-governance development includes the popularization of citizens' participation in the government decision-making [26].

Concerning the research questions, we can say the following.

RQ1: At the moment, the declared aims of some initiatives in the EAEU countries (e-interaction between citizens and government) are not supported by the functional facilities.

We can see some similar features of the EAEU countries approaches to e-participation. Policy papers (strategies and programs), as well as the legislation, contained similar aims and were adopted at the same time. However, the legislation should be developed by normative formalization of e-commerce, e-learning, as well as other aspects. Development in this direction will contribute to improved integration and social interaction. However, the EAEU countries e-governance development are often not coordinated, do not have detailed programs and development strategies, has internal contradictions. [26] At the state level, the development strategy should correspond to the digitalization's main goals and priorities. Experts note that institutional immaturity associated with the overall ongoing transformation of state institutions as negative factors affecting the e-government development in the EAEU. [26] Currently, it is hard to effectively facilitate the integration in the region through e-governance tools.

RQ2: During the studies, it was found that many institutions are responsible for the development of electronic control in the EAEU countries. This is a negative factor that causes functions duplication, difficulties in determining responsibilities in the course of their work, and also causes difficulties in launching e-participation and governance projects.

In the course of future research, institutional maturity level of e-government services in the EAEU countries should be determined. However, this research question is extremely difficult, since there are no generally accepted criteria for determining institutional maturity. There is also no large-scale research in this area. Note that this issue

---

[1] At the moment "E-Government Portal of Kyrgyzstan" is under development.

was not discussed at the state level, since services are only being introduced into the state system. Therefore, a number of systemic studies in this area are required.

It is extremely important for future research to analyze Eurasian region integration processes against the background of e-participation and governance services development. In order to ensure the Eurasian region sustainable development and integration, on the basis of planned studies, an optimal e-government model will be developed.

Digitalization is now becoming a cross-cutting topic for most subject areas of research in humanities and socio-economic sciences, in the social challenges study and institutions that contribute to the human capital development. The proposed list of topics does not include the technical and technological aspects of digitalization, but focuses on relevant interdisciplinary research areas. International experience shows that it is at the intersection of disciplines that centers of excellence and expertise are formed.

1. Digital transformation of socio-economic processes.
2. Digital transformation and human capital development.
3. Digital transformations of the branches of human life.
4. "Smart city" and research into the specifics of the design, implementation and development of complex socio-technical projects.
5. Big data for the study of complex socio-technical systems.
6. Artificial intelligence for digital transformation of socio-economic processes.
7. Development of standards and conceptual framework, development of a competence centers network in the field of digital transformation.

The seven thematic blocks presented above, in our opinion, do not cover the entire spectrum of possible areas of scientific and technical cooperation within the EAEU. However, they can form the basis for the elaboration of an important area related to the promotion of the implementation of the EAEU Digital Agenda in the context of the tasks of socio-economic integration in order to increase the quality of citizens life and the growth of total human capital.

References

1. The Chiefs of EAEU Member-States Ratified New Structure of EEC Collegium. http://www. eurasiancommission.org/ru/nae/news/Pages/22-12-2015-5.aspx
2. Tolbert, C., Mossberger, K.: The effects of e-government on trust and confidence in government. Public Adm. Rev. 66(3), 354–369 (2006)
3. Chugunov, A., Kabanov, Y., Bolgov, R., Kampis, G., Wimmer, M., et al.: Communications in Computer and Information Science, vol. 674. Springer, Cham (2016). https://doi.org/10. 1007/978-3-319-49700-6
4. Bolgov R., Filatova O., Golubev V.: E-government in the eurasian economic union: a comparative study of member states. In: 11th International Conference on Theory and Practice of Electronic Governance, ACM International Conference Proceeding Series, ICEGOV 2018, pp. 27–33 (2018). https://doi.org/10.1145/3209415.3209435
5. Haas, E.B.: The study of regional integration: reflections on the joy and anguish of pretheorizing. Int. Organ. 24(4), 607–646 (1970)

6. Kubicek, H., Aichholzer, G.: Closing the evaluation gap in e-participation research and practice. In: Aichholzer, G., Kubicek, H., Torres, L. (eds.) Evaluating e-Participation. PAIT, vol. 19, pp. 11–45. Springer, Cham (2016). https://doi.org/10.1007/978-3-319-25403-6_2

7. Feeney, M.K., Brown, A.: Are small cities online? Content, ranking, and variation of US municipal websites. Gov. Inf. Q. **34**(1), 62–74 (2017). https://doi.org/10.1016/j.giq.2016.10.005

8. Elsherif, M., Azab, N.: A framework to measure e-participation level of government social media accounts. In: ICIST 2019: Proceedings of the 9th International Conference on Information Systems and Technologies (2019). https://doi.org/10.1145/3361570.3361572

9. Chugunov, A.V., Kabanov, Y.: Evaluating e-participation institutional design. a pilot study of regional platforms in Russia. In: Edelmann, N., Parycek, P., Misuraca, G., Panagiotopoulos, P., Charalabidis, Y., Virkar, S. (eds.) ePart 2018. LNCS, vol. 11021, pp. 13–25. Springer, Cham (2018). https://doi.org/10.1007/978-3-319-98578-7_2

10. Kassen, M.: Understanding Systems of e-Government: e-Federalism and e-Centralism in the United States and Kazakhstan. Lexington Books, Lanham (2015)

11. UN E-Government Development Index. Country Data. 2020. https://publicadministration.un.org/egovkb/en-us/Data-Center

12. Belyi, V., Smirnova, P., Chugunov, A.: Implementation of electronic state services in the economic and demographic conditions of the COVID-19: citizens survey results in St. Petersburg. Int. J. Open Inf. Technol. **8**(11), 97–109 (2020). (In Russian)

13. Chugunov, A., Kabanov, Y., Panfilov, G.: Regional e-participation portals evaluation: preliminary results from Russia. In: CEUR Workshop Proceedings, 2797, 2020 Ongoing Research, Practitioners, Posters, Workshops, and Projects of the International Conference EGOV-CeDEM-ePart, EGOV-CeDEM-ePart 2020, Virtual, Linkoping, 31 August 2020–2 September 2020, pp. 71–78 (2020)

14. Chugunov, A., Kabanov, Y., Fediashin, S.: Development of the electronic "reception desks" in the Russian regions: pilot survey results of 2017–2018. Inf. Resour. Russia **3**, 32–36 (2019). (In Russian)

15. Berntzen, L., Olsen, M.G.: Benchmarking e-government - a comparative review of three international benchmarking studies. In: Proceedings of Third International Conference on Digital Society, pp. 77–82 (2009). https://doi.org/10.1109/ICDS.2009.55

16. Fedotova, O., Teixeira, L., Alvelos, H.: E-participation in Portugal: evaluation of government electronic platforms. Procedia Technol. **5**, 152–161 (2012). https://doi.org/10.1016/j.protcy.2012.09.017

17. Vidiasova, L.: The applicability of international techniques for e-participation assessment in the russian context. In: Chugunov, A.V., Bolgov, R., Kabanov, Y., Kampis, G., Wimmer, M. (eds.) DTGS 2016. CCIS, vol. 674, pp. 145–154. Springer, Cham (2016). https://doi.org/10.1007/978-3-319-49700-6_15

18. Ostling A.: How democratic is e-participation? In: Proceedings of the International Conference for E-Democracy and Open Government, CeDEM 2011, pp. 59–70 (2011)

19. Radina, N.K. (ed.): Digital Political Participation: The Effectiveness of Electronic Petitions of the Internet Platforms Change.org and ROI (Russian and Cross-Cultural Perspectives). Nestor Istoria, St. Petersburg (2019). (in Russian)

20. Xenakis, A., Loukis, E.: An investigation of the use of structured e-forum for enhancing eparticipation in parliaments. Int. J. Electron. Gov. **3**(2), 134–147 (2010). https://doi.org/10.1504/IJEG.2010.034092

21. Bohman, S.: Information technology in eparticipation research: a word frequency analysis. In: Tambouris, E., Macintosh, A., Bannister, F. (eds.) ePart 2014. LNCS, vol. 8654, pp. 78–89. Springer, Heidelberg (2014). https://doi.org/10.1007/978-3-662-44914-1_7

22. List of instructions following the meeting of the Council for the Development of Local Self-Government. President of Russia. Documentation, 1 March 2020. http://kremlin.ru/acts/ass ignments/orders/62919

23. Feedback platform. Unified portal of state and municipal services. https://www.gosuslugi.ru/ 10091/1

24. For the implementation of regional management centers in the Russian Federation, the Autonomous Non-Commercial Organization "Dialogue Regions" was created. Expert Center of the Electronic State. https://d-russia.ru/dlja-vnedrenija-centrov-upravlenija-regionami-v-rf-sozdano-ano-dialog-regiony.html

25. Reception of messages has been stopped. The portal "People's Expertise" is being replaced by "POS". People's Expertise of the Leningrad Region. https://xn--80aaaogmgoxcjqhhmt5p9a. xn--p1ai/news/66/

26. Bolgov, R., Karachay, V.: E-participation projects development in the e-governance institutional structure of the eurasian economic union's countries: comparative overview. In: Chugunov, A.V., Bolgov, R., Kabanov, Y., Kampis, G., Wimmer, M. (eds.) DTGS 2016. CCIS, vol. 674, pp. 205–218. Springer, Cham (2016). https://doi.org/10.1007/978-3-319-49700-6_20

The Impact of M-Learning on Sustainable Information Society

Radka Nacheva[1](✉) ⓘ, Vladimir Sulov[1] ⓘ, and Maciej Czaplewski[2] ⓘ

[1] University of Economics – Varna, Varna, Bulgaria
{r.nacheva,vsulov}@ue-varna.bg
[2] University of Szczecin, Szczecin, Poland
maciej.czaplewski@usz.edu.pl

Abstract. The rapid development of information and communication technologies (ICT) comprises the development of the information society on many different levels. One of them is connected with sustainability. The concept of a sustainable information society has been hotly debated by researchers for the last fifteen years. In this paper we focus on the education's point of view and specifically on one of the ways to increase student motivation – m-learning. The purpose of the publication is to propose a conceptual model of a m-learning system that integrates approach to information society and the views of the stakeholders (i.e. teachers, students, university management, etc.). Such model is crucial for the best use of m-learning and its potential to reduce the digital division which subsequently leads to a more sustainable information society. To achieve this goal, we surveyed the opinion of academics at Polish and Bulgarian universities. For the processing of opinions, we have applied the tools of statistical, sentiment and emotional analysis.

Keywords: m-learning · Higher education · Sustainability · Information society · Emotions mining

1 Introduction

The topics of information society development and sustainability are not new. Additionally, they are gaining more and more popularity due to the rapid development of information and communication technologies. The 2020 pandemic situation is forcing the processes of digitalization in all fields of public spheres, including education. There is an increase in the use of Internet and consumption of digital services, which in turn enhances the rapid information growth through the exchange of data between users online. The statistical portal Statista.com reported 4.66 billion active internet users worldwide at the beginning of 2021 – which translates into 59.5% of the global population [1]. 92.6% (4.32 billion) of all users accessed the internet via mobile devices. There is an increase of almost 400 million users compared to 2019 or the period before the pandemic [2]. One the other side, global internet penetration rate as of April 2021 is much higher for Europe and North America (between 82 and 97%) than for Asia, South America and Oceania (between 60 and 70%). The lowest internet consumption is in African countries (between 24 and 60%) [3]. In 2021, the number of mobile devices

© Springer Nature Switzerland AG 2022
A. V. Chugunov et al. (Eds.): EGOSE 2021, CCIS 1529, pp. 244–262, 2022.
https://doi.org/10.1007/978-3-031-04238-6_19

used by consumers worldwide increased by one billion, compared to 2020 - from 14 to 15 billion. [4] The increased use of digital devices also leads to an increase in the volume of data generated. For 2021 it is reported that there are 79 zettabytes of data, and this number will be more than double by 2025 [5]. For comparison, a year earlier it was reported that they were 64.2 zettabytes [6]. This increase is attributed to the pandemic and to the need to reorient many activities in the Internet space. However, 90% of the data in the global data sphere is replicated data, while only 10% is unique [5].

Against the background of the growing use of the Internet and digital devices, there is still a tangible gap between low- and high-income countries. Digital connectivity, especially in a state of emergency, is extremely important for the most vulnerable society groups. Without modern infrastructure, people with special needs or those who are poor remain isolated, both in terms of employment opportunities as well as education. The World Bank states that "more than 600 million people live without access to the Internet, a far cry from the United Nations' Sustainable Development Goal target of universal and affordable access to the Internet." [7].

All these data lead to the conclusion of a large growth of the amount of techno-logically mediated information. It is about almost 80 zettabytes, which are expected to double in just 3–4 years. The development of technology is far from enough to form a sustainable information society. In the context of sustainability, at the international level United Nations (UN) has identified 17 Sustainable Development Goals (SDGs), the implementation of which is monitored at national and organizational levels too. Their goals are to reduce world poverty and hunger, to ensure gender equality, to improve health and education, to increase economic growth and more. UNESCO invokes for ensuring inclusive and equitable quality education and promoting lifelong learning opportunities for all [8]. Their analysis shows that inequalities in education are significant and have deepened during the coronavirus pandemic. About 500 million students were not part of the online training. According to UN statistics, 34% of the world's poorest students have failed to complete their academic commitments due to the COVID-19 crisis [9]. That is why more and more goals and indicators of success are set for educational institutions.

Goal 4 - Quality education has not yet been fully achieved. There are many challenges for teachers, especially in low-income countries. The UNESCO Global Education Mon-itoring Report of 2021 is one of the tools for monitoring and reporting on Goal 4 and on education in the other UN goals. The analysis covers Central and Eastern Europe, the Caucasus and Central Asia. It reaffirms that "should be prepared and supported to rec-ognize student needs, ensure rich learning environments, and cooperate with colleagues to provide high-quality education for all" [10]. The authors point out that the teachers from the studied areas are prepared to teach mainly in their native language by traditional methods, which do not require the obligatory participation of digital devices. Estonia is the most prepared in terms of e-learning, where the provision of e-services is about 99%, including in terms of students' access to online materials in all schools and universities.

According to the same study, in Poland 85% of school teachers indicated that they had no experience with distance learning before the pandemic outbreak, and 52% reported some difficulty using digital tools [10]. The report points out that inequalities in online learning are particularly pronounced among poorer students. Low-income families can-not provide adequate facilities for their children's education. Whether it is a pandemic, deteriorating political situation or a situation of difficult access to the school environment, digital and broadcast remote learning programs are not available around schoolchildren worldwide [11]. Ministries around the world are developing "policies regarding the provision of at least one form of distance learning that involved digital and/or broadcast instruction" [11]. Some of these policies are related to the implementation of m-learning due to the fact that the majority of students have at least one mobile device, most often a smartphone.

The technological progress and the development of the information society are not unequivocal. The advantages, as the above-mentioned authors point out, are mainly related to economic progress, capitalist growth, development of employees' skills in order to find new fields of professional realization, environmentally friendly methods of dissemination of information, integration of new teaching methods in education systems worldwide, etc. At the other pole are the negatives of the much-desired sustainability in the information society. The digital division between low- and high-income countries, between rich and poor, between disadvantaged and special needs people and people with high social status is widening.

These problems raise a number of questions among researchers, which purpose is to reduce digital inequalities between people and strengthen the digital inclusion of vulnerable groups in society. One of the solutions we can offer for building digital bridges in education is mobile learning, as the most accessible option for online learning. M-learning has the potential to reduce the gap between rich and poor, the digital division and in consequence lead to a more sustainable information society.

On this basis, **the aim of this paper** is to propose a conceptual model of a m-learning system that integrates approach to information society and the views of the stakeholders. Such model is crucial for the best use of m-learning and its potential to reduce the digital division which subsequently leads to a more sustainable Information Society.

Based on the goal we can formulate the following research questions:

- (RQ1) What technologies and tools are used to implement m-learning?
- (RQ2) To what extent is m-learning adopted by teachers in higher education?

To answer research questions, the paper should meet the following objectives:

- To research of sustainability in the information society;
- To study of m-learning systems and frameworks;
- To survey of the opinion of university professors on the adoption of m-education;
- We process the results by means of statistical analysis and opinion mining tools.

2   Literature Review

The issues of sustainability of information technology are considered by a number of researchers. Christian Fuchs summarizes approaches to sustainability and information society policies. These are: reductionism, projectivism, dualism, and dialectic. According to him, they "classify information society policy discourses according to how they relate the domains of ecology and the economy to the realms of politics and culture" [12].

The dimensions of Sustainability that Christian Fuchs summarizes are: Ecological, Technological, Economic, Political, Cultural, Sustainability of Mass Media, Science, Art, Education, Ethics, Medicine, Sports and Social Relationships [13].

As Fuchs points out, the concept of sustainability comes from the field of the environment and the environmental dimension should play a key role in defining this term [12]. The leading forces that define the information society in the Reductionism approach are ecology, economy, or technology. As an example, the author gives GDP investment in information technology and the information economy. The physical aspects of the information society are important. For example, projectivism is an approach found in ICT policy discourses on sustainability. It tends to be linked to the interests of industry because politics and/or culture are the driving forces behind this approach. Dialectic approaches, on the other hand, are based on a number of dimensions that see the information society as interdependent, mutually causally linked, and only relatively autonomous. Contrary to this notion, dualistic approaches rely on multiple dimensions that are not necessarily related to each other. It suggests that ICT development can be achieved simultaneously through capitalist growth and social equality. The investment in ICT is linked to capitalist growth.

Ziemba et al. examine maturity of a sustainable information society. They define the information society as "evolved from a narrow observation and assessment to a more holistic approach <...> which has access and is able to use ICTs and information and knowledge to achieve collective and individual goals in an efficient and effective manner, in economic, social and cultural dimensions" [14]. On one hand, according to some authors, the information society has a direct bearing on economic growth and sustainable development, movements of goods, information and people [14, 18]. This is confirmed by Fuchs' research, which we quoted. On the other hand, Ziemba et al. point out that the information society is also responsible for digital exclusion, the formation of new social divisions, economic diversification, loss of privacy, cybercrime [14, 16, 17].

A conceptual model of a sustainable information society is proposed in [15]. It involves several levels of interaction. The main players in the model are ICT, stakeholders (citizens-governments-businesses) and the data, information and knowledge that is exchanged. First of all, these are current emerging trends, which are expressed in the growing importance of ICT, the processing of big data and the acceleration of digitalization processes. We are witnessing huge changes in this direction since 2020, when the pandemic accelerated the development of ICT in order to achieve a sustainable information society. At the next level, Ziemba defines the principles that are observed in the information society: trust, partnership, networking, transparency, openness, creativity, adaptability and entrepreneurship. Success factors in the information society are of course directly related to the use (economic, technological, social, organizational, culture, politics) and access to ICT and competencies of their stakeholders. From these factors derive the metrics with which the development of the information society is measured. In this regard, we do not establish formal metrics for measuring the sustainability of the information society. They should be entirely related to ICT and their adoption by stakeholders.

The development of the information society is a direct task of the United Nations Group on the Information Society (UNGIS), which deals with the development, implementation and support of "policy coherence and program coordination on matters related to information and communications technologies (ICTs) in support of internationally -agreed development goals " [19]. UNGIS hosts the annual World Summit on the Information Society (WSIS) Forum, which in 2020 focuses on ICT for the development of societies around the world, including the use of new technologies by young people, the elder generation and people with disabilities. In the conditions of COVID-19 one of the most discussed topics is e-learning. Some of the problems that are identified in low-incoming countries are related to quality education, lack of infrastructure, technology and trained teachers [20]. In remote areas, students often do not have access to online learning. Due to the popularity of mobile technologies, one of the possible solutions to the problems with e-learning is mobile learning.

To answer the RQ1, we must explore researches that work on the problems of m-learning. Some of them also offer models of such systems. For example, Todoranova and Penchev offer in their study a detailed conceptual framework for mobile learning development in higher education [21]. These authors prioritize the factors that influence mobile learning. They divide them into external and internal ones. The first group includes policies imposed by governments and educational institutions, as well as the rules of the business environment. The internal factors influencing m-learning are the policies imposed by university management, IT infrastructure and the development environment. The authors also pay attention to the security of m-learning platforms. This problem is also addressed by researchers who identify security based on the completeness-determining indicator [22].

Two author teams are researching the application of M-Learning as a New Interactive Technology in higher education and Vocational Education. Sizova et. al. work on the advantages and disadvantages of m-learning [23]. They also explore commonly used mobile applications in the learning process. Such are, for example, interactive books, language quizzes, travel applications, applications to help programmers, biologists and others. specialized professions. Berestova et. al. emphasize the impact of m-learning on students [24]. According to them, it leads to the implementation of new learning strategies and the integration of tools close to students, such as social networks. On the other hand, it is an indicator of increased stress due to the inability to acquire knowledge without a direct connection with teachers. The research of other author teams focuses on the changes of m-education in higher education in the conditions of a pandemic. Marunevich et. al. explore the tools used to implement m-learning [25]. According to them, these are mainly LMS and social networks. Valeeva and Kalimullin explore the challenges facing teachers in Russia during the lockdown in Russia [26]. According to them, the pandemic has led to an increase in the experimental work of teachers, the study of new digital technologies in order to improve didactic skills.

In their publication, Petrova and Sulova touch on the application of artificial intelligence as a technology for measuring and controlling the quality [27]. They offer a new technique to handle the issue. Another author team is researching data mining algorithms for knowledge extraction [28]. They can be used in a number of areas, including education. They are often used in combination with artificial intelligence and machine learning. [29] and [30] work on the application of augmented reality in education. As [29] points out, AR visualization relies on tracking, which comprises a set of very different technologies with the determining of the goals. In our opinion, these technologies can be used as an extension of the new m-learning system model.

Bankov is working on the principles of gamification in web applications [31]. The author proposes a model that in our opinion can be applied in the development of mobile applications for educational purposes. Gaming software is characterized by high user engagement due to receiving various rewards as a result of their tasks. According to Bankov's model, the gamification of complex systems depends on four main components: motivation, actions, rewards, achievements. The model is applied in the training of bachelor's and master's students at the University of Economics - Varna.

Many publications offer m-learning application architecture. They offer m-learning software architecture [32–37]. In the general case, the architectural models are based on a multi-layered model of software systems, which consist as standard of a presentation layer, a service layer, a business layer, a data layer and external data sources. [36] suggested the so-called "human layer" which consists of learners, administrators and instructors. In our opinion, this can also be described as a layer of human resources management, an idea that we have set in another of our publication [38]. The difference between the models lies in the technologies that the authors offer for the implementation of the systems. In [37] the model is based on Moodle, while in [33] it is based on so-called "Software Product Line". [36] relies on the combination of JAVA or.NET platforms; both communicating using standard sets of protocols such as HTTP, XML and SOAP, and repository is accomplished through UDDI. Another author's vision is for responsive mobile learning, which is based on fog computing architecture [32]. What is special about this type of architecture is that the system consists of cloud and fog layers, i.e., applications are completely cloud-based. The cloud layer contains all historical/backup storages and batch mining intelligences. The fog layer consists of "lightly NoSQL data storages and various internal network operations" [39]. The system is directly dependent on educational policy publishers, institutions, teachers and learners. The latter, in turn, can be related to the already mentioned human layer or human resources management layer.

We believe that the development of a m-learning system is not only related to technological implementation. The views of stakeholders must also be considered, which would only help to improve the user experience. On the one hand, these are the learners. On the other hand, these are the academics. Both sides are the ones most involved in the educational process.

We studied the opinion of the students in another paper [40], which we have in mind when realizing the current purpose. The opinion of the academics is summarized in the next section of this paper.

3   Method

3.1   Material

To answer the RQ2, we must define a research method which purpose is to investigate academic representatives' views on improving the "student-teacher" communication by integrating modern mobile technologies in the learning process. That is related to study the adoption of m-learning in higher education. There are investigated Bulgarian and Polish lecturers. We explored their opinion about the attitude towards mobile learning and experiences with m-learning tools.

3.2 Design

The study used partially within-subject design, with the two main factors being the participants' academic position and the country of residence (Bulgaria or Poland). The independent variable is the stated benefits of mobile learning, and the dependent one is the rating of the characteristics of mobile devices that can hinder the successful implementation of mobile learning. They are detailed in the next sections of the paper.

This study has some limitations:

- the scope of the studied countries is narrowed in order to test the research methods, and not so much to study the adoption of m-learning in different countries around the world;
- the number of participants cannot be considered as a representative statistical sample of academics from both countries. On this basis, no general conclusions can be drawn;
- the representativeness of the participants in the different age groups is not enough to make a differentiation by that criterion.

3.3 Participants

The number of Bulgarian respondents is 80 (47 female) who are academics at University of Economics – Varna (UEV). Total number of Polish participants is 57 (30 female) who are academics at University of Szczecin (USZ). Two of them (one Bulgarian and one Polish participant) did not agree to use their data for research purposes. Their answers were excluded from the statistics below.

The respondents were divided into five age groups and six academic positions (Table 1).

3.4 Process

We have developed a bilingual survey in English and Bulgarian. We used email and university channels to distribute it among the academics. The study contains the following groups, marked with Gn, and the related questions, marked with Qn:

- (G1) Participant data: containing questions about academic position, age group, gender, teaching experience (in years) and field of study.
- (G2) E-Learning experience:

- (Q1) Do you have experience with e-learning?
- (Q2) Please write approximately how many years you have been participating in e-learning.

Table 1. Statistics on survey participants.

Country of residence	Age group	Percentage	Academic position	Percentage
Bulgaria	25–34	10.13	Professor	6.33
	35–44	29.11	Associate Professor	29.11
	45–54	41.77	Chief Assistant Professor	41.77
	55–64	12.66	Assistant Professor	15.19
	65+	6.33	Senior Lecturer	5.06
			Lecturer	2.53
Poland	25–34	10.71	Professor	10.71
	35–44	46.43	Associate Professor	17.86
	45–54	25	Chief Assistant Professor	10.71
	55–64	10.71	Assistant Professor	42.86
	65+	7.14	Senior Lecturer	7.14
			Lecturer	10.71

Source: own elaboration

- (Q3) What learning content management platforms do you have experience with?
- (Q4) What e-learning platforms do you have experience with?
- (Q5) Do you access e-learning platforms via mobile device?

- (G3) E-learning platform of the University:

- (Q6) Do you use the e-learning platform of the University?
- (Q7) If you use the platform, how many courses do you manage through it?
- (Q8) Do you use the platform via mobile device?
- (Q9) According to you the e-learning platform of the University is: easy and intuitive to work on mobile devices; not optimized for mobile; I cannot evaluate.
- (Q10) In what form do you most often use study materials in the platform?
- (Q11) Do you conduct tests via the e-learning platform?

- (G4) Mobile devices and platforms:

- (Q12) Do you use mobile applications/platforms to support the learning process in the courses you teach?
- (Q13) Would you use mobile apps/platforms to help the educational process in the courses you teach?
- (Q14) Please list the names of mobile learning applications/platforms you have experience with. (open-ended question)
- (Q15) How often do you use your mobile device to access e-learning applications/platforms?

- (G5) M-learning benefits:

 – (Q16) Please note the benefits of mobile learning.
 – (Q17) In your opinion, which of the characteristics of mobile devices can hinder the successful implementation of mobile learning?
 – (Q18) Please share your recommendations on the successful implementation of mobile learning at the university. (open-ended question)

We processed the two questionnaires independently of each other to compare the results. We used survey software that supports the automatic generation of graphs of closed questions. The open questions were processed through data mining tools – Orange and MeaningCloud. They were sent as unstructured text and therefore require the application of text mining methods. The techniques of sentiment and emotional were applied for studying the level of satisfaction with the successful implementation of mobile learning at academic environment.

4 Results

4.1 Statistical Analysis

The participants answered the questions from group G2 as follows (Table 2):

Table 2. Results of G2 group.

	UEV	USZ
Q1	96,4%: yes	85,71%: yes
Q2	1–5 years: 53,16% 6–10 years: 36,71% 10+ years: 10,13%	1–5 years: 67,85% 6–10 years: 14,29% 10+ years: 17,86%
Q3	Moodle: 84,62% Google Classroom: 32,97% Blackboard Learn: 5,49% Other: 13,92%	Moodle: 67,85% Google Classroom: 21,43% Blackboard Learn: 8,93% Other: 17,86%
Q4	Udemy: 26,37% Coursera: 28,57% Open-edX: 12,09% WizIQ: 6,59% LearnWorlds: 9,89% Other: 27,47%	Udemy: 25% Coursera: 25% Open-edX: 7,14% WizIQ: 7,14% LearnWorlds: 3,57% Other: 21,43%
Q5	61.54%: yes	60,71%: yes

The participants answered the questions from group G3 as follows (Table 3):

Table 3. Results of G3 group.

	UEV	USZ
Q6	88,61%: yes	57,14: yes
Q7	1–3: 68,57% 4–6: 8,57% 6+: 22,86%	1–3: 68,74% 4–6: 15,63% 6+: 15,63%
Q8	48.35%: yes	85,71%: yes
Q11	94,95: yes	75%: yes

Additionally, participants answered Q9 in relation to Q6. 60,71% of the Polish participants and 50,63% of the Bulgarian respondents cannot evaluate their universities' e-learning platforms. According to 21,43% of the Poles and 44,3% Bulgarians it is easy and intuitive to work on mobile devices. The rest 17,86% of the Polish and 5,06% of the Bulgarian participants think their universities' e-learning platforms not optimized for mobile operation. On the Q10, academics said that they mostly share study material as: presentations (71,43% USZ and 87,34% UEV), PDF/DOC files (64,28% USZ and 97,47% UEV), audio/video content (21,43% USZ and 48,1% UEV), text files/pages (32,14% USZ and 63,29% UEV) and forums/chats (32,14% USZ and 54,43% UEV).

The distribution of G4 questions is comparable for the USZ and UEV participants. To question Q12 57,14% of USZ respondents answered that they use mobile applications/platforms to support the learning process in the courses they teach. 29.67% UEV participants answered positively to the same question. To Q13 50% of USZ respondents use mobile apps/platforms to help the educational process in the courses they teach. 45.05% UEV participants answered positively to the same question. To question Q14, participants from both universities answered similarly to Q3 and Q4. They use mobile applications on these e-learning platforms. As a result of Q15, 42,86% USZ respondents use their mobile device to access e-learning applications/platforms 1–5 times a day, and 14,29% 5–10 times per day. Only few of them use every other day or once a week - 8,93%. 31,65% UEV participants use mobile devices for the same purpose 1–5 times per day, 12,66% - 5–10 times per day. The rest of them answered they do not use mobile access and prefer desktop version of e-learning platforms.

The data show that the participants from both universities answer almost identically. They have experience with e-learning, and the most commonly used platforms are Moodle and Google Classroom. Most prefer to access e-learning platforms via a computer, but would also use mobile applications. In Q18, some users say that the main reason for their reticence about m-learning is related to the age factor. Experienced academics prefer traditional forms of e-learning. Their motives are that only in this way will a full-fledged, high-quality learning process be conducted, and not for its bilateral deprivation of depth. Lecturers occupying lower levels in the academic hierarchy point out that: this type of training will support the overall educational process; it is the possibility of direct involvement of each student; it ensures better organization of time and use of resources; it can be useful during a pandemic or during the temporary absence of a lecturer/student. Some respondents believe that in order for m-learning to be successful, both parties need to be prepared for it, finding a flexible approach that can be combined with other forms of learning.

4.2 Sentiment Analysis

The sentiment analysis of the open questions was made by applying MeaningCloud – a Microsoft Excel plugin. We used its built-in basic WordNet model. The analysis confirms that the attitudes of all participants towards implementation of mobile learning at the academy are predominantly positive. 63.29% of Bulgarian and 42.86% of Polish respondents express a positive opinion about successful integration of mobile learning in the academic environment (Table 4).

Table 4. Results of MeaningCloud's sentiment analysis of open questions.

Polarity	UEV	USZ
P+	7,59	17,86
P	55,70	25
NEU	17,72	14,29
N	13,92	32,14
N+	5,06	10,71

Source: own elaboration

The main reason for the failure of mobile learning, which participants point out, is the excessive workload of students when using mobile devices. Although students use them too much for personal purposes, according to some respondents, the use of mobile applications in the learning process would drastically reduce face-to-face communication.

4.3 Emotional Analysis

We made the analysis of emotional attitudes was performed by using the Orange's Tweet Profiler module (Fig. 1), which supports several methods of content classification. These are classes based on the classifications of Plutchik, Ekman and Profile of Mood States (POMS). Each of them identifies a different number of basic emotions.

Fig. 1. Configuration of emotion analysis in Orange. Source: own elaboration.

According to Plutchik these are: anticipation, acceptance, joy, surprise, anger, disgust, fear, sadness [41]. Ekman distinguishes joy, surprise, anger, disgust, fear, sadness [42]. POMS classify the emotions of tension, anger, vigor, fatigue, depression, confusion [43]. The common emotion for the three classifications is anger, which is considered a primary negative emotion, thanks to which individuals defend and survive, both physically and verbally.

The results generated by Orange after applying the Plutchik classifier are shown in Fig. 2 and Fig. 3. It is noticed that the positive emotions joy and trust are the highest percentage – 50,63% of Bulgarian participants' answers and 96,43% of Polish participants' answers.

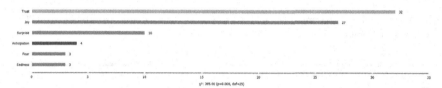

Fig. 2. UEV results of the emotions analysis in Orange according to the classifier of Plutchik. Source: own elaboration.

Fig. 3. USZ results of the emotions analysis in Orange according to the classifier of Plutchik. Source: own elaboration.

The results according to the Ekman classifier (Fig. 4 and Fig. 5) are similar to the previous one – again, positive emotions prevail. Orange identifies emotion joy in 50.63% of UEV answers and 75% of the USZ answers.

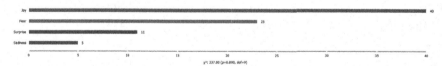

Fig. 4. UEV results of the emotions analysis in Orange according to the classifier of Ekman. Source: own elaboration.

In Fig. 6 and Fig. 7 it is noticed that the diagram changes when applying POMS. The reason is that this classification is oriented entirely to negative emotions.

The differences in the results of the application of the different classifiers also arise from the pre-defined set of words that is applied for sentiment analysis of Orange. The results of the emotional analysis are slightly different compared to the sentiment analysis. Plutchnik's and Ekman's classifiers of Orange tool show that the percentage of positive opinions is higher among Polish participants.

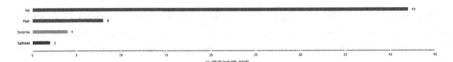

Fig. 5. USZ results of the emotions analysis in Orange according to the classifier of Ekman. Source: own elaboration.

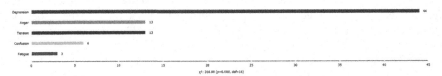

Fig. 6. UEV results of the emotions analysis in Orange according to the classifier of POMS. Source: own elaboration

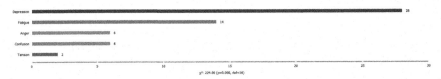

Fig. 7. USZ results of the emotions analysis in Orange according to the classifier of POMS. Source: own elaboration

For comparison, we applied the emotional analysis model maintained by MeaningCloud (Table 5). It is based only on Plutchik's classifier. It is part of the Deep categorization module of MeaningCloud.

Table 5. Results of MeaningCloud's emotional analysis of open questions.

Emotion	UEV	USZ
Anger	8,25%	12,50%
Anticipation	29,90%	19,44%
Disgust	3,09%	5,56%
Fear	4,12%	4,17%
Joy	15,46%	13,89%
Sadness	6,19%	13,89%
Surprise	5,15%	8,33%
Trust	13,40%	11,11%
NEU	14,43%	11,11%

Source: own elaboration

Compared to Orange, MeaningCloud recognizes the full set of emotions from the Plutchnik classifier, with some of the open answers marked with two or three emotions.

The table shows that between 11 and 14% of the responses were identified as neutral (NEU).

However, emotional analysis confirms sentiment analysis of open questions made by MeaningCloud. As mentioned above, the positive attitudes prevail at both universities. This is an indicator of the adoption of m-learning in both universities.

5 Discussion

Summarizing the results of the research in this paper, as well as our previous research [38, 40, 44] and some aspects of [29, 30, 33], we can suggest a conceptual model of a m-learning system. We are developing the idea of a layered architectural model composed of subsystems with the integration of augmented reality (AR) to find application in the development of system modules to add elements of gamification (Fig. 8). We believe that the motivation and commitment of students to the learning process will increase.

The system must be based on the following principles: adaptability; gamification; ease of use; user oriented; security; sustainability; quality. The layers should integrate: basic pedagogical methods; data and knowledge management methods; business processes management methods; modern technologies to increase students' motivation; educational policies.

The system consists of two hardware tiers located on the client side and on the server side. The **User Experience Subsystem** is located on the client side. This is exactly the Presentation layer at the standard software architecture. It is used for visualizing the components of the user interface. The main elements are dashboards and views of the individual components that are part of the business process management subsystem.

On the server-side tier are located: cross-cutting, human resources management, policy, business processes management and data management subsystems. The **Cross-cutting Subsystem** groups all the components that affect the performance of the components of the other layers, which largely depends on the proper functioning of the system. These are modules for managing the authentication and authorization of users (security access), user accounts and sessions, quality management. It contains a Services module that consists of all APIs through which external systems are able to use the services of the proposed system. This is the interface that performs connection with the application that users install on their mobile devices to send data to the system.

The **Human Resources Management Subsystem** is based on basic postulates in human management related to the administration of knowledge, skills, productivity, as well as the principles of gamification. Here it is important to mention that human knowledge is key to the successful development of m-learning. As [31] points out, badges and pins are part of the gamification tools. Users collect rewards for their achievements in the learning process.

The **Policy Subsystem** integrates all legal frameworks at national, international and university level, which restrict stakeholders in using the system, but also the protection of their personal data. Strict adherence to the legal framework guarantees all parties that their rights are protected and that digitalisation guidelines are followed.

The **Business Processes Management Subsystem** contains all system components that implement the system's business logic. It includes Education Management module

User-side Tier

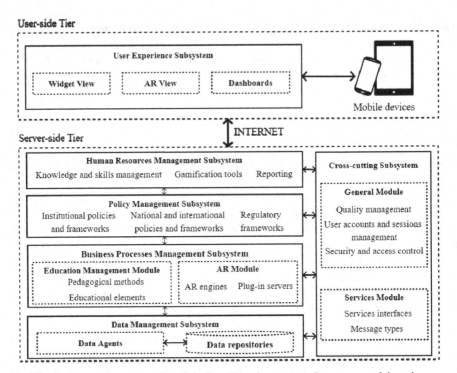

Fig. 8. Proposed conceptual model of a m-learning system. Source: own elaboration.

and AR module. The first one is responsible for successful pedagogical methods application through their educational elements. As [33] wrote, the educational elements are the entities that encapsulate the business logic and data necessary for representing real world elements, such as learners, teachers, classes, courses. AR module consists of AR engines and plug-in servers. The AR engine is in charge of user's behaviour tracking and scene augmentation/rendering [30]. It contains methods for image thresholding, markers detections, perspective computation.

The **Data Management Subsystem** groups all system components that combine into a logic necessary to access the data repositories.

The development of the system will be discussed in future papers. The exact technologies for its realization are not considered in the present study.

We can define the system we offer as an integrated system for m-learning, as it is based on various ICT technologies and teaching methods. We believe that it should implement the following basic principles of the information society [45]:

– promotion of ICTs for development;
– ICT for an inclusive information society;
– access to information and knowledge;
– building confidence and security in the use of ICTs;
– ICT applications benefits in all aspects of life.

6 Conclusions

In summary, regardless of the type and implementation of the architecture, it can be concluded that mobile learning has its positives (Q16). Among them are:

- applying a new paradigm of learning "on the go";
- immediate access to study materials at any time of the day and from anywhere in the world;
- opportunity to apply the principles of gamification in order to increase the motivation of learners;
- ad hoc collaboration and informal interaction between students;
- lifelong learning opportunities or non-age dependable possibilities;
- low cost, easy for understanding and adopting by young people.

As the participants in our study point out on Q17, mobile learning also has its drawbacks, which must be considered contextually, both in terms of learners and in terms of the learning environment and opportunities. Among them are:

- lack of adoption on the part of adult teachers;
- technical difficulties arising from the characteristics of mobile devices, such as screen size, data entry methods, battery capacity, and resource storage.
- connectivity issues, such as the amount of mobile data available or the speed of the Internet connection.

Here we had to add the problem with the coverage of mobile networks in remote mountainous areas, where access to a stable internet connection and mobile network is still low not only in Bulgaria or Poland, but also worldwide.

Despite those weaknesses, mobile learning remains one of the most affordable ways that can be integrated into the educational environment. In this regard, more needs to be done to develop information and communication technologies so as to contribute to overcoming the gap between societies and to ensuring a sustainable information society. WSIS Forum participants and scientists around the world are working to bridging the digital divide and connecting the unconnected [46]. The potential of new digital technologies contributes to building new, healthier and more interconnected societies. We believe that in the future we can improve our proposed model of m-learning system and integrate a wider range of technologies.

Acknowledgment. The reported study was supported by project NPI-36/2019 "Contemporary Approaches to The Integration of Mobile Technologies in Higher Education". We kindly thank all participants in our study.

References

1. Global digital population as of January 2021. https://www.statista.com/statistics/617136/dig ital-population-worldwide/. Accessed 21 Aug 2021
2. Global internet penetration rate as of April 2021, by region. https://www.statista.com/statis tics/269329/penetration-rate-of-the-internet-by-region/. Accessed 21 Aug 2021
3. Number of internet users worldwide from 2005 to 2019 (in millions). https://www.statista.com/statistics/273018/number-of-internet-users-worldwide/. Accessed 21 Aug 2021
4. Forecast number of mobile devices worldwide from 2020 to 2025 (in billions). https://www.statista.com/statistics/245501/multiple-mobile-device-ownership-worldwide/. Accessed 21 Aug 2021
5. Big data - Statistics & Facts. https://www.statista.com/topics/1464/big-data/. Accessed 21 Aug 2021
6. Volume of data/information created, captured, copied, and consumed worldwide from 2010 to 2025 (in zettabytes). https://www.statista.com/statistics/871513/worldwide-data-created/. Accessed 21 Aug 2021
7. Connecting the world - World Development Report 2021. https://wdr2021.worldbank.org/sto ries/connecting-the-world/. Accessed 21 Aug 2021
8. Quality Education – United Nations Sustainable Development. https://www.un.org/sustainab ledevelopment/education/. Accessed 21 Aug 2021
9. Ensure inclusive and equitable quality education and promote lifelong learning opportunities for all. https://unstats.un.org/sdgs/report/2020/goal-04/. Accessed 21 Aug 2021
10. Antoninis, M., et al.: Global Education Monitoring Report. Central and Eastern Europe, Caucasus and Central Asia. Inclusion and Education: All Means All. UNESCO (2021)
11. COVID-19: Are children able to continue learning during school closures? https://data.uni cef.org/resources/remote-learning-reachability-factsheet/. Accessed 21 Aug 2021
12. Fuchs, C.: Information technology and sustainability in the information society. Int. J. Commun. **11**, 2431–2461 (2017)
13. Fuchs, C.: Sustainability and the information society. In: Berleur, J., Nurminen, M.I., Impagli azzo, J. (eds.) Social Informatics: An Information Society for all? In Remembrance of Rob Kling, vol. 223, pp. 219–230. Springer, Boston (2006). https://doi.org/10.1007/978-0-387-37876-3_18
14. Ziemba, E., et al.: New perspectives on information society: the maturity of research on a sustainable information society. Online J. Appl. Knowl. Manag. **1**(1), 52–71 (2013)
15. Ziemba, E.: Discussion on a sustainable information society. Informatyka Ekonomiczna Bus. Inform. **1**(31), 13–25 (2014)
16. Ziemba, E.: The ICT adoption in government units in the context of the sustainable information society. In: Proceedings of the Federated Conference on Computer Science and Information Systems, pp. 725–733 (2018)
17. Ziemba, E.: Exploring levels of ICT adoption and sustainability – the case of local governments from Poland. Procedia Comput. Sci. **176**, 3067–3082 (2020)
18. Schneider, F., et al.: Eco-info-society: strategies for an ecological information society. In: Hilty, L.M., Gilgen, P.W. (eds.) Sustainability in the Information Society, pp. 831–838. Metropolis, Marburg (2001)
19. United Nations Group on the Information Society (UNGIS). https://sustainabledevelopment. un.org/index.php?page=view&type=30022&nr=1953&menu=3170. Accessed 21 Oct 2021
20. WSIS Forum 2020 Outcome Document. Fostering digital transformation and global part nerships: WSIS Action Lines for achieving SDGs. https://www.itu.int/net4/wsis/forum/2020/Files/outcomes/draft/WSISForum2020_OutcomeDocument_DRAFT-20210201.pdf. Accessed 21 Oct 2021

21. Todoranova, L., Penchev, B.: A conceptual framework for mobile learning development in higher education. In: Proceedings of the 21st International Conference on Computer Systems and Technologies, CompSysTech 2020, Ruse Bulgaria, New York, pp. 251–257. Association for Computing Machinery (2020)

22. Cristescu, M., Vasilev, J.: Specialized applications used in the mobile application security implementation process. In: Orăştean, R., Ogrean, C., Mărginean, S.C. (eds.) Organizations and Performance in a Complex World, pp. 39–49. Springer, Cham (2021). https://doi.org/10.1007/978-3-030-50676-6_4

23. Sizova, D., et al.: M-learning as a new interactive technology in education. Adv. Soc. Sci. Educ. Humanit. Res. **437**, 328–334 (2020)

24. Berestova, A., et al.: New tendencies in studies within vocational education in Russia. Int. J. Instr. **13**(1), 886–900 (2020)

25. Marunevich, O., et al.: E-learning and m-learning as tools for enhancing teaching and learning in higher education: a case study of Russia. In: SHS Web of Conferences, vol. 110, no. 03007 (2021)

26. Valeeva, R., Kalimullin, A.: Adapting or changing: the COVID-19 pandemic and teacher education in Russia. Educ. Sci. **11**, 408 (2021)

27. Petrova, R., Sulova, S.: AI governor for the quality and the strength of bridges. In: Proceedings of the 21st International Conference on Computer Systems and Technologies, CompSysTech 2020, pp. 78–85. Association for Computing Machinery (2020)

28. Stancu, A., Cristescu, M., Stoyanova, M.: Data mining algorithms for knowledge extraction. In: Fotea, S., Fotea, I., Văduva, S. (eds.) Challenges and Opportunities to Develop Organizations Through Creativity, Technology and Ethics, pp. 349–357. Springer, Cham (2020). https://doi.org/10.1007/978-3-030-43449-6_20

29. Turkan, Y., et al.: Mobile augmented reality for teaching structural analysis. Adv. Eng. Inform. **34**, 90–100 (2017)

30. Bifulco, P., et al.: Telemedicine supported by augmented reality: an interactive guide for untrained people in performing an ECG test. Biomed. Eng. Online **13**, 153 (2014). https://doi.org/10.1186/1475-925X-13-153

31. Bankov, B.: Game design principles in enterprise web applications. In: Proceedings of International Multidisciplinary Scientific Geoconference, SGEM 2020, Informatics, Geoinformatics and Remote Sensing, 18–24 August 2020, Albena, Bulgaria, vol. 20, issue 2.1, pp. pp. 161–167. STEF92 Technology Ltd., Sofia (2020)

32. Trifonova, A., Ronchetti, M.: A General Architecture for M-Learning. Department of Information and Communication Technology. University of Trento (2003)

33. Marcolino, A., Barbosa, E.: Towards a software product line architecture to build m-learning applications for the teaching of programming. In: Proceedings of the 50th Hawaii International Conference on System Sciences, pp. 6264–6273 (2017)

34. Sharma, S., Kitchens, F.: Web services architecture for m-learning. Electron. J. e-Learn. **2**(1), 203–216 (2004)

35. Shanmugapriya, M.: Design and development of m-learning framework based on learning management system architecture. Int. J. Adv. Sci. Technol. **29**(8s), 2585–2596 (2020)

36. Zaman, W., Basu, P.: A framework of web service based architecture for m-learning of a university consortium education system. Am. J. Comput. Sci. Eng. Surv. **3**(1), 11–20 (2015)

37. Casany, M., et al.: Moodbile: a framework to integrate m-learning applications with the LMS. J. Res. Pract. Inf. Technol. **44**(2), 129–149 (2012)

38. Nacheva, R., Jansone, A.: E-learning in a pandemic: the Bulgarian and Latvian experience in higher education. Izvestiya J. Univ. Econ. **64**(4), 311–331 (2020)

39. Parlakkılıç, A.: Responsive mobile learning (m-learning) application design and architecture in fog computing. Int. J. Mod. Educ. Stud. **3**(2), 82–94 (2019)

40. Todoranova, L., Nacheva, R., Sulov, V., Penchev, B.: A model for mobile learning integration in higher education based on students' expectations. Int. J. Interact. Mobile Technol. (iJIM) **14**(11), 171–182 (2020)

41. Plutchik, R. A general psychoevolutionary theory of emotion. In: Plutchik, R., Kellerman, H. (eds.) Emotion: Theory, Research, and Experience, vol. 1, pp. 3–31. Academic Press, Cambridge (1980)

42. Ekman, P.: Emotion in the Human Face, 2nd edn. Cambridge University Press, New York (1982)

43. Renger, R.: A review of the profile of mood states (POMS) in the prediction of athletic success. J. Appl. Sport Psychol. **5**(1), 78–84 (1993)

44. Nacheva, R.: Architecture of web-based system for usability evaluation of mobile applications. Izvestiya J. Univ. Econ. **61**(2), 187–201 (2017)

45. Declaration of Principles. Building the Information Society: a global challenge in the new Millennium. https://www.itu.int/net4/wsis/forum/2020/Home/Outcomes. Accessed 21 Oct 2021

46. Highlights and Outcomes of the WSIS Forum. https://www.itu.int/net4/wsis/forum/2020/Home/Outcomes. Accessed 21 Oct 2021

Digital Government and Economy

Improving eGovernment Services with Blockchain: Restoring Trust in e-voting Systems

Solomon Negash$^{(\boxtimes)}$

Kennesaw State University, Kennesaw, GA 30144, USA
snegash@kennesaw.edu

Abstract. Trust in e-voting systems has declined due to claims of fraud. The trust-less blockchain technology offers new hope to restore elector's trust on e-voting systems. The distributed ledger technology, often referred to as blockchain, provides desirable e-voting characteristics including provenance, immutability, security, and finality. Several technological, organizational, and environmental factors impede the adoption of blockchain technology, such as, its novelty, the perception that it is an unproven technology, its association with the seamier side of cryptocurrency, and uncertainty among prospective stakeholders about how to configure and implement blockchain solutions to serve their unique needs. However, evidence demonstrates that a socio-economic effect or benefit will catalyze the adoption of blockchain technology. This paper presents a modified framework for eGovernment blockchain technology adoption and a use case to help educate the public. The paper recommends field study for the proposed framework and more use cases to help familiarize the public about voting in a blockchain-based platform. Governments leading the way by adopting blockchain-based eGovernment services goes a long way in facilitating blockchain technology adoption by the public, hence, restore trust in blockchain based e-voting systems.

Keywords: Blockchain · Distributed ledger technology (DLT) · Trust · Trustless · e-voting · Socio-economic benefits · Decentralization · Immutability · Privacy · Provenance

1 Introduction

Trust on e-voting systems gets eroded when claims of voter fraud persists [5]. Unprecedented number of false claims were seen in the 2020 U.S. Presidential Election alleging election fraud [30]. A survey conducted three days after Biden was declared the winner, 40% of survey participants said they will continue to view Biden as illegitimate [30] and the partisan spite and endorsement of violence between Trump and Biden voters was equivalent [30]. This widespread of unfounded election fraud claims culminated in violence inside the U.S. capitol [11]. This erosion of trust in e-voting systems is disconcerting. A large segment of the U.S. voter, a country that boasts moral superiority, is

This is a U.S. government work and not under copyright protection in the U.S.; foreign copyright protection may apply 2022
A. V. Chugunov et al. (Eds.): EGOSE 2021, CCIS 1529, pp. 265–275, 2022.
https://doi.org/10.1007/978-3-031-04238-6_20

misled and distrusted the e-voting system. Would the public adopt e-voting system built on the blockchain technology that promises a trustless platform?

Trustless is a blockchain concept which means that you don't have to trust a third party: a bank, a person, or any intermediary that could operate between you and your cryptocurrency transactions or holdings.

Blockchain is a type of Distributed Ledger Technology (DLT) promising trustless platform that is immutable and collaborative [27]. DLTs serve as enablers for digital transformation [36, 39, 43]. Key characteristics of DLTs are consensus, provenance, immutability, and finality [17, 37]. DLT characteristics are defined by many sources including [45].

Consensus: agreement among all participants that the transaction is valid.

Provenance: always knowing ownership of the asset, where it came from and the ownership changes over time.

Immutability: a guarantee that recorded transactions in the ledger are not altered or tampered. No deletes. Agreed upon corrections to errors will be appended instead of deleting the prior record.

Finality: the current record in the ledger serves as a single source of truth, completion of transaction and its ownership are confirmed in one place.

DLT characteristics enable many eGovernment services like issuing entitlements, attestations and certifications, identity, and delegated authority. For example, current issuance processes are often paper based, non-interoperable and are susceptible to loss, destruction, forgery, and counterfeiting. Other digital mediums, like email, still have issues including loss of authenticity, provenance and audit trail. DLT technology can overcome these limitations and enable secure e-services for certificates, degrees & diplomas, badge, rewards points, documents, entitlements, and notarizations.

Greater transparency and trust are the mainstay of DLTs. Other benefits include enhanced security (tamper proof & immutable), improved traceability (full audit trail), and reduced costs (no middlemen/third party). These DLT characteristics enable government to improve service efficiencies; authenticity, audit trail, data analytics & tamper-proof to all documents; issue credentials on different blockchains (public or private) based on costing needs; and easily integrated into existing workflows.

Despite the technical and operational benefits, there is a gap in the literature on why the blockchain technology is not widespread? This study focuses on the research question: What are the factors hindering the adoption of blockchain e-voting platforms? Following [35] we use a technology, organization, and environment framework (TOE framework) to evaluate the challenges and expectations of adopting a blockchain technology to address the research question.

The rest of the manuscript is organized as follows, the background section summarizes the history of voting systems, followed by sections on literature review, discussions, and conclusion.

2 Background

This section provides a brief history of voting in the United States[1]. Casting votes has taken many different forms. When the first citizens began voting for government candidates, they "used different colored beans or kernels to cast votes" [20]. The methods of voting gradually changed over the years until people were actually calling out their votes to "tallying clerks" who were overseen by officials. This method of voting was exploited by the candidates that would stand next to the clerks while soliciting themselves to the citizens about to cast their votes.

It was not until the late nineteenth century that the U.S. government adopted the use of the paper ballot. This new form of voting allowed the concept of confidentiality to be incorporated into the voting process. In addition, it also allowed the voter to cast a vote without having to worry about others finding out what candidate she/he had chosen to support. The limitation of this method was that voters had to rely on the people counting the vote to properly handle their ballots as well as make accurate counts of the candidate's supporters. This possibility of fraud paved the way for the implementation of different voting techniques throughout the 1900s that would help reduce the possibility of someone tampering with the votes after they had been cast.

One of the first innovations to fix this problem was the lever machine. This type of machine was introduced at the end of 1800s. It used a series of levers that would turn counting wheels that would count the number of times each lever had been flipped. When the machine was checked the value on each counting wheel would represent the number of votes for a choice on a ballot. This method, unlike the paper ballot, kept the people who recorded the votes from being able to recount the vote, and any lost votes resulting from a defective machine would not be subjected for the final count [12].

By the 1960's the new technology of punch cards was introduced. These were brought into use to further speed up the tallying process as well as to address the concern that lever machines were having including the issues with keeping a proper count of votes. However, punch cards also had inherent flaws. Dented marks and not completely punched holes on the ballots made it difficult for the machines to count some ballots. If the ballot was evaluated by hand it was also difficult in some cases to determine the voter's intent.

Optical scans came out a few years later with the intent to fix the problems that occurred with punch cards. As it turned out, this method still had inherent flaws with the reading of the ballots much like that of the punch cards, but the technology reduced the number of failures in comparison.

It was at the turn of the century that a direct-recording electronic (DRE) devices began to be used in the United States' presidential elections. Few states adopted the idea in the 2000 election out of fear for lack of security with the machines being used. With improvements coming rather quickly to these machines, the number of votes cast greatly increased for the 2004 presidential election. Around 30% of the votes cast in the 2004 election were from electronic media [20].

Even with the introduction of newer, faster, and more accurate forms of voting, paper ballots, lever machines, and punch cards lingered in the United States until mid-2000s

---

[1] The earlier e-voting account in the background section is drawn from a 2008 unpublished class project by Alex Hough and Solomon Negash at Kennesaw State University.

[10]. The older voting systems, punch cards, lever machines, and paper ballots, have been showing a significant decline in use from 2000 to 2004, while the newer systems, optical scans and electronic systems, have been showing a significant increase in usage. Punch cards have decreased from 16.93% to 9.39%, lever machines from 13.94% to 8.67%, and paper ballots from 11.89% to 9.60% while optical scans have increased from 41.09% to 45.54% and electronic systems from 9.93% to 21.40% [13].

One of the main concerns with this new electronic voting technology is the lack of security built-in to the systems [4, 38] including programming codes, which was used to change the outcome of a 2002 gubernatorial election [13]. To further complicate the problem, there are a limited number of regulations that control the quality of the machines being used to capture the citizen's votes. For example, the programming error in Union County, Florida in September of 2002 that caused thousands of votes to be misrepresented [13]. Another example is the flawed voting machine chip in South Dakota that caused the votes to count twice [13]. Regulations are still trying to catch up with the systems being used [13].

Paper ballots had the lowest error rate at 1.9% rate of failure, followed closely by optical scanning at 2.1%, electronic systems at 2.9%, and punch cards at 3% [20]. Most of the problems from the electronic voting systems are due to programming logic errors [13]. In [12] the author explains the outdated lever machines to remove from use in New York to comply with HAVA (Help America Vote Act). The 2000 U.S. presidential election debacle and similar incidents show the importance of retaining a level of confidence in the voting systems [9].

In the 2016 U.S. presidential election optical scans were used 70%, 25% DREs, and 5% mixed devices [10]. In the 2018 midterm elections, West Virginia became the first state in the U.S. to allow select voters to cast their ballot on a mobile phone via a proprietary app that used a permissioned blockchain [33, 39] and again in 2020 in Utah county, West Virginia [39].

In the 2020 U.S. Presidential election mixed tabulation methods were used by the 50 states: 24 states used optical scan only, one state used DRE only, 11 states used a mix of optical scans and DRE, eight states used a mix of optical scan and hand count, and six states used a mix of optical scan, DRE, and hand count [40].

3 Literature Review

Voters are understandably concerned about election security. News reports of possible election interference by foreign powers, of unauthorized voting, of voter disenfranchisement, and of technological failures call into question the integrity of elections worldwide [28].

A traditional voting system relies on tallying authority. To the contrary, in Blockchain e-voting the platform itself provides complete proof of the votes casted, and the proofs are open for scrutiny by the public [42].

Blockchain applications are being developed or explored for governmental functions, such as homeland security (specifically border patrol), electronic citizen ID cards, and e-voting. In light of the allegations that elections are plagued by fraud, the use of blockchain for e-voting is significant. As Bashir (2018) notes, while the voting machines that have been built-in recent years promise security and privacy, they nonetheless have weaknesses that can be exploited and/or manipulated, thereby casting doubt on the validity of the voting process and distrust for the government itself.

Many of the vulnerabilities can be eliminated via the use of blockchain technology that could provide comprehensive security and transparency (Bashir, 2018). Security in the form of public key cryptography that is standard in a blockchain system would ensure the integrity and authenticity of the votes. In addition, blockchain immutability would ensure that no vote is cast more than once. This is accomplished via the use of smart contracts that track the votes already cast. This is done in tandem with the use of biometric identification, such as a fingerprint. A system utilizing these features was used during the 2018 presidential election in Sierra Leone (Bashir, 2018; Del Castillo, 2018). Since then several countries have experimented a blockchain-based voting system including the United States, Sierra Leone, Japan, and Russia and more countries are conducting proof of concept include South Korea, Thailand, and India [39].

Blockchain based voting systems has its critics too. In [28] the authors posit that malware, zero day, and denial-of-service attacks continue to persist in blockchain-based voting systems.

Centralized systems that evolved from TCP/IP protocols and the Internet are being replaced by distributed ledger technologies [1]. We have three generations of DLTs.

First generation DLTs: Bitcoin pioneered the first distributed infrastructure – blockchain [24]. The [24] paper mentions the term "block" (or blocks) 67 times and the term "chain" (or chains) 27 times, but it never once uses the term blockchain. The process of blocks in a chain was later popularized as "blockchain". Not all DLTs use the blockchain process, nevertheless, many publications use blockchain and DLT interchangeably.

Second generation DLTs: Ethereum used the blockchain process and made it programmable. But the speed of transaction verification used in blockchain consensus algorithm – Proof of Work (PoW) – is slow [23], consumes massive energy [14, 22, 23], expensive [6, 21, 29], lack of transaction finality [15, 44] are limitations of DLTs that use the blockchain process.

Third generation of DLTs: Directed Acyclic Graph (DAG) effectively solves the performance limitation that had a chock hold on the widespread adoption of the DLT/blockchain technology [16]. DAG-based consensus protocol is used by blockchain systems including IOTA, Nano, Byteball, and Hashgraph. The performance bottleneck created by the sequential architecture of the Blockchain technology has motivated the creation of next generation blockchains without the blocks [19, 32]. For example, Hashgraph uses the gossip method for sharing information and consensus [32].

Blockchain technology has proven to reduce security attacks and manipulation of votes while providing transparency [7]. Potential blockchain weakness include its architecture and validation by voters [7]. The potential of blockchain-based e-voting systems to provide integrity, privacy, and consensus is proven in a review of 63 scientific papers [34]. While advocating these benefits we also need to be cautions of potential downsides regarding transaction speed and privacy protections [34]. We posit that third generation DLTs have solved the transaction speed issue.

In [3] the authors investigate the contributions of blockchain technology for secure e-voting and conclude that it gives peace to electors. Blockchain based e-voting has already solved issues of fairness, eligibility, usability and privacy; but capabilities of voting protocols including receipt-freeness (a voter cannot create a receipt which proves how she voted), in coercibility (impossible to coerce or control forcibly), and universal verifiability (the need for cryptographers to balance usability with strong security guarantees) are harder to implement [11]. The use of tokens makes the blockchain platform resistant to coercion [11] the use of append-only instead of delete function of blockchain ensures universal verification. [11]. The decentralization of the core data makes it resistant to alteration because of its presence on multiple servers in which the ledgers, or data blocks, are connected to each other in chainlike fashion; fraudulently changing the data in one place does not change it elsewhere, where it exists in hundreds, or even thousands of devices [31].

4   Methods

To identify a sampling of the academic and trade-related literature available about DLTs and blockchain technology a variety of search terms were utilized via the advanced search feature of https://scholar.google.com/. For example, terms such as e-voting systems, blockchain, and distributed ledger technology were used singularly or in pairs, using the Boolean operators "and"/"or", with an all source filter or a peer-reviewed, academic journal filter. When a search resulted in an unwieldy number of hits, searches were narrowed down using terms specific to the technologies, singularly or in multiples, with Boolean operators, such as trust, trustworthy, trustworthiness, trust-based, reliability, credibility, veracity, integrity, secure, security, immutable, immutability, ledger immutability, permission(s), and privacy.

5   Discussion

Corroborating the findings by [7] we posit that election stakeholders and government policy makers do not yet have adequate examples to base their understanding of potential risks regarding blockchain-based voting systems.

Technology, organization, and environment challenges for blockchain are captured by [35]. We adopt these challenges for eGovernment and modify the ecosystem expected value constructs removing two of the four and modifying the factors. We removed start-up & entrepreneur and organization & industries constructs. We modified the public sector construct to include coordination and horizontal integration of data, public services efficiency, business process improvement, decentralization, developing new capabilities, and disintermediation. We also modified end-users and society construct to include transparency, speed of transactions, data and ID control, empowerment, social and financial inclusion, new jobs opportunities, economic growth, and data protection and privacy.

This paper posits that the modified eGovernment blockchain technology adoption framework provides a succinct model describing the value and benefits of using blockchain based e-voting. This model paves the way for educating the public. The modified framework is depicted in Fig. 1.

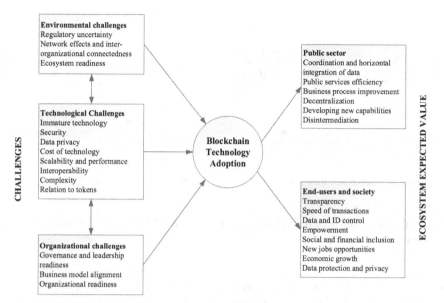

Fig. 1. eGovernment blockchain technology adoption framework

Figure 1 is a framework adapted for eGovernment blockchain technology adoption adapted from [35] and modified through our literature review.

Explaining electronic voting systems through ease, trust, and social opposition has found acceptance across all age groups and educational levels [9]. Scholars agree that the focus of blockchain technology adoption should be less on the technology per se and more on its practical aspects or socio-economic aspects or benefits, in which blockchain can be customized to meet [26, 35].

In [41] the authors run an A/B-testing experiment at a university election and concluded the suitability of blockchain e-voting system as a technical solution to establish transparency and create trust. They found interrelation between distrust and familiarity with blockchain technology and recommend voter education to take advantage of the technology's potential [41]. To increase trust, we propose a use case from the business world that may help familiarize the public. We chose a use case on Board of Directors election depicted in Fig. 2.

The following steps illustrate e-voting in a Board of Directors use case implementing a blockchain-based voting system [25]. The steps are described here, citing from the author's prior work,

1. Identify the voting objectives.
2. Create ballot using Smart Contract.
3. Secure the ballot with cryptography and setup immutable blockchain record.
4. Validate eligible voters and record their votes.

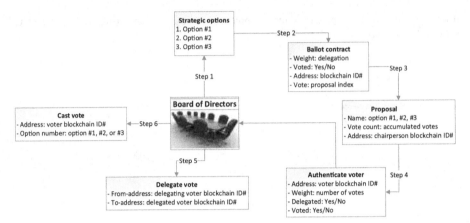

Fig. 2. Blockchain-based Board of Directors e-voting use case (adapted from [25]).

5. Design to eliminate duplicate votes while accommodate delegated votes.
6. Cast and record votes.

As for the environmental conundrums blockchain must address before gaining wider acceptance, blockchain-related decentralization and the de-necessitation of intermediaries present legal challenges, and the pace at which governmental entities develop regulatory and tax structures either could hinder or hasten blockchain development and/or adoption.

Another problem inherent in the blockchain ecosystem that might deter respectable actors from jumping onto the blockchain bandwagon is the anonymity of cryptocurrency transactions. Hailed at first as a positive, the anonymity of cryptocurrency transactions harbors a dark side. For example, Bitcoin transactions have been linked to the financing of terrorists, ransomware attackers, drug cartel transactions, money laundering, human trafficking, and other unsavory practices.

The impasse can be overcome by wholesale adoption of blockchain by the public and governmental sectors which could demonstrate the benefits that can be accrued by the adoption of blockchain technology [35]. The U.S. government was in the forefront in the adoption of the Internet, a similar public sector embrace may advance the adoption of blockchain.

6   Conclusion

DLT has trust built-in within the base technology. Its distributed data storage, consensus mechanisms, provenance, immutability, security, and finality are ready to bring trust back to e-voting systems. The socio-economic challenge, however, is wanting. We anticipate significant success in the adoption of blockchain technology will be gained by educating the public about the value and benefits.

Governments can play a significant role in facilitating the adoption of blockchain technology by embracing its use in eGovernment services. Just like the Internet era of the

1980s and 1990s lead role by governments help ease the adoption by the general public. This paper has enumerated several blockchain-based eGovernment services that add value in the public sector. Government investment in adopting these blockchain-based services will go a long way in realizing the socio-economic benefits to the public.

We presented a modified eGovernment adoption framework for blockchain. We have also provided a use case many may relate in familiarizing them about a blockchain-based voting process. Conducting field study on the proposed eGovernment blockchain technology adoption framework is among the limitations of this study. We presented a single use case for educating the public. Future studies may conduct field study to validate the framework and provide additional use cases to educate the public. Another future study may be the process for government to create blockchain applications.

References

1. Akhtar, Z.: From blockchain to hashgraph: distributed ledger technologies in the wild. In: 2019 International Conference on Electrical, Electronics and Computer Engineering (UPCON), pp. 1–6. IEEE (2019)
2. Bashir, I.: Mastering Blockchain: Distributed Ledger Technology, Decentralization, and Smart Contracts Explained. Packt Publishing Ltd., Birmingham (2018)
3. Baudier, P., Kondrateva, G., Ammi, C., Seulliet, E.: Peace engineering: the contribution of blockchain systems to the e-voting process. Technol. Forecast. Soc. Change **162**, 120397 (2021)
4. Benjamin, B., Lee, B., Sherman, R., Herrnson, P., Niemi, R.: Electronic voting system usability issues. In: Chi 2003, vol. 5, no. 1, pp. 145–152 (2003)
5. Berlinski, N., et al.: The effects of unsubstantiated claims of voter fraud on confidence in elections. J. Exp. Polit. Sci. 1–16 (2021)
6. Conoscenti, M., Vetro, A., De Martin, J.C.: Blockchain for the Internet of Things: a systematic literature review. In: 2016 IEEE/ACS 13th International Conference of Computer Systems and Applications (AICCSA), pp. 1–6. IEEE (2016)
7. Daramola, O., Thebus, D.: Architecture-centric evaluation of blockchain-based smart contract e-voting for national elections. In: Informatics, vol. 7, no. 2, p. 16. Multidisciplinary Digital Publishing Institute (2020)
8. Del Castillo, M.: Big Blockchain: The 50 Largest Public Companies Exploring Blockchain. Forbes (2018). https://www.forbes.com/sites/michaeldelcastillo/2018/07/03/big-blockchain-the-50-largest-public-companies-exploring-blockchain. дата обращения 06 Feb 2019
9. Delwit, P., Kulahci, E., Pilet, J.: Electronic voting in Belgium: a legitimised choice? Politics **25**(3), 153–164 (2005)
10. Desilver, D.: On Election Day, most voters use electronic or optical-scan ballots. Pew Research Center (2016). https://www.pewresearch.org/fact-tank/2016/11/08/on-election-day-most-voters-use-electronic-or-optical-scan-ballots/. Accessed 28 Aug 2021
11. Dimitriou, T.: Efficient, coercion-free and universally verifiable blockchain-based voting. Comput. Netw. **174**, 107234 (2020)
12. Edelstien, W.: New York State Law and Lever Voting Machines. New Yorkers for Verified Voting, pp. 1–3 (2006)
13. Evan, W.: Voting technology, political institutions, legal institutions and civil society: a study of the hypothesis of cultural lag in reverse. Hist. Technol. **20**(2), 165–183 (2004)
14. Eyal, I.: Blockchain technology: transforming libertarian cryptocurrency dreams to finance and banking realities. Computer **50**(9), 38–49 (2017)

15. Falazi, G., Hahn, M., Breitenbücher, U., Leymann, F., Yussupov, V.: Process-based composition of permissioned and permissionless blockchain smart contracts. In: 2019 IEEE 23rd International Enterprise Distributed Object Computing Conference (EDOC), pp. 77–87. IEEE (2019)

16. Gao, H.: Performance Benchmarking of DAG-based Blockchain Applications (Doctoral dissertation) (2021). http://hanyang.dcollection.net/common/orgView/200000485659

17. Godbole, S., Lead, I.B.M.: How blockchain can transform global trade supply chains. IBM Center for Blockchain Innovation IBM Research (2017). https://www.unescap.org/sites/default/files/3_IBM%20Blockchain.pdf

18. Gonzalez, R.M.: Cell phone access and election fraud: evidence from a spatial regression discontinuity design in Afghanistan. Am. Econ. J. Appl. Econ. **13**(2), 1–51 (2021)

19. Hoxha, L.: Hashgraph the future of decentralized technology and the end of blockchain. Eur. J. Eng. Formal Sci. 86 (2018)

20. Jacobovits, T., Kroepsch, A.: Making Each Vote Count: A Research Agenda For Electronic Voting. American Association for the Advancement of Science (2004)

21. Lee, W.Y.: Cost minimization of solidity smart contracts on blockchain systems. Int. J. Adv. Smart Converg. **9**(2), 157–163 (2020)

22. Li, J., Li, N., Peng, J., Cui, H., Wu, Z.: Energy consumption of cryptocurrency mining: a study of electricity consumption in mining cryptocurrencies. Energy **168**, 160–168 (2019)

23. Mingxiao, D., Xiaofeng, M., Zhe, Z., Xiangwei, W., Qijun, C.: A review on consensus algorithm of blockchain. In: 2017 IEEE International Conference on Systems, Man and Cybernetics (SMC), (pp. 2567–2572). IEEE (2017)

24. Nakamoto, S.: Bitcoin: a peer-to-peer electronic cash system. Decent. Bus. Rev. 21260 (2008). https://bitcoin.org/bitcoin.pdf. Accessed 25 Aug 2021

25. Negash, S., Thomas, D.: Teaching blockchain for business. In: 2019 IEEE Canadian Conference of Electrical and Computer Engineering (CCECE), pp. 1–4. IEEE (2019)

26. Ølnes, S., Ubacht, J., Janssen, M.: Blockchain in government: benefits and implications of distributed ledger technology for information sharing (2017)

27. Pandey, P., Litoriya, R.: Promoting trustless computation through blockchain technology. Natl. Acad. Sci. Lett. **44**(3), 225–231 (2021). https://doi.org/10.1007/s40009-020-00978-0

28. Park, S., Specter, M., Narula, N., Rivest, R.L.: Going from bad to worse: from internet voting to blockchain voting. J. Cybersecur. **7**(1), tyaa025 (2021)

29. Partz, H.: Bitcoin transaction fees in US dollars near all-time high levels (2021). https://cointelegraph.com/news/bitcoin-transactions-fees-in-us-dollars-near-all-time-high-levels. Accessed July 14 2021

30. Pennycook, G., Rand, D.G.: Examining false beliefs about voter fraud in the wake of the 2020 Presidential Election. Harvard Kennedy Sch. Misinf. Rev. 2(1) (2021). https://doi.org/10.37016/mr-2020-51

31. Roberts, J., Karras, J.: What is blockchain? Econ. Dev. J. **18**(4), 5–10 (2019)

32. Schueffel, P.: Alternative distributed ledger technologies blockchain vs. tangle vs. hashgraph-a high-level overview and comparison. Tangle vs. hashgraph-a high-level overview and comparison, 15 December 2017

33. Specter, M.A., Koppel, J., Weitzner, D.: The ballot is busted before the blockchain: a security analysis of voatz, the first internet voting application used in us federal elections. In 29th {USENIX} Security Symposium ({USENIX} Security 20), pp. 1535–1553 (2020)

34. Taş, R., Tanrıöver, Ö.Ö.: A systematic review of challenges and opportunities of blockchain for e-voting. Symmetry **12**(8), 1328 (2020)

35. Toufaily, E., Zalan, T., Dhaou, S.B.: A framework of blockchain technology adoption: an investigation of challenges and expected value. Inf. Manag. **58**(3), 103444 (2021)

36. Treiblmaier, H., Önder, I.: The impact of blockchain on the tourism industry: a theory-based research framework. In: Treiblmaier, H., Beck, R. (eds.) Business Transformation Through Blockchain, pp. 3–21. Palgrave Macmillan, Cham (2019)

37. Tsoulias, K., Palaiokrassas, G., Fragkos, G., Litke, A., Varvarigou, T.A.: A graph model based blockchain implementation for increasing performance and security in decentralized ledger systems. IEEE Access **8**, 130952–130965 (2020)

38. Vaidhyanathan, S.: Afterword: critical information studies, a bibliographic manifesto. Cult. Stud. **20**, 292–315 (2006)

39. Della Valle, F., Oliver, M.: Blockchain enablers for supply chains: how to boost implementation in industry. IEEE Access **8**, 209699–209716 (2020)

40. Vinnakota, R.: Which countries are casting votes using blockchain? (2021). https://hacker noon.com/which-countries-are-casting-voting-using-blockchain-s33j34ab. Accessed 28 Aug 2021

41. Voting method. Voting methods and equipment by state. Verified Voting (2020). https://bal lotpedia.org/Voting_methods_and_equipment_by_state. Accessed 28 Aug 2021

42. Vysna, N.: The impact of blockchain technology on the trustworthiness of online voting systems - elections and trust (Doctoral dissertation) (2020). https://1library.org/document/zgx r1r8q-impact-blockchain-technology-trustworthiness-online-voting-systems.html. Accessed 25 Aug 2021

43. Yang, X., Yi, X., Nepal, S., Kelarev, A., Han, F.: Blockchain voting: publicly verifiable online voting protocol without trusted tallying authorities. Future Gener. Comput. Syst. **112**, 859–874 (2020)

44. Yrjölä, S.: How could blockchain transform 6G towards open ecosystemic business models? In: 2020 IEEE International Conference on Communications Workshops (ICC Workshops), pp. 1–6. IEEE (2020)

45. Zhao, Q., Sun, Y., Zhang, P.: Design of trust blockchain consensus protocol based on node role classification. In: 2019 IEEE International Conference on Service Operations and Logistics, and Informatics (SOLI), pp. 104–109. IEEE (2019)

46. American Society of Business and Behavioral Sciences. http://asbbs.org/. Accessed 17 Nov 2021

Gender Disparity in the Usability of E-Government Portals: A Case Study of the Saudi Job Seeking Web Portal

Asma Aldrees$^{(\boxtimes)}$ ⓘ and Denis Gračanin ⓘ

Department of Computer Science, Virginia Tech, Blacksburg, VA 24060, USA
{aaldrees,gracanin}@vt.edu

Abstract. The rapid growth of e-government systems presents several challenges, including addressing gender differences in adopting the technology. We focus on the impact of gender and gender disparity on the usability of e-government systems. Our case study is the Saudi job seeking web portal called 'Taqat', which provides Saudi citizens access to available job opportunities. The portal is a part of the Saudi government development plan called "Vision 2030" to support Saudi society and accelerate its improvements. We aim to identify potential gender-based disparity in the portal's usability. We conducted a user study with 200 participants. We adopted Nielsen's ten heuristic principles and a survey instrument with twenty close-ended questions using a five-point Likert scale. Then, the Mann-Whitney test has been applied to measure the gender disparity of the portal's usability. The findings showed significant gender disparity among Saudi citizens regarding the usability of the 'Taqat'. Therefore, further research is required to investigate the social and cultural factors that might influence gender disparity to ensure the efficiency of Saudi e-government services.

Keywords: E-government · Gender disparity · Usability evaluation · Nielsen's heuristics · Comparative analysis · Quantitative method · Saudi Arabia

1 Introduction

The adoption of technology in government systems has provided many positive changes and brought significant developments in enhancing the citizen's engagement with their governments [37]. According to the United Nations report "E-government development continues to advance, with the global average of the E-Government Development Index (EGDI) increasing from 0.55 in 2018 to 0.60 in 2020" [34]. However, the rapid growth of e-government systems presents many challenges, such as gender differences [35], that need to be addressed to increase citizens' adoption of e-government services by all genders [31]. Gender factor is a fundamental component that must be evaluated to ensure that everyone has equal opportunities to access and adopt e-government services regardless of any issues or barriers.

E-government projects need to take into consideration the gender analysis process to avoid any gender disparity while offering their services [8].

© Springer Nature Switzerland AG 2022
A. V. Chugunov et al. (Eds.): EGOSE 2021, CCIS 1529, pp. 276–290, 2022.
https://doi.org/10.1007/978-3-031-04238-6_21

Therefore, investigating the gender disparities and the factors that mainly affect them in adopting e-government services has become highly required in line with the current global gender equality trend, which would positively improve the user experience of e-government services for all genders. Hence, in this paper, we focused on the gender impact on the usability evaluation of e-government systems.

Herein, the Saudi job seeking web portal, called 'Taqat', is adopted as a case study. This portal is a part of Saudi e-government development efforts towards electronic initiatives that started in 2005 by establishing the first electronic program called 'Yesser', which is a Saudi national project that manages the implementation of e-government programs and controls the transformation process [38]. In general, Saudi e-government initiatives aim to enhance the interaction with the government and increase the cooperation between public and private sectors to leverage and ensure the efficiency of their offered e-services [23]. Additionally, in 2016, Saudi Arabia has initiated its development plan "Vision 2030" as long-term goals and expectations to plan for the strength of the country [30]. It guides Saudi society's aspiration towards a new phase of development in which all citizens can fulfill their hopes and thrive in their jobs.

In the labor market, the Saudi Vision 2030 aims to reduce the unemployment rate for Saudi citizens by 9% which is at 15.4% in 2020. This paper contributes by investigating the usability evaluation of the Saudi job seeking web portal, 'Taqat'. However, according to the survey's findings on the Saudi labor market by the General Authority for Statistics (GASTAT) for the fourth quarter of 2020, the total male population's participation rate reached 80.6%, up from 79.4%. Whereas the females' participation rate increased to reach 32.1%, compared to 30.0% [16]. Due to the significant gap in the participation rate in the labor market between Saudi males and females, we investigated the usability of the 'Taqat' web portal from the lens of gender disparities among Saudi citizens. The Saudi government seeks in its Vision 2030 to serve all citizens equally and fairly regardless of their gender. Therefore, a user study was conducted to evaluate the usability of the 'Taqat' web portal from the gender perspective and to explore any potential gender differences among Saudi citizens.

The remainder of this paper is organized as follows: Sect. 2 elaborates on the Saudi e-government employment services and reviews the Saudi studies regarding the gender disparity in e-government systems. The research methodology is articulated in Sect. 3 while the analysis and results of the empirical study are provided in Sect. 4. Section 5 discusses the implications of the results of the study conducted in the previous section. Finally, we summarize and conclude the study of this research paper in Sect. 6.

2 Background and Related Work

Many research studies have investigated the critical issue of gender disparities between males and females in adopting e-government systems. In [10], the authors proposed a hypothesis stated that the adopters of e-government in Qatar are more likely to be male than female. They showed that gender is one of the direct determinants that influence e-government adoption.

Moreover, [24] focused on the gender digital divide in East Africa. They confirmed the continuance of gender disparities towards using e-Government services. The study's findings revealed that many social, cultural, and economic factors are the primary reasons hindering women's access to ICT systems. Moreover, [1] discussed the e-government issues and barriers from general perspectives; they conducted a user study investigating the impact of gender and education level on adopting e-government services in Turkey. The study emphasized that men were more likely to be lenient than women, which indicated significant gender differences in accepting and adopting e-government services.

In the Saudi context, the government introduced significant amendments that cause dramatic changes in Saudi society, especially for Saudi women, for the past two years (2019–2020). During Saudi Arabia's history, women's rights have been limited in some sectors, especially the government sector. Women did not have full access to government services as some services required a male guardianship (father, brother, husband, or even a son) to use them, such as issuing an ID card or passport. Also, women needed their guardian's consent to apply for a job.

However, 2019 was the turning point for all Saudi women, as the amendments have changed to protect women's rights and empower them in different government positions [29]. Saudi women have widely embraced new laws that allow them to drive, travel, get a job, and use all government systems with no restrictions the same as Saudi men [22]. Since 2019, the Saudi government has committed to supporting Saudi women and protecting their rights at national and global levels [28]. This dramatic change in Saudi women's lives motivates us to adopt Saudi e-government employment services and investigate the gender disparity in the usability evaluation behavior.

2.1 Saudi E-Government Employment Services

The Human Resources Development Fund (HRDF) is a Saudi governmental authority that was established in 2000. This authority works under the Saudi Ministry of Labor and Social Development. HRDF has mainly focused on financially supporting organizations that train and prepare Saudi citizens for working in the private sector. During the time over 2000–2010, the Saudi government represented by HDRF authority established many programs to support the labor market in Saudi Arabia and ensure its prosperous future [33]. In 2011, HDRF established job placement centers, which intend to promote a productive employment process by providing inclusive training for Saudi citizens and developing employment strategies for citizens with disabilities to help them be an active part of society. They also enable employers to participate in the labor market and respond to its changes, ensuring positive impacts on economic growth.

In the continuous participation and contribution to thrive the labor market, HRDF established the job seeking web portal, 'Taqat', in 2016 [21]. 'Taqat' is the Saudi National Labor Gateway that delivers job offers and helps Saudi job seekers find the right jobs with care and concern. It also facilitates smooth communication channels between citizens and employers. This web portal serves as an employment support channel that encompasses all necessary information regarding the Saudi labor market.

It tends to provide a high-level labor market to improve the Saudi workforce, enhance transparency, empower job seekers, and support employers in their decision-making [33].

In 2019, the Saudi government established the Ministry of Human Resources and Social Development after merging the Ministry of Labor and Social Development with the Ministry of Civil Service. This new Ministry is responsible for offering the Saudi citizens and legal residents support, development, and protection in their work. It is also in charge of labor affairs, issues, and rights by creating legislation and laws to regulate the Saudi labor market [27].

2.2 Gender Disparity and Saudi E-Government

The current efforts of the Saudi government have led to the rising importance of evaluating the government e-services from the lens of the gender factor to ensure its usability and suitability to all Saudi citizens. Many researchers have investigated the impact of gender differences in adopting the technology [35]. Gender has been identified as a significant predictor of public e-services and technology use [36]. In the e-government context, several studies have explored the significance of gender differences in adopting e-government services [1, 10, 11, 24].

However, in the Saudi context, the current state of Saudi women has highly motivated further research in investigating any potential gender disparities between males and females to explore the adoption behavior of Saudi e-government services from a gender perspective. From prior Saudi studies, gender differences have been mentioned in their findings as an obstacle that hinders an equal experience of Saudi e-government services. For instance, [9] revealed that the Saudi society's characteristics have an impact on the adoption of e-government services, which reflects the small number of female participants due to the lack of their interests, as many females are completely dependent upon male relatives to deal with government services and transactions.

Another study also discussed the study's limitations regarding the biased sampling of participants in favor of males over females, with 92.4% Saudi males and only 6.7% Saudi females [3]. They claimed that it is due to the Saudi society where males usually conduct more government transactions than females. That is because Saudi males have full access to all e-services and are in charge of their female relatives by law. As for many government transactions, Saudi females need authorization or consent from one of their male family members to conduct such transactions themselves. Although the study revealed no significant differences between males and females regarding the adoption of e-government services, the imbalanced sample size in gender prevents generalizing the study's findings to potential female users.

Additionally, another study revealed that Saudi female participants have a stronger attitude and intention to use e-government systems than males [7]. Due to Saudi society's regulations, many Saudi females prefer to conduct their transactions electronically. They feel free while using e-government services because it is difficult for them to conduct a face-to-face transaction. Moreover, a recent study revealed a significant gender gap in the sample size, with 88.1% males and only 11.9% female participants [5]. They claimed that this gap is due to the low uptake of Saudi e-government services from females than males.

Another Saudi research study was published after the amendments of Saudi women's rights in 2019 [6]. It revealed that the number of Saudi females conducting e-transaction is more likely to increase due to the current law that allows them to conduct government transactions themselves without any authorization from their male family members. Although the study showed more Saudi males accessing e-government services than females, the percentage of females adopting and accessing e-government services is more likely to increase and be very close to males' percentage shortly.

In conclusion, due to the findings of the research studies discussed above and the dramatic changes of Saudi society regarding Saudi females' rights, it is highly essential to preview the current state of Saudi e-government systems and understand the e-government adoption behavior from the perspectives of males and females equally. Hence, the findings of this research study could be useful and support the development of the promising Saudi e-government initiatives.

3   Research Methodology

This research expands on the user study that investigated the cultural differences in the usability of Saudi and the US job seeking web portals from the perspective of Saudi and US citizens [2].

3.1   Usability Evaluation Method

In the e-government context, usability is considered the essential indicator that positively affects and enhances users' acceptance and adoption of e-government services. It evaluates how useful and user-friendly the offered e-government services are, to promote the system and increase citizens' satisfaction [20]. A recent study found that the critical success of the e-government system is measured by reduced efforts required from users [4]. Therefore, perceived easiness alongside effortless systems would increase users' willingness to adopt the offered services.

There are diverse usability evaluation methods to evaluate the usability of e-government web portals. However, we adopted a widely known and effective usability heuristic evaluation method designed by Jacob Nielsen to evaluate the usability of 'Taqat' Saudi web portal based on a set of ten usability principles [25]. We developed a survey with 20 questions, as described in Table 1.

3.2   Research Design

'Taqat' is the Saudi government official job seeking web portal that requires Saudi citizens to register using their real information to use it, such as national ID number, full name, and date of birth. This study aims to provide the participants a complete experience of the job application process starting from registering in the system until applying for a job, which is not possible to perform using the actual web portal with their information. Participants may not be current users of the 'Taqat' web portal or are unwilling to provide their information and apply for a job to participate in this study.

Therefore, we designed an exact-match web prototype of the 'Taqat' web portal. The prototype functions the same as the original web portal. It allows participants to browse the portal and apply for the preferred job by following the same job application process in the 'Taqat' web portal and submit the request.

Moreover, the web prototype is only a user interface design of the original web portal. It does not have any back-end structure, database, or servers. Participants do not

Table 1. Nielsen's ten heuristic usability principles [25], and the number of related survey questions.

No	Principle	No. of Questions
1	Visibility of system status	3
2	Match between system and the real world	4
3	User control and freedom	2
4	Consistency and standards	1
5	Error prevention	3
6	Recognition rather than recall	1
7	Flexibility and efficiency of use	1
8	Aesthetic and minimalist design	1
9	Help users recognize, diagnose, and recover from errors	1
10	Help and documentation	3
Total		**20**

have to provide any private information to use them, and their job applications are not saved, which makes them more likely to participate in the study. Additionally, to ensure the credibility and reliability of responses, we anonymized the web prototype as we removed the portal's title and logo. We also removed identifiers that refer to specific names or locations. Hence, the web prototype replicates the design of the 'Taqat' web portal but without identifying information to prevent any biased incline by participants towards their country's web portal.

This study followed the quantitative approach using a web-based questionnaire instrument that encourages participants to browse the web prototype and provide their evaluations regarding the usability of the web prototype. Web-based surveys are mostly used due to their quick and accurate features of assessing information [40]. The questionnaire was designed based on the ten usability heuristic principles, as shown in Table 1. The questionnaire comprises close-ended questions to facilitate easy coding and analysis. Therefore, twenty questions were measured on a five-point Likert scale, from strongly disagree (1) to strongly agree (5).

There is a difference between the number of principles, ten, and the survey questions, twenty because we added a different number of questions to each usability principle to make the survey clearer and cover all principles adequately. As some principles can be covered within one question, others need more than one question to elaborate on them. The questionnaire was reviewed by four expert researchers (two English speakers, two Arabic speakers) to ensure that the questionnaire is focused and brief and can be completed within a reasonable time limit. The number of questions per each principle is mentioned in Table 1. The questionnaire consisted of three parts. Part one asked about demographic characteristics. Part two provided a set of job application tasks and asked the participants to go through the web prototype and perform these tasks. Finally, the last part listed the twenty close-ended questions and asked the participants to evaluate the web prototype's usability based on their experience from the previous part. After getting the participants' responses regarding the web prototype's usability, we will measure the average responses for each principle; therefore, we will end up with ten questionnaire items.

3.3 Research Setting and Sampling

The target sampling is males and females of Saudi citizens whose age range is 18–37 years old. This age range represents the majority of Saudi users of the 'Taqat' web portal. However, according to the Saudi General Authority of Statistics [17], the total population is around 35 million, with around 22 million Saudis and 13 million non-Saudis. However, the Saudi job seeking web portal 'Taqat' is limited only to Saudi citizens. The population of Saudi males and females is almost the same, around 11 million Saudi males and around 11 million Saudi females. Hence, the number of male and female participants in this study is the same.

Participants were recruited through random sampling strategies. In [14], the authors suggested having at least 100 participants. That suggestion was considered to determine the sample size, with 100 male and 100 female Saudi citizens participating. The participants were recruited by widely sharing the questionnaires link across the web and social media channels. Also, Google ads campaigns were used to promote the survey's link among Saudi citizens [18]. However, participants had to confirm their nationality and age to be allowed to participate in this study.

3.4 Data Collection

The data collection was driven by a web survey using Qualtrics online survey Software [26]. To maintain confidentiality, data collection was free of participants' names or identifiers. Participants spent approximately 15–20 min exploring the web prototype and evaluate its usability. Participation in the study was voluntary. Participants were allowed to choose to quit the survey any time they want without saving their responses. Social desirability might lead to inaccuracies of results when participants feel uncomfortable providing sincere answers that might make them viewed unfavorable by others. To reduce the potential effect of social desirability, the researchers included a confidentiality clause with the survey, guaranteeing that all answers will be completely confidential. As a result, a total of 200 valid and complete responses were received from Saudi citizens (100 males and 100 females), out of 235 received responses.

4 Analysis and Results

4.1 Demographic Data

The demographic distributions of the participants were presented in Table 2. The age range was encoded into four age groups with a five-year period. Since the participation in this study was limited to Saudi citizens aged 18–37 years old, there is no significant difference among the age groups. Regarding the educational level, we did not notice a significant difference between Saudi males and females. Overall, the undergraduate degree represents approximately half of the total participants with 53%, 45 males and 61 females, followed by the graduate degree with 20%, 26 males and 14 females.

Most participants from both genders are undergraduates, as mentioned above, with age ranges 18–22 and 23–27 years old, which means that most participants are younger and undergraduates. Regarding the male participants, most of them are undergraduates whose age range is 23–27 years old with 16%, followed by the graduates of the age range 33–37 years old with 15%. On the other hand, the majority of female participants are also undergraduates whose age range is 23–27 years old with 24% and 18–22 years old with 23% of total female participants.

90% of the total population of 'Taqat' target users hold either high school or undergraduate degrees. According to the recent Saudi education and training survey [15], among the Saudi population of the same age range as Taqat's target users, 56% have high school degrees (30% males, 26% females), 34% have undergraduate degrees (16% males, 18% females), 4% have associate degrees (6% males, 2% females) and only 1% have graduate degrees.

Table 2. Demographic data.

Demographics	Category	Male	Female	Total
Sample size		100	100	200
Age	18–22 years old	24	44	68
	23–27 years old	20	32	52
	28–32 years old	29	17	46
	33–37 years old	27	7	34
Education level	High school degree	16	18	34
	Associate degree	13	7	20
	Undergraduate degree	45	61	106
	Graduate degree	26	14	40

4.2 Reliability Analysis

We evaluated the survey's reliability based on the received valid responses by using Cronbach's alpha indicator, considering a minimum value of 0.7 [13]. Reliability is the internal consistency of a scale that gauges the degree to which the survey items are reliable. The survey consists of twenty items developed based on Nielsen's ten usability heuristic principles to evaluate the usability of the Saudi web prototype from the perspective of Saudi citizens. Therefore, we first measured the Cronbach's alpha value of composite usability principles which consist of more than one survey item, which are: first, second, third, fifth, and tenth usability principles. The Cronbach's alpha values for these composite principles show the acceptable values, which are above 0.7.

The Cronbach's alpha values are respectively: 0.750, 0.778, 0.760, 0.720, and 0.843. After that, we merged the survey items that belong to the same principle and ended up with ten questionnaire items corresponding to Nielsen's usability heuristic principles.

Since all Nielsen's usability principles are used to evaluate one latent variable, which is the overall usability of the system, we evaluated the reliability of the ten questionnaire items to evaluate this variable. Hence, Cronbach's alpha value for the overall usability evaluation of the Saudi web portal is $\alpha = 0.889$, indicating that the survey's items are reliable and consistent.

4.3 Descriptive Analysis

The overall usability evaluation of the Saudi web portal from the perspective of Saudi citizens is illustrated in Table 3. The inspection of the usability results indicated that male and female participants equally strongly agreed (17%). However, the majority (62%) of females agreed compared to 44% males. 7% of males disagreed (6%) or strongly disagreed (1%), while only 2% of females disagreed. Regarding the education level, the majority of participants who agreed or strongly agreed (70%) have undergraduate degrees (41%: 31% males, 51% females), followed by high school degrees (12.5%: 12% males, 13% females), graduate degrees represent (11.5%: 13% males, 10% females) and associate degrees (5%: 5% males, 5% females). Male participants who generally disagreed have associate, undergraduate, and graduate degrees (3%, 2%, and 2%, respectively). Only 2% of female participants who have undergraduate degrees disagreed.

Table 3. Overall usability evaluation of 'Taqat' web portal.

	Strongly agree, %	Agree, %	Neutral, %	Disagree, %	Strongly disagree, %
Male	17	44	32	6	1
Female	17	62	19	2	0

4.4 Inferential Analysis

As stated earlier, this research aims to investigate to what extent the 'Taqat' web portal is equally usable and accepted by Saudi citizens, males, and females. In this vein, the inferential analysis of the data has been used. A non-parametric test was adopted in the analysis with no normal distribution of data as they are ordinal. We used the Mann-Whitney U test to measure whether there is a gender difference between two independent samples (male and female) of Saudi citizens regarding the usability of the 'Taqat' web portal. The test illustrated a null hypothesis before conducting the analysis, which states that the usability of the Saudi web portal is the same across categories of participants (males and females), with the significance level at 95%, ($p < 0.05$) [19]. Based on the obtained results, there is a very significant gender difference between Saudi males and females in the usability evaluation of 'Taqat' web portal with ($p = .036$). Hence ($p < 0.05$), the null hypothesis has been rejected, as shown in Table 4.

Table 4. Mann-Whitney U test results of the Saudi web portal's usability.

Null hypothesis	Significance	Decision
The usability of the Saudi web portal is the same across categories of Gender among Saudi participants	**.036**	**Reject** the null hypothesis

5 Discussion

This research study is mainly motivated to discover the potential gender disparities in the usability of e-government portals, using the Saudi job seeking web portal, 'Taqat', as a case study. The quantitative empirical study was conducted, and Mann-Whitney U test was adopted to detect gender differences in the usability of 'Taqat' web portal to apply further improvements. To this end, we analyzed a unique dataset from a randomized 200 Saudi citizens, 100 males, and 100 females, whose age is between 18–37 years old, considering the age limit of job seekers provided by the Saudi government. We measured the participants' responses according to Nielsen's usability heuristic principles and inspected the difference of their responses based on gender.

Overall, the results showed significant gender disparities between Saudi males and females in the usability evaluation of the 'Taqat' web portal with (p = 0.036). They revealed that Saudi females considered the web portal more usable than Saudi males. Below we provided the discussion for the web portal's usability based on the usability evaluation by all Saudi participants. Then we shed light on the potential gender disparity in the usability evaluation between males and females.

5.1 Usability Evaluation of 'Taqat' Web Portal

Table 5 illustrates the usability evaluation of 'Taqat' web portal based on each Nielsen's usability principle and compares the usability evaluation between Saudi males and females. For a more focused discussion, we summed up the 'Strongly Agree' and 'Agree' scales into an overall agree statement, and 'Strongly disagree' and 'Disagree' scales into an overall disagree statement. Overall, more than 50% of participants from both genders consider the web portal usable, with a higher percentage of Saudi females regarding all the ten usability principles. Also, Saudi males show a high percentage of disagreement on the web portal's usability throughout the ten principles. However, we focus on the usability issues of the web portal by discussing the overall disagreement evaluation of the web portal's usability.

According to the first principle, visibility of the system status, around 11.5% of all participants struggled with the portal's visibility (19% males, 4% females).

The second principle, matching between system and the real world, shows almost the same usability disagreement evaluation from participants as the first principle with 10.5% of all participants disagreed with the usability of the web portal regarding this principle (16% males, 5% females). 9.5% of all participants disagreed in reference to the third principle, user control and freedom (17% males, 2% females).

Table 5. The usability evaluation based on Nielsen's usability heuristic principles.

Principle	Gender	Strongly agree, %	Agree, %	Neutral, %	Disagree, %	Strongly disagree, %
1	Male	16	45	20	13	6
	Female	20	59	17	4	0
2	Male	24	32	28	13	3
	Female	22	58	15	5	0
3	Male	17	32	34	17	0
	Female	26	46	26	2	0
4	Male	19	31	28	19	3
	Female	22	47	22	9	0
5	Male	23	35	27	14	1
	Female	26	45	20	9	0
6	Male	27	25	27	18	3
	Female	28	46	15	10	1
7	Male	22	23	31	21	3
	Female	18	37	34	11	0
8	Male	22	31	30	12	5
	Female	18	51	20	10	1
9	Male	19	29	36	13	3
	Female	22	40	23	10	5
10	Male	22	31	21	22	4
	Female	24	45	22	8	1

However, a noticeable percentage of participants believed that the web portal needs more efforts to improve its consistency and standards, the fourth principle, with 15.5% of all participants (22% males, 9% females). Regarding the fifth principle, error prevention, 12% of all participants disagreed with its usability (15% males, 9% females).

The sixth principle, recognition rather than recall, shows a high disagreement evaluation among participants with an overall 16% (21% males, 11% females). Similarly, the seventh principle, flexibility, and efficiency, shows 32% of all participants disagreed (24% males, 11% females). The eighth and ninth principles, aesthetic design and help to recover from errors, demonstrate similar disagreement evaluation with 14% (17% males, 11% females) and 15.5% (16% males, 15% females).

The tenth principle, help documentation, shows the highest percentage of disagreement with 17.5% of all participants disagreed (26% males, 9% females).

To summarize the usability evaluation of the web portal 'Taqat', Saudi females consider it more usable than the Saudi males, as mentioned before. The overall issues or disagreement with its usability show that the web portal lacks the successful application of half of the principles: the fourth, sixth, seventh, ninth, and tenth principles. A noticeable percentage of participants, more than 30%, considered the web portal not usable based on these principles. They could not feel the consistency of its design, the fourth principle. They also failed to recognize the portal's functions, the sixth principle. Similarly, the flexibility and efficiency of its features were not satisfying as the participants did not accept their design, the seventh principle.

Participants also struggled when they made mistakes, they could not recover successfully, as articulated in the ninth principle. Moreover, they found the help documentations not helpful and not clear enough, the tenth principle. Therefore, developers and designers of Saudi e-government teams should pay more attention to these five principles to improve the web portal's design and make it more usable to the target users.

5.2 Gender Disparity in the Usability Evaluation

There is a considerable gender gap among Saudi participants in evaluating the first, third, and tenth principles with 15%, 15%, and 17% respectively. The results showed that designing for Saudi males require more efforts related to these principles compared to Saudi females. The first and third principles share the same percentage of the gender gap. The first principle refers to the system's ability to keep users visually informed about where they are and their overall progress. While the third principle measures the control and freedom that users feel while using the system. The results imply that Saudi males require clear visual designs to keep them aware of their location and progress and to allow them to freely exit without going through any extended process.

These results are aligned with the results from a previous study [39], which explored the gender differences in evaluating the usability of tourism websites. The study showed that the first and third principles were the common usability heuristics that males require the most. Furthermore, another study supports the findings of this research study [12]. It proved that males are more sensitive to the layout structure of a website and pay more selective attention to it than females do. The study results showed that males and females perceived the visual design of a website differently. They proved that the visual design quality and the navigation quality evaluation of a website were stronger for males than females.

Regarding the tenth principle, around 26% of Saudi males struggled when reading the help documentation compared to only 9% of Saudi females. In [32], the study implied that females have different reading behaviors and techniques than males. They interpret reading documents according to their reading identity and the socio-cultural factors that affect their reading style.

Similarly, the study [39] supports the findings regarding this principle, as it showed a significant gender difference in evaluating the usability of help documentation of tourism websites. Therefore, e-government developers should create help documentation with considering the gender differences in cognition and reading behaviors.

To wrap up, the gender factor is usually affected by social and cultural determinants that influence e-government adoption [9, 24]. Similarly, in our related research, we found significant cultural differences in the usability of the 'Taqat' web portal. Likewise, this study revealed gender disparities in the usability of 'Taqat'. It leads to the hypothesis that there might be a correlation between cultural and gender factors, which in turn influence the usability of the offered e-government services. Practitioners and designers should make significant efforts to develop the Saudi e-government system and improve the web portal's design to narrow the cultural and gender gaps.

Further investigation is required to explore potential correlations between socio-cultural contexts and gender factors. Therefore, we plan to conduct follow-up research for investigating the socio-cultural contextual influence on the gender disparity on adopting e-government services.

6 Conclusion

Our main goal was to contribute to understanding the impact of gender and gender disparity on the usability of e-government systems. The case study was the Saudi e-government system, specifically the job seeking web portal, 'Taqat'. We conducted a quantitative user study that assessed the usability of 'Taqat' to detect any potential gender disparity from the perspective of Saudi citizens, males and females. Nielsen's usability heuristic principles were adopted for the usability evaluation of 'Taqat' web portal by developing twenty close-ended survey questions with a five-Likert scale ranging from strongly disagree (1) to strongly agree (5). The Mann-Whitney U test was used to inspect the potential gender disparity in the overall usability of 'Taqat' web portal, which showed a significant gender disparity between Saudi males and females regarding the usability of 'Taqat' web portal ($p = 0.036$). It indicated that Saudi females consider the web portal more usable than Saudi males.

The described results could be used to support for the Saudi government's "Vision 2030" plan by shedding light on the design gaps such as the gender disparity and recommending prompt actions to narrow the gaps. Practitioners and designers in the Saudi government teams should increase their efforts and improve the design of the Saudi web portals to accelerate their development and acceptance by all Saudi citizens, which holds great promise if administered properly. We hope our findings will encourage further investigation into the power of digital interventions to serve the Saudi job seeking population.

Finally, this case study is only a first step in examining the effect of gender factor on evaluating the usability of e-government services. Thus, for future research, we suggest expanding this study's findings by investigating the underlying dynamics for the behavior difference between Saudi males and females in evaluating and adopting such e-government services. Researchers might investigate the factors influencing the adoption behavior from the perspective of Saudi males and females separately to understand the target users and narrow down any potential gender gap in adopting any Saudi e-government service.

References

1. Akman, I., et al.: E-government: a global view and an empirical evaluation of some attributes of citizens. Gov. Inf. Q. 22(2), 239–257 (2005)

2. Aldrees, A., Gračanin, D.: Cultural usability of e-government portals: a comparative analysis of job seeking web portals between Saudi Arabia and the United States. In: Soares, M.M., Rosenzweig, E., Marcus, A. (eds.) HCII 2021. LNCS, vol. 12780, pp. 3–17. Springer, Cham (2021). https://doi.org/10.1007/978-3-030-78224-5_1

3. Alghamdi, S.A.: Key Factors Influencing the Adoption and Utilisation of E-Government Systems and Services in Saudi Arabia. University of Sussex (2016)

4. Alhammad, M., Elmouzan, A.: Factors influencing citizen's adoption of m-government: the case of Saudi Arabia. J. Manag. Strategy. 11(3), 43 (2020)

5. Almukhlifi, A.F.: Investigating the Critical Factors for the Adoption of E-Government in Saudi Arabia. RMIT University (2019)

6. Alonazi, M.: MGAUM: a new framework for the mobile government service adoption in Saudi Arabia. University of Sussex (2019)

7. Alotaibi, R.S.: Factors Influencing Users' Intentions to Use Mobile Government Applications in Saudi Arabia. Griffith University (2017)

8. Al-Rababah, B.A., Abu-Shanab, E.A.: E-government and gender digital divide: the case of Jordan. Int. J. Electron. Bus. Manag. 8(1), 1–8 (2010)

9. Alsaif, M.: Factors affecting citizens' adoption of e-government moderated by socio-cultural values in Saudi Arabia. University of Birmingham (2013)

10. Al-Shafi, S., Weerakkody, V.: Factors affecting e-government adoption in the state of Qatar. In: Proceedings of the European and Mediterranean Conference on Information Systems – EMCIS 2010, EMCIS 2010, Abu Dhabi, UAE, pp. 1–23 (2010)

11. Bélanger, F., Carter, L.: The impact of the digital divide on e-government use. Commun. ACM. 52(4), 132–135 (2009)

12. Cho, S.-H., Hong, S.-J.: Blog user satisfaction: gender differences in preferences and perception of visual design. Soc. Behav. Pers. Int. J. 41(8), 1319–1332 (2013)

13. Cronbach, L.J.: Essentials of Psychological Testing. Harper & Row, New York (1984)

14. Gall, M.D., et al.: Educational Research: An Introduction. Pearson, USA (2006)

15. General Authority for Statistics: Education and Training Survey, Saudi Arabia (2019)

16. General Authority for Statistics: Labor Market Statistics Q4 2020. General Authority for Statistics (GASTAT), Saudi Arabia (2020)

17. General Authority for Statistics: Population Estimates, Riyadh, Saudi Arabia (2020)

18. Google: Google Ads (2021). https://ads.google.com/. Accessed 10 Aug 2021

19. Hettmansperger, T.P., McKean, J.W.: Robust Nonparametric Statistical Methods (1998)

20. Huang, Z., Benyoucef, M.: Usability and credibility of e-government websites. Gov. Inf. Q. 31(4), 584–595 (2014)

21. Human Resources Development Fund: TAQAT The National Labor Gateway (2021). https://www.taqat.sa/en/web/guest/individual. Accessed 10 Aug 2021

22. Jessie, Y., Hamdi, A.: Saudi Arabian women finally allowed to hold passports and travel independently (2019). https://cnn.it/2Yv6QWb. Accessed 10 Aug 2021

23. Khan, G.F., Park, H.W.: The e-government research domain: a triple helix network analysis of collaboration at the regional, country, and institutional levels. Gov. Inf. Q. 30(2), 182–193 (2013)

24. Mumporeze, N., Prieler, M.: Gender digital divide in Rwanda: a qualitative analysis of socioeconomic factors. Telemat. Inform. 34(7), 1285–1293 (2017)

25. Nielsen, J.: 10 Usability Heuristics for User Interface Design (2020). https://t.ly/7YPA/. Accessed 10 Aug 2021

26. Qualtrics: Qualtrics Online Survey Software (2021). https://www.qualtrics.com/. Accessed 10 Aug 2021

27. Saudi Labor Ministry: The Ministry of Human Resource and Social Development (2019). https://hrsd.gov.sa/en. Accessed 10 Aug 2021

28. Saudi Press Agency: Enabling Saudi women and increasing their share in the labor market cuts the gap between the two genders, official report says (2020). https://bit.ly/3ln3lKy. Accessed 10 Aug 2021

29. Saudi Press Agency: KSA Emphasizes Promotion of Strategies Supporting Advancement of Women (2019). https://bit.ly/3AlNYpL. Accessed 10 Aug 2021

30. Saudi Vision 2030 (2016). https://www.vision2030.gov.sa/en. Accessed 10 Aug 2021

31. Shaouf, A., Altaqqi, O.: The impact of gender differences on adoption of information technology and related responses: a review. Int. J. Manag. Appl. Res. 5(1), 22–41 (2018)

32. Singh, M.: Factors contributing to reading literacy differences between males and females. Int. J. Learn. 15(3), 337–2344 (2008)

33. The National Observatory of Labor: Human Resources Development Fund Annual Report (2019). https://nlo.sa/. Accessed 10 Aug 2021

34. The United Nations: E-Government Survey 2020 Digital Government in the Decade of Action for Sustainable Development. The United Nations, New York (2020)

35. Venkatesh, V., et al.: User acceptance of information technology: toward a unified view. MIS Q. 27(3), 425–478 (2003)

36. Venkatesh, V., Zhang, X.: Unified theory of acceptance and use of technology: U.S. vs. China. J. Glob. Inf. Technol. Manag. 13(1), 5–27 (2010)

37. West, D.M.: Digital Government - Technology and Public Sector Performance. Princeton University Press, New Jersey (2005)

38. Yesser: e-government Program (2021). https://www.yesser.gov.sa. Accessed 9 Aug 2021

39. Huang, Z., Yuan, L.: Gender differences in tourism website usability: an empirical study. In: Marcus, A., Wang, W. (eds.) DUXU 2017. LNCS, vol. 10290, pp. 453–461. Springer, Cham (2017). https://doi.org/10.1007/978-3-319-58640-3_32

40. Zikmund, W.G., et al.: Business Research Methods. South-Western, Cenage Publishing Co., Boston (2013)

Success and Success Factors of the Estonian E-Residency from the State and Entrepreneur Perspective

Mohammed Saber H. A. Sallam[ID], Silvia Lips[✉][ID], and Dirk Draheim[ID]

Information Systems Group, Tallinn University of Technology, Akadeemia tee 15a, 12618 Tallinn, Estonia
{silvia.lips,dirk.draheim}@taltech.ee
http://www.taltech.ee

Abstract. Estonia has created an effective, stable and transparent digital society, where most government services are accessible online. As the first country in the world, Estonia launched in 2014 an e-residency program that can be considered as an extension of its digital society. Estonia provides digital identity card (digiID) for third country nationals enabling electronic authentication, digital signature and encryption functionalities. After seven years, the e-residency program has achieved a level of maturity that presumes a revised approach to the strategy. Therefore, we decided to research the topic more in-depth with a particular emphasis on the assessment of the project strategic goals. We conducted 12 semi-structured interviews with public and private sector representatives to evaluate the current e-residency strategy and propose future directions. The research approach is oriented towards the case study methodology and bases on qualitative data collection. We identified three main strategic areas: communication, support and engagement that need further investigation and development.

Keywords: Electronic identity · e-residency · Identity management

1 Introduction

Estonia was able to handle effectively the COVID-19 crisis thanks to its current electronic identity (eID) infrastructure and well-developed e-service platforms. As a result, it is fair to say that Estonia was digitally ready to face those challenges. This makes Estonia an interesting and unique case from the e-governance research perspective.

Estonia also provides its digital infrastructure to third-country nationals through a pioneering "e-residency" program. Estonia was the first state to provide the completely functioning eIDs to third-country nationals in addition to its residents, allowing the development of new enterprises and providing digital resources for freelancers, developers and investors [1].

The e-residency digital identity card (also known as digiID) allows users to authenticate themselves in a variety of online service platforms and environments and provides them access to Estonian e-services equally to residents.

A. V. Chugunov et al. (Eds.): EGOSE 2021, CCIS 1529, pp. 291–304, 2022.
https://doi.org/10.1007/978-3-031-04238-6_22

Users may digitally sign documents (the signature is legally binding in every EU Member State), execute internet-banking transfers, encrypt documents and declare taxes online among other items [2]. However, it is important to mention that digiID does not guarantee access to the physical entrance to the country[1]. The project has received a lot of positive attention on the international level and even considered a tool of soft power [3]. However, the project has encountered several obstacles, some internal and others external that have influenced the state to overlook the program strategic goals.

The aim of the research is to investigate the Estonian e-residency program and improve it by evaluating the achievement of the strategic goals of the project from the public sector and entrepreneur's perspective. Those two viewpoints play the most significant role in the e-residency program context by shaping its development directions. We believe that by re-designing some of the aspects of the program it is possible to turn Estonia into an appealing business environment by using the e-residency. General economic impact assessment of the e-residency program is not in the scope of this research.

Based on the previously described situation, we formed main research question: in how far (and in how far not) and why is the Estonian e-residency initiative successful from the state and the entrepreneur perspective?

To answer this research question we identified the main strategic goals, how they have developed and how these goals were met. We also identified the expectations of the e-resident entrepreneurs and how they are met. We analyzed different available official documents and conducted semi-structured in-depth interviews with the state representatives and e-resident entrepreneurs.

Moreover, based on the research results, it is possible to identify the entrepreneur's expectations and the companies that are the most promising to succeed later (in service of approaching them as leads in the sense of CRM in selling the e-residency program).

2 Background

2.1 E-Residency Related Literature

E-residency related literature focuses mostly on the project evaluation and analysis from different perspectives starting from the marketing point of view to the business and economical perspective.

The key purpose of the e-residency project was to enhance Estonia as a competitive e-state, raise revenue and investments and support the country's economy [4]. The e-residency has an impact on smart rural development as well as the entrepreneurs. It facilitates the development of the country's business environment. The e-residency concept eases the development and the implementation of industry 4.0, additionally offering more opportunities to the business models as well as the logistics solution and supply chain and product distribution [5].

On the other hand, the e-residency enhances the opportunities for running location-independents businesses that can run within the EU legal framework. The e-residency is

---

[1] Identity Documents Act, 2000. Available: https://www.riigiteataja.ee/akt/108072021002?lei aKehtiv.

the option that tackles the shortage of the local policies or infrastructure, furthermore, develops the integration with the world trade [6].

From the applicants' point of view, individual socio-demographic characteristics and macro-level characteristics assessing digital and economic growth in the applicant's country of origin influence individual motivations to apply for the e-residency [7].

Some sources see the Estonian e-residency program as a marketing project or a national branding case and focus on this aspect. Estonia's e-residency program is a communication tool through which national branding is directly linked to the country's ICT policy [8].

The Estonian e-residency program has been also investigated as a soft power that develops the state position. The program as a digital tool can be considered as a tool that enhances the political capital of the state [3].

Some papers focus more on the philosophical aspects of the e-residency. The e-residency does not change the characterization of the state. One paper mentions that the Estonian e-residency provides the model to create the European e-resident model [9].

2.2 E-Residency Project and Product Overview

On December 1, 2014, entered into force the changes of the Identity Documents Act that enabled the implementation of the e-residency concept. Based on this legal act it is possible to issue a digital identity card for e-residents.

The first strategic goals of the e-residency program were ambitious. The goal was to have 10 million e-residents by 2025. Soon it was clear that initial plan needs revision. According to the former director of the e-residency program, the original goal of the project was to establish a digital community of 10 million e-Estonians by 2025.

In 2018, new vision document e-residency 2.0 white paper was created with a focus on the quality aspects of the program followed by the action plan approved by the government of Estonia. Currently, Estonia has more than 70 000 e-residency digital cardholders from 165 countries. Digital identity card enables electronic authentication, eIDAS compliant electronic signature and data encryption [10].

DigiID is a part of the Estonian eID ecosystem – a complex public key infrastructure (PKI)-based e-governance system managed by the public sector and operated in cooperation with public and private sector authorities. Starting from December 2018, Estonia issues the fourth generation of eID documents, including digiID's for e-residents with a new layout [11].

2.3 Profile of E-Residents

According to the public e-residency statistical dashboard, Estonia has over 79,588 e-residents[2]. Over 14 200 companies have been licensed in Estonia because of the involvement of 20% of these e-residents. In 2018, more than 20 500 people became e-residents. Every month about 1,700 people apply for e-residency. In 2019, the number of new e-residents was about three-quarters of that, with an average of 1,300 people per month. Estonian e-residents come from 173 different countries. Most of the e-resident come

---

[2] e-Residency dashboard. Available: https://e-resident.gov.ee/dashboard/.

from Finland, Russia, Ukraine and Germany. However, China, the United Kingdom, India, the United States, Japan and France are also in the top ten.

Companies of the e-residents focus mostly on three types of business activities. At the time of registration, 39% worked in information and communication technology field, 24% in technical, academic and technological projects and 17% worked in wholesale and retail trade area. The top three economic activities have been consistent over time and their share of the economy has risen. Whereas these three economic operations accounted for 70% of all new businesses in 2015, they now account for 82% of new businesses this year. Two-third of licensed information and communication companies established by e-residents offer data engineering, consulting and similar services.

2.4 E-Residency Strategy

Before it is possible to evaluate meeting the strategical goals, it is important to see how the strategical goals have developed over time. There is not much literature available about this topic. Therefore, we had to use expert interviews with public sector representatives to fill this gap. Based on the interviews, it is possible to say that the understanding of the strategical goals varies depending on the interviewee's field of expertise. Therefore, it is important to clarify the strategic scope of the e-residency program.

The first strategic goals can be found from the very early stage of the program from the "10-Million E-Estonian" concept developed by a small group of people from the Ministry of Economic Affairs and Communication and Ministry of the Interior [1]. This was rather a vision and a dream where this program could develop in future. The aim was to enable as many people as possible from third countries to benefit from the Estonian eID ecosystem. The interviewees also mentioned that in the beginning the residency program was quite similar to the private sector start-up initiatives. It means that there was lot of uncertainty and the strategic perspective of the project was not completely clear. Therefore, it is understandable that after four years of the program implementation, the necessity for more concrete strategical directions raised.

In 2018, Enterprise Estonia initiated a process engaging different public and private sector authorities to improve the e-residency program and to overlook the strategic directions of the program. According to the interviewees, the following authorities were engaged in the e-residency 2.0 white paper building process:

- The Office of the President of the Republic of Estonia.
- The Ministry of the Interior.
- Ministry of Foreign Affairs.
- Enterprise Estonia (EAS).
- The e-Residency Council.
- Police and Border Guard Board (PBGB).
- Tax and Customs Board.
- Ministry of Economic Affairs and Communications.
- The Chamber of Service Economy.

The work was organized in different working streams/groups and every working group had a leader who was driving the discussion. After several meetings and based on the conclusions of the working groups e-residency 2.0 white paper was formed[3].

By issuing the e-Residency 2.0 white paper Estonia aimed to improve the efficiency of e-residency. Action plan was created that will mitigate the security risks related to the applicants while issuing the eID for the e-residents. It also aimed to increase the value created by the e-residents for the public sector. The white paper 2.0 e-residency action plan supports local businesses and the Estonian state by generating more value for the state[4].

In August 2019, the Estonian government approved the e-residency 2.0 action plan. Agreed directions gave the input to the yearly work plans for authorities involved in the management and development of the e-residency program (e.g., EAS, PBGB etc.). Previously mentioned documents express the latest strategical approach of the e-residency program.

3   Methodology

E-residency is a complex phenomenon comprising different aspects starting from the organizational view to the technological framework. E-Residency is not a separate phenomenon but a part of other nationally important systems (e.g. eID ecosystem). Therefore, we rely on the institutional design for complex technological systems designed by Koppenjan and Groenewegen to understand the e-residency phenomenon in a more systematic way [12]. The model bases on the institutional framework proposed by Oliver Williamson [13].

Following figure presents the relation between the e-residency technological, institutional, and process design.

During this research, we focus mainly on the institutional design part and the development of the e-residency strategical goals. To improve the e-residency process, it is important to describe and analyze both - the technological and institutional aspects.

This research follows the case study methodology; more specifically, we have chosen the explanatory case study as a research strategy [14]. Throughout the research, we link together different data sources like qualitative interviews with public and private sector entities, documentary sources etc. to answer the main research question [15] (Fig. 1).

We identified the research need and set the focus on this particular case based on the existing documentation, especially on the Estonian National Audit Office Report "Effectiveness of the e-Residency program".[5] Based on the first findings, we organized an additional meeting with EAS to clarify research related details. After the meeting, we formed the research strategy and started planning the data collection activities.

To understand if the strategic goals of e-residency were met, it is important to cover the public and private sector (entrepreneurs) perspective and analyze different statistical,

---

[3] E-residency 2.0 White Paper. Available: https://bit.ly/3B9j04F.

[4] The new e-Residency action plan helps to create more added value for local entrepreneurs and the Estonian state. Available: https://www.mkm.ee/en/news/new-e-residency-action-plan-helps-create-more-added-value-local-entrepreneurs-and-estonia.

[5] Report is available: https://bit.ly/3vF2W9P.

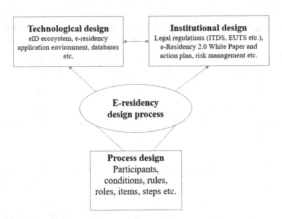

Fig. 1. Institutional design of the e-residency program.

documented and legal sources. We used qualitative research approach and prepared two different semi-structured interviews to understand the public and private sector views [16].

We choose the qualitative research approach mainly because it enables to research more deeply the relations between the strategic goals and expectations between different sectors. Therefore, we conducted five semi-structured interviews with the public sector representatives who were involved in the e-residency strategy-building process.

We conducted seven interviews with the e-resident entrepreneurs to research their initial expectations towards e-residency and to find out how the program met their expectations.

Due to the data protection rules, it was challenging to reach e-resident entrepreneurs. All contacted authorities refused to give out company names established by e-residents referring to different legal and data protection constraints. Finally, we decided to use publicly available sources to schedule the interviews (e-Residency Facebook groups and other publicly available sources).

We conducted all interviews in English using online communication channels (Teams or Skype for Business), recorded based on the interviewees' prior consent and later transcribed. The duration of the interviews remained between 45 min up to one hour. We transcribed the interviews and used thematic data analysis method [17].

We identified the most relevant themes and mapped all interesting characteristics into different codes. In the next stage, we conducted in-depth analysis of the transcribed material [17].

4 Research Findings

This chapter presents the research findings relevant from the e-residency white paper building process perspective. We analyze the expert interview results and presents in detail the most interesting and significant research findings from the public sector and entrepreneurs' point of view.

4.1 Public Sector

The semi-structured interviews with the public sector aimed to identify the strategic goals and the development as well as meeting the goals. We conducted five in-depth expert interviews with Estonian public sector representatives. Table 1 presents the profile of the public sector interview participants and their relation to the e-residency strategy development. We divided the interview into three logical sections: introduction, development of strategical goals and meeting strategical goals.

The first section focused on the years of experience and relation to the Estonian e-residency area as well as the performed tasks. All interviewees provided an approximate number of years they work in this field. The public sector had a median experience of 7,2 years. Maximum years of experience was twenty-four years and the minimum years of experience was two years. All interviewees were actively involved to the e-residency strategy development process.

Table 1. Interview participants - public sector.

Organization	Position	Relation to the Strategy
Enterprise Estonia	Head of Legal, Risk and Compliance	Involved expert
Police and Border Guard Board	Chief Expert	Involved expert
SITA (previous PBGB official)	Senior Business Development Manager	Involved expert
Ministry of the Interior	Head of Citizenship and Migration Policy Department	Conceptual founder of e-residency program
Enterprise Estonia	Marketing and Communications Team Lead	Involved expert

The second part of the interview focused in-depth on the development of the strategic goals. Firstly, we asked interviewees what was in their opinion the most important areas while building the strategy from the state and their own perspective.

One interesting finding was that all public sector representatives brought out the importance of the economic development and profitability of the program. They all mentioned that there is a need to increase the financial benefits for the national income as well as reduce the costs. Interviewees considered these three aspects as the most important topics for the state while developing the strategy.

From the economic side, they also emphasized positive contribution to the Estonian economic environment while helping e-residents to set up companies in Estonia.

The other benefit that interviewees mentioned was the market expansion. Public sector authorities constantly try to find ways how to increase the number of established companies. Furthermore, the focus is on customer acquisition channels and wider coverage of e-residency in different markets.

However, interviewees mentioned several other important strategic topics during the interviews but not by all interviewees. For example, reputation of the advanced Estonian digital society was one of these strategic topics in addition to the number of pick-up locations mentioned by the interviewees while discussing the strategy development.

During the interviews, participants mentioned that during the e-residency 2.0 white paper discussion process the overall need and they evaluated continuity of the program. It was important to understand whether the e-residency is something that the state has to pursue and is the program beneficial for the country.

We asked interviewees to name e-residency top strategic goals. Interviewees had different vision regarding previously mentioned question. Interviewees pointed out the following important strategic issues:

- Making Estonia more visible in the world.
- Cybersecurity and digital identity issues.
- Giving people a chance to have a better life.
- Risk management and risk mitigation.
- Legal compliance correspondence to the legal acts.
- Getting more e-residents with an interest to establish a company and increasing the economic impact.

Interviewees found difficult to evaluate the success of the program. For example, PBGB was not able to evaluate the achieved value of the program. At the same time, EAS found the program valuable. According to EAS, the program generates indirect revenue by promoting the e-residency. PBGB found challenging to assess the risks, as it is not possible to ask from applicant about their business activity and background. Therefore, this aspect should have received more attention during the e-residency white paper discussions.

Additionally, interviewees found important to identify the correct target groups. It is important to understand the types of entrepreneurs who benefit the most from the program.

The top strategic goals mentioned in the context of the e-residency white paper 2.0 varied from one expert to another. Interviewees brought out following main strategic goals:

- The impact on the national economy.
- Increasing the number of e-residents.
- Increasing the convenience.
- Making Estonia more visible.
- Enhancing the economic side.
- Having a secure identity in the Internet.
- Digital identification of the applicants.
- Risk-based pre-and after control checks of the applicants.

Increasing convenience means increasing the pick-up locations and helping e-residents to understand their taxation more by developing things like a business guide or knowledge base and providing more tax-related information in other countries.

The last part of the interview focused on the meeting of the strategic goals. Firstly, we asked from the interviewees to evaluate the achievement of the e-residency 2.0 strategical goals on a 10-point scale, where one meant that the strategical goals were not met and 10 that the strategical goals were fully met. The average of the overall assessment points for the achievement score was 5.4 points.

The interviewees think that there are no fully unmet strategical goals. However, taxation and bank issues need still more attention. The most important factor that influenced the achievement of the goals was political support.

Evaluation of the sufficiency of the current e-residency 2.0 strategy, three out of five interviewees found it sufficient. One could not evaluate all aspects. The other interviewee mentioned that there are still issues that need improvement. For example, the banking, taxation and pick-up locations.

The last question focused on the elements in the e-residency program/strategy that still need improvement. All interviewees believe that several elements of the program need improvement. One interviewee brought out that there is no specific implementation plan. The other believed that when the program grows the more important comes risk management and the question of how to combine different ecosystems and different digital identities. Two of the interviewees agreed that the pick-up locations and the market expansion are the top elements that require further development together with banking and taxation areas.

4.2 Private Sector

The main goal of the semi-structured interviews with the e-residents was to clarify their expectations towards the program and if the program meets their expectations. We divided the interview with the private sector into two parts: the warm-up part and motivation and evaluation part.

The first part was introductory part and aimed to identify the interviewees, their company profession area, position in the company etc.

The second section aimed to clarify the expectations of the e-resident entrepreneurs towards the program. We tried to find out how the Estonian state has met the entrepreneurs' expectations and what factors affect it. Furthermore, we assess the entrepreneurs' knowledge regarding the state strategy and its impact on their business. We examine the level of participation of the e-resident entrepreneurs in the strategy building and their interest in this process. Finally, we collect proposals to improve the current e-residency program.

On average, the interviewees have been e-residents of Estonia for approximately 3,2 years. Four of the interviewees had been e-residents for more than 4 years. The interviewees were mostly founders or co-founders of the company and having different responsibilities in their organization.

The business area of the selected companies varied from education and research field to the information technology sector and digital marketing, digital consultation and real estate services.

Most of these companies use outsourcing while performing their projects. Meaning, that in most cases they do not have employees until they have a project. They hire employees on a need basis and prefer to pay for actual working hours. However, some of these companies have a fixed number of employees. They use the same method and employ additional specialists on need basis. This supports the idea of cost reduction and gaining profit. The companies mostly outsource the expertise outside of Estonia, as it is cheaper.

The second part of the interview focused on the motivation and evaluation. It started with the question regarding the motivation that encouraged them to become an e-resident of Estonia. Answers of the interviewees varied. However, they all agreed that the most important motivator was the independence from the work location. Additionally, interviewees named different motivators that encouraged them to join the program, such as tax residency and possibility to run the company between different countries more easily. In one case, the key driver was Brexit [18].

Interviewees found the whole e-residency package quite appealing. Probably there will be a new piece of business on boarded via holding a European company with an EU VAT number. It is a European bank account and European business address. Having a company in Europe and legally secured infrastructure offered by Estonia, in addition to the Estonian reputation on digital initiatives on the international level, is motivating. Especially for countries with less digital security. Furthermore, interviewees found that the digital environment of Estonia eases the establishment of companies and encourages transparent atmosphere.

In addition to the work location, independence, the accessibility and easy use of public services were the expectations that the interviewees had before applying for the e-residency. Interviewees brought out that the security of the digiID cards guaranteeing access to the services is important for running a business besides the digital signing functionality. Entrepreneurs considered the possibility to do things remotely in a fast and secure way important. One interviewee added networking and community, where e-resident entrepreneurs can market and support their business and offer their services to other companies, to the list of their expectations.

When it comes to the evaluation of the program and how it meets the entrepreneurs expectations on the 10-point scale (where 1 meant that the expectations were not met and 10 that the expectations were fully met), three out of four e-residents gave 7 points out of 10 to meeting the expectations. The other four interviewees evaluated the program up to 4 points out of 10. The average score in total was 7,4 points. Those interviewees, who evaluated the program more than 7 points mentioned that everything the program promised was granted.

Some interviewees were critical due to the transparency laws and security that creates additional legal work and legal complexities requiring much time and money in their origin.

When we asked the question regarding the non-met expectations, interviewees' answers were different according to their regions.

Some of them had issues regarding to the tax register and taxation in general. It seems that in some cases local laws affect the salary payments from their Estonian companies.

One remarkable observation was that entrepreneurs are all satisfied with the provided services. However, they expected a bit more support for their business from the Estonian state.

They expected direct communication with the program representatives to increase their networking. Interviewees believe that the state should be closer to them, on one hand, to listen to them and understand their needs and on the other hand enhance the efficiency of the program.

This answer explains the gap between the e-residents and the state vision. Since not all e-residents have this simple expectation towards the program. The author asked from the interviewees to whom they recommend becoming an e-resident.

Interviewees recommend the status of an e-resident to the freelancers and self-employees as well as small businesses. Especially if the partners are from different countries, the e-residency program will be suitable and beneficial for them.

Additionally, the interviewees believe that the e-residency program is beneficial for entrepreneurs, especially when the company has grown and expanded its work on an international scale. However, the state support for the entrepreneurs is still the point that needs improvement from their point of view.

There was a remarkable observation concerning the Estonian e-residency 2.0 initiative or Estonian e-residency strategy. Only two out of seven interviewees knew about it. Those, who have read the e-residency 2.0 white paper initiative, mentioned that this strategy was just reflecting the interests of Estonia, not focusing the business or entrepreneurs perspective. Although, it shows the government plans regarding the program it would be good to take into account the expectations of the end-users of the e-residency program.

One of the elements in the e-residency program/strategy that still needs improvement to meet the entrepreneur's expectations was the cross-border salary payments. In addition, the program coordinators should pay more attention to the legal compatibility between countries. It is important to have more connection with the program delegates. The growth strategy is one of the elements that the interviewees believe that needs improvement by more financial solution and marketing support as well as the networking support within the e-residency community.

All interviewees found that state should involve e-residents more in the development of the strategic goals of the e-residency program. Interviewees mentioned that involvement could be achieved for example through the Estonian e-Residents International Chamber Association (EERICA). This association has elected board discussing with e-residents all topics regarding the program and e-residency status. Furthermore, the organization enhances their networking. Based on the interviews e-resident entrepreneurs want to connect more to the program through direct connection and shape their future as e-residents.

5 Discussion

We identified the gap between the e-residents and the state vision. Both parties have slightly different expectations. As the initial expectation of the e-residents was just to create a company in the EU. However, not all e-residents have this simple expectation towards the program since they are expecting further support to their business.

To evaluate the strategic goals, it is important to look at the most important strategic directions from both perspectives. Table 2 summarizes the main strategic goals of the e-residency white paper 2.0 as the latest document reflecting the public sector strategic view.

Based on the entrepreneurs' feedback, we identified positive aspects of the program and factors that need improvement. Table 3 presents the summary of the factors affecting the achievement of the strategic goals. The research results show that e-residents consider positive that they can establish their business and obtain the business independent location, besides they can save time and work in a transparent environment. However, they are facing some challenges that may affect their future business plan in their Estonian companies.

Table 2. The main goals of the e-residency white paper.

Secure	Beneficial	Convenience
Improved information exchange	More opportunities to connect	Advances in technology
Better use of data	More opportunities to grow companies	More user-friendly
Greater oversight and control	More opportunities to share Estonian culture	

Table 3. Feedback and expectations of the entrepreneurs.

Positive comments	Expectations
Establishing company	Tax confliction and the complying with their regions' tax regulations
Business location independent	Tax advisors
Transparent	Direct connection
Saves time	Engagement in the discussion for the future of the program
Clear process	Support the community through the business advisors Platform interface and available languages

After a comparison of public and private sector strategic goals and expectations, it is possible to say that there are no contradictory aspects. However, both sectors accent different topics. For example, communication is a common strategical goal, but technological development is more on the public sector focus. During the research, we identified three main areas that are important for the e-residents and what public sector should consider while setting strategic goals. These areas are communication, support and engagement.

The results of interviews with the e-residents show that they have some challenges with the networking and marketing solutions because of the lack of support from the program side. There is not many events or direct connection to them to enhance the communication element, which affected to the growth of their business. E-residents would like to benefit from the existing e-residency network from the communication perspective. There are existing social media channels where it is possible to communicate (e.g. Facebook groups etc.). However, the state should approach more systematically to the different available communication channels.

The platform and the lack of advisors were marked as a challenge that the e-residents most commonly face. E-residents expect support from the legal and taxation point of view. Moreover, the government on-boarding platform needs improvement with better interfaces and different available languages. Based on this information, the public sector should focus on the improvement of different support programs and services. It does not mean that the state should offer all support by itself or without fees. It is more about developing the enabler services infrastructure that supports the businesses of the e-residents.

Engagement was one of the most mentioned topics during the interviews. One of the e-residency 2.0 initiative goals was to offer more opportunities to share the Estonian culture, which is one of the e-resident goals. However, the program authority does not invite them to participate while setting the program strategic goals. They were not involved to the discussions regarding the e-residency strategy and the future development of the program.

The research team was aware that EAS has launched different questionnaires and surveys to map the e-residents view. However, the responses from the interviews show that there is still enough room for improvement. For example, considering how to engage e-residents through the EERICA to the strategy shaping process.

6 Conclusion

Based on the conducted research it is possible to say that Estonian e-residency program has reached the maturity level where it is necessary to revise the followed approach of the strategy.

We assessed from the public sector and e-residents perspective, whether the strategic objectives were met based on the e-residency white paper 2.0, which was the only publicly available source that contained e-residency program strategic goals. Research results provided valuable feedback for re-designing certain elements of the program.

The findings of the study indicate that e-residents are positive about their ability to start a company and run their businesses remotely, as well as the ability to save time and operate in a transparent atmosphere. However, they confront with certain obstacles that influence their potential market plans in Estonian businesses. We gathered the best practices, made recommendations for the future process and mapped further possible research topics.

It is important to note that there are no conflicting factors after comparing the policy priorities and aspirations of those two sectors. Both sectors clearly emphasize and focus on different issues. Based on the research results communication, for example, is a general strategic aim, but technical development is mostly a public-sector concern.

Based on the research, it is possible to say that communication, support and participation are the three key areas that e-residents and the public sector should address when setting strategic targets. Strategy development is collaborative process that needs the engagement of all stakeholders. Meaning that the state achieves its strategic goals as far and as successfully as the state can meet the goals of e-residents. We believe that despite the fact that the e-residency program has faced some criticism; the program still has many potential and success opportunities.

References

1. Kotka, T., Vargas, C., Korjus, K.: Estonian e-residency: redefining the nation-state in the digital era. University of Oxford Cyber Studies Programme Working Paper 3 (2015)
2. Särav, S., Kerikmäe, T.: E-residency: a cyberdream embodied in a digital identity card? In: Kerikmäe, T., Rull, A. (eds.) The Future of Law and eTechnologies, pp. 57–79. Springer, Cham (2016). https://doi.org/10.1007/978-3-319-26896-5_4
3. Blue, A.: Evaluating Estonian e-residency as a tool of soft power. Place Brand Public Dipl. **17**, 359–367 (2020). https://doi.org/10.1057/s41254-020-00182-3
4. Kimmo, M., Pappel, I., Draheim, D.: E-residency as a nation branding case. In: Proceedings of the 11th International Conference on Theory and Practice of Electronic Governance, pp. 419–428 (2018)
5. Prause, G., Boevsky, I., et al.: E-residency: a business platform for smart rural development. Ikonomika i upravlenie na selskoto stopanstvo/Bul. J. Agric. Econ. Manag. **61**(2/4), 80–89 (2016)
6. Godoy, D.G.S., Heal, A.: Trade in the digital age: can e-residency be an enabler for Asia-Pacific developing countries? UN ESCAP: Trade Insights 1–13 (2016)
7. Tammpuu, P., Masso, A.: Transnational digital identity as an instrument for global digital citizenship: the case of Estonia's e-residency. Inf. Syst. Front. **21**(3), 621–634 (2019)
8. Tammpuu, P., Masso, A.: 'Welcome to the virtual state': Estonian e-residency and the digitalised state as a commodity. Eur. J. Cult. Stud. **21**(5), 543–560 (2018)
9. Roots, L., Dumbrava, C.: E-citizenship opportunities in the changing technological environment. In: Kerikmäe, T., Rull, A. (eds.) The Future of Law and eTechnologies, pp. 45–56. Springer, Cham (2016). https://doi.org/10.1007/978-3-319-26896-5_3
10. Lips, S., Pappel, I., Tsap, V., Draheim, D.: Key factors in coping with large-scale security vulnerabilities in the eID field. In: Kő, A., Francesconi, E. (eds.) EGOVIS 2018. LNCS, vol. 11032, pp. 60–70. Springer, Cham (2018). https://doi.org/10.1007/978-3-319-98349-3_5
11. Lips, S., Aas, K., Pappel, I., Draheim, D.: Designing an effective long-term identity management strategy for a mature e-state. In: Kő, A., Francesconi, E., Anderst-Kotsis, G., Tjoa, A.M., Khalil, I. (eds.) EGOVIS 2019. LNCS, vol. 11709, pp. 221–234. Springer, Cham (2019). https://doi.org/10.1007/978-3-030-27523-5_16
12. Koppenjan, J., Groenewegen, J.: Institutional design for complex technological systems. Int. J. Technol. Policy Manag. **5**(3), 240–257 (2005)
13. Williamson, O.E.: The institutions of governance. Am. Econ. Rev. **88**(2), 75–79 (1998)
14. Yin, R.K., et al.: Case study research and applications: design and methods (2018)
15. Runeson, P., Host, M., Rainer, A., Regnell, B.: Case Study Research in Software Engineering: Guidelines and Examples. Wiley, Hoboken (2012)
16. Creswell, J.W., Creswell, J.D.: Research Design: Qualitative, Quantitative, and Mixed Methods Approaches. Sage Publications, Thousand Oaks (2017)
17. Clarke, V., Braun, V.: Thematic analysis. In: Michalos, A.C. (eds.) Encyclopedia of Quality of Life and Well-Being Research, pp. 1947–1952. Springer, Dordrecht (2014). https://doi.org/10.1007/978-94-007-0753-5_3470
18. Clarke, H.D., Goodwin, M., Goodwin, M.J., Whiteley, P.: Brexit. Cambridge University Press, Cambridge (2017)

E-Court Transition Process: Identifying Critical Factors and Recommendations for Developing Countries

Jesujoba Tolulope Adeleye[1]($\boxtimes$) ⓘ, Rozha K. Ahmed[2] ⓘ, Katrin Nyman-Metcalf[3] ⓘ,
and Dirk Draheim[2] ⓘ

[1] Tallinn University of Technology, Tallinn, Estonia
jeadel@taltech.ee
[2] Information Systems Group, Tallinn University of Technology, Tallinn, Estonia
{rozha.ahmed,dirk.draheim}@taltech.ee
[3] Department of Law, Tallinn University of Technology, Tallinn, Estonia
katrin.nyman-metcalf@taltech.ee

Abstract. Many countries across the world have adopted the electronic court system to various degrees. Likewise, many others are either in the process of adopting it or contemplate transitioning to the use of e-court. However, developing countries have not had much success with developing e-government services so far, one of which is the e-court system. This research engages in a thorough analysis of the court system and its scope. It uses qualitative research methodology to study the e-court transition process of two chosen case studies: Estonia and the Kurdistan Region of Iraq (KRI). A detailed review of relevant literature was combined with in-depth interviews of experts involved in the transition processes and users of the e-court systems in each of these case studies. The research uncovered many accomplishments of the e-court system in Estonia and the KRI, which are meant to serve as prospects for countries planning to adopt it. The result presents several critical factors to the success of a transition process to an e-court system, i.e., an active information system, functioning interoperability platform, user-friendly interface, electronic ID and signature, support of stakeholders, end-user participation, thorough plan and analysis, updated legal framework, and organizational change. Finally, as a recommendation directed mostly at developing countries, authors developed a set of critical steps to be accomplished at different specified phases of the transition to the e-court system.

Keywords: E-court · E-justice · E-governance · Digital transformation

1 Introduction

For centuries, the court system has engaged in traditional ways of adjudication, with the parties and witnesses at a physical location and in the presence of a judge or judges, using hardcopy (paper-based) documents and records. However, with the introduction of e-governance technologies in recent years, there has been a fusion of the judicial

© Springer Nature Switzerland AG 2022
A. V. Chugunov et al. (Eds.): EGOSE 2021, CCIS 1529, pp. 305–317, 2022.
https://doi.org/10.1007/978-3-031-04238-6_23

system and information and communications technology (ICT) in justice delivery as the "e-court" system. The e-court system provides an avenue for filing court processes, presenting evidence, and receiving the testimonies of parties and witnesses remotely [1], resulting in a faster case dispensation process and a more efficient and effective court system [2]. The need for an effective electronic court system is increasingly being discovered, especially in developing countries, resulting in more clamors for its adoption [3]. However, developing countries particularly have difficulties and a high failure rate regarding the implementation of e-government solutions. The mere adoption or replication of e-court, like most other e-government solutions, does not guarantee its success in a new country regardless of its success rate in the foreign context. This presents the fear of undertaking such a seemingly hydra-headed project from the beginning, only to flounder.

There is a knowledge gap in research on steps to transition to the e-court system, especially in developing countries since they have had a relatively low success rate at the implementation of e-services. There is a need to discover whether processes and strategies can be built from successful case studies for developing countries that want to adopt the e-court system to their contexts. Hence, this research seeks to examine the e-court system of two different countries that have attained different levels of development economically, socially, and technologically, and make analysis and recommendations that may be useful for developing countries to unpack how and why e-court has worked so well in the digitally advanced European country, Estonia, and its similar, relatively recent success in a developing area such as the Kurdistan Region of Iraq (KRI). This unpacking leads to the detailing of necessary tools and solutions to implement at each step of the transition to e-court.

The outcome of this study presents critical factors that could make up the transitioning process for the successful implementation of e-court. Additionally, by comparing the e-court system's implementation in both case studies - Estonia and the KRI - the authors developed a guideline for intending implementers of the e-court system to be accomplished at different phases of the transition process.

Section 2 presents the relevant work on the digital transformation of court systems. Section 3 presents the research approach and background of both case studies and research methodology and data sources. Section 4 provides the results of the analysis. Section 5 presents discussions and the developed implementation guide for e-court system transition. Finally, Sect. 6 concludes the research and presents research limitations and future directions.

2 Introduction to E-Courts

E-Court refers to the adoption of technology by the courts to improve the judiciary's service delivery through automated courtroom processes [2]. This digital transformation of courts can manifest through different features. A major feature is electronic filing, which allows for the filing or submission of documents in electronic form, as against paper form [4]. Also, an electronic case management system is required for efficient monitoring and administration of the flow of cases throughout their lifecycle and for the exchange of data among courts, parties to suits, and other institutions involved [2]. This can help improve courts' efficiency and curb corruption [5].

E-court can also involve the use of virtual trials. A virtual trial could either refer to the conduct of a trial entirely electronically - through some video conferencing platform and in real-time- or to the conduct of merely some parts of trials electronically, like remote testification of witnesses [6]. Very commonly, e-court involves using appropriate electronic hardware machines and gadgets, including visual display mechanisms, within the courtroom itself.

While ICT has the potential to create or facilitate transformational change in the courts, relevant works have shown that tangible results might not be seen so often due to the absence of institutional competence and readiness [7, 8]. Competence not only refers to the existence of organizational structures for easy implementation and adoption of services but also the presence of trained, qualified human capital. Therefore, the needed capacity and competencies are ensured through proper human resource management, not merely possessing ICT or ICT skills [7].

Since it is the duty of the court to interpret the law, a plan to adopt e-court raises questions about the relationship between law and technology. It has been argued that the law cannot always catch up with the fast pace of technological advancement, and this leaves for possible over-regulation or under-regulation of technology. This conundrum affects e-court, in that, a hazy framework regarding technology and the law can adversely affect the application of an e-service [9]. Hence, the validity of trials conducted in e-court can be called to question [6]. The foregoing suggests that the desire to transition to e-court must be met with a structured and informed e-court transition process, for the achievement of effective and desired results.

3 Background and Research Approach

3.1 E-Court in Estonia

Although Estonia launched its court information system, e-File, in 2006, the development of e-governance in the country had begun well before then. Therefore, the e-court system, called "e-justice" in Estonia, was a logical upshot of the e-governance mechanisms that were already existing or budding at the time. As [10] traced the progress of e-governance in Estonia to the development of internet banking by the private sector, by 2002, about half of all payments for e-government services in Estonia were already being made through internet banking. Subsequently, the electronic identity function came with the ID cards given to the country's residents [11]. Thus, users of online governmental services could only access them with an electronic identity. Within the same time, the national data exchange layer, X-road, was created. X-road connected government agencies and departments' information systems and databases, allowing for seamless, secure interoperability and exchange of information [12].

With the introduction of the first set of e-services, several other digital tools, structures, and policies were needed to implement new services like e-court, e-taxation. Some of these digital tools were introduced simultaneously with those initial services—one of such tools as digital signatures. The introduction of digital identities to Estonian residents availed them the opportunity to sign electronically.

The e-court system began with developing the 'e-File' by Estonia's Centre of Registers and Information Systems. The e-File system is an information system that allows parties to a suit to file documents and monitor their cases remotely, online. It is a central platform for the storage of electronic documents and communications from different other information systems. It utilizes the X-road infrastructure, which ensures that information entered once on the system, is exchanged among all involved parties, like the police, court officials, citizens, and lawyers, depending on their relevance to the suit. As with other e-services in the country, the e-file system can only be accessed with the electronic identity of the users. The system also allows for payments to be made electronically.

The e-Justice system has improved the productivity of justice service delivery in Estonia. Center for Security Studies' report showed that by 2008, the country had been out-performing most other countries in Europe regarding digital tools of their e-justice systems [13]. The study assigned points to countries based on computer facilities provided in three areas: assistance rendered to judges and clerks, case management and administration, and communication between courts and parties. As a result, court cases are now dispensed faster and with less administrative burden than before developing the e-justice system.

In a bid to speed up the dispensation of justice even further, the Estonian Ministry of Justice and Estonia's Chief Data Officer developed an AI software to hear and decide on small claims disputes [13]. This incorporation of AI into the justice system ("robot judges") is expected to give human judges the time to deal with more complex cases. This project is being done in furtherance of the existing e-court system.

3.2 E-Court in the Kurdistan Region of Iraq (KRI)

The e-court system has been implemented in the Sulaimaniyah Appellate Court, one of the four Appellate courts in the KRI [2]. As reported by Ahmed et al., the operation of the e-court system involves an interoperability network, allowing the flow of information among the courtroom, its departments, and the public prosecution and law enforcement institutions [2]. This facilitates the ability to feed the system with information only once while all participants can simultaneously access information required for their duties. In addition, the case management system allows for electronic registration of cases; the use of electronic summons; electronic, automated allocation of cases to judges; electronic notifications to parties involved regarding the case; and the availability of court documents in three different languages.

Furthermore, they detailed the new processes, functions, and tools introduced to the court system in KRI as e-court. Some of them are, the use of monitor TV screens by the courtrooms to display to parties and visitors the details of cases; allocation of cases to judges automatically by electronic means as against the previous manual allocations; provision of an easy electronic interface, allowing the public, court officials, lawyers, and other parties to see their roles and permissions; availability of a better management system for service of court summons; electronic notification of persons related to cases regarding adjournments, fees to be paid and other important notices; the ability for lawyers to search for previous cases electronically; and the availability of the system's contents in Kurdish, Arabic, and English.

Functionalities such as the implementation of bar codes to link digital files of cases with physical files where such files need to be printed on paper helps faster creation and registration of documents; judges can now review case files simultaneously unlike the paper system where judges had to wait on each other to pass on case files before being able to study them. This burden of the paper system persists in many countries and is a major cause of delay in the disposition of cases. Moreover, in some other parts, parties have to make a large number of copies of the same document for the court, each party, and each judge. The e-court process, therefore, saves a lot of time and resources.

The court system is the first e-service in Sulaimaniyah city [2, 14]; this indicates that other e-services such as digital identity and digital signature were absent from the system at its inception. Furthermore, Ahmed et al. in [14] argued that while the e-court system has the impressive features earlier mentioned, the absence of e-signature is a critical factor missing. This absence made the system not entirely be paperless since users still have to sign on paper before uploading online [7, 14].

While the challenges show that there is room for development and lessons to learn, the e-court system in KRI has had a high level of user satisfaction because of the significant improvements which it has introduced over the paper court system [2, 7].

3.3 Research Methodology

The roadmap for a successful implementation of e-court systems in developing countries may require strategic plans as well as analysis and studying other experiences to follow the right steps in the transition processes from different countries that have already adopted the system. Hence, this research examines the e-court system implementation of two different countries that have attained different levels of development and successfully passed the transformation process in order to answer the following research question:

– What are the critical factors and recommendations for e-court system implementation in developing countries?

This research employs a qualitative case study approach that presents the detailed exploration by researchers of an idea within one or more defined contexts [15]. The qualitative case study is best used when present-day is studied in detail and its real-life context, and the phenomenon is not easily separable from its context [16]. The research is intended at getting a balanced picture of the existing contexts. The topic necessitates the use of qualitative rather than quantitative research, as there are few examples of e-courts, and these are not mutually comparable in all aspects. Thus, the aim of the research is to identify and evaluate relevant factors that can serve as inspiration in a situation in which there is no large sample to use for comparison.

Data were collected using two methods: a review of existing literature and semi-structured, in-depth interviews of essential stakeholders to implement the e-court in the two case studies. The interviews were conducted on three respondents from Estonia and two from the KRI. The respondents were taken from different fields critical to implementing the e-court system in the case studies.

The respondents were legal practitioners and judges, a top official at the company that worked with the government to implement the service, and a top-level government official responsible for the process. For this reason, this research used the purposive sampling method in its choice of participants with adequate knowledge and experience about the subject matter being studied, and data is to be collected according to the research aims [17]. The collected data through semi-structured interviews and existing data were analyzed using thematic analysis to elicit patterns of themes from the gathered data without preconceived biases. This promotes the audience's trust in the validity of the results arrived at by the research [18].

4 Research Results

This section presents our results of the analysis, as shown in Fig. 1.

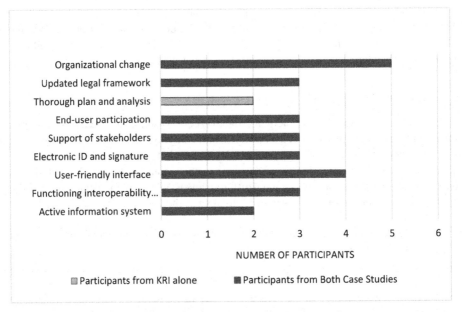

Fig. 1. Number of participants' reference to critical factors.

As can be seen, Fig. 1 shows nine identified critical factors from the e-court transition processes of Estonia and the KRI, along with the frequency of the participants' reference to each of these factors during the interviews.

4.1 Active Information System

Participants expressed the need for a centralized system where electronic data will be collected and stored. For example, participant 4 from the KRI noted that data and court files that were previously held in paper form have now been digitized and kept in a digital database. Similarly, Participant 1 from Estonia stated that Estonia developed a centralized database for all data. Therefore, the courts, law enforcement agencies like the police and prosecutor's office can have one central system to share critical data.

"So, we have one centralized database with courts because the criminal procedures and misdemeanor procedure starts from mainly from police and then end up in court finally. So, we developed a centralized database for all data. That was called "e-file." (Participant 1, Estonia).

4.2 Functioning Interoperability Platform

The participants from Estonia identified the X-Road platform as an important system through which the transfer of data across information systems with the e-court system was made possible. This interoperability system was noted to be a tool for the entire e-governance framework.

"And we have a decentralized system, but that's not only for the court system, but that's for the whole Estonian e-governance - the X-Road." (Participant 2, Estonia).

4.3 User-Friendly Interface

Participants 1 from Estonia, and 4 from the KRI, directly identified the need for a user-friendly interface. According to them, this user-friendliness is necessary so that users can easily maximize the e-service. In their opinion, this factor was present in the making of e-court systems in their countries.

"Then we developed the portal for our citizens and lawyers. And then, we also developed a specialized tool for people working for court files as lawyers, including judges and also attorneys. This is publicly accessible. This tool is systemizing electronic files in some more logical ways and representing in a way it's easier to access them and read them and make comments and do searches inside them. So, it's easier to work with electronic parts." (Participant 1, Estonia)

"This system was... implemented in a way that it will be a very modern integrated system, that to be very friendly for all the court staff to use" (Participant 4, KRI).

4.4 Electronic ID and Signature

Three participants underscored the roles that electronic ID and digital signatures played or could have played in implementing the e-court system in their countries. It was noted that digital signatures keep the system more secure and further help eliminate the need for papers in court procedures.

"We have secure authentication with our ID card or mobile ID or ... smart ID, whatever you use." (Participant 2, Estonia)

"It would be better if you have a digital signature in place; it would be better if you have electronic ID to identify all participant or all users in the system digitally." (Participant 4, KRI).

4.5 Support of Stakeholders

The interviewees equally made references to the importance of collaboration with the private sector. For example, participant 4, from the KRI, being an employee of the company that implemented this system in the KRI at the time of the implementation, highlighted that, while the government financed the project, the private sector organization carried out a large part of the hands-on implementation. The participant also expressed the close communication and joint effort the company had with the court staff. Likewise, participant 2 expressed that the lawyers using the system are mostly from the private sector; therefore, the system's success was largely hinged on their participation and cooperation.

Participant 1 underscored the partnerships between the private and public sectors on the project thus:

"During years, we used different companies from the private sector to make technical IT work. But we had, like, main public sector partner, like Justice IT Enterprise, I think, how you call it. But they used subcontractors, depending on the issues, from the private sector."

The attitude of the majority of the users was also said to be positive towards the adoption of the process.

"In general, like Estonian public authorities and also companies are very open to digitalize everything." (Participant 3, Estonia)

"I also know that opinions were asked from different law firms and different courts as to how well is the court system functioning. And there has been some cooperation in that regard." (Participant 3, Estonia)

Lastly, as a major stakeholder in the adoption process, the will and support of the government were emphasized, especially by Participant 4, from the KRI.

4.6 End-User Participation

Participant 2 from Estonia, having been personally involved in many stages of tests of the e-court system in Estonia over the years, expressed how different versions of the system were brought to be tested by the end-users, and many changed were made over the years to make the system further suit users' needs.

"All these structures or developments were also tested very closely with the user, with the end-users." (Participant 2, Estonia)

"We had to meet multiple court staff from judges, from clerks, from prosecutors, lawyers and all the roles inside the court," *"they established like different committees, one committee of clerks, and one committee of judges. And we had to do to kind of take data from all of them. So huge amount of meetings, like took six months or one year even"* (Participant 4, KRI)

In corroborating this, Participant 5, from the KRI, acknowledged being the head of one of the committees set up to participate in the process.

4.7 Thorough Plan and Analysis

Two participants identified the need for proper analysis of the project before the commencement of the implementation.

"Study the project well before starting implementation by the presidency of the court" (Participant 5, KRI)

Participant 4 from the KRI expressed this need for proper, prior analysis and suggested that this was to make the system of better standard and more suited to the users' needs.

4.8 Updated Legal Framework

The interview participants observed that the laws need to be reviewed and updated where necessary to accommodate, legalize, or enforce the e-court system. For example, participant 2 from Estonia noted that the legislature enacted laws to compel legal professionals – judges, lawyers, and other persons using the services of the court – to use the e-court system and other e-governance tools, like digital signatures on court documents. It was also noted that the laws gave users the leave to make signatures on paper and send documents by post where the electronic process was not feasible. The participant found this step to be the most critical factor responsible for the success of the e-court system in the country.

Likewise, Participant 1 from Estonia highlighted the importance of legislative enactments and internal organizational regulations in facilitating the adoption of e-court. Lastly, Participant 4 from the KRI noted that the e-court system needed to have the force of law.

"And I think that the most crucial change was when it was made obligatory for legal professionals to use e-court system, especially lawyers, prosecutors, and also, for example, notaries or, and state institutions for the administrative court." (Participant 2, Estonia)

"There is definitely need for legislative support... like in-laws... but some of them, you need to have some internal regulation." (Participant 1, Estonia).

4.9 Organizational Change

Lastly, all the participants said that the system necessitated a lot of organizational changes. For example, participant 1 from Estonia stated that there were many changes to the old institutional arrangements for the system to be implemented in Estonia. Specific references were made to merging old structures and reducing personnel in some areas to effectuate more efficiency. These changes were to increase efficiency and eliminate redundancy.

"quite a lot of training for everybody who wanted to be trained. We have within the court... a support person.", "There is also online support." (Participant 2, Estonia)

Participant 4, from the KRI, also referred to the training lasting about two years which had to be done in the justice system. Also, Participant 5 from the KRI noted that he was personally involved in the skills development course to be proficient in using the technology.

5 Discussion

The data obtained from interviews were analyzed and revealed critical factors responsible for the successful transition to e-court in both case studies. Comparing the discoveries from the review of relevant literature with the findings from the interviews presents a consistent identification of these factors as critical.

The factors are 1. Active information system 2. Functioning interoperability platform 3. User-friendly interface 4. Electronic ID and signature 5. Support of stakeholders 6. End-user participation 7. Thorough plan and analysis 8. Updated legal framework 9. Organizational change.

According to Bwalya [19], trust is a major component of culture awareness, contributing to citizens' acceptance of an e-service [19]. However, none of the participants made any specific reference to trust in government as a major determining factor for the success of e-court implementation. The participants had revealed that some users were resistant to adopting the service and needed further persuasion to use it. Not all the reasons for this resistance were given; therefore, Bwalya's proposition involving users' trust in government cannot be invalidated [19]. Culture awareness was presented, firstly in terms of proper understanding of the context where the e-service is to be adopted and tailoring the service to suit that context, and secondly, the sensitization of the users to adopt it [20]. Therefore, the use of different languages predominant among the court users in the e-court systems of both KRI and Estonia and the consistent training and involvement of users in both case studies show a high level of cultural awareness. These manifest as organizational change, end-user participation, and user-friendly interface in this research.

Moreover, the findings revealed that the existence of an e-governance system in a country facilitates the smooth implementation of e-court in that country or setting and further allows for its optimized use. E-Government tools and services such as electronic signature, digital identity, and a functioning interoperability platform have been critical factors to the implementation. Bwalya in [19] had postulated the need for an adequate and inexpensive IT infrastructure. While this infrastructure can readily refer to the existence of the needed hardware, the findings from the case studies show that these e-services, software, and tools are equally as vital to e-court implementation.

Lastly, organizational changes conducted by the case studies were highlighted in the findings of this research. These changes included training of staff, restructuring of organizational structures, and collaborations with the private sector. This correlates with the statement in [8], which underscored the importance of institutional readiness and competence. It has been found from the interviews that the mere introduction of ICT to the court without the necessary changes will not result in the achievement of the desired results. The managers, staff, and users of the e-court system need to be built with the requisite skills they need, and administrative and internal processes need to be reorganized. Likewise, the work of Lʼohmus et al. in [21], which emphasized the need for collaborations between the public sector and the private sector, was proven true, as both case studies in this research engaged the services of the private sector companies, especially for the technical aspects.

Furthermore, from comparing both case studies, the authors identified considerable similarities between KRI and Estonia's successes through their adoption of the e-court system. For example, both cases have had improved efficiency and effectiveness in how court cases are handled. Likewise, they have both experienced a better, more transparent system for case distribution among judges. However, the research shows that Estonia has experienced more flexibility in its legal system through e-court than the KRI as remote work for staff is possible with the Estonian system. Also, users have more than one option to perform the electronic signatures through their eID in Estonia, while this feature is not available yet in the KRI.

Table 1. Implementation guide.

Phase	Activities	Details
Pre-Implementation	Budgeting	Conduct cost-benefit analysis Source for funds
	Updated legal framework	Study existing laws Amend/enact new laws
	Functioning e-governance system	Have functioning interoperability platform Put e-governance tools in place
	Collaborations with private sector	Involve private sector technocrats
	Developing stakeholders' will	Will/support from government and end-users
	Thorough plan and analysis	Study-specific context and current situation Identify aims and KPIs Identify possible challenges and solutions
Implementation	Active electronic information system	Set up necessary database
	User-friendly interface	Create a non-complex, well-organized interface
	Organizational change	Train end-users Restructure departments where necessary Hire skilled staff
Post-implementation	Organizational change	Train and re-train end-users
	Constant system improvements	Deliver updates and upgrades
	Increase size/scale of service	Broaden the scope of implementation

Similarly, some challenges are common to both case studies. Both case studies experienced some resistance of some users, budgetary challenges, and lack of ICT skills among users. Both were able to surmount the challenge of lack of ICT skills among users by engaging in constant training. However, due to budgetary challenges, the KRI has not scaled the system to other regional courts which were initially planned. Meanwhile, Estonia got its funds from the regular budgetary allocations to the justice sector.

Finally, in addition to identifying the critical factors, the authors presented their recommendations and developed a guideline for developing countries that are on the way to implementing the e-court system. As shown in Table 1., the guideline is divided into three phases for the successful implementation of the e-court system.

6 Conclusion

This research investigated the critical factors that facilitated the successful e-court transition process of Estonia and the KRI and analyzed their accomplishments, prospects, and challenges to make recommendations for developing countries that have either started or are considering starting their transition to e-court. The analysis was based on the qualitative approach. Data were collected from reviewing existing literature and semi-structured in-depth interviews of important stakeholders to implement the e-court system in both case studies. Findings presented nine significant factors for the successful implementation process of e-court systems: active information system, functioning interoperability platform, user-friendly interface, electronic ID and signature, support of stakeholders, end-user participation, thorough plan and analysis, updated legal framework, and organizational change. Consequently, the authors developed a guideline to serve as a checklist for countries intending to implement an e-court system. The practical implication of this research lies in providing the foundation for practitioners and implementors of the e-court system that are on the way to the digital transformation of their justice systems. A limitation of this research includes a limited number of case studies and interviewing a small sample of experts. However, the authors' desire in the future is to do more comprehensive studies by exploring experiences from more advanced countries. Likewise, a more indepth analysis can be done on the national e-court plans, policy documents, and actions of countries or regions intending to implement or already beginning implementation to analyze their prospects of success and identify areas of possible inadequacies.

References

1. Dillon, M., Beresford, D.: Electronic courts and the challenges in managing evidence: a view from inside the international criminal court. Int. J. Court Adm. **6**(1), 29–36 (2014)
2. Ahmed, R.K., Khder Hassan, M., Ingrid, P., Draheim, D.: Impact of e-court systems implementation: a case study. Transform. Gov.: People Process Policy **15**(1), 108–128 (2021)
3. Kagbala, T.I., Bethel, O., Fems, K.M.: The role of technology in recalibrating the legal profession to meet the entrepreneurial exigencies of modern legal practice in Nigeria. Int. J. Recent Innov. Acad. Res. **2**(4), 36–44 (2018)
4. Fenwick, W.A., Brownstone, R.D.: Electronic filing: what is it - what are its implications? Santa Clara High Technol. Law J. **19**(1), 181–227 (2003)
5. Saman, W.S.W.M., Haider, A.: Electronic court records management: a case study. J. e-Gov. Stud. Best Pract. **2012**, 11 (2012)
6. Lederer, F.I.: The road to the virtual courtroom? A consideration of today's - and tomorrow's - high technology courtrooms. In: William & Mary Law School Scholarship Repository (1999)

7. Ahmed, R., Draheim, D., Pappel, I., Muhammed, K.H.: Challenges in the digital transformation of courts: a case study from the Kurdistan region of Iraq. In: Conference: International Conference on eDemocracy & eGovernment (ICEDEG), Buenos Aires, Argentina (2020)
8. Hunnius, S., Schuppan, T.: Competency requirements for transformational e-government. In: Proceedings of the 46th Annual Hawaii International Conference on System Sciences (2013)
9. Touray, A., Salminen, A., Mursu, A.: ICT barriers and critical success factors in developing countries. Electron. J. Inf. Syst. Dev. Countries (EJISDC) 56(1), 1–17 (2013)
10. Kitsing, M.: Explaining the e-government success in Estonia. Policy Interest 3(1), 1–21 (2011)
11. Martens, T.: Electronic identity management in Estonia between market and state governance. Identity Inf. Soc. 3, 213–233 (2010)
12. McBride, K., Toots, M., Kalvet, T., Krimmer, R.: Leader in e-government, laggard in open data: exploring the case of Estonia. Revue Française D Administration Publique, 613–625 (2018)
13. Center for Security Studies. E-tools for criminal case management within selected EU Member States. Center for the Study of Democracy (CSD), Zurich (2011)
14. Ahmed, R.K., Lips, S., Draheim, D.: eSignature in eCourt systems. In: Fourth World Conference on Smart Trends in Systems, Security and Sustainability (2020)
15. Rashid, Y., Rashid, A., Warraich, M.A., Sabir, S.S., Waseem, A.: Case study method: a step-by-step guide for business researchers. Int. J. Qual. Methods 18, 1–13 (2019)
16. Yin, R.K.: Case Study Research: Design and Methods, vol. 5, pp. 1–219. SAGE Publications, Inc., Thousand Oaks (2014)
17. Robinson, R.S.: Purposive sampling. In: Michalos, A.C. (eds.) Encyclopedia of Quality of Life and Well-Being Research. Springer, Dordrecht (2014). https://doi.org/10.1007/978-94-007-0753-5_2337
18. Braun, V., Clarke, V.: Using thematic analysis in psychology. Qual. Res. Psychol. 3(2), 77–101 (2006)
19. Bwalya, K.: Factors affecting adoption of e-government in Zambia. Electron. J. Inf. Syst. Dev. Countries 38(4), 1–13 (2009)
20. Al-Jaghoub, S., Al-Yaseen, H., Al-Hourani, M.: Evaluation of awareness and acceptability of using e- government services in developing countries: the case of Jordan. Electron. J. Inf. Syst. 13(1), 1–8 (2010)
21. Lõhmus, K., Nyman-Metcalf, K., Ahmed, R.K., Pappel, I., Draheim, D.: The private sector' s role in e-government from a legal perspective. In: Proceedings of the Fourth International Congress on Information and Communication Technology (2019)

Author Index

Printed in the United States
by Baker & Taylor Publisher Services